Artemis C

Artemis Cooper is the author of *Writing at the Kitchen Table*, the authorised biography of Elizabeth David, and *Patrick Leigh Fermor: An Adventure*, shortlisted for the Costa Biography Award, the National Book Awards and Waterstones Book of the Year. With her husband Antony Beevor she wrote *Paris After the Liberation, 1945–1949*. As well as two collections of letters, she has edited *Words of Mercury*, a collection of pieces by Patrick Leigh Fermor, and, with Colin Thubron, *The Broken Road*, the final volume of Patrick Leigh Fermor's walk from the Hook of Holland to Constantinople.

Praise for *Cairo in the War 1939–1945*

'Much more than a lively and amusing social history. With enormous skill she has shaped it into a gripping account of the progress of the war itself and of the fortunes of its major protagonists. Even more remarkably, she has given her book an additional dimension by drawing on a great many Egyptian sources to tell us their side of the story, too. The result is bracing and salutary and very readable indeed' *Sunday Times*

'This informative and enjoyable book puts political history side-by-side with the personal sub-history of the characters who determined it . . . a mine of entertaining anecdotes' *Observer*

'Much more than a collection of wartime gossip . . . The author's clear and well-researched account of the desert war and of the political and diplomatic developments which served as a background to it is as good in its way as anything I have read on the subject. At the same time she provides us with a highly entertaining picture of the numerous remarkable things that . . . were going on in Cairo at the time . . . lucid and compelling prose . . . a most enjoyable experience' *Scotsman*

'Ranges over matters requiring the combined gifts of the military historian, the political commentator, the social columnist, and also – for juicy anecdotes punctuate the narrative – the convivial raconteur . . . I can assert . . . that no one could have done a better job' *The Spectator*

Cairo in the War
1939–1945

ARTEMIS COOPER

JOHN MURRAY

First published in Great Britain in 1989 by Hamish Hamilton Ltd

This paperback edition first published in Great Britain in 2013
by John Murray (Publishers)
An Hachette UK Company

8

A CIP catalogue record for this title is available from the British Library

ISBN 978-1-84854-884-8
Ebook ISBN 978-1-84854-885-5

Typeset in Bembo by Servis Filmsetting Ltd, Stockport, Cheshire

Printed in Italy by Elcograf S.p.A.

John Murray policy is to use papers that are natural, renewable and recyclable
products and made from wood grown in sustainable forests. The logging and
manufacturing processes are expected to conform to the environmental regulations
of the country of origin.

John Murray (Publishers)
338 Euston Road
London NW1 3BH

www.johnmurray.co.uk

To Antony
who probably knows it by heart

Contents

Maps

Acknowledgements

This book began with a telephone call from Hugo Vickers. At that time he was working on his biography of Cecil Beaton, and had just written the chapter on Cecil in Egypt. 'It is quite extraordinary what was going on in Cairo,' said Hugo, 'and everybody you have ever heard of was there at one time or another during the war. What a subject!' I congratulated Hugo on having found his next book. 'No, I think not,' he said. 'But why don't you do it?' I would therefore like to thank him first; not only for the idea, but for all his help, and (in his capacity as literary executor) for access to the papers of Cecil Beaton and Sir Charles Johnston, and allowing me to quote from them.

Next I would like to thank those who were so good to me in Cairo: Alexander and Zein Baring, Alice Brinton, Dr John Rodenbeck, Abdel Salaam Osman, Wagih Kotb, Professor Magdi and Mrs Wahba. Particular thanks go to Adel Mahmoud Sabit, who was so generous with his time and hospitality. I would also like to thank Luis Awad; Mirrit Boutros Ghali; Walter and Mitzie Duhring; Ibrahim Farag; Fayed Farid; Yusuf Idris; Prince Hasan Aziz Hasan; Samiha Hansa; Samih Moussa; Jean Papasian; Fares Serafim; Dr Hamed Sultan; Mahmoud Muhammad Mahmoud; Teddy Maggar; Iris Khoury; Marie Louise Khomsi; General Sallah ed Din Sadek el Moghy; Victor Simaika; Samir and Dimiana Wahba; and Samiha Wahba.

John and Josie Brinton, Edward Hodgkin and Gertrude Wissa have given me invaluable material and advice, for which I am immensely grateful. I would also like to thank Sir Philip and Lady Adams; Susan Mary Alsop; Julian Amery MP; Dr Christopher Andrew; Joan Astley; Brigadier Bagnold; Sir Harold Beeley; John and Mary Beevor; Kinta Beevor; Mr and Mrs Walter Bell; Ralph Bennett; Mary Benson; Roger Bowen; Lady Bowker; June and Neville Braybrooke; Ion Calvocoressi; Viscountess Camrose; Field Marshal Lord Carver; Mr and Mrs Walter Clarke; Hilda Clouet des Péruches (née Khyatt); Anthony Contomichaelos; Pamela Cooper (formerly Hore-Ruthven); Company Sergeant Major T. Cosgrove, In Pensioner of the Royal Hospital, Chelsea; Aidan Crawley; Harriet Crawley; Elizabeth David; Michael Davie; Dan Davin; Eric Dawson; Lord Dunsany; Eve Durrell; Lawrence Durrell; HRH Prince Ahmed Fuad of Egypt; Christopher Fawcus; Renée Fedden; Xan Fielding; Fergus Fleming; Professor M. R. D. Foot; Sir Edward Ford; Martin Gilbert; Mrs V. Greer; Irene Guinle; Shusha Guppy; Michael Haag; Mr H. Habergam, In Pensioner; Mary Hadkinson; Sir Denis Hamilton; Mr C. Hancock, In Pensioner; Max Harari; Alastair Horne; Penelope Hope; Albert Hourani; Jean Howard; Mollie Izzard; Lord Jellicoe; Joseph E. Jeffs; the late Sir Charles Johnston; Dalu Jones; Jacqueline, Lady Killearn; Commander Bill King; Francis King; Joan and Patrick Leigh Fermor; the late Anita Leslie; Robert Liddell; Penelope Lively; Admiral Lucas; Sir Fitzroy Maclean, Bart.; Ian MacNiven; Dr Philip Mansel; Aurion de Meaupou; Lady Menuhin; Sophie Moss (formerly Countess Tarnowska); Brigadier and Mrs Edmund Myers; Lesley O'Malley; Princess Osmanoglu (née Abu'l Huda); Burnet Pavitt; Stewart Perowne; Barrie Pitt; J. Enoch Powell, MP; Shervie Price; David Pryce-Jones; Sir James Richards; Sir Frank and Lady Roberts; Dr Michael Rogers; André Rouxel; Malise Ruthven; Hoda Saada; the late Christopher Scaife; Rodney Searight; Colonel David Smiley; Diana Smith; Colonel David Stirling; Peter Stirling; Sadika Tancred; Major Patrick Telfer-Smollet; the late Terence Tiller; Jeremy Trafford; Ivor Treavett; Dr Charles Tripp; Mr Turner, In Pensioner; Sergeant S. Tweedale, MM, In Pensioner; Richard Usborne; Professor P. J. Vatikiotis; Elia Warner; the late Gordon Waterfield; Professor J. H. A. (Adam) Watson; Ian Weston-Smith; Sergeant L. Williams, In Pensioner; Gwyn Williams; Sir Peter Wilkinson; Nolly Zervudachi; Kyril Zinovieff; and Mme I. Zulficar. Particular thanks go to Mrs Nicholas Elliott and Mrs Walter Clarke, who were kind enough to lend me their wartime scrapbooks.

ACKNOWLEDGEMENTS

I am most grateful to Lord Killearn, for allowing me to publish extracts from his father's diaries; and Lord Kinross, for allowing me to publish extracts from his uncle's letters. I would also like to thank Gillian Grant, Derek Hopwood and Diane Ring of the Middle East Centre, St Antony's College; Douglas Matthews, and the staff of the London Library; and Iain Brown, of the National Library of Scotland.

Right from the start I have enjoyed the stimulating support of my literary agent, Felicity Bryan, and my editor, Christopher Sinclair-Stevenson. My parents were tireless in their quest for people to enrich this book, and I am very grateful for the interest they managed to sustain in what, at times, must have seemed my only topic of conversation. Lastly I would like to thank my husband and military adviser, Antony Beevor, an 11th Hussar of a later generation. This book has been immeasurably improved by the hours of work he put in on the early drafts, and his constant encouragement.

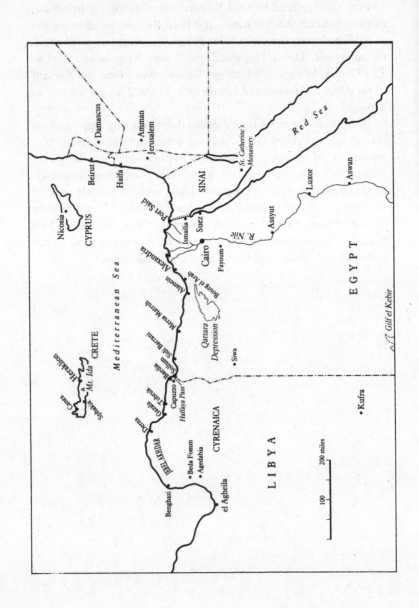

PROLOGUE

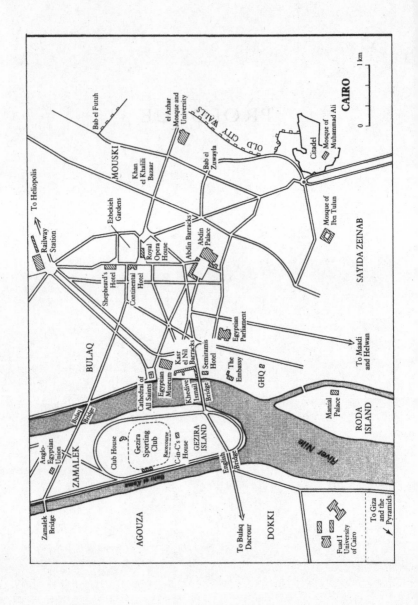

CAIRO

0   1 km

To Heliopolis

Railway Station

Bab el Futuh

el Azhar Mosque and University

MOUSKI

Khan el Khalili Bazaar

Bab el Zuwayla

OLD CITY WALLS

Citadel

Mosque of Muhammad Ali

Mosque of Ibn Tulun

SAYIDA ZEINAB

Ezbekieh Gardens

Royal Opera House

Shepheard's Hotel

Continental Hotel

Abdin Barracks

Abdin Palace

Egyptian Parliament

To Maadi and Helwan

BULAQ

Cathedral of All Saints

Egyptian Museum

Kasr el Nil Barracks

Khedive Ismail Bridge

Semiramis Hotel

The Embassy

GHQ

Bulaq Bridge

Anglo-Egyptian Union

ZAMALEK

Zamalek Bridge

Club House

Gezira Sporting Club

C-in-C's House

Racecourse

GEZIRA ISLAND

Bahr el Ama

English Bridge

Manial Palace

RODA ISLAND

River NILE

AGOUZA

DOKKI

To Bulaq Dacrour

Fuad I University of Cairo

To Giza and the Pyramids

When the Luftwaffe was forced to change its tactics to night raids on London in September 1940, the British in London and Cairo were separated by Axis forces stretching from Norway to Libya. But the division between the two cities was, above all, one of imagination.

In his office in GHQ Cairo, the Director of Military Intelligence, Brigadier Eric Shearer, looked at the plans brought from London by Captain Gordon Waterfield, and wondered why the War Office had accorded this mission such extraordinarily high priority. Britain was facing the possibility of a German invasion, and was painfully short of aircraft: yet one of the chief reasons for flying Captain Gordon Waterfield out to Egypt was so that he could blow up the Addis Ababa–Djibuti railway. Its destruction now would certainly damage enemy supply lines; but in the long term, this rail link between the Ethiopian capital and the narrow mouth of the Red Sea might be useful to the Allies. The DMI laughed. 'But we don't want the Djibuti railway blown up, and if we did we could blow it up ourselves, without the War Office flying somebody out from London!'[1]

Humiliating as it was to find out that his mission was considered a waste of time, Gordon Waterfield could not help feeling that Brigadier Shearer's careless laughter was misplaced. Nobody who had not experienced the Blitz could know what it was like to have their sleep frayed by the sound of sirens, planes, guns, then the hideous whistle followed by a dull explosion. In the morning, the bombed areas reeked of damp, dust and charred wood. Thousands, mainly in the East End, found themselves homeless. Every fire brigade, hospital and first aid station was working flat out and every shelter was packed, as Londoners endured the savage bombardment of their capital.

Incessant air-raids and the threatened invasion of the South Coast exaggerated the anxieties of the War Office, heightened their perception of danger, and provoked a strong urge to strike back at the enemy wherever he could be found. This was the atmosphere in which the planners had thought up a number of daring operations, including that on the Addis Ababa–Djibuti railway.

However, it was not the place of a junior officer to explain all this to the DMI – even though Gordon Waterfield was in a good position to do so. Before training as a commando, he had covered the fall of France for Reuters, and written a book called *What Happened to France*. As well as this, his journey between London and Cairo by Wellington bomber had taken under a week: the contrast between London and Cairo was more vivid to him than it was for the majority of men, who arrived by troopship and train after a long voyage round the Cape which might have taken up to seventy days. Frustrated and depressed, Waterfield stepped out of GHQ into the hot white light, and realised that the war was still very far from Cairo.

Having been a journalist on the *Egyptian Gazette* for seven years, Waterfield knew the city well. In the autumn of 1940, the half million strong population of Cairo had been increased by only a few thousand British and Empire troops; by the following spring, these numbered 35,000. The bobbing line of turbans and tarbooshes that threaded its way along the pavements was speckled by khaki caps in a variety of styles, but the city was still pervaded with the familiar smell of the urban Middle East: a blend of exhaust fumes, over-worked pack animals, cheap incense, and manure.

The ancient Thorneycroft buses and trams were as tired and battered-looking as the donkeys – and like the donkeys, they were adorned with blue beads to ward off the evil eye. The Cairo traffic, which included creaking carts piled high with vegetables, nervous flocks of fat-tailed sheep and the small Fiats and Austin Sevens of the European community, now had to share the streets with an ever increasing number of staff-cars, motor-bikes and military trucks.

In the large department stores like Cicurel's, Chemla's or Le Salon Vert, business carried on as usual with lavish displays of glass, crockery, fabrics and cosmetics. Groppi's, the most famous café in

4

Cairo, was fragrant with the smell of roasting coffee and fresh pastry cooked in clarified butter. In Shepheard's Hotel, the stocks of decent hock and champagne did not run out till 1943. Even then, there was no shortage of Algerian, Palestinian or South African wine. Rationing had been in force for nine months in England; but the corner shops and Greek groceries of Cairo were packed with butter, sugar, eggs, and paraffin. Oranges and dates were piled into round baskets in the greengrocers, as were great mounds of beans, maize, and the gigantic cauliflowers and cabbages produced in the rich warm soil of the Delta.

Waterfield made his way to the Continental Hotel, where he proposed to dine; but, on entering the restaurant, he was told that the Continental did not serve officers wearing shorts. He protested that he had just arrived by air, and had no other clothes; and in the throes of a war in which Great Britain was fighting for her life, could it really matter what an officer on urgent military business was wearing? When he expressed his irritation to a group of crisply-ironed officers in the Turf Club later, he was pleased to see that his audience included the Assistant Provost Marshal. Not only was the APM unimpressed by the story, but a lieutenant-colonel sprang to his feet, and said hotly that captains had no right to an opinion on the matter.

Even more alarming than the extent to which the military in Cairo were inhabiting an unreal world was their apparent reluctance to leave it. Waterfield proposed to deliver a broadcast which would describe conditions people were living in under the Blitz and the gallantry of the Londoners; but once again he found himself up against Brigadier Shearer, as draft after draft of the broadcast was turned down for being too explicit. Waterfield, who felt strongly that Cairo needed shaking up, argued that as one of the first eye-witnesses of the Blitz to arrive in Egypt he was constantly being questioned about life in England. People wanted to hear the truth, and they would be inspired by London's heroism – but the Brigadier remained firm, saying that the troops would be upset to learn the strain their families and friends were living under.

But this insipid excuse hid another reason. A broadcast describing London in the Blitz would create a bad impression locally. The

British occupation of Egypt was not popular; and if Egypt realised how weak Britain was, she might show herself reluctant to provide the labour and facilities on which the British war machine in the Middle East was to depend.

THE BRITISH IN EGYPT

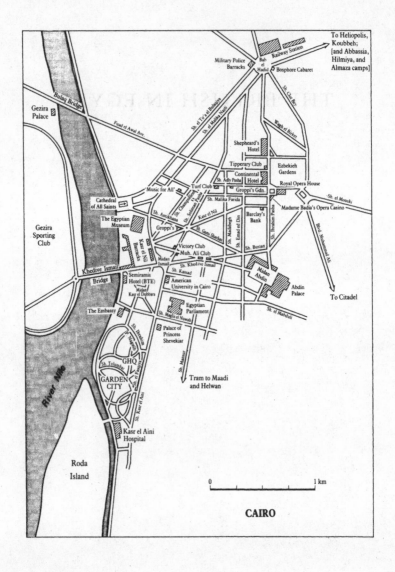

CAIRO

An Egyptian, looking at his country in the late nineteenth century, did not have to be a passionate nationalist to reach the conclusion that it was being run for, and by, foreigners. There was nothing new in this. Egypt had come under Ottoman rule in 1517 and, by the time Napoleon launched his brief campaign in 1798, she had dwindled into a provincial backwater of the Ottoman Empire. The Egyptians had known taxation and oppression, droughts and plagues without end. The magnificent medieval city of Cairo was falling to pieces, and all that remained of her former glory was the University of el Azhar, the oldest and most respected centre of Islamic study.

Then, in the years following the departure of the French in 1801, the Egyptians found a leader in Muhammad Ali, commander of the Ottoman Sultan's Albanian troops in Egypt. With the help of the people, Muhammad Ali overthrew the Mamluks* and made himself master of the Nile valley. He pulled Egypt out of centuries of stagnation, and awakened it to the benefits, as well as the painful complexities, of Westernisation. However, he did not manage to shake free of Ottoman suzerainty.

His descendants were essentially Turks, living in a foreign country. They married Circassian women, and kept villas on the Bosphorus. Turkish was the language of the Egyptian court, and Turks held every position of social, military and administrative importance.

In their wake came the Europeans: not only British and French,

---

* The word Mamluk means 'owned'. The Mamluks were an élite warrior caste of slaves imported into Egypt, who overthrew the ruling dynasty in 1250. They were defeated by the Ottomans in 1517; and from then on, until their final destruction by Muhammad Ali, they were vassals of the Sultan of Turkey.

but Italian, Greek, and Maltese. They worked as merchants, dealers, teachers, doctors, lawyers, and every kind of financial and technical consultant. Under an Ottoman system known as the Capitulations, they paid no taxes, and could only be tried in their own courts – which put them beyond the reach of Egyptian law. Their presence in such strength dated from the late 1850s, when Ferdinand de Lesseps – after years of persuasion – finally got the concession from Muhammad Ali's son Said to build the Suez Canal.

Although dug by forced labour recruited through a tax known as the *corvée*, the Canal was to prove ruinously expensive for Egypt. By using the carrot of future profit and the whip of Egypt's irreversible commitment, de Lesseps made Said underwrite the venture and give concessions to the Suez Canal Company that were too heavy for Egypt to bear, as well as being absurdly generous to the concessionaires. The revenue from the Canal was insufficient to steady an economy that had lost its balance, and Said was obliged to start borrowing money.

Said's successor did not seem unduly worried by his inherited debts, however, when the Suez Canal was opened in a blaze of glory in November 1869. Ismail the Magnificent spent a fortune on entertaining the Empress Eugénie and all the European royalty he could assemble for the great occasion. The centre of Cairo was rebuilt in the style of Haussmann, complete with opera house, for the arrival of his distinguished guests. A few years later, a second fortune was spent on gifts to the Sublime Porte, getting Istanbul to issue a *firman* which proclaimed his family the hereditary rulers of Egypt, with the title of Khedive, or viceroy. During Ismail's reign, hundreds of miles of railway had been laid, telegraph poles planted, irrigation canals dug, schools and hospitals built, training colleges founded. The modern Egypt that his grandfather Muhammad Ali had dreamed about was at last a reality, but Egypt was over a hundred million pounds in debt.

In order to finance his plans, Ismail had borrowed money from European banks at vastly inflated rates of interest. The fellahin,* already exhausted by poverty, were crushed by overwhelming tax-

---

* The name given to the peasants who, for thousands of years, have cultivated the Nile Valley.

ation. The European creditors realised that, unless they took control of the Egyptian economy, the debt would only get more unwieldy. Ismail knew it, and it was one of his frantic efforts to raise money that gave Disraeli the opportunity to buy the Khedive's shares in the Suez Canal Company, for four million pounds. In 1876, England and France formed a commission to take over the Egyptian economy until the debt was repaid, and three years later the Khedive was deposed.

Ismail was succeeded by his son Tewfik, a weak man who tried to co-operate with the European powers, and with the Ottoman Empire of which Egypt was still a part. The Turks saw this as a chance to reassert their authority in Egypt, and one of their demands was that the Egyptian army be severely reduced. Cuts in both pay and personnel had hit the Egyptian officers hard. They became increasingly rebellious, and united behind Colonel Ahmed Bey Arabi, who was determined to see these injustices redressed. A great wave of popular support for this big, honest man who had the courage to challenge the Turks forced the Khedive to accede to his demands. But when Arabi and the Army joined hands with those seeking a more liberal constitution, and campaigned for Egyptian control of that part of the budget not set aside for paying off the debt, Britain and France decided that the time had come for a show of strength.

In May 1882, British and French warships gathered off the coast of Egypt, and on 10 July Admiral Sir Beauchamp Seymour ordered Colonel Arabi to stop building earthworks in Alexandria. His ultimatum was ignored and, when the French were informed of what the British planned to do next, they withdrew their ships. On 11 July, Alexandria underwent twelve hours of bombardment from the Royal Navy. Arabi's army retreated, and a few days later the Khedive and his followers took refuge in British-occupied Alexandria.

That August a force of 20,000 under the command of Sir Garnet Wolseley moved quickly up the Canal to Ismailia, eighty miles east of Cairo. Arabi's army of between ten and fifteen thousand fought well at Qassassin; but, on the night of 13 September, Wolseley attacked them in their sleep at Tel el Kebir. About a third of Arabi's men were killed, and the rest scattered. The British occupation of Egypt had begun.

The French, Russians and Germans, and especially the Turks, were furious at Britain's intervention and demanded that she formally state her position and intentions concerning Egypt. The British refused, and said they would leave as soon as the authority of the Khedive and financial stability had been restored. However, once in Egypt, they found several good reasons for staying. The re-establishment of political and financial stability took longer than anticipated, while the Suez route to India became increasingly important to the security and prosperity of the British Empire. There was also the Sudan.

Geographically, Egypt is a ribbon of cultivation either side of a broad river, that runs for 700 miles through the desert. Since the water that feeds Egypt has to pass through the Sudan, the Egyptians naturally look on that country as an extension of the Nile Valley, and Muhammad Ali had brought it under Egyptian control. The Sudanese had been in revolt since 1881. Several bloody Anglo-Egyptian campaigns, and the dramatic stand of General Gordon at Khartoum, were at last avenged by victory at Omdurman in 1898. Lord Kitchener became a hero in Egypt; but, when Khartoum was taken, the Egyptians were not pleased to see the Union Jack flying over the city alongside their own flag. The Sudan remained a bone of contention between Egypt and Britain for the next fifty years, while the British ruled it with such efficiency that it became a model of colonial administration.

Sir Evelyn Baring, later Lord Cromer, was British Consul General in Egypt between 1882 and 1907. During that time the debt was paid off, financial equilibrium was established, and the taxation of the fellahin reduced. Any money left over was invested in projects that would earn a quick return. To satisfy Egyptian sensibilities, the façade of a Khedive ruling through a parliamentary government with Egyptian ministers was scrupulously (if transparently) maintained. Everybody knew that behind each Egyptian minister was a British civil servant.

Egypt under the 'Veiled Protectorate' worked extremely well. Apart from public health and education, which were sorely neglected, the Egyptians were still better off than they would have been under the Turks – and still resentful. Like the Turks, the new rulers gave the best jobs to their own young men, not to Egyptians.

The British attitude towards the latter ranged from good-humoured exasperation to benign contempt, and despite the benefits of British rule the Egyptians felt oppressed.

In June 1906, some British officers on their way from Cairo to Alexandria went pigeon-shooting near a village called Denshawi, without bothering to ask permission from the headman. Pigeons were part of the fellahin's meagre economy, and the British habit of indiscriminate bird-shooting near villages was detested.

Trouble broke out when the wife of the local imam was accidentally wounded by one of the officers. This led to a fight in which several people were badly injured, and one man from each side killed. Fifty-two villagers were arrested by the British, and for those found guilty the punishments were savage: four were executed, many were given long prison sentences with hard labour, and the rest were publicly flogged. The incident provoked widespread rioting among the outraged Egyptians, and aroused new fervour in the nationalist leader Mustafa Kamil and the Islamic fundamentalists, who wanted the British out at all costs. Mustafa Kamil died young in 1908. He is remembered as the man who first inspired the Egyptians to fight for independence, and persuaded them it was possible.

A more lenient approach to governing Egypt was taken by Cromer's successor, Sir Eldon Gorst; but the unrest in the country continued on and off until the appointment of Lord Kitchener in 1911. Although he put through some important reforms and was popular in Egypt, by the time he returned to England on the outbreak of war he had made a sworn enemy of the Khedive, Abbas Hilmi.

The Khedive was in Constantinople in 1914, and decided to throw in his lot with Turkey and the Germans. In Egypt, the nationalists and Islamic fundamentalists also sided with Turkey, but the Prime Minister Rushdi Pasha declared the country neutral and pro-Allies. Despite this support, Britain realised that she could no longer afford to keep up an unspecified relationship with Egypt; and, in December, the country was declared a British Protectorate.

Britain undertook to shoulder all responsibility for the war, including the defence of the Nile Valley, the Delta, and of course the Canal. Troops poured into the country, and the campaigns in

Gallipoli and Palestine were launched from Egypt. The people were asked to co-operate with the British, and they did so. Huge supplies of corn and fodder, plus thousands of camels and donkeys, were requisitioned. The British tried to be fair both in the requisitioning and the reimbursement, but the system was plagued with inefficiency and corruption. A Labour Corps was established, to lay lines of supply and communication. Wages were high to encourage volunteers but, as the war progressed, conscription to the Labour Corps was introduced. This was particularly hateful to the Egyptians, who saw it as a British version of the *corvée*.

Four years of war completely changed the face of the Middle East. The fledgling nations that grew out of the ashes of the Turkish Empire were untried. This state of affairs inclined Britain to strengthen rather than loosen her ties with Egypt, in order to maintain her influence in the region and protect the Suez Canal. But, in declaring the Protectorate in 1914, the British had sugared the pill by undertaking to consider the long-term possibility of Egyptian self-government. From this, the Egyptians understood that the Protectorate was temporary; and, having supported Britain loyally throughout the war, they wanted to discuss independence.

A new sort of nationalism had emerged in Egypt which, though more moderate than its predecessors, had the public support and the moral determination to become revolutionary. It was headed by Saad Zaghloul, a lawyer and former minister of Education and of Justice under Cromer. In 1918 he formed a delegation, which he proposed to take to London to discuss the future of his country. The Arabic word for a delegation is *wafd*, and Zaghloul's Wafd evolved into a political party that could justly claim to be the democratic voice of Egypt.

Not only did the British refuse to see Zaghloul, but Egypt was not represented at the Peace Conference – although the Hejaz, Syria, Iraq and Ethiopia were. In the spring of 1919, the Egyptians gave vent to their feelings in a series of riots and demonstrations that started in Cairo and spread through the country. The Egyptians count 1919 as their first revolution, though there were too many British troops to allow it any hope of success.

Although they had stamped out the rebellion and exiled Zaghloul, the British realised that they would never restore order until they came to an agreement with him. This stern, white-haired patriarch of peasant origins commanded tremendous support all over Egypt. Since he stubbornly insisted on the evacuation of British troops and Egyptian sovereignty of the Sudan, the British decided to bypass him altogether.

In 1922, Egypt was given qualified independence, and a constitution that greatly increased the power of the throne: for, with the dissolution of the Ottoman Empire, Muhammad Ali's dynasty had been raised to a monarchy. The British made certain 'Reserved Points', which might be discussed in the future but were at present under British control. These were the administration of the Sudan; the defence of Egypt and the route to India, which meant that the troops would not be evacuated; and the protection of foreign nationals.

Zaghloul, who returned from exile the following year, was disgusted by this travesty of independence, and he saw the new constitution as a grave danger to Egyptian unity. The power granted to the monarchy would inevitably attract supporters, which would sooner or later come into conflict with the Wafd. Energy would be squandered in political struggles, while the British sat back in overall control.

Most Egyptians, however, were happy with their new status as a sovereign country. The first elections brought the Wafd to power with a vast majority, and Zaghloul became Prime Minister, though this did not deter him from continuing his campaign for real independence. In May 1924, he reminded Parliament that an Englishman was Governor General of the Sudan, and Sirdar (commander-in-chief) of the Egyptian army. Three days later, the Sirdar, Sir Lee Stack, was murdered by nationalist extremists. The massive clampdown that followed marked the end of the revolutionary period that had begun in 1919. Zaghloul was deeply shocked by the assassination, and his first and only ministry was dissolved in December.

With the Wafd temporarily in eclipse, the other political parties came into the light. The most important party after the Wafd was that of the Liberal Constitutionalists. If the Wafd was the party of the people, the Constitutionalists represented the interests of the propertied classes and the old Turkish families. The Unionist Party was founded in 1925 by Nashaat Pasha, who was to become Egyptian Ambassador to London during the Second World War. However, the real leader of this party was never seen in Parliament; everybody knew it was the King.

King Fuad had co-operated with the British in 1919, rather than stand by the majority of his subjects and Zaghloul. The constitution of 1922 gave him power, which he fully intended to use. When Zaghloul, the founder of the Wafd, died in 1927, King Fuad silently hoped that the occasion would mark the decline of Egypt's popular party.

The leadership of the Wafd devolved on Nahas Pasha. Like Zaghloul he was of peasant stock; but this comfortable, paunchy politician who suffered from a severe astigmatism seemed the very antithesis of the distinguished statesman he succeeded. Everyone in Egypt had a jolly uncle like Nahas, and he achieved what Zaghloul never had – a workable treaty with the British.

The years between the death of Zaghloul and the signing of the Anglo-Egyptian Treaty in 1936 were increasingly uneasy, as the authoritarian King and the Wafd struggled for control of Egypt. Political instability led to waves of riots, strikes and demonstrations, followed by the inevitable clamp-down initiated by the Palace.

In October 1935 Italy invaded Ethiopia, and Egypt realised that she could not defend herself against the Italian threat without British help. An Anglo-Egyptian treaty was vital, but the British – although as keen as the Egyptians to have a solid base to their relationship – were unwilling to negotiate with anything less than a constitutionally elected government.

Elections were set for May 1936, and back came Nahas, to form his third ministry in eight years. The Anglo-Egyptian Treaty was negotiated and signed by August.

Only one of the four Reserved Points that had stood in the way of complete independence in 1922 had been resolved in Egypt's favour: the Capitulations, that had given the entire foreign community the privileges of a *corps diplomatique*, were abolished. The British still held the right to defend Egypt and the route to India, and the Sudan was to stay under British administration. But the Treaty was considered a victory for Nahas and the Wafd, for Egypt did gain a greater independence from the British. She became a member of the League of Nations; the British relinquished their hold on diplomatic affairs, and the High Commissioner, Sir Miles Lampson, became merely an Ambassador. However, the pre-eminence of Britain's diplomatic representative was underlined by the fact that he headed the only Embassy in Egypt. All other countries had legations or consulates, headed by diplomatic ministers or consuls.

Provision was also made for the expansion of the Egyptian armed forces. The Royal Military Academy, which had hitherto chosen its cadets from the rich upper classes, now opened its doors to a far wider section of society. Both Gamal Abdel Nasser and Anwar Sadat were part of this new intake of students. Coming from relatively poor and uninfluential families, they could never have hoped for such an opportunity before 1936.

King Fuad had not lived to see these developments, having died in April. It is ironic that his devoted work to improve higher education in Egypt had greatly increased the number of politically articulate Egyptians, for the old autocrat had never believed in democracy, and no doubt thought that he was doing his best for Egypt in trying to draw all power to himself. He found it easier to exert his authority on his family than on his country, but the effects were equally unsatisfactory.

THE KING AND THE CITY

An only son in a family of girls is usually indulged; if the family is Muslim and the son will one day be king, he will be shamelessly spoilt. King Fuad was aware of this, and so instituted a régime for the young Prince Farouk that kept him at his studies from morning till night. His son must have the best education, and he must speak demotic Arabic: the lack of which had been an embarrassment to Fuad, who – though King of Egypt – spoke only French, Turkish and Italian. Farouk was a bad scholar, but he learnt early that there were two sorts of people: those who dominated him, like his father and his tutors, and those he could dominate, like his doting mother Queen Nazli and the fawning palace servants. He ran to the latter whenever he could, to be petted and fed with cakes. When he grew too fat – for even as a child Farouk had a large appetite, and a tendency to corpulence – his father put him on a diet. Farouk later told a friend that he was sometimes so hungry, he would eat food put out for the cats. There was no one he knew as an equal. In the vast grounds of the Koubbeh Palace, on the beach of the palace of Montazah in Alexandria, the only children he played with were his little sisters, Fawzia, Faiza, Faika and Fathia. (Both the King and Queen were very superstitious, and a fortune-teller had once told Fuad that the letter F would bring his family luck.)

In 1935, at the age of fifteen, Farouk was sent to England to study at the Royal Military Academy in Woolwich. At the entrance examination, he waited for the answers to appear on his desk, as they always did in Egypt. This time they did not materialise. Farouk failed, though he was allowed to attend classes on two afternoons a week.

The royal party was installed at Kenry House, Kingston, where the Prince spent more time in the jewellery shops and tea parlours of the town than he did at his studies. Meanwhile, his Egyptian tutors argued about how to handle him. Aziz el Masri Pasha was a soldier and nationalist, who hated the British and admired the Germans. He believed in discipline. Hassanein Pasha, on the other hand, took a more indulgent view. Charming and sophisticated, he had made a name for himself as a desert explorer – and had won the Medal of the Royal Geographical Society for being the first to cross the Sahara from the Mediterranean to Darfur. He was also a courtier: and in the interests of securing his future sovereign's goodwill, he argued that the boy should be given his head. After only seven months in England, the Prince was hurried back to Egypt on the death of King Fuad.

It was one of Farouk's great misfortunes that he had barely turned sixteen when he found himself the richest and most powerful person in Egypt. As head of the royal family, even his mother and uncle were (technically) subject to his will. It was an immense burden for one who had not begun his adult life, and was emotionally weak; but as the King could only be advised, not told what to do, there was no one to share it with him. The isolation of his position, and a deep sense of inadequacy, made him awkward and given to absurd boasting in the company of his own social class: a boasting that often showed signs of an overheated fantasy. The first time he went duck-shooting he was the guest of Sir Miles Lampson, who was an experienced sportsman and a first-class shot. The Cairo papers, however, were told that His Majesty had shot two hundred and eight birds: sixty-eight more than his host, and a great many more than anyone else.

Farouk's father had been educated in Geneva and the Turin Military Academy. He had spent his happiest years in Italy and, on returning to Egypt, had retained a number of Italian servants. They had always been kind and indulgent to Farouk, who kept them in his immediate entourage; Antonio Pulli, the palace electrician, became the King's shadow, accompanying him everywhere when he was off duty. The palace Italians cushioned Farouk's sense of inadequacy with a back-slapping bonhomie, spiced with schoolboy pranks and smutty jokes. Theirs was the only companionship in which the young King felt at ease; and, compared with their easy laughter and flattery, the voices of his family and counsellors sounded like constant and unbearable nagging.

A young English tutor called Edward (later Sir Edward) Ford was appointed to Farouk's staff, and it was hoped that he might have a healthy influence on His Majesty. It was an impossible job. Farouk did not think he needed much tutoring – he claimed to have exhausted most subjects, from the American Civil War to the Theory of Relativity. Ford saw that what the King really needed was a friend, and made it known that if ever His Majesty should feel like a game of bridge or tennis, he would be delighted to oblige. But Farouk rarely summoned him, preferring to drive cars at terrifying speed around the palace grounds.

Edward Ford accompanied the royal party, which included Farouk and his mother, on a cruise to Upper Egypt in January 1937. In his diary, he recorded what happened when he told Farouk that his astonishing success at duck-shooting was not believed in Cairo.

'Farouk's answer was that he was not sure of the 8 but he himself had certainly shot 200 with his own gun! The facts apparently are that, shooting very well for a beginner, he brought down 40 or 50 duck but that there were two or three good Bedouin shots behind him who put the rest into his bag.'[1]

Farouk's emotional stability was not helped by the behaviour of his mother. The late King Fuad had held very strict ideas on the seclusion of women and, once her husband was dead, Nazli took on a new lease of life. On holiday in Europe she was seen at the theatre, in restaurants, at parties, even dancing. She could not behave so freely in Egypt; but it was no secret that her most constant companion – both at home and abroad – was Farouk's old tutor, Hassanein Pasha, whom Nazli had made her Chamberlain. The King took great exception to their liaison. On one occasion he was tipped off that a man was in Nazli's apartments in the *haramlek*.* Farouk stormed in, brandishing a pistol – and caught Hassanein in the act of reading the Koran to his mother. It is said that they were secretly married in

---

* Muslim houses are divided into the *salamlek*, the more public side of the house which includes the reception rooms, and the *haramlek* or women's quarters.

1937; and that, when Hassanein died in a car crash in 1946, Farouk ordered the marriage contract to be destroyed.

In those early days of his reign, Farouk was very good-looking. Tall and well-built, he also had the light hair and pale eyes so admired in the Orient, which made him an ideal of masculine beauty to his subjects. They were deeply proud of this beloved son; and in July 1937, more than two million people from all over the country poured into Cairo, to celebrate the crowning of the first King of independent Egypt.

The people of Egypt were equally jubilant when in January 1938, a month before his eighteenth birthday, Farouk married the sixteen-year-old Safinaz Zulficar. Her father, Yousef Zulficar, was Vice-President of the Mixed Courts of Appeal in Alexandria, and her mother had been lady-in-waiting to Queen Nazli. In accordance with the family fondness for the letter F her name was changed to Farida, 'the only one'. Farida became very popular in Egypt, where she appeared in innumerable magazines – her pretty features framed by the *hotoze*, a Turkish headdress of white gauze which was still *de rigueur* for royal ladies.

It was Queen Nazli who had brought the couple together and encouraged their relationship (though both she and the Zulficars had tried to persuade them to postpone marriage until they were a little older). She hoped to dominate her daughter-in-law by constantly reminding her of who was responsible for her elevation, but Farida resisted her with spirit, and furious rows were not uncommon between the two Queens. Nevertheless, Farida was high in her husband's favour – certainly higher than the Queen Mother. It was said (though it was probably no more than a rumour, encouraged by Farida's entourage) that the King gave her a present of jewels every day, which had to be stored in special chests of drawers since no jewel box could contain them.

Until such time as the King had a son, the heir to the throne was his cousin, Prince Muhammad Ali. He was a neat and fussy man with charming manners, a trim figure, and a well-clipped white beard. He wore his tarboosh at a jaunty angle, and on his hand there was always a ring set with a huge cabochon emerald. This stone had a strange story. In his youth Prince Muhammad Ali had been very sickly, and his doctors had given up all hope of improving his constitution. However, the Prince had sought the advice of a wise woman who told him to invest everything he had in a single object. He bought one flawless emerald, which had cost him more than he could afford; but he had never had a day's illness from that moment on. Prince Muhammad Ali had written a book called *The Breeding of Arabian Horses*, but his principal interest now was his collection of antique treasures, and the cultivation of his garden at the Manial Palace, said to be the most beautiful in Cairo.

He was extremely pro-British, and often dropped in at the Embassy for a chat with Miles Lampson, who would have to drop everything at a moment's notice to receive His Royal Highness. Prince Muhammad Ali thought that the British Ambassador was far too soft, both with the Egyptians and his young cousin Farouk, of whom he complained incessantly.

There were two principal figures in Farouk's public life: his staunch political supporter Ali Maher Pasha, and the British Ambassador. Sir Miles had been appointed High Commissioner for Egypt in 1933, having been Minister to China before that. The Egyptians, pleased with the part he played in the construction of the Anglo-Egyptian Treaty of the previous year, had asked that he be kept on as Britain's first Ambassador to Egypt. Harold Macmillan described him as 'a man of considerable personality – strong, unscrupulous and entertaining',[2] but his undoubted shrewdness and powers of observation were sometimes dulled by a refusal to see both sides of the question – particularly Egyptian questions. Sir Miles stood an impressive six-foot-six. He wore grey frock coats with spotted bow ties, and had a no-nonsense, avuncular manner to go with his commanding bulk.

He had scant respect for Farouk, whom he referred to as 'the boy' – not only in his diaries, but in public as well. To Farouk, who called Lampson 'the Schoolmaster' or '*Gamoose** Pasha', the British Ambassador represented everything he hated most: a ponderous authoritarian father-figure, and the foreign occupation his country yearned to be rid of.

---

* water buffalo

The knowledge that Sir Miles did not approve must have made Farouk all the more inclined to listen to Ali Maher Pasha, who had served his father and was now the new King's closest political adviser. Small, fastidious, and well-scented, Ali Maher suffered from dyspepsia and was never without his pills. As well as being efficient and well-organised he had a remarkable skill for intrigue, for which he was feared; and among parliamentarians and democrats, he was hated for his pro-monarchist machinations in 1923. In late 1937 he had started to capitalise on the King's youth and popularity, which was then at its height – for Ali Maher's ambition was to be the power behind the throne, with Parliament kept on a short leash through a web of informers.

The Prime Minister, Nahas Pasha, was very concerned by the King's rising popularity, which was – as Ali Maher intended – undermining that of the democratic Wafd Party. Nahas had already stood in Farouk's way on a couple of occasions, and the rift between the Palace and the Wafd grew wider. In December 1937, Nahas attempted to block the King's power once and for all. The result was a massive anti-Wafd demonstration, mounted by the Islamic University of el Azhar, and the students of the (secular) University of Cairo. Thousands of people gathered outside the Abdin Palace, all shouting for the King, and pushed Nahas and the Wafd ignominiously out of power. The Palace had won; and in August 1938, Ali Maher became Prime Minister.[3]

Like those other great trading cities of the Middle East – Aleppo, Damascus and Istanbul – Cairo was made up of a cluster of different communities. Muslims, Copts, Jews, Syro-Lebanese Christians, as well as French, Italian, Maltese, Cypriot and Greek expatriates, all did business together over endless little cups of sugary coffee, and glasses of syrupy tea. Good manners prompted a Muslim to offer his Christian friends the compliments of the season at Christmas and Easter, and they did likewise at the feasts of the Muslim New Year and the Prophet's Birthday.

There was remarkably little racial or religious discrimination; but the banks and department stores in the smarter parts of town tended to favour employees of European origin, and young European women worked as shop assistants and secretaries. Their families lived far better in Egypt than they could have done in Europe: taxes were minimal, food was plentiful and cheap, and most households had more than one servant. They were educated at the French, Italian and American mission schools, of which there were several – and this was one area where the British lagged far behind. Apart from the excellent Victoria College in Alexandria, the Gezira Preparatory School and the work of the British Council, the British had neglected education in Egypt. It was a policy started by Lord Cromer, who positively disapproved of education on the grounds that a little learning was a dangerous thing.

The visitors to King Farouk's capital found their expectations of Cairo well-satisfied by the donkeys, street vendors, bazaars and cafés that go to make up the jingling cacophony of Arab street life; but the Egyptian middle classes were closer in spirit to provincial France than to the *Thousand and One Nights*, and a veneer of French culture was necessary for anyone aspiring to refinement.

At the time of the Khedive Ismail, Turkish and French had been the languages of the ruling classes. Since independence Arabic had taken the place of Turkish as the language of government and, although more and more English was spoken, French was still dominant in business and social life. Much of private education, and a substantial portion of the press, was in French; it was also the language of cafés and tea-rooms, department stores and learned societies, museums, banks and cotton-houses. As one Cairene scholar put it, 'To be French-speaking was to think of Cairo as home, but to believe that Paris was the navel of the world.'[4] The Comédie Française and the Paris Opera came regularly to Cairo and Alexandria, and the French style – in everything except gentlemen's tailoring – was usually preferable to the English. Elaborate French furniture and porcelain were particularly popular, in a society where the home is an exclusively feminine preserve.

The Egyptian middle classes also favoured a foreign education, and it was not unusual for Muslims to send their sons to the Catholic mission schools. Then the brightest went to the American University in Cairo, or Fuad I University on the Giza side of the Nile. From there, the lucky ones would follow their fathers into the family business, or become teachers, lawyers, and government officials; but there was very little industry in Egypt at the time, and plum jobs still tended to go to Europeans. No wonder many students turned to politics, and vented their frustrations in nationalistic and anti-British demonstrations.

At the top of the Egyptian social scale was a cosmopolitan society that did not aspire to be Europeanised – it already was. English nannies and French governesses had ensured that its members spoke both languages with equal ease. Their sons went to Victoria College in Alexandria and then on to Oxford or Cambridge, while their daughters were finished in Switzerland. They could speak Arabic, but it was used mostly to communicate with the servants. Time was divided between their villas in Alexandria and Cairo, and the hottest months were spent abroad, in Geneva or Paris.

'*Je vais vous présenter la haute Juiverie, la haute Copterie, et la haute Mussulmanie du Caire,*' declared one observer of Cairene society to a newcomer.[5] Strictly speaking she should have added '*la haute Levantinerie*' and '*la haute Grecquerie*', but the flourish of the sentence would have been lost.

The '*haute Mussulmanie*' of Cairo was dominated, naturally enough, by the royal family. The older generation was headed by Prince Muhammad Ali, the heir to the throne, and Prince Omar Toussoun. By strict descent from the founder of the dynasty, both were senior to Farouk, and both deplored the decadence of the younger generation – but Prince Omar Toussoun was the more old-fashioned. He had exquisite manners, scholarly interests, and was a devout Muslim. Prince Omar Toussoun had never forgiven King Fuad for disobeying the Koranic injunction against copying natural forms, by allowing his image to appear on Egyptian currency.

Prince Omar Toussoun had two sons, who despite, or perhaps because of, their strict upbringing quickly developed corrupt Western tastes. For as long as they lived under his roof the old Prince never discovered that the whisky smuggled into his house was purchased on his account, where it appeared as '*Eau d'Evian*'. The Prince was astonished at the quantity of mineral water his sons managed to consume.

The eldest, Prince* Said, married Mahavesh Shirin in 1931; while the younger son, Prince Hasan, married Fatma Sherifa in 1940. Fatma and Mahavesh Toussoun were young, beautiful and high-spirited. King Farouk would often ring Mahavesh or Fatma to find out what parties were taking place that week, and they would suggest which ones he might like to drop in on. Towards the end of the war, it was widely rumoured that Princess Fatma Toussoun had become Farouk's mistress. She was supposed to have borne him an illegitimate daughter, who was known as '*Mademoiselle Roi*'.

The husbands of Fatma and Mahavesh were constantly scolded by their father for not keeping their wives under control; and Prince Omar Toussoun was disappointed by the refusal of his only surviving daughter, Princess Emine, to sit in the *haramlek* all day like a respectable woman. At the age of twenty-two, Emine had been one of three princesses to appear unveiled at the Cairo Opera House in 1925, which caused a sensation.

The Princess's first husband (from whom she had been divorced for over a year before the famous unveiling) was Prince Omar Halim, a keen polo player. Her second marriage lasted barely a year, and after the war she married a United States naval officer, Captain Cornelius Bretsch.

Among Muslim women of the upper classes at this time, one could find extraordinary variations in lifestyle – particularly in the royal family. Princess Nimetullah Mukhtar kept herself in comparative seclusion in her palace at Maarg. She received the occasional male visitor, but was never seen at mixed parties, and her social life revolved around female friends and family. She was frequently visited by King Farouk, over whom she was supposed to have had a far greater influence than either his mother Queen Nazli, or his wife Queen Farida. However, Farouk was also very fond of his father's first wife, Princess Shevekiar, who was famous for some of the most spectacular parties in Cairo.

---

* Technically the sons of Prince Omar Toussoun were not princes, but *nabils*: a title beneath the rank of prince, accorded to those who were of royal blood but not closely related to the reigning family. To avoid confusion this book does not make the distinction, and refers to all members of the Egyptian royal family (below Kings and Queens) as Prince or Princess.

The young princes had little to do but pursue fashionable pleasures. In Cairo these included a love of intrigue, horse-racing, and
clothes, for they set the pace in this clothes-conscious society. They
also gambled with the King at the Royal Automobile Club, or the
Muhammad Ali Club – the grandest and most luxurious establishment of its kind in Cairo. It was largely patronised by Egyptians;
but a great many Allied officers joined during the course of the war,
particularly since it boasted one of the best restaurants in the city.

One or two princes, however, had more serious ambitions.
Prince Abbas Halim had fought for the Germans in the First War,
admired the ideology of National Socialism, and involved himself
in trade unions. The British did not approve of his pro-German
sympathies, for which he was interned in 1942; but in the meantime
they enjoyed going to the parties he gave with his wife Tahida Halim
in Garden City. Ironically one of Abbas Halim's palaces, at 6 Sharia
Rustum, acted as the American Legation in Cairo.

Outside the royal family, Muslim women were less visible. Nahed
Sirry, whose husband became prime minister in late 1941, was not
seen in public until after his appointment. There were also a number
of Muslims who had married women of other religions, to whom
the Islamic code of conduct did not apply. Ahmed Bey Sadik, shortly
to become the Sequestrator of German property in Egypt, was married to a beautiful red-haired Jewess called Vicky who was said to
have had an affair with Feisal of Iraq. The Sadiks were among the
rich Cairenes who had a houseboat or *dahabiya* moored on the Nile,
which they used for entertaining. Mamduh Riaz Bey had married a
Frenchwoman, Marie Cavadia, who was among the most flamboyant hostesses in Cairo; while Abboud Pasha, one of the richest men
in Egypt, had married a Scottish girl of humble origins. The British
sniggered at the studied refinement of Madame Abboud Pasha; but
they took to Katie, a plump blonde barmaid with a Cockney accent
who had married the Wafd politician Sir Amin Osman Pasha. When
asked what it was like to be Lady Amin Osman Pasha, she replied,
'Ever so nice – I get to be a lady at both ends.'

The '*haute Juiverie*' – the Cattauis, the Rolos, the Hararis and
the Menasces – were the financiers of Egypt. They moved in royal
circles: Madame Joseph Cattaui Pasha and Valentine Rolo, wife of

Sir Robert, were both said to have been mistresses of King Fuad. Sir Robert Rolo was Director of the National Bank of Egypt. He had a son called Simon, whose taste in dress was considered a shade too loud; but his taste in women was impeccable, and his half-Italian, half-American wife Consuelo was one of the most beautiful women in Cairo. Sir Victor Harari Pasha was a brilliant financier who had worked with Lord Cromer, and had devoted his life to business and philanthropy. He was continually urging his son Max to take a more serious view of life; but, like so many rich young men in Cairo, Max preferred playing polo at the Gezira Sporting Club. He would serve with the 8th Hussars in the coming war. The Menasces had been ennobled by the Emperor of Austria. Baron Georges de Menasce was very disturbed by hands – other people's and his own: he always wore gloves, and would only play the piano if the audience could not see his fingers. Georges de Menasce's brother Charles was extremely proud of his family's nobility, and displayed the Patent from the Emperor on a magnificent lectern in his front hall.

If any modern inhabitants of Egypt can claim to be the descendants of the Pharaohs, it is the Copts. Their ancestors were the indigenous Egyptians to whom St Mark brought Christianity, and who clung to that religion after the Arab conquest of Egypt in 640 AD. The words Copt and Egypt come from the same root. The great Coptic families of Egypt were landowners and politicians – and, in Cairene society, the most visible were the Wissas, the Wahbas, the Ghalis and the Khyatts. Traditionally they were pro-British, and all four families were immensely hospitable. The Wissas held weekend parties for their British friends in their family house at Assyut, and shooting parties at Abouxa in the Fayoum; while Bobby Khyatt's Christmas party was one of the highlights of the social year. Being Christian, they had no objections to their daughters enjoying the pleasures of Anglo-Egyptian society, and among the most social were two sets of sisters: Gertrude (more often known as Gertie), Farousa, and Philae Wissa, and their cousins Samira and Samiha Wahba. One of the most popular members of the '*haute Copterie*' was Victor Simaika, who was blessed with good looks and an ebullient love of life. Men admired his excellent polo, while with women he was charming, witty and romantic.

The important Greek families in Egypt – the Salvagos, Benachis, Zervudachis, and Rodocanachis – had come to Egypt in the latter half of the previous century, and lived mainly in Alexandria. The Mosseris were Greek Jews; and Elie Mosseri's widow Hélène, who entertained in the sumptuous Mosseri house in Cairo, specialised in entertaining royalty. Prince Peter and Princess Irene of Greece were to become frequent visitors in the latter half of the war (though Crown Prince Paul and Princess Frederica were never seen there, since the latter strongly disapproved of Peter and Irene's morganatic marriage). Hélène Mosseri was also a close friend of King Farouk's. It was said that the King had installed a private telephone line on which he would ring her up, at any hour of the day or night. Farouk also gave her a magnificent emerald and diamond bracelet, of which she was very proud – but, when she tried to sell it in harder days, the stones turned out to be false.

Cairene society also included a number of Syro-Lebanese Christians, among whom were the Lotfallah brothers and the Nimrs. Dr Fares Nimr had founded the newspaper *el Mokkatam*, and he and his family lived in the green suburb of Maadi, linked to Cairo by a long avenue lined with pepper trees. His daughter Amy married the British Oriental Councillor Walter Smart, while his daughter Katy married one of the great scholars of Arab nationalism, George Antonius. The main distinction of George and Habib Lotfallah, apart from their popularity as great party-givers, was that they lived in Gezira Palace (now the Marriott Hotel), which Ismail the Magnificent had erected in a matter of months to accommodate the Empress Eugénie during her visit to open the Suez Canal.

These rich and hospitable people mixed easily with the upper echelons of the British community, whose most distinguished member was Sir Thomas Russell Pasha. As Chief of the Cairo Police, he was best known for smashing the Egyptian narcotics trade. He retired in 1946, by which time he was the last British officer in the Egyptian Civil Service. His knowledge of Egypt and the Egyptians was born of a deep love of the country and respect for its inhabitants. Tall, elegant and urbane, Russell Pasha enjoyed the pleasures of life in Cairo; yet the most beautiful passages of his memoirs describe the days he spent hunting in the green fringes of the desert.

Russell Pasha was one of the characters in *The Gentle Men*, a *roman à clef* by Miriam Vogt, the wife of the Norwegian Counsellor, which describes her experiences with four of her many lovers in Egypt. (The other three were the writer Gordon Waterfield; Major the Hon. Cecil Campbell, who managed the Marconi Radio and Telegraph Company in Egypt; and Professor Robin Furness, of the English Department of Cairo University.) The book was printed by the aptly-named Obelisk Press in Paris, and seems to have been sold in large numbers at the station bookshop of the Gare du Nord. From the moment his formidable wife Dorothea found out, some said that Russell Pasha was never allowed to leave the house with more than 20 piastres* in his pocket; yet others claimed she was rather pleased to discover there was life in the old dog yet.

The leaders of the British community had nearly all been in the service of the Egyptian government. Sir Alexander Keown-Boyd had been Director General of the European Department in the Egyptian Ministry of the Interior. With a group of Egyptian pashas he founded the Egyptian dyeing industry, and it was said that these connections gained him inside information about what was going on in Egyptian politics – information that was passed to the British Embassy.

Sir Robert Greg[6] was another prominent feature on the social landscape; his mannered pomposity earned him the nickname 'Pompy' Greg. Under the Protectorate he directed the Ministry of Foreign Affairs, and served as Commissioner for the Public Debt for ten years before his retirement in 1940. Sir Robert was a connoisseur, and luckily his wife Julia was a wealthy American who loved beautiful objects as much as her husband did. Their large villa in Sharia Ibn Bakil, Giza, was a showcase for his collections. Archaeology was another of Sir Robert's interests; and this, plus his skills as a diplomat, made him just the person to approach the estate of the late Howard Carter in March 1940, and persuade them to return objects from the tomb of Tutankhamun which rightfully belonged to the Egyptian Museum.

---

* Since 1885, the unit of currency in Egypt has been known as the Egyptian pound (£E) – then valued at £1. 0s. 6d. in English currency. The Egyptian pound is divided into 100 piastres, each piastre being worth 10 milliemes.

Apart from those who moved in the highest Anglo-Egyptian social circles, most of the British in Egypt were more integrated in the economic than the social life of Egypt. Working for the government, there was the permanent British staff of the Egyptian State Railway, irrigation inspectors, and (lowest in the pecking order) teachers of the Department of Public Instruction. There were also merchants, doctors, bankers, businessmen, lawyers, and every other profession which could find itself a lucrative niche in Egypt. They were catered for by certain shops which specialised in goods of an unmistakably British flavour – Roberts Hughes for shoes, and Davies·Bryan's department store, full of sensible clothes, huge tins of Huntley & Palmer's biscuits and bales of chintzes. However, not all the British felt the need to isolate themselves from the everyday life of Egypt. Two lecturers of Cairo University had converted to Islam, and lived in Giza when most British lived in Zamalek. They were known as Abu Bakr Serag ed Din Lings, and Hussein Nur ed Din Patterson.

In Cairo, the life of the élite – social, commercial and political – took place within a mile radius of Midan Ismail Pasha (now renamed Midan Tahrir). The commercial centre of the town lay between Midan Ismail Pasha and Ezbekieh Gardens: an area of broad streets lined with offices, apartment blocks and the occasional modern department store. The architectural styles of these buildings were either Viennese, Italian, Art Nouveau or flamboyant neo-Arab; obscured at street level by window-displays, large signs in French and Arabic, banks, cinemas, cafés, and cocktail bars.

Roads were busy; but traffic moved far more freely than it does today, and there was no trouble parking. However, all cars without chauffeurs were subject to the urchins of Cairo: and, unless the driver was willing to have his automobile 'guarded', he might well return to find the air let out of his tyres. Most submitted to this small-time protection racket; and, when giving the boys a few coins at the end of an evening, the inevitable question from the recipient was *'Fein el cocktail bokra?'* (Where is the party tomorrow?). For those who did not have cars, both taxis and horse-drawn gharries were frequent and inexpensive.

Immediately to the south of Ezbekieh Gardens was the immense royal palace of Abdin, the chief residence of King Farouk, built by the Khedive Ismail in 1863. This was surrounded to the north and east by the offices of the Household, inspectorates, and barracks for the Palace Guard; while the rest of the Abdin quarter was distinguished by a large number of mosques, schools, and the HM King Fuad Museum of Hygiene.

Westwards towards the Nile lay the parliament buildings, ringed by a constellation of ministries; and between them and the river was a fashionable quarter which took its name from the Midan Kasr el Dubbara. There, the richest Egyptians and members of the royal family lived in large, imposing mansions; while just to the south lay the winding, tree-lined streets of Garden City. Here the houses were just as substantial but closer together, and interspersed with office and apartment blocks. Although both British and Egyptian families lived in Garden City, it was mainly favoured by Egyptians, who liked its proximity to the centre of town. The British tended to prefer Zamalek, immediately to the north of the Sporting Club. Being on an island in the Nile, it had a fresher feel than Garden City. Zamalek was made up of long straight boulevards lined with plane trees, and its houses and apartments were simpler and airier than those on the east bank.

There were two smart suburbs beyond the central circle. Baron Empain had built Heliopolis to the north-east of the city; and his own house, modelled on a Hindu temple, is a landmark on the present-day journey from Cairo airport into the city. A few miles to the south lay Maadi, with its large villas set in spacious, luxuriant gardens. Beyond these two, and in between the fashionable areas of the central circle, Cairo was a Muslim rather than a cosmopolitan city. Contact between the two worlds was restricted to commercial transactions. Neither the British nor the French- and English-speaking Egyptian upper classes had any social contact with the ordinary, Arabic-speaking people of Cairo.

The main streets of Shubra, Bulaq, and Sayida Zeinab, the lower class areas of Cairo, were prosperous and filled with little shops, cafés and businesses; but, beyond them, architectural order disintegrated. Dwellings of brick and mud were piled together without drainage or running water, and the streets split into a labyrinth of narrow alley-ways where children played in the dust. Among the adults, men were willing to travel wherever there was work; but the women rarely went beyond the well where they fetched their water. Large areas of these districts were uncharted – even on the huge, linen-backed, 1:5,000 maps of the Survey of Egypt; and whole communities lived among the tombs and mausolea of the City of the Dead.

However, there were landmarks in this little-known city. To the north-east, in the Mouski district, stood the tenth-century Mosque of el Azhar and the great courtyard of the Islamic University, where the students sat in small groups on the ground to hear the discourses of their religious teachers. Just beyond el Azhar was the Khan el Khalili bazaar, where tourists and residents alike came to buy faience beads, silver, alabaster, rugs, spices, and perfumes. Both the bazaar and the Islamic University lie between the gates of Bab el Futuh in the north, and Bab el Zuwayla to the south, which guard what is left of the greatest medieval capital in the world. How long the remains of this city will survive the pace of modern life is debatable; but it was meticulously recorded by Professor Archibald Creswell, Professor of Muslim Art and Architecture at Fuad I University.

The British garrison in Cairo was housed in the Citadel of Muhammad Ali, a vast complex which included married quarters, tennis courts, stables and training grounds. There was also a smaller barracks on the edge of the Nile at Kasr el Nil which could house about 1,000 men. Every incoming British regiment blamed its pre-decessor for the bedbugs in the Kasr el Nil barracks, which seemed remarkably resistant to every form of insecticide.

As well as being protected by this large garrison, the British way of life was enshrined in five magnificent institutions, two of which looked directly onto the Nile: the British Embassy in Garden City, and the Cathedral of All Saints, Bulaq. The Cathedral had been built by Adrian Gilbert Scott, and looked as heavy and purposeful as a power station. It was eventually pulled down in 1975, to make way for the 6 October Bridge.

A sadder loss, claimed by the Corniche, was the bottom half of the British Embassy's lawn in Garden City which spread from the terrace down to a low wall at the very edge of the Nile. The Embassy itself is unchanged: an ample colonial house, protected from the sun by a wide columned verandah on two storeys and guarded by wrought iron railings adorned with the cypher of Queen Victoria. The portico is flanked by stone lions, and a short flight of stairs leads up into the house. In Sir Miles Lampson's day, its lofty rooms hung in silk damask provided an impressive setting for the antique chests and chairs he had brought back from China, and his collection of Persian rugs.

Between the Cathedral and Ezbekieh, the area that could be described as Cairo's West End, was the Turf Club – an exclusively British, all-male establishment at 32 Sharia Adly Pasha which would not have looked out of place in St James's Street. A few minutes' walk from there brought one to Shepheard's Hotel – which, after the Pyramids, was the most famous tourist landmark in Cairo.

The founding of Shepheard's Hotel in 1841, and its profitable association with the earliest 'expeditions' organised by Thomas Cook in the 1870s, had provided the base camp for travellers journeying all over the Middle East. Beyond the famous terrace, set with wicker chairs and tables and commanding a lofty and shaded view of Ibrahim Pasha Street, lay the Moorish Hall. It was deliciously cool and dimly lit by a dome of coloured glass that hung above it; and, to the small groups sitting comfortably in plump, anti-macassared chairs round little octagonal tables, it gave a feeling of intimacy and discretion. The ballroom featured lotus-topped pillars modelled on those of Karnak, which prompted one writer to describe the hotel's style as 'Eighteenth Dynasty Edwardian'.[7] Some found it oppressive. One visitor wrote that it was like living in the British Museum, and 'even the lavatories have something monumental about them . . . you feel as if you were sitting in the central chamber inside a pyramid.'[8] From the Moorish Hall the great staircase swept upwards, flanked by two tall caryatids of ebony with magnificent breasts, which were subjected to humiliating indignities on boisterous evenings. Presiding over the Long Bar of Shepheard's Hotel was Joe, the Swiss barman, probably one of the best-informed people in Cairo. The fact that women were not allowed in the Long Bar made its patrons notoriously indiscreet; and, during the Desert War, it was said that anyone who wanted to find out the Order of Battle for the next offensive only needed to sit in the Long Bar for a while, and keep his ears open. Perhaps it was to encourage discretion that the rumour was put about that Joe was a spy. If he was, he never gave himself away.

For the British privates and NCOs in Egypt, life in Cairo was a hotter version of the square-bashing and weapon-cleaning they could expect at Aldershot or Catterick, with the occasional game of football on some dry and dusty pitch. Their officers, however, had access to the most magnificent sports grounds ever seen in the heart of a capital city. The Gezira Sporting Club was laid out on land given by the Khedive Tewfik to the British Army. It covered the entire southern end of Gezira Island with gardens, polo fields, a 5,250-yard golf course, a race course, cricket pitches, squash courts, croquet lawns and tennis courts. A new club house was built in 1938, consisting of a square stuccoed building, painted cream and dark red, flanked by two wings angled around a terrace known as the Lido, since the swimming pool was directly in front of it. From their stuffy offices or their houses in Zamalek, people gathered under the awnings of the Lido for lunch. It has been said that the Sporting Club was exclusively British, which is not true. Many members were drawn from the richest and most Westernised Egyptian families, though they were greatly outnumbered by British members. There was also a garden, in one corner of which was a pets' cemetery, and a playground where nannies and their charges would congregate in the afternoons. This was kept well away from the serious business of the Club, which centred around racing and polo.

While the Egyptians could understand the care and attention devoted to valuable horses, they found the overwhelming British sentimentality for downtrodden beasts of burden quite incomprehensible. They also saw nothing wrong with selling a fine horse once it was past its prime, and allowing it to pass down the scale of owners; until, as the property of a poor carter, it would be half-starved and crippled with back-breaking loads until it died of exhaustion.

This had been the fate of hundreds of old war horses in Egypt, which had been shipped out from England with the cavalry and sold off at the end of the First War. It was to save them from such pain and misery that Dorothy Brooke, the wife of a British Army officer who came out to Egypt in 1930, founded what the poor Egyptians considered the craziest institution they had ever heard of. Once a week the carters of Cairo would bring their beasts to a sale: when the mad English woman and her friends would buy up the very worst, put them in a deliciously comfortable stable with as much food as they could eat, and – if they were past healing – kill them. Dorothy Brooke bought up as many of these pathetic wrecks as she could; but she looked out for old war horses in particular – recognisable by their huge frames, and the arrow-shaped brand on their mangy flanks.

Such was the support for the Old War Horse Memorial Fund that when the Second World War broke out, the British Army promised that cavalry horses sent out to the Middle East would be humanely killed rather than sold. War horses are now a thing of the past; but Dorothy Brooke's work still continues at the Brooke Hospital for Animals, Cairo, where the mules and donkeys of the poor are treated free of charge.

In fact, there were very few cavalry horses in Egypt during the Second World War. Mounted cavalry and yeomanry regiments were mostly kept for patrol work in Palestine and Transjordan, while cavalry regiments in Egypt were largely mechanised. The 11th Hussars were to become one of the most battle-seasoned units in 7th Armoured Division, the Desert Rats. They had arrived in Egypt for a tour of duty in 1934; and, in the five years' training up till the outbreak of war, had learnt more than any other unit about handling armour in the desert. They also took their polo very seriously. Forty-six polo ponies had been sent out a year in advance of the regiment's arrival to become acclimatised, and another twenty-two were bought in Alexandria. The regimental history expresses grave disappointment that, due to armoured car patrols in the desert, trouble in Palestine and the Desert War, the entire regiment was never in Cairo long enough to get a proper team together.

1939–1940

Preparing for War

A war on two fronts had destroyed Germany in the First War, and Hitler was determined not to make the same mistake again. The Nazi-Soviet non-aggression pact of August 1939, followed by the invasion and dismembering of Poland, had secured his eastern front; and he could now turn his attention to the west.

Britain and France, unprepared as they were, could only hope to hold Hitler off while they built up their own strength and supply base. This meant bringing oil from the Middle East, and men and materials from Canada, South Africa, Australia, New Zealand, India, and Indo-China. Whoever was in command of the Middle East was going to have to defend the Suez Canal, the Red Sea, and the Eastern Mediterranean, as well as prepare for war with the Italians. Their armies in Libya, Ethiopia and Italian Somaliland could not be expected to remain neutral for ever.

General Sir Archibald Wavell arrived in Egypt on 2 August 1939. He was fifty-six, and had served in France, Russia and Egypt in the First War. Behind his formidable reserve, which articulate and emotional people like Churchill found baffling, was a mind both lucid and profound. As Commander-in-Chief Middle East, a title confirmed in February 1940, he was responsible for the land forces in Egypt, Transjordan and Cyprus, which would be increased to British Somaliland, Aden and Iraq in time of war. He was to liaise with all the Ambassadors, High Commissioners and Governors General in that enormous parish, and co-ordinate Britain's battle plans with those of her allies over an area that stretched from Syria to Ethiopia, and from the Western Desert to Baghdad. His force in Egypt consisted of one armoured division in the process of formation (later to win fame as 7th Armoured Division) and eight battalions of infantry.

He was to concentrate on building up the defences of the Delta and the Western Desert, without in any way provoking the Italians.

Mussolini's invasion of Ethiopia had shown that he was not beyond fabricating an excuse to go to war. And his maps would look much tidier if the Italian Empire in Africa, now in two pieces, were joined together by the inclusion of Egypt and the Sudan. The Italian forces in Cyrenaica were estimated at 215,000 men, and in Ethiopia the Duke of Aosta's army numbered a quarter of a million. Wavell did not, however, expect the Italians to attack in the immediate future. Intelligence reports indicated that their men had no wish for a fight; but the fact remained that they outnumbered his men by five to one, and were considerably better equipped.

Lieutenant-General Sir Henry Maitland Wilson, more usually known as Jumbo Wilson, arrived a few weeks ahead of Wavell on 21 June to take up his appointment as General Officer Commanding British Troops in Egypt. His brief was to prepare plans for the invasion of Libya and build up the defences of Egypt, particularly Alexandria. He also had to prepare for the reception of an army of fifteen divisions, which would mean providing accommodation for some 300,000 men. Throughout that winter he worked tirelessly, hampered by slim resources and a sluggish administration.

As a large-scale military base, Egypt possessed a number of advantages. It had three deep-water ports, and a railway between Suez and Palestine's deep-water port at Haifa. Cheap labour was plentiful. And, however inhospitable the desert, there was plenty of room for military installations without wasting precious agricultural land.

Almost all the military infrastructure the British had left behind in 1918 had been dismantled or let go to ruin, so new workshops and ammunition depots had to be constructed in the area of Tel el Kebir and Qassassin, to the west of Ismailia, where they could make use of the railway and the Sweet-Water Canal. New roads, airfields and lines of communication had to be built, pipes laid to take Nile water into the desert, and water-purifying plants installed to treat it. Training schools, permanent base camps, canteens, and field hospitals had to be organised. The unloading, handling and storage of cargo had to be drastically increased, and Egypt and Palestine were combed for desert-worthy vehicles, particularly trucks.[1] Tanks designed for muddy European fields were found to seize up in the desert, their tracks torn by the rocky ground, their air-filters choked with sand.

Since Egypt had almost no raw materials except food, the problem of supply was enormous. GHQ Middle East lost no time in putting in all the orders they could, to the Far East, Australia, South and East Africa. All the British government funds available were turned into steel, pumps, pipes, tools, explosives, petrol, and heavy machinery for docks and workshops.[2]

When Britain declared war on Germany in September 1939, the Egyptian Prime Minister Ali Maher appeared to move swiftly. Diplomatic links with Germany were broken off, and the internment of adult German males and the sequestration of their property were begun at once.

There were under one thousand Germans in Egypt, most of whom were members of the Nazi Party; and those who were not, amounting to some 20 percent of the German community, had been under great social and economic pressure to join. All these people were now in the hands of the official sequestrator, Ahmed Bey Sadik – who was very pro-British and a familiar figure on the Anglo-Egyptian party scene. Members of the Nazi Party and their leaders were interned in the Italian School in Alexandria, and non-Nazis in the German School in Bulaq, Cairo. The two groups were united later on in the war, a decision which led to savage fights between the Nazis and the handful of German Jewish internees; but the latter were released in late 1942.

Martial law was established in Egypt, making the Prime Minister Lieutenant of the Realm. All railways and aerodromes were put at Britain's disposal, communications and the press were censored. In accordance with the terms of the Anglo-Egyptian Treaty, as Ali Maher kept telling Sir Miles Lampson, Egypt was co-operating fully with her ally: but she would not declare war.

In the new year, the men Wavell so desperately needed started to arrive: from India, New Zealand, England and Australia. The Indians, New Zealanders and British seemed well-behaved, but the Egyptians were very nervous of the Australians, whom they remembered rampaging through Cairo at the end of the last war.

The Egyptian government insisted that the Australians be billeted outside the country – so, for the first few months, they were kept in Palestine. Work on the new military infrastructure was also making progress, for the British paid well. But, although things were beginning to move for Wavell, Sir Miles Lampson's efforts to push the Egyptian government into a more active role were being continually thwarted by Ali Maher.

The Embassy soon realised that Ali Maher's actions were designed to tell the Axis powers that, although forced to co-operate with Britain, he was covertly thwarting them wherever possible. Egyptian officials who had co-operated with the British (like the General Manager of the Egyptian State Railways, Shaker Pasha, who had sold them 17,000 tons of coal from his stocks) were soon replaced by Ali Maher's men.[3] By mid-January 1940, several civil servants and junior ministers had been sacked, and it was well-known that to be friendly with the British was to court political disaster under the present régime. A cartoon appeared, showing the Rector of the Egyptian University on his knees in front of Sir Miles Lampson, begging to be spared the KBE.[4]

Ali Maher was, however, forced to do something about Aziz el Masri, once tutor to Farouk and now Chief of Staff of the Egyptian Army. A patriot and idealist, now in his mid-sixties, he had always been a close friend of Ali Maher's. Many of his officers were suspected of having contacts with the enemy. The Head of the British Military Mission, General Macready, found him impossible to deal with. He was always praising the French and German armies, while scorning that of the British. He manipulated appointments, criticised the Military Mission's every move, and refused to answer letters.[5] (According to Anwar Sadat, Aziz el Masri further infuriated Macready by saying that the British Military Mission was more interested in trade than in the defence of Egypt: an order for Bren guns for the Egyptian Army had been given to Britain, though the Czechs were offering them at far lower prices.)[6] Lampson demanded that el Masri be removed from office – but Ali Maher would do no more than put him on indefinite leave.

Groups of Islamic fundamentalists were also adding to the general anti-British trend, especially the members of Young Egypt – whose leader, Ahmed Hussein, was an indefatigable pamphleteer and organiser of demonstrations. Ali Maher agreed with Sir Miles that Ahmed Hussein should be 'stamped out like a poisonous beetle',[7] and left it at that.

On 9 April 1940, the Germans occupied Denmark and Norway; a month later, they launched their assault on the Low Countries. On 17 May they captured Brussels, and on the following day they were well on their way to Arras and Amiens. Events had moved with terrible speed, and Britain – now under the leadership of Winston Churchill – was in immediate danger. Mussolini had still not declared himself, but in a letter to General Sir John Dill of 22 May Wavell compared him to a man who has made his way to the top of a high diving board: 'I think he must do something; if he cannot make a graceful dive, he will at least have to jump in somehow; he can hardly put on his dressing gown and walk down the stairs again.'[8]

On 30 May, Ali Maher drew up a proclamation declaring Cairo an Open City. This measure, designed by international law to protect the urban population of a neutral state from enemy bombardment, would not technically come into force while British troops were in the Citadel and the Kasr el Nil barracks, both inside the city limits. The Ambassador and the Service Chiefs, furious at being taken by surprise, had no intention of moving their troops; Cairo's status remained ambiguous.

At the beginning of June, guards were doubled at the Palace and the Ministries, and there was another round-up of suspicious persons. Hundreds of people were banished from Alexandria to Upper Egypt, fourteen Germans were arrested for fifth-columnist activities, and a hundred cabaret artistes were deported. Six thousand children were evacuated from Alexandria, in anticipation of heavy air-raids.[9]

Mussolini waited until 10 June before declaring war on the Allies: twelve days after the BEF and 90,000 Frenchmen had been evacuated from Dunkirk. Canada immediately declared war on Italy, and was followed by Australia, New Zealand, and South Africa. The Italian Ambassador, Count Mazzolini, was asked to leave Cairo, which he did – telling his servants he would be back in two weeks. Hundreds of Italian men of military age were interned, which caused great inconvenience to everybody since they were mostly mechanics and electricians. On 12 June, the press revealed that the names of several prominent Italian residents of Alexandria were found on a document outlining the post-war government of Italian-occupied Egypt, along with maps showing Egypt as an Italian possession.

Towards the end of the month, the Ethiopian Emperor Haile Selassie, in European exile since the Italian invasion of his country four years before, returned to Africa. To draw attention away from his arrival, the security forces provoked a demonstration in another part of Alexandria; for his presence was to be kept secret until he crossed the mountains into Ethiopia. At a private reception in the Royal Yacht Club, the Emperor gave a gold watch to the pilot who had brought him safely over the Mediterranean. He then urged his hosts to come and visit him in Addis Ababa, before being whisked off to his preliminary headquarters in the Sudan.[10] From there he would enter his own land with a British force, and call on his people to join him in hounding the Italians out of East Africa.

For the Egyptians, it looked as if their country was threatened with a similar fate to that of Ethiopia. They were cheered by the news of 30 June, which announced that the Commander-in-Chief of the Italian Army in North Africa, Italo Balbo, had been shot down while flying over Tobruk two days before. This was seen as a bad omen for the Italian Empire; but the moment of hope was dashed when they heard that he was to be replaced by Marshal Rodolfo Graziani. Ten years before, Graziani had quelled the rebellion in the Fezzan in Libya with savage cruelty. Stories of the raping, burning and looting that the Libyans had suffered at the hands of Italian soldiers, who pushed them off their land to make way for the colonisers, lost nothing in the telling. Compared to the previous summer, when they had been shouting 'L'Eggitto sarà a noi!', the Italian Fascists in Suez, Alexandria and Cairo were suspiciously quiet.[11]

While the Egyptians were grateful for British help in keeping the Italians out of their country, they had no wish to be involved in the war between England and Germany. Nahas Pasha described the situation in terms of an Arab proverb: it was a war 'in which we have neither a male nor a female camel' – in other words, it has nothing to do with us.

But, whereas the Italian threat had been growing gradually since 1936, the surrender of France on 16 June 1940 came as a complete shock. Only a few months before, the Egyptian correspondent Mahmoud Abul Fath had gone on a tour of the Maginot Line. He had been very impressed, and described its invincible strength to the readers of the *Misri* and the *Bourse Egyptienne*. When the dreadful news reached the beaches of Alexandria, where people had gone to escape the unbearably hot weather in Cairo, they could hardly believe it. From now on, the Egyptians felt that they were caught up in a series of events over which they had little control.

To the Service Chiefs in Cairo, the military implications of the fall of France were disastrous. The co-operation of the French Navy in the Mediterranean, the French Army in Syria, and the air-bases in France could no longer be relied on. The only spark of hope came from General de Gaulle, and it was too early to estimate the success of his call to free Frenchmen everywhere.

In June 1940 Baron de Benoist, the director of the Suez Canal Company which employed a large proportion of the Frenchmen and women working in Egypt, was determined that the fight should go on – as were most of the Company's executives, including Capitaine de Vaisseau Lucas. 'From now on,' he told his children, 'we must think of ourselves as British.' His ten-year-old son remembers going out by himself into the garden of his family's house in Ismailia, to sing the 'Marseillaise' for what he thought would be the last time. Thanks to the initiative of men like Lucas and Benoist, the majority of Frenchmen in Egypt rallied to General de Gaulle; they were one of the first overseas communities to do so. However, the French Minister in Cairo and the Consul at Alexandria were among those who remained faithful to Vichy. The latter was also profoundly anti-Semitic: in a secret report intercepted by Field Security, he wrote that the Egyptian newspapers in French were only pro-de Gaulle because they were in Jewish hands and under British influence.[12]

The French Navy in the harbour of Mers el Kebir, Algeria, was crippled by a British force on 3 July 1940. The reason for its destruction was that, though the armistice forbade the deployment of French ships against the Allies, Hitler would not have hesitated to force France to use her fleet had occasion demanded. The British did not take the decision lightly and, despite the loss of over 1,000 French lives, even General de Gaulle admitted it was necessary. What he found unforgivable was the way the British gloated over Churchill's show of resolution. He condemned the action as detestable, but urged the French to understand why it was taken.

Until Mers el Kebir, pro- and anti-Vichy Frenchmen had indulged in heated arguments; now they were divided by a gulf of icy silence. Jeanne de Schoutheete (pronounced Skouteet), the French wife of the Belgian Minister, was disturbed to see how hatred of Britain had become so strong among the Levantine French in Beirut that their real enemy was quite forgotten. Mme de Schoutheete was told that the outrageous vandalism of the British at Mers el Kebir was inexcusable, in view of the scrupulously correct behaviour of the Germans in Paris.

Back in Cairo at the end of the month, Jeanne de Schoutheete found herself presiding at a lunch in the P'tit Coin de France Restaurant. Also present was Colonel de Larminat, recently escaped from Syria, and fifteen other Frenchmen. They had come from as far away as Russia and Tunisia to the one country where there was still an active front on which to fight, and had been turned away from the French Legation. Since it was so suffocatingly hot in town, Mme de Schoutheete decided to entertain these brave and bewildered men the following evening to a picnic in the desert, by which time their ranks had swelled to thirty. Once out in the open, their spirits rose a little with the food and wine, and they watched the spectacular Egyptian sunset. *Le cafard* was kept at bay, until a young lieutenant from Toulon started singing Provençal songs in the shadow of the Pyramids.

Of the 37,000 men of the French Army of the Levant, based in Syria and Lebanon, only a handful left Syria to continue the war beside the British. They arrived at the border of British-mandated Palestine with no idea of the real situation, since they had heard only Vichy broadcasts. All they knew was that they could not stomach the armistice. By the time they left Palestine for Egypt, they were about 1,000 strong. They were camped at Tahag near Ismailia, the administrative centre of the Suez Canal Company, where they were warmly greeted by the French community.

At the time of his first broadcast from London, de Gaulle had also contacted military commanders and administrative governors all over the French Empire. The only one willing to follow him was General Georges Catroux, who had been Governor General of French Indo-China, and the fact that a five-star general was prepared to put himself under de Gaulle's orders gave the Free French movement weight at a crucial stage in its development. Catroux and his formidable wife, known as 'la Reine Margot', moved to Cairo in October. They had an apartment in one of the two blocks of flats in Zamalek known to British residents as Elephant and Castle. He was to be paid the salary of an ambassador *en poste*, which was appropriate, since he was more of a diplomat than a soldier. At first he was incognito, under the name of Monsieur Charretier (a name chosen because a cart has *quatre roues*). Within a short time he had resumed his real identity; and Adam (now Professor) Watson, the Embassy's liaison officer with the Free French, put Catroux onto a very good Greek tailor from whom he ordered some uniforms. The Greek tailor was not convinced by Catroux's rank, and thought it worth checking: 'A general, sir?' Watson assured him that Catroux was a general. 'But *five* stars, sir?'

Catroux was a trim, fastidious man, whose tactful and courteous disposition contrasted sharply with de Gaulle's. Soon after he arrived in Cairo he was received by Sir Miles Lampson, who liked him at once. However, his status as the Free French Representative in Egypt was not acknowledged by everyone. At a reception in the French Legation, the King's uncle Prince Muhammad Ali asked if Catroux was received in diplomatic circles. There was an uncomfortable silence. The French Minister, Monsieur Pozzi, answered: 'Although it seems incredible, a certain friendly legation [i.e. the British Embassy] does open its doors to a French general stripped of his rank, who has been condemned to death by his government, and to a rabble which would, in normal times, be shot.'[13]

One man who felt the humiliation of Mers el Kebir more than most was Admiral Godfroy, in command of Force X: this consisted of a battleship, four cruisers and three destroyers of the French fleet in Alexandria Harbour. Ever since the signing of the armistice, when he had been ordered home and Admiral Cunningham had refused to allow him to leave Alexandria, he had been co-operating with the British admiral whom he liked and respected.

Godfroy had begun discharging his fuel-oil, as a proof of his goodwill, when he heard about Mers el Kebir. The outflow of fuel-oil was stopped, he renounced every undertaking he had made to Cunningham, and the French ships began getting up steam and clearing their decks for action. Godfroy was evidently planning to smash his way out of Alexandria Harbour, which was the worst possible place for a naval battle as far as Admiral Cunningham was concerned. Quite apart from the damage that might be done to the docks and harbour facilities he did not want another Mers el Kebir on his hands, and begged Godfroy to think again.

When Godfroy remained adamant, an appeal was made to the officers and ships' companies – a message written on large placards, which were set on boats that floated round the French ships. The officers and men were in favour of accepting the terms offered to them; and in the face of this pressure, and that of the French Minister in Cairo, Admiral Godfroy yielded.

The consideration with which Force X was treated, thanks to Admiral Cunningham, was generous. Godfroy was allowed to use Vichy codes to transmit information from the Levant. His men were fed and paid by the British, and they had permission to take shore leave in Alexandria. For over two years, during which the British fleet saw victory at Matapan, suffered massive losses in Crete, kept Tobruk supplied in the face of terrible danger and fought to control the Eastern Mediterranean, Admiral Godfroy stuck to his principles and played tennis. Without so much as a scratch on their paintwork, the French ships looked brazenly sleek and shiny compared to the battered British fleet. However, Godfroy never failed to send a courteous message of congratulation or sympathy to Admiral Cunningham, after every British naval engagement.

The men of Force X went on leave in Syria and Lebanon, where the company of the pro-Vichy French Army of the Levant re-fuelled their hatred of the Free French. The feelings of the latter were equally hostile, and resentful: the men of Force X not only lived a soft life, but they could send money home – which no Free Frenchman could do through the regular channels. Fights were common in the streets of Alexandria, where the Free French would taunt the sailors – '*Vous avez des moules ou des huîtres à vendre?*' – at which point *la bagarre* would begin in earnest.

A more thought-provoking challenge came from Georges Gorse, who broadcast radio programmes aimed at converting the sailors of Admiral Godfroy's fleet to Free France. One of these featured the results of a competition to find the greatest absurdities of the war (Gorse had in fact composed all the entries himself). He declared a tie between the crowning of Tomislav II of Croatia, and men of Vichy singing the 'Marseillaise'.

The soldiers of the British Empire cultivated a heroic flippancy, which expressed cheerfulness, and – when things got rough – bravery and endurance. This was reflected in the hearty colloquialism of the propaganda movies: 'Well, we certainly gave Jerry a pasting that time, he won't be coming back for more in a hurry!' This tone was in marked contrast to that of the Free French, whose heroic mode was far more serious.

Poles, Belgians, Yugoslavs – all the nationalities who fought in the Middle East while their country was occupied by the Germans longed for the day of liberation as much as the Free French did; but the Free French were the only ones to be utterly repudiated by their home government: they had disobeyed authority, and were not only outlaws, but traitors. Though they could be seen relaxing and joking, usually among themselves, their commitment to the cause was so fervent that there seemed little room for frivolity.

The speed of events had brought a measure of confusion to Anglo-Egyptian relations. While the strength of the Axis made the Egyptians uncertain of the extent to which they should commit themselves to Britain, the British were equally uncertain about how much they should expect from Egypt. After the defeat of France, Whitehall felt the need for more fighting allies, and looked to Egypt. But though the Service Chiefs and Sir Miles Lampson agreed in principle with their superiors in London, and urged Egypt to declare war, they had reservations about the prospect of Egypt as a combatant ally.

The Service Chiefs felt that nationalist elements in the Egyptian Army might cause trouble and refuse to fight under British officers, while Lampson knew that full participation would make Egypt vulnerable to indiscriminate bombing. If that happened to Cairo, one of the sacred cities of Islam, the rest of the Islamic world would undoubtedly blame Britain for forcing Egypt into a war against her will. The British could not afford to lose the goodwill of neighbouring Arab countries. There seemed no good reason to coerce Egypt into war, when the Anglo-Egyptian Treaty already pledged her full co-operation.

The British were very concerned, however, when Ali Maher stated that even if Egypt were invaded by Italy he would not declare war straight away but would have the matter debated in Parliament. Diplomatic relations with Italy were broken on 12 June; but the Arabic press was not allowed to print any anti-Italian propaganda. Only a handful of Germans had been interned, and their firms – particularly the Dresdner Bank – seemed to be taking a long time to liquidate.[14] Despite their protestations, it was obvious that both the King and Ali Maher wanted to stay friends with the Axis; and Lampson and the Service Chiefs knew that, sooner or later, they would have to get rid of the Prime Minister.

Luckily for the British, Ali Maher was very unpopular. He had not been elected, but appointed by the King; and, with martial law, he became more powerful than any previous Egyptian Prime Minister. Ali Maher had incurred a good deal of resentment in his few months of office. He governed by intrigue, threats, and the manipulation of administrative posts, rather than through ministers, for whom he held a barely concealed contempt. Thus Parliament made little attempt to defend him when the British demanded his dismissal, and King Farouk reluctantly accepted his resignation on 23 June.

Despite the Wafd's occasional bouts of anti-British fervour, Lampson knew that it was the only party that could keep the country stable during the course of the coming war. The British Ambassador therefore asked the King to summon its leader, Nahas Pasha, to form a government. Farouk hated Sir Miles, and he hated Nahas, who had impudently tried to curb his power. He quibbled and prevaricated with such persistence that it became obvious that he had no intention of asking the Wafd to take office. But Egypt could not go on indefinitely without a government, and Hasan Sabry Pasha – who represented a compromise – was appointed Prime Minister. Over the next few months his administration saw to the sequestration of Italian property, increased the Egyptian Army by 5,000, and passed a law giving the police powers to arrest anyone spreading false rumours.

The false rumours spreading in late August, however, were entirely due to GHQ, which at that time decided to evacuate the wives and children of all British military personnel stationed in Egypt – only wives involved with official war work were allowed to stay. Service families were not in immediate danger; but it was thought that a soldier could better concentrate on winning the war if his wife and children were safely out of the way. It was bitterly resented by the women, especially when they saw exceptions being made for those with the influence, income, or sheer determination to stay put. These became known in Cairo as the 'illicit wives', though that term rarely included the most blatant exceptions of all – Lady Wavell and her daughters. Brigadier McAndlish, who dealt with the evacuation, said later that he had had a dreadful war. First he had to separate the 'clingers' – families and newly-weds for whom separation was intensely painful; and, when the fighting was over, his was the job of reuniting people who would have been much better left apart.

The news that all military families were leaving for South Africa caused consternation in the civilian community. Sir Alexander Keown-Boyd had already written a paper on the evacuation of British women and children, which ended with a plea that arrangements should not be left to the last minute. What was the Embassy going to do? Lampson managed to reassure the British Community Council without actually committing himself to an answer. In his opinion the military had needlessly provoked alarm – not only in the British community, but among the local population as well.[15] As for the evacuation, he later described it as 'illogical, inconsistent and unfair'.[16]

As the British geared themselves for war, the Egyptians could say that they had honoured their commitments under the Anglo-Egyptian Treaty. If anyone should be criticised for not adhering to it it was the British, for the agreement guaranteed Egypt's rights to order her own internal affairs – a term the British chose to gloss over when they ousted the Egyptian Prime Minister. But, with the Italians on the doorstep, this was not the time to argue.

The Benghazi Handicap

At midnight on 10 June – the moment at which Mussolini decreed that war against the Allies would begin – the 11th Hussars made the first move in the Desert War by cutting out their way through the Wire. This was the frontier fence between Egypt and Libya, which consisted of metal posts and coiled barbed wire three lines deep, and ran for hundreds of miles in a straight line across empty wastes of sand and rock. Once inside Libya, they launched a series of raids on the camps at Fort Capuzzo and Fort Maddalena that took the Italians completely by surprise. As well as destroying a number of guns, tanks and lorries, their prisoners included General Lastucci, the Engineer in Chief of 10th Army. He was captured in his staff car, with two 'lady friends'.*

The British continued their harrying tactics; but the Italians, apart from carrying out regular if not very effective air-raids on Egypt and Palestine, made no serious move till 13 September. On that day, with much trepidation, Marshal Graziani moved his 10th Army sixty miles into Egypt, occupying Sollum and Sidi Barrani. Here he stopped, and built a series of semi-permanent defensive camps. It was hardly the sign of an offensive strategy; but the Axis radio

---

* The Italian Army routinely supplied their larger garrisons with prostitutes. Fourteen of them were found in Tobruk when the Australians captured it in 1941; and, since the women could not be put in the prison cages along with the POWs, they were sent to Alexandria. Here, to his acute embarrassment, they were handed over to the Roman Catholic Chaplain of the Forces, who found a convent in Cairo prepared to take them in. Their clothes were taken away and replaced by shapeless gingham uniforms, they had no sweets or cigarettes, and were utterly miserable – but neither the Church nor the Army could bear the moral responsibility of turning them out on to the streets.

broadcast that the Italian Army of Liberation, inspired by Mussolini who dubbed himself 'the protector of Islam', was on its way to free Egypt from the British oppressors.

The Egyptians were under no illusions. Newspaper reports estimated the Italian strength at 250,000 men, supported by nearly a thousand aircraft; censorship prevented them from estimating British numbers, but everyone knew they were less than 50,000. Wavell, under increasing pressure from Churchill to begin the campaign, refused to be hurried. The RAF kept the Italians under constant attack and, to demonstrate its effectiveness and reassure the local population, a captured Italian plane was exhibited in Alexandria. The idea was that the spectators would be filled with admiration for its British captors; but, in their eyes, the aircraft only confirmed the power of the Italian Empire. There was a general mood of what the British called 'defeatism', which their unimaginative propaganda could do nothing to dispel. On the night of 19 October Italian planes roared over Cairo, and the suburb of Maadi was bombed.

Wavell had placed Western Desert Force under the command of Lieutenant-General Richard O'Connor. Over the next two months, this small, wiry, unassuming commander established a number of supply-dumps in the open desert, so that his limited transport could be used exclusively for the troops, when all was ready. Secrecy was vital, for Cairo swarmed with enemy agents. To keep up the impression that nothing was happening, the Commander-in-Chief, Lady Wavell and their two daughters went to the races at Gezira on the afternoon of Saturday, 7 December. That evening, Wavell gave a party for senior officers at the Turf Club. His guests said he had looked very relaxed.

The Italians in their camps were no match for the light, mobile forces that O'Connor unleashed upon them on 9 December. After three days' fighting, O'Connor had retaken Sidi Barrani.

This came as a tremendous boost to morale in Cairo and London. For the last few months, Churchill had been extremely impatient with Wavell, who refused to move until he was ready. All that had vanished in the glow of victory, but the Prime Minister's delight prompted two rather ill-judged statements. The speech in which he said that the Italians had invaded Egypt 'which was under British protection' infuriated the Egyptians, for whom the word 'protection' had humiliating associations.[1] There was a flurry of embarrassed apologies from the Embassy. Another speech led Wavell to believe the Prime Minister was being incorrectly briefed, an impression the CIGS Sir John Dill made haste to rectify in a signal to Cairo:

'21 December 1940. Yes of course I realise Australian Light Horse Regiment is mechanised. Fear that PM having seen reference to Australian cavalry ... in a moment of exuberance, and forgetting desert, distance and water, jumped to conclusion that dashing cavalry charge had taken place and said so in the House.'[2]

A little later, a serious breach of security was discovered. A copy of a secret memorandum from General Wilson, concerning the British defence of Siwa Oasis, was found among papers belonging to the captured General Pescatori. Dated October 1939, it had been sent to the Egyptian Minister of Defence. But those suspected of passing it on to the Italians were Ali Maher, then Prime Minister, or Aziz el Masri, in his capacity as Chief of the Egyptian General Staff.[3] Since both were out of high office and under surveillance already, there was little Lampson could do; but the incident served to silence protests, however, when the British took back equipment they had promised to the Egyptian Army.

The new Prime Minister Hasan Sabry had no chance to prove himself, for he dropped dead of a heart attack while reading the Speech from the Throne to the assembled Parliament on 14 November. Lampson was not surprised to find that the King still baulked at appointing Nahas – but he was extremely displeased when he heard that Farouk wanted to reinstate Ali Maher. The only candidate acceptable to the Embassy, Parliament and Farouk was Hussein Sirry Pasha – an engineer who had been Minister of Public Works and Commerce. Sir Miles was not very impressed; but Sirry seemed willing to co-operate with the British, and was also the King's uncle by marriage. The Embassy hoped he would exert a certain influence on His Majesty, if only by keeping Ali Maher as far as possible from the Palace.

This, however, was easier said than done. Farouk had not dismissed any of his Italian servants, through whom he maintained links with Ali Maher and Rome. There were rumours of a powerful radio-transmitter at the palace of Inchasse, and Sir Miles once had to warn the King that, despite the blackout ordered in Alexandria, powerful lights had been seen coming from the palace at Montazah. The King smiled, and said it would not happen again.[4]

By 23 December 24,000 Italians had been taken prisoner, and O'Connor seemed unstoppable. Not only had the Italians been pushed out of Egypt, but during that autumn they had also failed to take Greece. When the Italians declared war on Greece in October 1940, fights between the two communities in Egypt had at once broken out. The enthusiasm of the Greeks in Egypt to rush to the aid of the homeland had been remarkable: fourteen thousand had enrolled at once and sailed home to fight; while the newspaper *el Mussawar* stated that, in one night, the Greek community had raised more money than the whole of the national defence budget for Egypt, a country of sixteen million people. *El Mokkatam* reported that a high-minded Greek had broken off his engagement to an Italian girl.[5] Among the men, this patriotic fervour tended to overlook the conditions the Greek Army would be facing in the mountains. The women showed more foresight: Madame Capsalis, the wife of the Greek Minister, urged all Greek women to start knitting jerseys and socks for the brave troops in the coming winter. A month later the Italian advance had collapsed, and on 18 December the Greek Army launched its offensive, driving the Italians back into Albania. In December 1940, the Greeks and British in Egypt celebrated their triumph; it seemed that Cairo had never been so glittering and carefree as it was that Christmas.

Although the smart restaurants of Cairo were full of people congratulating each other, Britain's successes in the desert had led to a worsening of Anglo-Egyptian relations. The Egyptian newspapers were full of articles saying that Wavell could never have done it without Egyptian co-operation, and in return they wanted to see some concession towards their ultimate goal of *Istiqlal-el-tam* – complete independence. The British, on the other hand, thought that Egypt should be eternally grateful for having been saved from the Italians.

After a huge tea party for two to three thousand soldiers in the Gezira Club, with tea served by Lady Lampson, the Ambassador and his wife repaired to Upper Egypt for a few days' holiday with the writer and traveller Freya Stark. They visited the desert tombs and temples on donkeys, and danced in the evening with pashas in the ballroom of the Winter Palace Hotel – 'both the good ones,' wrote Freya, 'and the bad ones who looked as though they had backed a favourite and lost'.[6]

Jacqueline Lampson rejoiced in the desert victory as much as anyone in the British community, but the war had put her in a difficult position, for she was half Italian. Her father, Sir Aldo Castellani, was a distinguished Italian physician with a Harley Street practice. He had done valuable work on tropical diseases in Africa, was Surgeon General to the Italian forces during the Ethiopian War of 1935–36, and became Medical Adviser to the Italian High Command in 1942. For Lampson, the only real embarrassment came when Farouk made remarks like 'I won't get rid of my Italians till he gets rid of his' – a story that went round Cairo like wildfire.

Sir Miles's first wife had died while they were *en poste* in China, and he met Jacqueline when she came out on a visit to Egypt as a friend of his niece Miranda. Despite the considerable difference in their ages they were married in December 1934, when he was still High Commissioner. Dark and pretty, Jacqueline Lampson barely came up to her husband's shoulder. She was energetic and bossy, both excellent qualities in a diplomat's wife; and she also had the invaluable gift of being able to talk confidently and brightly to everyone, from the King to Tommy Atkins.

Chips Channon arrived to stay at the British Embassy in Cairo on New Year's Day 1941, on his way to Yugoslavia. 'I am exultant; the Cairene scene is just my affair, easy, elegant, pleasure-loving, trivial, worldly; me, in fact . . .'[7] Channon attended a race meeting at Gezira with his hosts, and was delighted by the ceremonial formalities – 'God Save the King' played as the Ambassador entered his box, dressed in a grey frock coat and topper, with Lady Lampson in a dress of silk ruffles and a picture hat. 'The paddock was crowded and it reminded me of Newmarket, with Aly Khan leading his horses and Charles Wood [later Lord Halifax] wandering about with Hughie Northumberland.'[8]

Not surprisingly, Wavell was the toast of Cairo and Channon was determined to meet him through Peter Coats, the General's ADC. Lady Wavell was not a natural hostess; and since his arrival in early 1940, Major Coats had taken over the organisation of the Wavells' social life, with great success. Both the food and the conversation at the General's table showed a marked improvement, and even the General himself seemed a little more talkative.

Peter Coats was delighted to see Channon again; but was rather nervous of introducing this professional socialite and bon viveur to Wavell, whose long bouts of silence were uncomfortable for those who were not used to them. On 4 January the Wavells gave a cocktail party for a hundred people at their house overlooking the Gezira race-course. Wavell had evidently taken a shine to Channon for he was asked to stay on for dinner, and he and Wavell had a long conversation after that. Channon told him he was a hero in England, '. . . and when I told him he was a second Nelson (a foolish remark) he retorted "Why? because I have only one eye?" We really made friends.'[9]

A few weeks later, on his way back from Yugoslavia, Channon made himself a firm friend of Lady Lampson, who was then involved with the Red Cross and Red Crescent Ball. Gala occasions took place almost every Saturday in aid of one war charity or another, and the organisers of this particular party were Lady Lampson, the Prime Minister's wife Mme Sirry, and the wife of the Greek Minister Mme Capsalis. They each took one third of the tickets to sell, and Lady Lampson sent a hundred to Lady Wavell, asking her to help distribute them. Lady Wavell immediately sent them back, without so much as a covering note. After much argument through inter-mediaries she could only be persuaded to take four – but, luckily for Lady Lampson, Channon cheerfully bought a hundred.[10]

The good news kept up in January: O'Connor captured Bardia on the 4th, and forged on to take Tobruk and Derna. The East African campaign began, and Kassala was in British hands on the 19th. However, there were alarming reports from Greece: her heroic but ill-equipped army was trapped in the Albanian mountains, enduring one of the fiercest winters in living memory. The Greek dictator Metaxas, who had declined Britain's offer of help, died on 29 January. By now the Germans were massing in Rumania, and

Metaxas's successor Koryzis immediately asked the Allies for every possible assistance.

Channon was sad to leave the gaieties of Cairo on 8 January, and anxious about his visit to Belgrade. His mission was to try and persuade the Regent Prince Paul, whom he had known for years, to join the Allies and stand by her neighbour Greece; but Paul could not bring himself to hand over a country at war to his young nephew Peter, who would reach his majority in a few months' time.

Back in North Africa, O'Connor cut off the Italians' escape south of Benghazi at Beda Fomm on 7 February. The exhilarating gallop across the desert, which the men of Western Desert Force had dubbed 'the Benghazi Handicap', was over. Five days later, on 12 February, General Erwin Rommel arrived in Tripoli.

SPRING 1941

Disaster in All Directions

When Rommel stopped off in Sicily on 11 February on his way to North Africa, he learnt that Rome had forbidden the bombing of British-occupied Benghazi because too many influential Italians had houses there. He promptly told the Luftwaffe commander General Geisler not to pay any attention to such ridiculous obstructions to military priorities. Air-raids on Benghazi began at once.

In Cairo that same day, Wavell received the instructions he had been expecting with such grave misgivings. From now on, Cyrenaica was to be held with the bare minimum of men and equipment, and the East African campaign was to be wrapped up as soon as possible. The defence of Greece was the highest priority.

Rommel wasted no time. His intelligence reports confirmed that the British position was weak and over-extended, and he knew that Wavell would be under pressure to send aid to Greece. Work was to proceed at full speed, round the clock, to get his troops and equipment unloaded and sent forward. However, the German High Command was considerably less enthusiastic. The demands of the huge army with which it was planning to invade Russia had relegated the Western Desert to a side show, and Rommel was told not to move until the arrival of the 15th Panzer Division in May.

Wavell, his attention now focused on the problem of putting 60,000 men into Greece, also thought he had a couple of months in which to build up his defences before the Germans made any serious moves in Cyrenaica. When Rommel attacked in late March, the British were as unprepared as the Italians had been in December. Both the Italians and the German High Command were dismayed by this headlong charge, but they were overruled by Hitler himself who gave Rommel his blessing. Confounded by the speed of the German advance, Western Desert Force began to disintegrate into confusion. On 3 April, General O'Connor – who had been enjoying some well-deserved leave – was sent up to assist Lieutenant-General Philip Neame VC, who had taken over command of Cyrenaica when General Jumbo Wilson was assigned to lead the Greek campaign.

Early on the morning of 6 April, Germany invaded Greece and Yugoslavia. Belgrade was subjected to an aerial bombardment comparable to that which Hitler had unleashed on Warsaw and Rotterdam, and the country fell within a week. In Greece, Wilson's little Allied force of Australian, New Zealand, English and Polish troops had barely assembled beside the defending Greeks, when twenty German divisions marched over the border from Bulgaria. The Allies found themselves fighting a rearguard action from the very beginning.

In the Western Desert that same night, after two days of fruitlessly trying to co-ordinate the movements of the British and Australian forces, Neame and O'Connor decided to pull back their headquarters. Since O'Connor had no car of his own, Neame gave him a lift in the huge white Cadillac that he had inherited from Jumbo Wilson. They set off in the main stream of British vehicles pouring east of the Jebel Akhdar, but before nightfall realised they were on the wrong track. After midnight, the car suddenly hesitated, and stopped. O'Connor woke up. Lights were flashing in their direction, and the voices behind the lights were German. Of all the commanders who might have been captured, O'Connor was the one who could least be spared; and it was not until Montgomery arrived a year and a half later that the British had a general of his calibre in the Western Desert.

When the Axis announced their invasion of the Balkans and the capture of Neame and O'Connor, GHQ tried to emphasise the good news – Addis Ababa had been taken with 10,000 Italian prisoners. But the success of the campaign in Ethiopia was of little interest as the Germans got closer, and Anglo-Egyptian relations got worse. The deterioration was largely due to conflicts arising from the war, public discussion of which was frozen by censorship; but the feeling of mutual hostility found expression in reactions to a proposal that all commercial accounts should be kept in Arabic. It was widely supported by Egyptians who were well aware of the upheaval it would cause, while it exasperated the British community, who dismissed the idea as the work of ungrateful fanatics.[1]

The British could hardly hide their anxiety, despite strong exhortations not to appear alarmist or defeatist – particularly in front of Egyptians. In darker moments they wondered what would happen when the Germans reached Cairo. The Chief of Staff, General Sir Arthur Smith, admitted to Lampson on 13 April that he thought the Germans would be at the Pyramids, only eight miles west of the capital, at any moment.

On that very same day, Rommel encircled Tobruk. The town had been well-fortified by the Italians, and the Australians inside had had time to organise their defence – which was far fiercer than the Germans had anticipated. Rommel seemed to be everywhere at once, furious at the lack of progress and driving every unit beyond the limit of its endurance. He spent nine days trying to force his way in until blinding sandstorms, heavy tank losses and the death of two of his most effective commanders obliged him to let up. The fact that he had failed to take Tobruk turned the fortress and its defenders into a powerful allegory which captured the Allied imagination. Only a month later, the troops' magazine *Parade* dedicated an issue to 'The Spirit of Tobruk', and every week that the siege continued made the myth more powerful. Although forced to leave the best harbour in eastern Cyrenaica in British hands, thus placing a considerable strain on his supply lines, Rommel was determined not to lose the initiative. By mid-May he had taken Sollum, on the westernmost edge of Egypt.

In late April, 21,000 British, Anzac and Greek troops were evacuated from Greece to Crete, to join the 6,000-strong garrison already there. These men were tired, and desperately short of guns, ammunition, signalling equipment, vehicles and tools; but the New Zealander General Freyberg estimated that if more convoys got through successfully, and if he had the full support of the Navy and the RAF, it would be possible to hold Crete.

From 14 May onwards the Germans launched repeated air attacks on the island and the convoys trying to reach it. This softening up process culminated on 20 May. Early that morning, the attack was fiercer than usual; then, through the dust and smoke, the defenders saw the sky speckled with parachutes. Hundreds of paratroopers were shot like so many pheasants; but, despite an enormous casualty rate, 5,000 Germans had landed safely on the island by sundown.

The capture of Maleme airfield the next day provided the toe-hold that the Germans needed, and the psychological strain of the next week's incessant fighting and air attacks brought the Allied troops to the edge of nervous exhaustion. On 26 May, Freyberg admitted that his forces were at breaking point, and the order to pull out was given the following day.

In a heroic effort which claimed over two thousand lives and five ships, the Navy managed to rescue 18,000 men from Crete between 28 May and 1 June;[2] 12,000 men remained on the island and were taken prisoner. From Cairo, the situation looked disastrous. Not only were the Balkans and Crete in enemy hands, but Rommel had now trumped all Wavell's winter victories. 'I don't think,' wrote Lampson in his diary on 29 May, 'I have ever seen our Archie look quite so gloomy.'

The news that an Italo-German force was on the Egyptian border raised considerable alarm, but nothing like the panic provoked by the very heavy bombing raids on Alexandria in mid-June. There was a mass evacuation of between fifty and seventy thousand people from Alexandria and Port Said, and the flight of dock-workers, in large numbers, caused chaos at a critical time for the military administration. Hussein Sirry did succeed in calming the country with reassuring speeches; but the Egyptians no longer had much faith in Britain. A month earlier the expeditionary force to Greece was assumed to be much greater than it actually was, and no one imagined that it had been raised by stripping Cyrenaica and leaving Egypt exposed to attack.

The airborne invasion of Crete proved so ruinously expensive in lives and resources that the Germans were never tempted to try anything like it again – but it did have the advantage of giving their prestige in the Middle East a tremendous boost. 'The fall of Crete,' wrote Lampson, '. . . has created a profoundly defeatist impression among the Egyptian public, which is inclined to regard this German overseas success as a serious blow to the hitherto unquestioned legend of British sea power. Explanations of aviation difficulties, lack of aerodromes nearby, etc., have not sufficed to counteract this impression.'[3] There was a general feeling that though the British were capable of beating the Italians, they would not be so successful against the Germans.

As well as directing three different fronts at once, Wavell also had to deal with constant harrying, prodding, bullying and questioning from the Prime Minister, whose ideas about warfare differed sharply from his own. All fire and action, Churchill thought a man was ready for the front as soon as he had been issued with a rifle. He believed in heroism, whereas Wavell relied on strong supply lines, sound equipment and good planning. This careful attitude made Churchill rank Wavell's remarkable abilities with those of 'a good chairman of a Tory Association'.[4]

The gulf between them grew wider over the Iraq crisis, which erupted at the same time as the Greek campaign. In the first days of April, four Iraqi generals known as the Golden Square seized power with the aid of the nationalist politician Rashid Ali el Ghalani. They searched the palace in Baghdad for the pro-British Regent, Emir Abdul Ilah (it was said that the search party included four doctors, who had already completed a certificate of death from heart failure); but the Emir had fled, and taken refuge on board a British ship in Basra. The rebels besieged the main air-base at Habbaniya, and surrounded the British Embassy in which 300 people had taken refuge. Since the aim of the coup was to free Iraq from British control it had the wholehearted support of Germany, which promised substantial military aid.

London felt that a brisk military intervention was the best way to bring Iraq to heel. General Sir Claude Auchinleck, recently appointed C-in-C India, offered to send a force to Iraq which would be up to division strength within a month; he was also willing to command the operation. Churchill accepted the first part of his offer, but insisted that Iraq was Wavell's responsibility.

Over-extended on every front, Wavell was extremely unwilling to launch another campaign for which he had neither the men nor the equipment, and felt that a diplomatic solution should be found for the Iraqi problem. However he scraped together various units to make Habforce, which entered Iraq through Palestine in mid-May. Wavell's force moving from the west towards Auchinleck's in the south-east succeeded in quelling the rebellion. The Iraqis were obliged to move before they were ready, and the reinforcements they had been promised by the Axis failed to materialise. On the night of 29 May, Rashid Ali, his colleagues and the German and Italian Ministers fled into Persia.

While he did not entirely blame Wavell for the disasters of the Greek campaign, which was undertaken for political rather than military reasons, Churchill could not forgive the reluctance and pessimism he had shown over Iraq. Sooner or later, Wavell would have to go.

The time that Britain had taken to get Iraq under control was seen in Egypt as yet another sign of military weakness. While many Egyptians would have wished Britain stronger to protect them from invasion, Rashid Ali's rebellion found some support in Egypt. On 16 May Huda Shaarawi, who had devoted her life to feminism and, in 1923, was the first woman to unveil her face publicly in Egypt, asked the British Embassy to allow her to send medical supplies to the rebels. Permission was firmly refused. (A year later one of her charitable soirées was attended by King Farouk, who presented her with the decoration of Al Kamal – a mark of favour the Embassy interpreted as approval of her anti-British activities.)

On the same day, the ex-Chief of Staff of the Egyptian Army, Aziz el Masri, made what was to be his second attempt to get out of Egypt to join the fight against the British. He had formed a secret, anti-British organisation within the Egyptian armed forces; and, with the help of two young air force pilots, he seized a plane from Abbassia aerodrome and took off for Baghdad. They had been in the air only a few minutes when the aircraft lost power – one of the pilots had turned the oil pump off instead of on. A forced landing was made at Qailoub, a few miles north of Cairo. In Qailoub, el Masri and his pilot told the Chief of Police that their car had broken down. This official willingly offered his own, and the two men vanished into the back streets of Cairo.

The day after their escape, the Egyptian government announced a reward of £E1,000 for their capture. But strong local support for el

Masri was demonstrated by the number of posters calling for revolution that appeared at bus and tram stops, and a rain of anti-British
leaflets. Death-threats were sent to newspaper editors who toed the
government line.

The story had an astonishing sequel, when Field Security finally
caught up with el Masri two months later. Although the slapstick
comedy of his escape was treated as a good joke, el Masri had been
considerably more clever than the British at first supposed. A preliminary inquiry was launched in order to prepare charges of treason;
but, when questioned, el Masri claimed that he had tried to reach
Iraq not to join, but to put an end to, the rebellion. He also stated
that his intervention had been solicited by a senior British officer.

To Lampson's horror, at least part of this story was true.[5] El Masri
had asked for a meeting with Brigadier Iltyd Clayton of Military
Intelligence; but since the latter was away, he agreed to talk to
Colonel C. M. J. Thornhill of the highly secret Special Operations
Executive. Thornhill worked in a section dealing with anti-fascist
propaganda, and his assistant Christopher Sykes was to describe him
as someone 'who literally could not resist being "in" every event
that came his way'.[6] Thornhill and Aziz el Masri lunched together
on 12 May and, according to Thornhill, el Masri proposed that he
should fly to Iraq. He would interrupt the rebellion by offering
Iraq Dominion status, which would also be offered to other Arab
countries including Egypt. Whatever he thought of the curious idea
that most of the Middle East should join the British Empire, particularly from a notorious nationalist like el Masri, Thornhill agreed to
present these proposals to Brigadier Clayton on his return; though he
insisted that he did not encourage el Masri to fly to Iraq.

However, the fact that Thornhill had had a meeting with el
Masri compromised the whole case. The suggestion that Iraq and
Egypt join the Empire – which el Masri stated was a British idea,
put forward by Thornhill – would create particularly dangerous
propaganda; and, rather than risk the consequences, the British
Embassy reluctantly dropped the idea of bringing el Masri to trial.
He was not officially interned until 1942. Thornhill himself was
dismissed from SOE.

With their successes in Greece and North Africa, it seemed only a matter of time before the Germans made a move into Syria, and aid to the Iraqi rebellion had provided the ideal opportunity. The country had been a French mandate since 1919, and was the home of the 38,000-strong pro-Vichy French Army of the Levant. The Germans were given landing rights in Syria, as well as permission to move men and equipment round the country.

By mid-May, both Churchill in London and the Free French in Cairo were pressing Wavell for a Syrian campaign; but, by the time a mixed force of British, Australian and Free French troops went into Syria on 8 June, the Germans had moved out. The expense of the airborne Cretan campaign and the futility of the Iraqi rebellion had both discouraged a stronger hold on Syria, and in Berlin all minds were focused on the imminent launch of Operation Barbarossa. The Germans also hoped that, after they had pulled out of Syria, the British would no longer have any reason to go in. The French, however, hoped that by confronting and talking to their countrymen they might convert the whole Army of the Levant to the cause of Free France.

Their reception by the Vichy forces was far worse than had been anticipated. They were called traitors and fratricides, and a few Free Frenchmen with white flags were shot while attempting to talk to their compatriots. The field hospital at Deraa was in turmoil, as wounded Frenchmen went for each other's throats. Syria eventually came under Allied control on 11 July, at the very beginning of Auchinleck's command; yet Operation Exporter, and the armistice negotiations that followed, held only disappointment and bitterness for the Free French.

There were no recriminations from Churchill after the terrible swiftness of Rommel's advance on the unprepared, under-equipped Western Desert Force. Against all advice, he gave orders that a huge convoy of tanks be sent directly to Egypt via Gibraltar, rather than round the Cape, which took another forty days. Operation Tiger was a terrifying gamble, for the convoy would have to cross the Mediterranean in full view of the enemy; but it would make up for the armour lost during Rommel's advance, and put heart into what Churchill called the Army of the Nile.

Of the five transport ships carrying a total of 295 tanks and fifty-three Hurricanes, only one was lost, sunk by a mine in the narrows south of Malta. The others reached Alexandria on 12 May. Churchill was delighted by the arrival of his 'Tiger Cubs', but as the month wore on he became increasingly impatient to know why they were not being sent up to the front. Wavell explained that the tanks needed to be camouflaged and modified for the desert, tank crews had to familiarise themselves with the new models, and that many of the light tanks arrived requiring a massive overhaul. But the pressure from Churchill did not let up. The Germans, he argued, were dangerously far from their supply base, and there was no time to be lost.

The tanks were handed over to their units by 9 June, and the second British offensive, Operation Battleaxe, began on the 15th. Unlike O'Connor's and Rommel's advances which had swept through hundreds of miles, Battleaxe took place within a fifteen-mile radius of Sollum.

Air Marshal Tedder, who had just taken over from Sir Arthur Longmore, had concentrated as many planes as he could to ensure that the RAF took and held air superiority. The fact that they duly did so was a source of great encouragement, in both London and Cairo. The Army, however, had no inkling of Rommel's 88mm guns which were about to be used in an anti-tank role for the first time in the desert.

They were horribly accurate. Tank after tank burst into flames and, as the day wore on, it became evident that Rommel had a far firmer grasp on this fast-moving and complicated battle than either Major-General Creagh of 7th Armoured Division, or his superior General Sir Noël Beresford-Peirse. The British withdrew on 17 June.

The collapse of Operation Battleaxe and the Tiger Cub losses represented a bitter blow for Churchill. Twenty-six cruiser tanks had been destroyed, and out of 100 Matildas only 36 remained. Wavell took full responsibility. He never suggested, either then or at any time in the future, that the Prime Minister's impetuosity had pushed him, and the Tiger Cubs, into action before they were ready.

The telegram that told Wavell that he and Auchinleck were to exchange appointments was delivered by his Chief of Staff,

Lieutenant-General Sir Arthur Smith, while he was shaving on the morning of Sunday, 22 June. It came as no surprise. He agreed with the Prime Minister that the job needed 'a new head and a new hand', and, tired as he was, he hoped that he would be allowed some leave in England. But Churchill decided that the ex-C-in-C Middle East would be an embarrassment in London, and five days after handing over to Auchinleck, on 8 July, Wavell flew to New Delhi to take up the post of Commander-in-Chief, India.

In Cairo, everyone from Sir Miles Lampson down felt that he had been most shabbily treated. Freya Stark was one of the small group of people who gathered on the tarmac to see him off. He looked sad and tired; and the huge empty aerodrome, with its little group of uniformed figures in the early morning light, reminded her strangely of a Highland farewell in the Stuart risings:

'. . . the image was not inspired by any thought of lost causes, but by an atmosphere of loyalty and devotion that hung about the scene, and with it an acceptance of all that comes.'[7]

New Arrivals

'Oh, I expect we shall meet again. The evacuation season's just getting underway.'

John Connell, *The House at Herod's Gate*

With the Balkans overrun, refugees began pouring into Egypt. As well
as the nameless and homeless, clutching their bundles and their children, there came a little procession of Balkan crowned heads. The royal
exodus was heralded by Joyce Britten-Jones, who arrived in Cairo on
1 April – six days before the invasion of Greece and Yugoslavia. She
was on her way to join King George of Greece in Athens.

In the period of his first exile after the revolution of 1923, King
George had come to England. During the years he spent there he
separated from his wife, Princess Elizabeth of Rumania, and Mrs
Britten-Jones became his mistress until his death in 1947. When the
Germans started massing in Bulgaria, King George asked that she be
allowed to join him, and that her journey be 'facilitated'; and, since
the Foreign Office considered her influence on the Greek King
entirely beneficial, it was. Anthony Eden sent a message to Sir Miles
Lampson, asking him to look after her and to treat her visit to Cairo
as very hush-hush.[1]

As it happened, she arrived in a blaze of glory. Peter Coats,
representing General Wavell, had been sent to Heliopolis airport
to meet General de Gaulle. All the Free French dignitaries of Cairo
had gathered on the runway: the door of the plane opened, the band
struck up the 'Marseillaise' – and out stepped Mrs Britten-Jones. She
had shared the General's flight on the last lap of her long journey
from London to Cairo, and he had courteously let her precede him
out of the plane.[2]

From the airport she went to the British Embassy for lunch, after which she and Sir Miles had a long conversation 'ending up on the not inappropriate subject of concubinage, during which I noticed she never moved an eyelid'.[3] A few days later, she continued her journey to Athens.

The first royal group to arrive in Cairo consisted of the ex-Regent of Yugoslavia, Prince Paul, with his wife Princess Olga and their three children, on 11 April – the day when the British heard that Rommel had taken all of Cyrenaica except Tobruk. The Prime Minister of Egypt, Sirry Pasha, had not been warned of their arrival, and – as Sir Miles put it – 'went up in a puff' about it, as the Ambassador feared he would.[4] '. . . it is becoming more and more embarrassing,' he had written on 28 March, 'the way London regards Egypt as a general dumping ground for political refugees etc.' The Embassy had been instructed to give them a cool reception, and most of the arrangements for their stay were arranged unofficially through friends – namely Peter Coats and Princess Joan Aly Khan. A house was found for the family in Heliopolis, though Prince Paul's biographers described it as 'filthy dirty and ridiculously small'.[5] A few days later they were visited unofficially by Sir Miles and Lady Lampson, who found them both very likeable and sympathetic. Sir Miles described Princess Olga as one of the most attractive women he had ever met, and had to remind himself that her husband 'had nearly sold the pass in Yugoslavia'.[6]

Prince Paul of Yugoslavia did not see his nephew King Peter, who had lunch in Alexandria a week later before going on to Palestine. However, a party of thirty Serbian notables – the men who had put King Peter on the throne and abolished the Regency – arrived at Heliopolis some time later, and had to be put up in Cairo until accommodation could be found for them in Palestine. (Once again, Hussein Sirry was furious that the Egyptian government had been given no notice.)[7] The Serbs asked Lampson to keep Prince Paul under close surveillance lest he should start intriguing against them, though this was an unnecessary anxiety. The ex-Regent had always preferred paintings and antiques to politics.

The new Yugoslav King and his ministers travelled to London, while Prince and Princess Paul were to be kept well out of the way in Kenya.* George of Greece escaped from Athens, in the words of Peter Coats, 'like Jesus Christ, on a donkey though wearing a tin hat'.[8] With him were the new Prime Minister, Emmanuel Tsouderos, and various members of the royal family: the King's younger brother Crown Prince Paul and his wife Princess Frederica, their two children, and the King's sister Princess Katherine. Mrs Britten-Jones was also of the party, described as 'lady-in-waiting to Princess Frederica'.[9] They all flew to Crete on 26 April, for the King wanted to remain on Greek soil until the last possible moment; and, in mid-May, they were evacuated to Cairo.

King George was a serious, soldierly man. He and his government in exile set to work to gather a Greek army, discuss the best use of the Greek Navy and Merchant Marine with the British, and arrange the infiltration of agents into occupied Greece. In early June, after the departure of Princess Katherine, he and Mrs Britten-Jones moved into Mena House. 'I must say,' wrote Lampson in his diary, 'I thought this slightly infradig on his part. In the days of Charles II there was no doubt a recognised protocol for royal mistresses, but nowadays I have a strong feeling that kings should keep that side more submerged.'[10] Fortunately for the Ambassador, King George and his family were only in Egypt for three weeks. Field Marshal Smuts invited them to South Africa; and after a short stay there, King George and his ministers proceeded to London.

For those who were not royal, the escape from Greece was considerably more uncomfortable. Once the wounded Greek, Anzac and British troops started limping back into Athens, panic spread. People jostled to get a passage on any ship willing to make the journey, while the Luftwaffe kept up their constant bombing on the capital's port at Piraeus.

The first refugees began to arrive in Egypt on 21 April, in a motley selection of tugs, caiques and small steamers. Over a thousand were settled on the beach at Alexandria, while the British and Egyptian authorities tried to speed up arrangements for their reception. Many

---

* They were lodged at Oserian, an isolated country house in Naivasha that had belonged to the recently-murdered Lord Erroll.

had no papers, and most had not eaten for forty-eight hours. Four thousand more were expected within the next few days.[11]

On the last civilian ship to leave Piraeus were the remaining members of the British Council, who included the novelists Robert Liddell and Olivia Manning, and her husband Reggie Smith. Their ship was a battered old steamer that had been used to transport Italian prisoners of war: berths were full of bedbugs, and some parts of the passageways had been boarded up to separate groups of prisoners. Also on board were two Greek poets: George Seferis, who went on to be the Greek Government in exile's Ambassador to South Africa, and Elie Papadimitriou.

Olivia Manning and Reggie Smith shared a small twin-berth cabin with Dr Harold Edwards, the Welsh poet, and his Greek wife Ettie. Olivia Manning took great exception to the latter's hatbox, and kept putting it in the passageway outside their cramped quarters. Since it was full of expensive Paris hats, Mrs Edwards kept bringing it back in. By the end of the voyage the two women were no longer on speaking terms.

The refugees had been told to bring food with them but, since there had been no food to buy in Athens, they did not eat for three days. In an article many years later, Olivia Manning recalled her first taste of food in Alexandria: '. . . we saw British soldiers on the quay and someone shouted down "Got anything to eat?" "To eat?" The soldiers were surprised at such a simple request. They went behind the cases of ammunition and came back with a bunch of bananas. They made a game of throwing the bananas up in ones and twos but we jumped and scrambled in earnest. I caught one, a small one, green outside, pink inside, and smelling of honey. I have never tasted another like it.'[12]

After the formalities they were given a proper meal of bacon, eggs and tea, which 'brought tears to our eyes'. That night, they were on the train to Cairo. Olivia and Reggie Smith moved into a refugee hotel, though it was more like a doss house. There were separate dormitories for men and women, and a single cold shower shared by both. The Smiths comforted themselves with the thought that it must be very cheap; but, when they asked for the bill, the doss house proved more expensive than Shepheard's. Harold and Ettie Edwards had not made the mistake of going to the refugee hotel; so Mrs Edwards was at least in a private room when she opened her hatbox and discovered Olivia's revenge: her precious hats had been crowned with the cabin's tin chamber-pot.

Lawrence Durrell, his wife Nancy and their infant daughter Penelope had been living in Kalamata in southern Greece, where he worked for the British Council. As the Germans approached, Durrell wrote to the Council asking for advice, and received the message, 'Carry on – Rule Britannia.' By the time the Durrells realised that they must get themselves and their child out of Greece, the Germans were approaching Athens. A friend with a large caique, of the sort used to transport goods around the islands, sailed them to Canea on the north-western coast of Crete.

The Durrells found Canea full of Australians in a very ugly mood, though they were mollified by a crate of beer from the hold of the caique. While talking to them, Nancy Durrell mentioned that she had run out of tinned milk for her baby; whereupon the Australians looted a nearby shop, and presented her with enough tins of Carnation to last her for months. From Canea they joined the passengers on the overcrowded steamship, and arrived safely in Alexandria a day or two later, at four in the morning.

One of the Field Security sergeants who met the boat was John Cromer Braun, a young poet who was delighted to find that the man in front of him was *the* Lawrence Durrell, writer and friend of Henry Miller. They talked literature in a slit trench through what remained of the night, until Durrell went off to join his wife. He and Nancy stayed a week in Alexandria before moving to the capital.

The Durrells found Cairo hateful and depressing. They had left Greece in the spring, when thousands of flowers soften the rocky landscape, and fill the parks and window-sills of Athens. In Cairo, it was the time of the *khamseen* – a hot, desert wind thick with sand and dust. (Egyptians say it commemorates the period of fifty days during which Cain carried the body of his brother Abel on his back, looking for a place to bury it.) The leaves of the municipal trees were choked in dust, which worked its way into Italianate plasterwork, wrought iron balconies, and modern apartment blocks with equal ease, and reduced every building to a warm camel grey. The dust hung in the air with the flies and the patches of hot summer stench, coated the skin in a fine gritty film, veiled the foetid puddles. Many cities juxtapose riches and poverty; nowhere did it seem so blatant, so indifferent.

'Such a country –' wrote Durrell; 'cripples, deformities, ophthalmia, goitre, amputations, lice, flies. In the streets you see horses cut in half by careless drivers or obscene dead black men with flies hanging like a curtain over their wounds . . . one writes nothing but short, febrile-like jets by this corrupt and slow Nile; and one feels slowly walked upon by the feet of elephants . . .'[13]

First impressions of Egypt for Olivia Manning were equally nightmarish. 'I believed the unreality had something to do with the light . . . It was too white. It flattened everything. It drained the colour out of everything. It lay on things like dust . . . we were shocked by the colourless summer delta. The squalor of the delta towns shocked us horribly – not only the squalor, but people's contentment with squalor. For weeks we lived in a state of recoil.'[14]

In the same article, Olivia Manning wrote that 'we did not suppose for a minute that we would remain there. We felt the town at once crowded and empty, for temporary use, like a railway station.' However great an upheaval, the war was finite. Everyone expected to go home and resume normal life sooner or later, and, in this sense, seeing Cairo as a temporary backdrop was not unusual. But, to the jobless, rootless refugee, it looked bleaker than to the men in uniform who had a positive reason for being there.

Women in uniform at that time were still very much of a novelty. One afternoon in March 1941, two young officers of the 7th Hussars, who had been sent back from the front to check on replacements, stood on a dock at Suez. The Canal was temporarily blocked by mines dropped by Italian aircraft, and what could be seen of the Red Sea was dark with the shapes of some two hundred ships waiting to be unloaded. In a compound behind the two subalterns was parked a group of Dodge delivery vans converted into two-stretcher ambulances. These vehicles had been purchased by voluntary subscription in America, and each bore a little plaque, with the name of the club or department store which had raised the money. They were destined for a new British medical unit, No. 11 Convoy of the

Motorised Transport Corps; and, as their drivers marched past, the two officers gasped in astonishment and then fell into fits of uncontrollable laughter: it was the first time they had ever seen women in khaki.

'Now, girls!' said their second-in-command. 'Even though you wear trousers, you must always sit as though you were in skirts.' However, the sixty women of No. 11 Convoy did not need to be reminded of their sex, which came as a dreadful shock to the Garrison Adjutant at Hilmiya Camp. Although tired and hungry, they had to listen to a lecture on the importance of behaving with propriety in an enclosed area containing several thousand men.

On further reflection, the Garrison Adjutant decided that their presence was too inflammatory without giving the men some warning, so they were moved to a hotel in Heliopolis. Here they fell into bed, only to be woken two hours later with instructions to meet the midnight ambulance train from the Western Desert. Work had begun.

The new ambulance drivers were on duty for twenty-four hours a day, for five consecutive days, the sixth day being free. Vehicle maintenance was carried out immediately outside their large mess building, which despite its size contained no sitting room. When the women were not on the road, loading and unloading wounded men and taking them from one place to another, they were working on the vans or snatching a cup of tea and something to eat.

Although the newspapers emphasised their fortitude and patriotism, most members of No. 11 Convoy had joined the MTC for one of two reasons: to meet up with a husband or boyfriend posted in Africa, or escape from one at home. In the latter category was Anita Rodzianko, née Leslie: a niece of Winston Churchill, a writer who was unhappily married to the Russian equestrian Paul Rodzianko. Her memoirs[15] vividly describe the five strenuous days of non-stop duty – but the sixth day of rest was never wasted in sleep. Whoever was on leave would hitch a lift into town in any passing military vehicle, and go straight to the hairdresser. The next stop was usually the Gezira Club; though Anita Rodzianko also had a friend who lived very close to Hilmiya Camp – Aziz el Masri. They had met when he had been Farouk's tutor in England; but her visits to his pleasant, shady house surrounded by trees were brought to an abrupt end by el Masri's attempted escape to Iraq.

One of Anita's more outrageous companions was Miranda Lampson, known to her family and friends as Betty, who joined No. 11 Convoy that summer from Kenya. Betty was blonde, and almost as tall as her uncle the Ambassador. Lampson had sent her back to England at the start of the war, with a certain sense of relief; for, though he was fond of Betty, her reckless exuberance had proved a strain. Now back, and in uniform, Betty swore she would behave – but trouble was her natural element. She adored parties, and nothing would stop her getting to them – even on those nights when she was supposed to be on call. She thought nothing of crawling under the barbed wire surrounding the camp in an evening gown of silver lamé, to meet her admirers who waited on the other side with pounding hearts.

Driver Lampson chafed under the strict military discipline imposed by Mary Newall, who ruled the Convoy of which she was Commandant with a rod of iron. Mrs Keith Newall was a striking woman. Her beautiful figure was emphasised by a well-cut uniform, which had the Springbok badge of her unit on the arm, and epaulettes embroidered with a golden rose. A blue chiffon scarf at the throat (worn, at her instigation, by all members of No. 11 Convoy) set off her prematurely white hair, and in a holster attached to a highly-polished Sam Browne belt she carried her father's revolver, which earned her the name of Pistol-Packing Mary Newall. By 31 July, Betty Lampson had had enough of her, and resigned. Mrs Newall was furious, and said that, if she did not return to work immediately, she would be deported. Sir Miles had Betty to dinner, and tried to persuade her to go back to Mrs Newall, though he doubted she would – being, as he put it, 'so wild and uncontrollable'.[16]

Betty Lampson indeed did not return to Mrs Newall and, despite the latter's threats, stayed on in Cairo as a driver. Her height, combined with the fact that she always seemed to be driving American generals about, meant that she became known as 'the Life Guard'.

Sir Miles was impressed by Mrs Newall, whom he described as a formidable woman with a reputation as a dangerous *femme fatale*. She was too hard for his taste;[17] but to some men she was irresistible, as Cairo was to discover at the time of the scandal that would rock the Minister of State's office the following year.

A Time of Ideas

The departure of Wavell marked the end of the first phase of the war, in which Britain had to face a formidable enemy with minimal resources. It was a time of ideas, which encouraged the development of small, highly specialised forces beyond the military and intelligence services that already existed. Wavell and Churchill might have very different views about warfare, but both were prepared to listen to any new and imaginative way of tackling the enemy.

Of the strange crop of 'private armies' that flourished in the Desert War, the most effective was the Long Range Desert Group. Its story began with the collision of two ships in the Mediterranean in October 1939. One of them was so badly damaged that it was forced to pull into Port Said for repairs; and Major Ralph Bagnold, a passenger on his way to East Africa to take up a routine appointment, thought he would use the few days' delay to visit some friends in Cairo.

For ten years between the wars, Bagnold had been the leader of a small band of enthusiasts who made regular expeditions into the Libyan Desert, paying their own way at £20 per thousand miles. In the course of these journeys, Bagnold perfected the use of the sun-compass, and developed special mats and ladders to release cars stuck in the sand. He became so adept in the techniques of desert driving and navigation, that he even managed to penetrate the Great Sand Sea: a vast range of powder-fine dunes, till then only traversable by camel.

Wavell heard of his arrival in Cairo, and summoned Bagnold to his office. He was extremely interested in Bagnold's idea of reviving the Light Car Patrols of the First War, making a mosquito force that would attack the enemy and vanish into the desert as soon as its work was done. Before long, the Major was on Wavell's staff.

In view of Wavell's initial enthusiasm, Bagnold was disappointed that the first proposal he put down on paper was stifled by an apathetic bureaucracy. He arranged for the second proposal to be put directly on Wavell's desk, a few days after Italy's invasion of Egypt, which resulted in a second interview with the Commander-in-Chief. Wavell argued that there was no need for patrols in the Sahara, for Egypt was far more vulnerable to naval attacks in the Red Sea. Bagnold's reply was, 'What about piracy on the high desert?'

He was thinking of Kufra, an oasis in Libya which lies roughly 700 miles west of Wadi Halfa. The Italians had established a garrison there ten years before, and it gave the enemy an ideal base for desert piracy. From Kufra they could reach Wadi Halfa, on the Egyptian–Sudanese border, in a few days – and its dock-yards and railway workshops could be attacked without warning.

According to Major Bagnold, the word 'piracy' clinched it. 'I want you to be ready in six weeks,' said Wavell, who then rang a bell at his side. To Bagnold's surprise, the man who answered the bell was not a secretary, but a Lieutenant-General. 'Bagnold needs a talisman,' said the Commander-in-Chief, and the Major was given the following note:

'To all Heads of Departments and Branches: I wish any requirement made by Major Bagnold in person to be met immediately and without question. Signed: A. P. Wavell.'

As well as recruiting several of those who had taken part in the pre-war expeditions, such as P. A. Clayton who worked for the Survey of Egypt, G. L. Prendergast, and W. B. Kennedy Shaw, Major Bagnold had a clear idea of the sort of man he would need for the new unit, and the New Zealand Command in the Middle East was asked to supply them. The reason for choosing New Zealanders was that they came from a rural rather than industrial tradition, which developed toughness, frugality and self-reliance. As farmers, and often owner-drivers, they were trained in the careful maintenance of machinery – unlike the average British soldier, who in Major Bagnold's view had a cavalier attitude towards government property.

Their transport consisted of 30-cwt Ford trucks and an assortment of cars, collected from various friendly organisations; the Army had none that were suitable. The work on modifying these vehicles to make them desert-worthy was given top priority, and by mid-August the Long Range Desert Group was ready. From then on patrols of five trucks, carrying five men each, made regular expeditions into the desert, usually for reconnaissance and survey. Considering the geographical and mechanical difficulties, it was astonishing how regular their missions were. The New Zealanders learnt their desert-craft with remarkable rapidity, and proved they had the inner strength to live in the desert.

Once the LRDG had cut its teeth, Major Bagnold contacted Lieutenant-Colonel d'Ornano, the Free French Commander at Fort Lamy, and suggested that together they attack Murzuk, the capital of the Fezzan in western Libya. Considerable damage could be done to the Italian garrison and their airfield, and d'Ornano – who, along with the rest of the province of Chad, had declared for Free France in August – accepted with alacrity.

The raid on Murzuk took place in early January. The airfield and hangars were left in flames, and petrol and ammunition dumps were blown up – but d'Ornano and an LRDG officer were killed in the attack.

Bagnold's second mission with the Free French was far more ambitious – the capture of Kufra. It would be led by one of the most inspiring leaders of the Free French, General Leclerc. An LRDG reconnaissance patrol set out for Kufra on 26 January; but since security was slack, and the French camp's toast for the past few weeks had been '*Vers Koufra*', they were expected.

The LRDG lost half its vehicles in the ensuing fight, seventy miles short of Kufra. P. A. Clayton was taken prisoner, and four men of the LRDG – assumed captured by their colleagues – had the choice of giving themselves up by walking north to Kufra, or heading south. In that direction, there was nothing but desert for hundreds of miles, with no wells or oases, and only the faintest chance of being picked up. This, they felt, was still preferable to an Italian prison camp – despite the fact that they had no food, and only one and three quarter gallons of water between them.

Nine days later, a second LRDG patrol heading for Kufra found the first of the survivors, and the search for his companions began at first light the next day. Fifty-five miles away they found the next man but, although still conscious, he died that evening. Sixty-five miles further on they came across another survivor, exhausted and delirious. The last man, Trooper R. J. Moore, was still walking when they caught up with him. Moore was confident that he could have reached the nearest source of water, eighty miles on – and was slightly annoyed that he no longer had the chance to prove it.

Stories like those of Trooper Moore were to give the LRDG an almost mystical status in the mythology of the Desert War. Articles about them with titles like *Desert Raiders Play their Part* and *Highwaymen of the Sahara* appeared in magazines whenever it looked as if morale needed a boost. Cecil Beaton went to take photographs of them at their base in Siwa in 1942, and remarked that 'the officers are serious, critical, and do not indulge in that rather child-like ragging, the easy laughter and small jokes which while away time in many messes . . .'[1] The LRDG officers were certainly critical of Beaton and his conducting officer, whom W. B. Kennedy Shaw referred to in his memoirs as 'The Official War Correspondent and his Boy Friend': 'A rough calculation showed that it must have cost about £50 in petrol alone for the Lysander which brought the OWC and his BF to visit us. We were not amused.'[2]

Since they were primarily engaged in gathering intelligence through observation, the LRDG did not appreciate the attention of war correspondents which sometimes gave away valuable information about their bases. But, although journalists were received with a certain gruffness, they were more than willing to co-operate with other irregulars working behind enemy lines. Among those who came to use the LRDG as a highly specialised taxi service was Vladimir Peniakoff, a middle-aged Belgian sugar manufacturer who had settled in Egypt. A man of immense and aggressive energy, Peniakoff had, between the wars, travelled deep into the desert both with Bagnold and on his own. Now, with a hand-picked band of Arab and British soldiers which eventually became known as Popski's Private Army, he worked there for months on end. With the help of the LRDG, he and his 'army' released prisoners of war and did whatever sabotage came their way. They also built up an important intelligence network with the desert tribesmen, who if caught by the Italians would be treated not as prisoners of war, but as collaborators: this meant being strung up with an iron hook through the jaw.

Whereas the LRDG and Popski's Private Army were formed by desert-lovers to make specific use of the desert, David Stirling's SAS – the most famous 'private army' of the Desert War – grew out of an idea that had been developed in England: the commandos. Stirling set out for Egypt in October 1940 as one of a 2,000-strong commando force known as Layforce, under Colonel Robert Laycock. Among the young subalterns he had trained with were Randolph Churchill, Edward Fitzclarence (later 6th Earl of Munster) and Evelyn Waugh, and a good deal of their long journey was spent playing an interminable variety of games. Evelyn Waugh – who had done his commando training with Stirling and Randolph Churchill in Scotland – described Stirling as 'a gentleman obsessed by the pleasures of chance. He effectively wrecked Ludo as a game of skill and honour. We now race clockwork motor-cars.'[3] As the long voyage progressed, the stakes got higher. Randolph Churchill lost £400 in a night, and by the time they arrived in Egypt he was £800 down. In the closed world of the ship, the men greeted this news with sardonic amusement: a private soldier's pay came to 14/– a week.

These young officers were typical of their class and education in that they did not have much faith in the older, professional soldier. In their eyes, he was a product of the blinkered system responsible for the carnage of the First War. They on the other hand, although new to the job, regarded themselves as the new, vigorous blood of the Army. They became very unpopular with the naval officers, particularly when they referred to the captain as 'the old bugger on the roof'.[4]

Layforce arrived in Egypt in early 1941. Its first task was the capture of Rhodes, which would prevent the Germans building an airbase on the island. The commandos were shock troops, trained to swarm over the target area and do their work with terrible speed, before the enemy knew what had hit him – but the flaw in their design was that they had to rely on someone else to get them to their objective: in this case, the Navy. Within a month of their arrival, the Navy was fully occupied in transporting men and equipment to Greece. The operation was called off, and by late April Rommel had advanced to the Egyptian frontier.

With nothing specific to do, Layforce struggled to maintain its identity against the inevitable tendency to split it amongst other units. Its arrogance gradually disintegrated into boredom and despondency, and even the series of raids planned by Colonel Laycock to harass the enemy did not raise morale. All too appropriately, these operations were given code names from the titles of successful Aldwych farces – Rookery, Nook, and Cuckoo.

Intense pressure on all military and naval resources meant that the programme had to be drastically scaled down. Three of Laycock's operations were called off at the last moment, to the intense disappointment of the men. One of the few missions that did reach its target was the attack on Bardia. Under cover of night, the raiding force slipped silently into the harbour, fully prepared to give the 2,000-strong Italian garrison an unpleasant surprise – only to find that the Italians had abandoned the town.

For men who had volunteered for especially dangerous service, and who had expected to see action within weeks of their arrival, these anti-climaxes were bitterly frustrating. The men were kept in dreary tented camps with little to do – though the young officers could alleviate their boredom at clubs, restaurants and dinner parties in Cairo and Alexandria.

While he lost no opportunity to criticise the bungling military machine, which he held responsible for holding back so many ardent young men, Randolph Churchill thoroughly enjoyed Cairo. He and the other young officers of Layforce had not been there long before they were introduced to Momo Marriott, daughter of the American financier Otto Kahn. Julian Amery, who arrived in Cairo that summer and became a close friend of hers, wrote that 'her routine was the same whether she lived in London, New York, Paris or wartime Cairo. She never rose before lunch. She spent an hour and a half reading in the bath before dinner. She gave luncheons and dinners almost daily and saw a constant stream of visitors in between and well into the night. She was, as a result, exceptionally well-informed.'[5]

Momo was just the sort of rich and sophisticated woman Randolph liked; and though Momo always denied it, Cairene society believed they were lovers. But whatever Randolph's relationship with Mrs Marriott it did not stop him enjoying the company of an ever-changing succession of elegant Levantine women, who sat in groups over tea in Shepheard's and the Continental waiting to be asked if they were doing anything that evening. He was often seen with them at Madame Badia's, the Kit Kat Club, and even the Muhammad Ali Club, which raised several eyebrows. On one occasion, he sat down with two of his girlfriends in the lobby, which was reserved exclusively for gentlemen – ladies were supposed to go straight upstairs. On being asked to move, Randolph flew into a rage that resounded through the building. The upshot was that the Club was forced to introduce a rule whereby members had to sign in their female guests, so that undesirable ladies be kept out. The pleasures of Cairo, however, did not lessen his frustration. After the defeat of Greece in late April, Randolph's tirades against the crass stupidity and inefficiency of the brass hats became notorious – especially after a dinner on 5 May at the British Embassy, when his blistering attack on the Army lasted an entire evening.

Evelyn Waugh was made Intelligence Officer in April, and spent most of his time at the camp in Sidi Bishr. He grew an unsatisfactory beard which he shaved off when he heard that the men called him 'the red-bearded dwarf', but held on to his moustache which was symbolic of the manly seriousness with which he took his duties. In late April he went to make his Easter confession, and arrested the priest for asking questions of a military significance. A similar incident happens to Guy Crouchback, in *Officers and Gentlemen*: 'Suddenly Guy was suspicious. He was shriven. The priest was no longer bound by the seal of confession. The grille stood between them. Guy still knelt, but the business between them was over. They were man and man now in a country at war.'[6]

Keen and earnest, Waugh was contemptuous of men like Edward Fitzclarence who while training in Scotland had made much of his lust to shoot Germans like rats, but wasted no time in getting himself a job on the staff once they got to Egypt. Waugh quotes Fitzclarence in his diaries as saying, 'You know, old boy, I don't like this idea of a spot being "forever England".'[7]

Weakness, fear, inefficiency – Waugh knew they existed; but, in the face of death and disaster, he believed the spirit of the British Army would make men into heroes. The moment of disillusion came the following month, when on 20 May he and 'A' Battalion of Layforce boarded a ship for Crete. On leaving Alexandria, they thought they were part of a massive reinforcement to push the Germans back; but once on the island, the realisation dawned that Layforce was not a reinforcement, but a doomed rearguard to protect a broken army in the course of its evacuation.

There was no plan to the march, as small knots of exhausted men dragged themselves over the mountains to the southern part of the island and Sphakia harbour. Military formations ceased to exist, and there was little food or water. In *Officers and Gentlemen*, Guy Crouchback sees more examples of meanness and cowardice than of gallantry, particularly in the moral disintegration of Major Hound.

Waugh was evacuated, and back in Egypt he made no secret of his feelings. They were recorded by his friend and future biographer Christopher Sykes, who was then working in the propaganda section of Special Operations Executive, Cairo. In 1936 Sykes had married Russell Pasha's only daughter Camilla, and he was part of that raffish set of young officers that gave such sparkle to Momo Marriott's parties.

'[Waugh] declared that Crete had been surrendered without need; that both the officers and men were hypnotised into defeatism by the continuous dive-bombing which with a little courage one could stand up to; that the fighting spirit of the British was so meagre and that we had no hope of standing up to the Germans; that he had taken part in a military disgrace, a fact that he would remember with shame for the rest of his life.'[8]

Waugh rejoined the Marines, and sailed back to England a few weeks after returning from Crete. In the reorganisation that followed the Cretan débâcle, No. 8 Commando was disbanded, and there was talk of doing the same to Layforce.

Randolph Churchill had not been part of the detachment sent to Crete, presumably because his superiors felt that the risk of his capture was too great. Randolph did not share these scruples. When a raid was planned on the Gazala airfield, Randolph found out the town boasted not one but two. He spent a lot of energy trying to organise a separate sortie for himself and Robin Campbell to blow up the other one. But the time to prove himself in action had not yet come, and in early June he began a new job as press relations officer.

David Stirling was the only one of the three who remained convinced that there was still a place for commando operations, if they could be made more mobile; which was why he seized the opportunity to join a fellow-officer called Jock Lewes, who had got hold of a consignment of fifty parachutes (addressed to India, but delivered to Egypt by accident) and permission to experiment with them. Stirling's first parachute drop was made from an old Valencia aeroplane on an airfield at Mersa Matruh, and he badly damaged his back. The next few weeks were spent in bed at the Scottish Military Hospital in Alexandria, where he wrote a proposal for a new, streamlined commando force.

His thoughts were drawn to the hundreds of miles of road that snaked round the coast of North Africa, carrying the lifeblood of both armies. Just off the road lay airfields, stores, ammunition dumps and petrol dumps. The RAF knew the area well and flew over it regularly. Stirling suggested that sixty men, divided into five groups of twelve and each carrying explosives, should be parachuted into the vicinity of the road on the night before the next major Allied attack. They could do a substantial amount of damage before vanishing into the desert, where they would hide until collected by an LRDG patrol.

Since he was not on social terms with anyone in high command at GHQ, his main option was to hand his proposal in at the gate of the compound; from where, as he well knew, it would end up in a waste-paper basket long before reaching anyone of importance. The only other alternative was to try and put it in the right hands himself.

On a boiling hot day in July 1941, David Stirling slipped past the guard on duty at GHQ Cairo and walked briskly towards the main entrance – though not without being spotted, for there were angry shouts behind him. He entered the first office he saw, mainly to evade his pursuers, but its occupant was very unsympathetic and told him what to do with his crackpot ideas. Stirling made a hasty exit when the officer's attention was drawn by the telephone, which announced that a uniformed trespasser was in the building. He knew that whoever was behind the next door he tried would be his last chance. The door was marked DCGS, and Stirling recognised the man who looked up from his desk as Major-General Neil Ritchie: Deputy Chief of Staff, Middle East Forces.[9]

Ritchie was intrigued by the proposal, and so was Auchinleck, the new Commander-in-Chief. Stirling was given the rank of Captain, and permission to recruit sixty men and six officers, among whom were Jock Lewes and a huge man from Northern Ireland called Paddy Mayne, who had been a rugby player of international standard before the war. The unit would be known as L Detachment, Special Air Service.

The SAS began as one of several fictions designed by A Force under Brigadier Dudley Clarke to make the enemy believe that the British too were capable of airborne invasions. To promote its existence, dummy planes had been constructed and dummy parachutists dropped to fool enemy reconnaissance. Stirling would add substance to what hitherto had been a myth, but he was not under Dudley Clarke's orders. Right from the start, Stirling had insisted that he be under the direct command of the C-in-C.

Although he had no difficulty in finding recruits to join such an exciting outfit, he had great trouble with supplies – but this was not allowed to hold up training. Stirling made up for the fact that he only had access to an aeroplane for a few hours a day by making his men roll out of trucks moving at thirty miles an hour, which resulted in innumerable torn muscles and fractures. Their training not only set new standards of toughness, but was also effective: Stirling claimed he could get into Heliopolis aerodrome and out again without being spotted, and was challenged to try it at the end of October. The guards had been warned to expect an invasion, yet the SAS detachment still managed to put labels on 45 planes.

On 16 November, with the second Allied offensive due to start in forty-eight hours, two raids were mounted against the Germans: one on Rommel's headquarters, and one on the airfields of Gazala and Tmimi – which was to be the first operation of the SAS. Turbulent weather and inexperience resulted in catastrophe: neither airfield was destroyed, and of the 62 men parachuted into the area only 22 managed to crawl back to the LRDG patrol that was waiting for them two days later.

Stirling realised that to go back to Cairo at that point would mean the summary dissolution of L Detachment by the military authorities, and decided to stay in the desert for the time being. He also saw that parachutes were too unreliable a means of getting his men to their targets. He had, though, been very impressed by the efficiency of the LRDG patrol that had picked them up. Would they be willing to take L Detachment to and fro over the desert? Major Don Steele, of the LRDG's A Squadron, said he was willing to take Stirling wherever he wanted to go. It was the start of an extremely successful partnership: by the end of the year, the LRDG had transported Stirling and his men during four missions, and 89 enemy aircraft had been destroyed.[10]

After the fall of France, it seemed inevitable that most of Europe would soon be occupied. Hitler's armies appeared invincible: the only way to undermine them was to create a whole new strategy, which had nothing to do with conventional warfare.

Special Operations Executive was designed to carry the lifeblood of European resistance. In its early days it hid behind any number of names and, officially, it did not exist at all. SOE's agents would make contact with resistance movements in occupied territories, spread propaganda, provide wireless sets, weapons and training, set up information networks, and mount sabotage operations. Little by little, the strength of Europe would be built up underground, while Britain concentrated on gathering her resources and defending herself. German forces, now at their most powerful, would gradually be eroded; and, when the enemy was weak enough, the whole of occupied Europe would rise in revolt.

These were the desperate hopes that were pinned to SOE, and this was the reason why so much money and energy were poured into it. The Minister for Economic Warfare, Hugh Dalton, was given responsibility for the organisation on 22 July 1940 by the Prime Minister. 'And now,' said Churchill, 'set Europe ablaze.'

SOE offices were established in Lisbon, Berne, Istanbul and other neutral cities. Each office had two branches, one dealing with propaganda, the other with operations. In the autumn of 1940, George Pollock was put in charge of the operational branch of SOE Cairo. It consisted of a small staff and a dump of supplies housed in a garage in Alexandria, collected by an offshoot of the War Office's D Section and destined for subversion in the Balkans. (Just before the French surrender, one of the last flying boats to cross the Mediterranean was filled with further supplies for this store.)

George Pollock employed a highly efficient secretary. Born Hermione Llewellyn, she had married Daniel Knox, 6th Earl of Ranfurly in 1939; and, when he was posted to the Middle East, she came out to join him. Lady Ranfurly had excellent secretarial skills, but did not have a job when the Army decided to evacuate military wives in August 1940 and was obliged to board the evacuation train to South Africa. She did not stay there long: telling the authorities that she had a job so secret they were not to ask her about it, Lady Ranfurly managed to return to Egypt.

Lady Ranfurly may have been recruited into SOE in South Africa, or perhaps she joined the organisation shortly after her reappearance in Cairo; but, whichever it was, she had to be very careful to stay out of sight of the military authorities. She arrived back in Cairo in the middle of the night, and went straight to the flat of her friends Captain Patrick and Pamela Hore-Ruthven. For the first few weeks she lay low, but gradually her presence in Cairo became known. In early December 1940, the Army approached Sir Miles Lampson for help in getting Lady Ranfurly out of Egypt. They wanted him to ask the Egyptian government not to give her a residence visa; but Lampson was entirely on her side, and noted in his diary that he was not prepared to ask the Egyptian government to do the Army's dirty work.[11]

One of the people working in SOE at this time was Colonel Thornhill (who was later to become involved in Aziz el Masri's abortive escape). Thornhill's work was intended to stimulate anti-fascist propaganda in Egypt, particularly among the Italians. He had written a paper designed to turn Italian prisoners into Allied sympathisers, and thought that among the thousands of POWs now filing into prison camps around Cairo and the Delta, there might be many who were already disillusioned with fascism. Some might even be willing to become SOE agents, and return to Italy to work for the downfall of Mussolini.

The job of recruiting and training the Italian agents was given to Yak Mission, a group of twelve men led by Peter Fleming (brother of Ian, then Personal Assistant to the Director of Naval Intelligence in London). Captain Fleming, who had shot to fame as a travel-writer with the publication of his book *Brazilian Adventure*, had gained some experience of undercover work in England, where he raised and trained small groups to 'stay behind' in the event of enemy invasion. He and the men of Yak Mission were given a crash course in assassination and explosives, and sent out to Egypt with large quantities of destructive devices, guns, and £40,000 in five pound notes – but Yak Mission was doomed to failure. In all the Italian prison camps, they could not raise one single recruit.

SOE had two successes in the spring of 1941. The organisation's contacts in Athens enabled General Wilson to communicate with the Greek Government, at a time when it was almost impossible to do this through the proper channels of the Legation; and, in Yugoslavia, some valuable links were forged with the Serb Peasant Party, through which encouragement was given to the coup d'état which ousted the Regent, Prince Paul. However, criticism against the organisation considerably outweighed its achievements. SOE had been in operation for almost a year, hampered by inexperi-ence, the hostility of other secret services, and continual pressure to produce results. Peter Fleming's was not the first SOE operation to come to nothing; and a growing number of people in Whitehall felt that, in view of the large staff employed and the amount of money spent, SOE had very little to show for it.

A similar discontent with SOE was felt in Cairo. Except for a handful of senior officers, nobody in staff circles in Cairo knew anything about SOE, nor precisely what it was meant to do; but this did not stop accusations of slack security, inefficiency, and extrava-gance. The person who felt most strongly that SOE was getting out of control was Wavell's Chief of Staff, General Sir Arthur Smith, and it is possible that Lady Ranfurly was recruited into SOE at his request. He complained that GHQ was not being kept informed, and other secret organisations pointed out that work was inevitably being duplicated.

There were certainly a handful of men in the Cairo office of the operational branch who seemed to have a very cavalier attitude to their work. Most were employed on a temporary basis, and they thought it great fun to have a hush-hush job. They swaggered about, ate at Shepheard's, laughed and drank immoderately at parties, and probably behaved no better or worse than any other young men about town. But rumour had it that they were an unacceptable security risk, and that it was disgraceful that they should be amusing themselves on apparently unlimited expense accounts while men were fighting and dying in the desert.

In March 1941, one of the men in O'Connor's much-depleted Western Desert Force was the Earl of Ranfurly, soon to be taken prisoner. For his wife Hermione, her nerves frayed by anxiety, the behaviour of the 'good-time Charlies' in the SOE office was particularly offensive. She felt that the organisation was getting out of control, as did Bill Stirling, David's elder brother, who had been involved with the ill-fated Yak Mission.

Shortly after lunch on 24 March (the day Rommel took el Agheila and began his thrust to the east), Sir Miles Lampson, Peter Fleming and Anthony Eden – who was in Cairo to deal with the Greek crisis – were sitting on the verandah of the British Embassy. A telephone message arrived from Lady Ranfurly, who asked to see the Foreign Secretary in private on an important matter concerning the war. It was then that Peter Fleming let slip that she worked for the same secret organisation as he did. Lampson thought it unfortunate that Fleming should witness one of his subordinates getting immediate access to the Foreign Secretary, and recorded the incident in his diary:

'She arrived in due course, and insisted on seeing A.E. alone. To him she imparted her feeling that the whole of this hush-hush organisation is not only in a state of chaos, but that any amount of public money is being wasted thereon. This, in point of fact, only confirmed what A.E. (as he subsequently told me) had already long suspected.'[12]

The military were equally suspicious. That summer, General Sir Arthur Smith summoned Sir Frank Nelson, head of SOE's London office, to Egypt. Smith had been very disturbed by a file he had been sent, on the state of SOE Cairo. Nelson was accompanied by an assistant, Bickham Sweet-Escott, who later wrote a book about his experiences in SOE. Sweet-Escott had the job of assessing the material in the file 'which, it was alleged, conclusively proved the incompetence or worse of our organisation'.[13]

He found the evidence far from conclusive, and suspected – since it was drawn from information in SOE Cairo's own files – that it was the work of Lady Ranfurly and Bill Stirling. However, there was no doubt that SOE Cairo had lost the confidence of its colleagues, and the first of its many purges was put into action.

George Pollock returned to England. Both branches of SOE were placed under the same roof in a huge block of flats called Rustum Buildings, under the direction of one man, Colonel Terence Maxwell. The purge left SOE Cairo very short of personnel, which prompted GHQ to suggest merging it with their own special operations staff. There were undoubted advantages to this arrangement, but SOE Cairo would continue to receive its policy directives from the Minister in London, while its operations would be controlled by the Commanders-in-Chief in the Middle East. Nobody could have foreseen the trouble this would unleash in two years' time.

Another of the ideas that grew up in that early, inventive stage of the war was an experiment in a new sort of persuasive propaganda, tailored for the Middle East – an area the British wanted to keep quiet, neutral and friendly.

When Freya Stark offered her services to the Ministry of Information in the autumn of 1939, she was in her mid-forties and had published four books on the Arab world. Her first mission to preach the Allied cause was to the Yemen, where people had been very responsive – particularly to her propaganda films. Films had the attraction of being forbidden fruit, for the rulers of Yemen were strict Muslims who disapproved of any representation of natural forms.

After two months in the Yemen, with spells in Aden as assistant to her future husband Stewart Perowne, Freya got herself posted to Cairo and had her annual salary doubled to £1,200. On her arrival in June 1940, one of the first things she did was to reprimand the men who worked in the editorial office of the publications department. None of them had stood up as she entered the room, and she would not tolerate such sloppy manners. She was equally indignant at Randolph Churchill, who turned his back on her as they were being introduced. In a letter to her mother she described him as an insufferable young man, and added, 'They say he is doing as much harm as any two Germans, just by being himself.'[14]

Since films were no novelty in Egypt and her style was so personal, it was decided that she should set up a sort of intimate Allied salon. Four times a week, over tea with Egyptian ladies, Freya spread the good word and thought about how to increase her audience beyond the confines of middle-class respectability. She moved into a flat overlooking the Bahr-el-A'ama, the branch of the Nile that flows past the western bank of Gezira Island. It had a terrace, and as the ibis flew upstream in the evening she would watch the sun go down 'behind a gentle line of desert, and a group of palm trees all suffused with gold dust'.[15]

Before long, one or two young Egyptian men with pro-Allied sympathies were coming to see her, sent by Christopher Scaife – actor, poet, and an inspiring teacher in the university's English Department. These students were encouraged to bring their friends, and the ensuing discussions covered every aspect of the war, its aims, and its effects on Egypt. Her new movement was called the Brotherhood of Freedom. Its message was that the Arabs and the British shared a common cause: what was good for one was, axiomatically, good for the other.

As the group got larger it was divided into cells, which in turn divided when they contained more than ten people. Christopher Scaife was made president, and Freya had two assistants, Pamela Hore-Ruthven (who had sheltered Lady Ranfurly after her secret return from South Africa) and Lulie Abu'l Huda. The latter was an Egyptian girl of Turkish ancestry, who had studied at Oxford and lived with her mother and sister in the flat next door to Freya's. Some of the stuffier members of her family were outraged that she should be working for the British – indeed, working at all. The organisation was run from Freya's dining room. Every week a broadsheet was distributed, with the news and information to be discussed at the meetings.

Meanwhile Freya worked extremely hard, travelling from village to village as well as to the major towns. She was sometimes speaking for ten hours a day – which put a severe strain on her health, particularly since she had low blood pressure.

New cells sprang up all over Egypt. 'Before another year was out,' she later claimed in *Dust in the Lion's Paw*, 'we had spread up and down the Nile, and Azhar University was being converted by seventy small "democrat" committees inside it. In Alexandria, in the commercial quarters and among labourers in the port, ten thousand members stuck to us through Rommel's invasion, publishing leaflets at their own expense.'[16]

Freya's genuine innocence was both her weakness and her strength. Though she exaggerated the achievements of the Brotherhood (el Azhar, for example, remained largely pro-Axis despite her claims of 'conversion'), the fact that she never questioned the justice of her cause or the sincerity of her listeners must have made her a powerful speaker. Freya knew as well as anyone that Egyptians are warm and emotional, easily inspired by noble words – yet she never doubted the ease of her success. She would return from visiting a new cell beaming with benevolent satisfaction, convinced that every person who had attended was from now on a firm supporter of the Allies.

There were plenty of people, however, who thought the Brotherhood of Freedom was nothing more than an exercise in preaching to the converted, made up of earnest young *effendis* (the clerical class, largely employed in government offices). Seton Lloyd composed the following irreverent verse to be sung to the tune of 'We Are the King's Navee':

> We don't want to sit in the coffee bars
> Lounge in the cinemas
> Looking at the movie stars
> We just want to ROOT for demo-cra-cee
> We are Miss Stark's Wee Free.

Freya would answer any criticism by saying that she was treating her Egyptian audiences as equals and allies, a novel experience for many of them and one to which they reacted warmly; she was also providing them with arguments to use against those who backed the Axis.

After a visit to Baghdad in April, where she and three hundred others were besieged in the British Embassy in the course of the Iraqi revolt, the Ambassador Sir Kinahan Cornwallis asked Freya to start a branch of the Brotherhood there. Since the message of British benevolence in the Middle East was so obviously in need of an airing, she agreed, and returned to Egypt to wind up her affairs. The Brotherhood of Freedom was left with Ronnie Fay, Pamela Hore-Ruthven, Christopher Scaife and Lulie Abu'l Huda, who felt they had been left holding a large and unmanageable baby at unreasonably short notice. Freya, however, was sure they would do very well. She left Cairo alone in her small car and headed off into the desert, wearing a large blue hat with a clock-face in Roman numerals picked out in pink velvet on the brim.*

For all its efforts, the Brotherhood of Freedom could not be expected to reach everyone in Egypt; but, considering the power of enemy propaganda, it was remarkable that the organisation achieved anything at all. Italy and Germany had been broadcasting in Arabic since 1936, and the German Arabic Service became particularly popular. It had an excellent announcer who stressed that the Axis were the friends of all Arab nationalists, while deriding the Allies with aggressive impertinence. There was plenty of music, an unmistakable Arab feel to the programme, and it broadcast on frequencies easily accessible to the average café radio which was on from morning

---

* Freya stayed in Baghdad for the next two years, during which time she paid a visit to the Wavells in India in February 1943. On Wavell's orders a car was found for her return journey, in which she drove from Delhi to Teheran, where she sold it. Freya always maintained she was entitled to sell it, since it had been given to her – but officials in Cairo and Aden took a dim view of what they saw as disposing of government property in wartime. Someone in the Ministry of Information insisted that Freya account for this action, and her reply came back in the form of a quotation from Rudyard Kipling: '*If you can make one heap of all your winnings/And risk it on one turn of pitch and toss . . .*' The Ministry of Information was left in baffled silence.

till night. The BBC's Arabic Service, which began in January 1938, was aimed at a more educated audience and was on the air for far less time. Compared to its German competitor it was genteel and highbrow; and, in an effort to tell Arab listeners about Britain, it occasionally offered talks on interesting topics like 'Tuberculosis in British cows'.[17] The Arab Service had the added disadvantage of not being able to vaunt the theme of Arab nationalism – for in Egypt, this had distinctly anti-British connotations. As John Connell put it in *The House by Herod's Gate*, 'We had used Arab nationalism to overthrow the Ottoman Empire; the Germans and the Italians were now determined to use Arab nationalism to overthrow the British Empire.'[18]

For the average Cairene, living far from the centre of town in poorer districts where British soldiers were never seen, the *inglisi* and their war existed somewhere far beyond the narrow confines of everyday life. His only contact with the war was through the radio, and the rumours that buzzed around Cairo – which always confirmed the two solid facts he knew about the British: they were responsible for the rise in the cost of living, and (like all foreigners) their pockets were full of money.

Have you heard? The British are starting up the Labour Corps again; they are not paying fair prices for the mountains of grain their soldiers eat; hoard sugar, hoard kerosene, there'll be none left in three days. You think the British pay well? They pay more if you're Coptic or Jewish, but that will change when the Germans come.

The Axis were responsible for many of these rumours, and as propagandists they were infinitely more imaginative than the British. One of the rumours spread by the Axis was that Hitler was Muslim (a ruse Napoleon had employed 140 years earlier, without much success) and impatient to liberate Egypt from the infidel British. To many illiterate Egyptians, Hitler – or 'Muhammad 'Ider', as he was known – became a shadowy hero, ever waiting in the wings to make his triumphant appearance. On one occasion, a great procession of German prisoners of war was marched from Cairo railway station to the prison camps. This impressive testament to Allied victory was, however, undercut by the rumour that the whole thing had been organised by Muhammad 'Ider, as a way of infiltrating himself into the city.

The rumours that worked against the British were fed by Islamic fundamentalists and extreme nationalists within the Egyptian community and, from without, by members of the diplomatic corps friendly to the Axis. These included people from the Spanish, Hungarian, and Rumanian Legations. The fifth-columnists soon found out that, in propaganda, it is always easier to undermine an idea than to promote it – particularly when the promotion was so inept. Alan Moorehead wrote that 'the British Empire was hawked through the mud villages of the Delta like a dud second-hand motor-car'.[19]

The Publicity section of the British Embassy called corrosive voices working for the Axis the Whispering Gallery. An attempt to counter this campaign by similar techniques was begun by Laurence Grafftey-Smith, a diplomat who knew Cairo and the Middle East well. He had been forced to leave Albania, where he was Consul General, when it was invaded by the Italians.

Grafftey-Smith knew that people are far more likely to believe – and repeat – what they have been told in the strictest confidence than what they read in a newspaper. He built up a corps of 350 Egyptian agents from all walks of life, who spread pro-Allied rumours and arguments; they also reported the latest rumours spread by the opposition. Among them were a number of fortune tellers, and holy men who sat outside mosques to dispense wisdom and prophecy. Their pronouncements carried weight among the poor of the city, and for a small fee they could be ensured to predict a future favourable to the Allies.

Patriots or Fifth-Columnists?

While Allied propaganda was able to exert some influence, particularly after 1942 when the war started going in the right direction,
it had no power over deeply held convictions – especially among
young idealists. They saw that, politically, Egypt was in the hands
of wealthy, land-owning pashas. There was talk of elections and
democracy, but their system was based on personalities rather than
policies. There was talk of reform, but the fellahin were still living
in squalor and misery. There was talk of getting the British out;
but despite the Anglo-Egyptian Treaty the British seemed more in
control than ever, and thousands of their red-faced soldiers swarmed
all over Egypt.

The vast majority of Cairo's student population was not drawn
from the pasha class, that rich élite which mixed socially with the
British. Most students felt that Egypt would never achieve greatness
and independence until she had a strong, nationalist government,
firmly rooted in the Islamic tradition. King Farouk commanded their
passionate loyalty, and symbolised all Egyptian aspirations.

Hitler's personal achievement held a profound message of hope
for these ardent young Egyptians: here was a former corporal in a
defeated army, who had defied the rest of Europe to make his country and its armed forces great again. He was also fighting the British
and French, who were perceived by many to be the enemies of Islam
and the Arabs. As the students saw it, Britain and France had promised independence to the Arab countries released by the dissolution
of the Ottoman Empire. Then they had treacherously gone back on
their word, and carved up the Levant between them.

These ideas were encouraged by the Muslim Brotherhood and
their eloquent Supreme Guide, Hasan el Banna. The Brotherhood

was organised into small groups, who swore absolute loyalty to Islam, and the movement which dominated their lives. As well as Koranic studies, there was a strong emphasis on physical exercise and weapons training for young men. The latter had to be done in secret, and the Cairo sections practised in the Mokkatam Hills to the east of the city.

By calling for a return to a pure Islamic society, free of corrupt Western influences, the Muslim Brotherhood exploited the huge gap between the sophisticated Westernised Egyptians who had money and power, and the ordinary people who had very little of either. For the fellahin, it promised social justice and an end to poverty. For the staunchly traditional town dwellers, it promised the re-establishment of strict Muslim values and an end to foreign domination. The movement had a wide following in the Military College and the Universities, in a country where students had a political voice far greater than their number would suggest. Illiterate Egyptians had a great respect for education, and students were listened to as the leaders of the future.

Even before the outbreak of war, the German officer was a paragon to be emulated: in 1938, Second Lieutenant Anwar Sadat was not the only young officer to wear his hair very short, and sport a swagger-stick and monocle. Beyond that he had nothing but his pay, and a home in his father's flat – whose inhabitants included his father's three wives, nine children, and Sadat's grandmother. At that time, Egypt was a country in which promotion depended largely on money and connections. Sadat was part of the first influx of officer cadets who had none, and despite the greater emphasis on personal abilities, those who had only their talents to depend on would feel the need for patrons. This was why Aziz el Masri (then Inspector General of the Egyptian Army) and Ali Maher took the opportunity to found a secret officers' association, both in the Army and the Air Force, later known as the 'Ring of Iron'. This would extend the Palace's protection to certain young men in return for their devoted obedience.[1]

The anti-British sentiments Aziz el Masri had cultivated throughout the Army were much strengthened after his dismissal in 1940, and Sadat was undoubtedly part of his group; but its aims were conspiracy and sabotage against the occupying British, rather than any long-term plan to achieve political power. This is the crucial difference between it and Nasser's Free Officers' Movement, a later development that had loose connections with the 'Ring of Iron'. Nasser and his followers became disillusioned with the government after the Palestine War of 1948, and from then on were dedicated to its overthrow.[2]

Sadat met Nasser in 1938, when they were both posted to Manqabad in Upper Egypt. Nasser's commitment to Egyptian nationalism was immensely serious, but he knew that the British would not be thrown out in a day. Sadat was impressed by Nasser but, being more hot-headed, he was keen to work against the British as soon as possible.

The Egyptian Army establishment at that time consisted of eleven infantry battalions, a regiment of light tanks, another of armoured cars and various anti-aircraft and anti-tank detachments.[3] The British were well-aware of the resentment they excited in the Egyptian Army, and it was considered too uncertain a quantity to rely on. Its officers might, at the last moment, refuse to serve under British command. The Egyptian and British governments therefore decided to keep the force in a defensive role. This consisted of manning anti-aircraft guns, and defending roads, communications, installations, and the Suez Canal.

Certain border posts were also in the hands of the Egyptian Army; and, in these remote spots, discipline and morale were particularly low – for salaries were based on the idea that the further a man was from Cairo or Alexandria, the less money he needed. Relegation to border duties was often seen as a punishment, as in the case of the King's cousin Prince Ismail Daoud, who was one of the few officers in the Egyptian Army who was pro-British. For this offence he had been banished to Mersa Matruh, and was later accused of sodomy on the evidence of five of his men. This canard was widely suspected of being an attempt by the Palace to get rid of him altogether.[4]

In April 1941, when Rommel was advancing on Egypt, the British ordered the Egyptian Army units back from the frontier and replaced them with Allied soldiers. (GHQ also saw this as a good opportunity to stop the gun-running which was going on in these far-flung outposts, between Egyptian soldiers and the Muslim Brotherhood.) Sadat was disgusted at how easily the Egyptian Army gave in and allowed the British to take over their weapons.

Only a short time before, Aziz el Masri had been contacted by the Germans; and in his autobiography *Revolt on the Nile*, Sadat wrote that he tried to persuade his mentor to rise up with the Egyptian Army: 'Now seemed to be the golden opportunity for General Aziz el Masri. No one could do more than he to hold the Egyptian forces together and to win vital German support for the Arab cause . . .'[5] El Masri was not about to attempt anything so foolish, but a month later he decided to accept the German overtures.

The extent to which Sadat was involved is difficult to assess, since his two autobiographies contradict one another. In the first, *Revolt on the Nile* (1957), he admits to supplying el Masri with a car, which broke down on the way to the distant airstrip where the Germans had planned to pick him up. In his second, *In Search of Identity* (1978), he says he was at Mersa Matruh at the time.[6] Whatever Sadat's involvement, Aziz el Masri's first escape came to nothing. His second, though more dramatic, resulted in his capture. Sadat however was still free, and impatiently waiting for another opportunity to strike at the British.

As the situation for the Allies worsened in the spring of 1941, Ali Maher and his thinly-veiled Axis sympathies threatened the interests of both Sir Miles Lampson and the Prime Minister, Hussein Sirry.

Hasan el Banna had been exiled to Upper Egypt, but Ali Maher still kept in touch with the Muslim Brotherhood, as well as other quasi-military organisations on whose support he could depend. In 1940 Azzam Bey had started the Territorials, whom he recruited from the overflow of conscripts in the Egyptian Army. The British Embassy had been worried by this development, for Azzam Bey's violent nationalist views were well-known; but the organisation was unpopular in the country, and the men's training was minimal. Another organisation that Ali Maher encouraged was the Special Police, raised by Taher Pasha, a nephew of King Fuad who was known to have close links with the Germans. This too had not achieved very much, though it might have done if Ali Maher had remained in power – but he was thrown out a few days after the first battalion had completed training.[7] Ali Maher was now doing his best to build up these organisations, and Lampson believed he was involved in the confection and distribution of a number of inflammatory anti-British pamphlets; but, as far as the Ambassador and Hussein Sirry were concerned, the most dangerous of Ali Maher's activities was the influence he was building up in the Palace.

In a later report, Sir Miles wrote that 'the offensive of Sirry Pasha against Ali Maher Pasha and his gang led to partial successes, and for a time Ali Maher seemed to have less influence ... But this proved to be a flash in the pan. Gradually, Ali Maher Pasha recovered lost ground, mainly because he was able to persuade the King that Hussein Sirry's loyalty to us constituted subserviency to British interests.'[8]

Since the King of Egypt wielded a power the British monarchy had not enjoyed since the days of George III, Sir Miles became so concerned about Ali Maher's growing hold on Farouk that he considered the possibility of having him abducted. 'If only we could get Ali Maher out of the way the internal political situation would be immeasurably easier to handle. I wonder if this is not a case for SO(2) [the operational branch of SOE]?'[9] In April 1941, Hussein Sirry made an ill-considered attempt to remove him from the scene by offering him a choice between the Egyptian Embassy in Washington, or exile to his country estate. He also made the mistake of telling Ali Maher that he was doing this at the request of the British. Not unnaturally, Ali Maher protested that this was an attack on his freedom as a member of Parliament, and threatened to bring the matter up in the Senate. Sirry was forced to assure him that the suggestion had only been intended as a bit of friendly advice.[10]

SUMMER 1941

SUMMER 1941

Troops

I've learnt to wash in petrol tins, and shave myself in tea
While balancing the fragments of a mirror on my knee
I've learnt to dodge the eighty-eights, and flying lumps of lead
And to keep a foot of sand between a Stuka and my head
I've learnt to cook my bully beef with candle ends and string
In an empty petrol can, or any other thing
I've learnt to use my jack-knife for anything I please
A bread-knife, or a chopper, or a prong for toasting cheese
I've learnt to gather souvenirs, that home I'd like to send
And hump them round for months and months,
        and dump them in the end
But one day when this blooming war is just a memory
I'll laugh at all these troubles, when I'm drifting o'er the sea
But till that longed-for day arrives I'll have to be content
With bully beef and rice and prunes and sleeping in a tent.

Lament of a Desert Rat, by N. J. Trapnell
From *Oasis into Italy*

The northern stretch of the Libyan Desert is a limestone plateau swept with sand and rocks. Near the coast, winter brings pouring rain and driving winds, churning the dust and sand into thick mud. In the summer away from the coast, temperatures rise to 112°, and sandstorms in this weather can whip the skin raw. Winter and summer alike, nights can be bitterly cold.

Every man who fought in the desert suffered the same extremes of heat and cold, boredom, and the constant chafing from fine sand in dirty clothes which caused lesions known as desert sores. The sand worked its way into every fold and crevice of the body; and if it got under the foreskin, which it frequently did, it could cause not

only great pain but complete incapacitation. Erik de Mauny records
the practical heroism of one New Zealand Medical Officer, who
decided to get to grips with the problem. Armed with a scalpel and
a good supply of local anaesthetic, he took up a position outside his
Regimental Aid Post and gave a short talk on the benefits of circumcision. He also declared that it was far less painful than one might
expect; and, to prove his point, performed the operation on himself
there and then.[1]

As well as sand, there were flies. The desert fly, *musca sorbens*, is
a smaller and much more aggressive insect than *musca domestica*, the
common European housefly. Brushing them off eyes, lips, mugs of
tea and food became almost a permanent tic. Sometimes men had
an urge to trap flies in large numbers, douse them in petrol and then
throw in a match; it felt like revenge, until the appalling smell from
the burning flies reminded their killers that they had fed on rotting
flesh.

The Italians hated the desert, and kept it at bay by building
stone houses in their camps, laying out paths and little gardens. The
Germans fought it with science: their stores were full of foot pow-
ders, eye-lotions, insect repellents, mouth washes and disinfectants.
The British, Australians and New Zealanders simply ignored the
desert. They slept in blankets on the ground, and were not unduly
worried about germs.

British Army rations consisted of M&V (meat and veg), fatty
bacon, cheese, marmalade, and the perennial bully beef. All these
substances came out of tins, and were eaten with bread, or hard tack
biscuits that turned to plaster of Paris in the mouth. They drank their
tea hot and sweet; and, provided there were regular 'brew ups' and
nips of whisky, they could put up with almost anything. Their food
was heated on Benghazi burners – large petrol tins filled with sand
and soaked with petrol. Other petrol tins full of sand acted as filters,
for those rare moments when there was enough water to wash or
shave in.

Information came largely from two sources: *Parade* magazine and
the BBC. *Parade* had been founded in 1940 by Lieutenant-Colonel
Howard Ruston, formerly Cairo correspondent for the *Morning Post*
and the *Daily Express*. Photographs of battle-stained and grinning

soldiers illustrated the latest war news, and were interspersed with articles about the sterling work being done by the women back home. There were notices of the latest fund drives for war charities, and a pin-up girl on the back. (Rita Hayworth was voted favourite pin-up of the Middle East.)

The initial gung-ho tone of the magazine had been mercifully subdued, after staff photographer Bela Zola entered a canteen in Cairo to be met with the cry, 'Hello! Come to show us happy again in your bloody paper, are you?' – but it did not contain much news until challenged by Randolph Churchill's first broadsheets in 1941. These proved that the men really did want to know what was going on: an idea so novel and subversive that one officer burnt the broadsheet in front of his men. Another assured Randolph that the ranks were quite happy with back numbers of *Tatler* and *Country Life*.[2]

The calm, upper-class tenor of the BBC announcer reading the news from London was of immense significance to the British in the desert, as a direct link with home – though news often lagged behind events. On returning from a successful engagement, it was more than likely that the soldiers would hear the last reversal described in sombre tones; while, in the exhaustion of defeat, they would tune in to a cheerful report that all was well in the desert, and Jerry had been dealt a staggering blow. German radio was listened to for the music – and especially 'Lili Marlene', which was the favourite song for both sides in the Desert War.

'Lili Marlene' had been recorded by a woman called Lale Anderson in Berlin before the war; nobody paid much attention at the time, and the song sank into oblivion until the night the Germans captured the radio station in Belgrade in the spring of 1941. A gap in the programming needed to be filled fast, and a soldier produced a battered record of 'Lili Marlene' – and since there was nothing else to hand, they played it. The response was astonishing: thousands of people wrote in, begging to hear it again. Lale Anderson, who had given up all hopes of a successful career, was pulled out of obscurity and became a star; while such was the demand for 'Lili Marlene' that it was broadcast three times a night.

The most infectious diseases suffered by the Allied troops in Egypt and Cyrenaica were malaria, dysentery, mumps and VD. Yet malaria never reached the epidemic proportions which (along with cholera) had so undermined the forces in East Africa; and, despite flies and lack of water, the clean, dry air of the desert made it a relatively healthy place. The horrors were all man-made: stepping on a mine, or being caught in a tank when it 'brewed up'. Not many people survived the ordeal, and those who did were disfigured for life.

The wounded were taken to hospitals in or around Alexandria and Cairo. The 9th General Hospital had a burns unit; one of the Egyptian ladies who worked there as a VAD remembered how the stench of burnt flesh permeated the ward in hot weather, and there was no way of adequately washing the patients. VADs and Red Cross volunteers patrolled the hospitals with tea, sandwiches, cigarettes, and books. Mrs V. Low (mother of the novelist Penelope Lively) started a library, mysteries and Westerns being the most popular. However, people cannot read all the time, and Mrs Low thought of another way to relieve their hours of boredom. She had regimental badges stamped onto canvas, brought coloured wools and needles, and suggested embroidery. At first, the men were indignant – 'What! Me *sew*, miss?' – but someone said he'd give it a go, and embroidery soon took on. People with large villas lent their spare rooms to convalescing soldiers, and they were entertained by English and Egyptian ladies who would give them tea and take them sightseeing.

It was rather tame compared to the few days' leave of the normal soldier, who came to Cairo to have a good time and slake his thirst for beer and women. Bars and brothels cost money; but, since there was nothing to buy in the desert except the occasional egg from a nomad child, the men usually arrived in Cairo with a considerable amount of back pay in their accounts. Some was sent home, some went into war savings – but most of it was to be spent.

At the start of the war, Wavell had had between 80,000 and 100,000 men. By November 1941, Auchinleck had 750,000 between Libya and Iraq, with over 140,000 in and around Cairo.[3] Basic uniform was a khaki bush shirt, a soft cap the British called a 'fore an' aft', and long baggy shorts to the knee. Also to be seen in the streets of Cairo were diamond-shaped Polish *czapkas*, Australian 'wide-awake' hats (pinned up on the left for formal occasions), the New Zealand slouch hat which looked like the Australian but had a conical crown, South African hats like solar topees, Indian *pugrees* with variations that indicated the wearer's tribe and religion, French *képis*, British and Canadian peaked caps, the berets of the tank regiments, the olive-green caps of the Greeks with their pale blue and white cockades, and the occasional 'Bombay Bowler'. Every nationality added its own flashes, regimental badges and symbols of rank to its dusty, desert-coloured khaki drill.

Major A. E. W. Sansom, recently appointed Chief Field Security Officer for the Cairo area, put two of his patrol-men into German uniform. They were to build up a picture of security-consciousness among the Allied troops, by making a list of those who attempted to arrest the 'Germans'; but, after wandering around Cairo for two days without provoking any reaction at all, they gave up.[4]

The troops were lodged in camps around the city: South Africans at Helwan, Indians at Mena, and a very well-appointed one at Maadi for the New Zealanders. The British were mostly in Heliopolis. The vast Abbassia barracks were solid buildings with married quarters; but Hilmiya camp, and the even bigger Almaza camp, consisted of row after row of square tents with one window, housing eight men to a tent. The summer temperature in Cairo is between 85° and 90°, the heat made more oppressive by the humidity caused by the surrounding cultivation and the Nile itself. Men slept through the warm, close nights as they had in the desert: on the ground, using their boots as a pillow.

Catering for so many thousands of sensitive, Westernised stomachs without poisoning them was a constant source of worry for the medical authorities. Milk always had to be boiled, even when fresh, and was often delivered dirty and copiously watered. Meat for the Middle East Forces came from Sudan and Abyssinia. The authorities had managed to hire decent slaughtering and storage houses. But the rest of the abattoirs used by the local population, and therefore by restaurants that catered for the troops, were in an appalling condition – and stayed that way despite regular remonstrations. As for the local sausages, they were not to be trusted under any circumstances.[5] Beyond board and lodging, other facilities in the camps included little more than a couple of football pitches and a bar; the latter furnished with one or two chairs and a battered refrigerated chest containing the local Stella beer, or (if one was lucky) Tennent's or McEwan's Red Label. Anyone who wanted more had to take the tram into Cairo.

A bar was usually the first priority, and plenty of these had sprung up in the last two years, selling beer, whisky and arak. Clubs that featured girls and music were popular but expensive, since one had to buy drinks for the girls as well. At Bab el Hadid was the Bosphore Club – a bit too close to Military Police Headquarters, but convenient for the main tram and train stations as well as the red light district. Other clubs and cabarets were clustered around Sharia Emad ed Din. Restaurants with names like Café-Bar Old England or Home Sweet Home served the closest that Egypt could get to English food. Those who ate water-buffalo steak with small musty eggs and chips at their rickety tables might grumble that it didn't taste the same, but it was a great deal better than bully beef.

Men coming from the chilly industrial towns of England, who had never seen anything more exotic than a banana, experienced a profound culture shock. Their senses were assaulted by a battery of powerful smells and noises; and, while there seemed to be an astonishing variety and abundance of fruit, vegetables and grains in the shops, there was poverty wherever one looked. They ate surrounded by begging children while pedlars and hawkers tried to sell them fly-whisks, razor-blades, or dirty magazines called *Zip*, *Laffs*, *Wam* or *Saucy Snips*, and young pimps called, 'Hi, George! You want my sister? Very nice, very clean, all pink inside like Queen Victoria.'

Similarly, the troops were something of a novelty for the Egyptians. Unlike the Greek and Italian communities which spanned several social classes, there were no English waiters, grocers or taxi-drivers in Egypt – only aloof, educated professionals. The Egyptians were very interested to see these examples of ordinary working Englishmen. Crowds used to collect in front of Kasr el Nil barracks, to watch the amazing and slightly shocking sight of British soldiers sitting on the window-sills, reading magazines and drinking beer while dressed in nothing but shorts and vests.

If called upon to lecture on the prevention of VD among troops, Regimental Medical Officers were advised to emphasise that, while the sexual urge was perfectly natural, it could be sublimated without injury to health. This could be achieved by 'concentration on games, general physical fitness, military duties and obligations, literature, hobbies and so on'.[6] But, while the British Army liked to pretend – at least officially – that sex could be safely ignored, they had set up seven VD centres attached to the main hospitals in the Cairo area. (These seem to have been very well attended. Between October 1941 and March 1942 when there were an average of 127,000 Allied troops in and around Cairo, No. 1 VD Centre alone clocked up 954 admissions; each of which needed an average of between ten and twenty days in bed.)[7] They also made certain brothels 'in bounds', but these seem to have been designed to depress rather than excite the senses. One was a great gloomy tenement with a wide stone staircase, where queues formed for the best girls. 'On the ground floor, sitting in his stall, was the RAMC man doling out one French letter, one tin of ointment, and one pamphlet to each suppliant.'[8]

The Cairo area medical report for the first quarter of 1941 notes gloomily that 'the increase in VD in March coincides with the return of 7th Armoured from Cyrenaica'. Sex-starved troops coming in from the desert had turned Cairo's oldest profession into a major service industry, focused on the run-down quarter of Clot Bey, just north of Ezbekieh Gardens. It is ironic that Antoine Bartélème Clot, who introduced Western ideas of public health and hygiene into Egypt and was rewarded with the title of Bey by his patron Muhammad Ali Pasha, should be commemorated in the most insalubrious area of the city. The street that bore his name ran parallel to the Wagh el Birket, known to English-speakers as the Berka.

The prostitutes sat fanning themselves on the hundreds of little balconies that overlooked the long narrow street, and called down to the men below, while at ground level there were little booths, screened by a single curtain. One of these bore the legend 'Esperanto spoken here'. The booths spilled into alleyways running off the Berka, with peep-shows and pornographic cabarets. The most famous of these was in Darling Street, and featured the outrageous coupling of a fat woman and a donkey.

The Berka was bounded by round white signs with a black 'X' through them, denoting that it was Out of Bounds to All Ranks. A visit there meant risking an encounter with the Military Police; but neither they, nor the high risk of venereal disease, seem to have been much of a deterrent. The Berka flourished until the summer of 1942, when the murder of two Australians prompted the authorities to close it down altogether. (Among Egyptians, the Australians not only had the reputation for being the rowdiest troops, but it was said that they threw prostitutes out of the window when they had finished with them.) The prostitutes of the Berka were evicted, a problem they overcame to some extent by doing business in the backs of horse-drawn gharries; but the medical authorities were well-pleased, since the closing of the Berka halved the monthly incidence of VD contracted in Cairo.[9]

It was considered bad form for an officer to visit a brothel. To go once or twice, for the experience, was forgivable, although it set a bad example to the men; but as a rule, it was humiliating to have to pay for something an officer ought to be able to get free. In the VD reports, most troops state they were infected in a brothel, while most officers say it was in a private house. This pious imposture was exploited very effectively by one racket, which consisted of introducing officers to a very beautiful and expensive woman; as they got out their wallets, they were knocked unconscious and robbed. This went on for some time, for no officer was willing to report that he had been robbed under such humiliating circumstances.[10]

To the average British soldier, the Egyptians were 'Wogs': a word they thought stood for Wily Oriental Gentleman, but which was in fact a relic of Lord Cromer's day, referring to those members of the clerical *effendi* class 'Working on Government Service'. There was 'wog' labour to do the most menial work in base camps and hospitals, 'wog' food for sale in the streets; the word was interchangeable as an adjective meaning anything Egyptian, or a term of abuse. Leaflets were issued stressing the importance of maintaining good relations with the Egyptians, but gave few hints on how these might be achieved.

With so many troops in the streets, many of whom were drunk and bored, hooliganism was not unusual; but, when a group of hard-drinking thugs brawled in a café, there was no compensation for the owner whose furniture had been smashed. The Egyptians still complained of British soldiers knocking off their tarbooshes (though the 'tarboosh game' had been far worse before the war, when pairs of young officers in open cars would compete to see who could grab the most tarbooshes in twenty minutes). It was not unusual for an Egyptian car to be hijacked by drunken soldiers, who would then force the owner to drive them wherever they wanted to go. Egyptians were frequently robbed and beaten up. Taxi-drivers went on strike, insisting on the right to take a friend in the front – a habit that always irritated foreigners, and had been banned a few years before. These were stories that never appeared in the papers, which were encouraged to show pictures of troops and gharry-boys laughing together.

'It was a long time since we last saw English people in crowds like that,' wrote Olivia Manning, who had travelled from Bucharest to Athens to Cairo since 1939, but had not been back home. 'Not ordinary, mixed English crowds of course – only young men. The streets were always full of them; sweat shining, hair bleached to a sameness, the pink burn of English skin disguising differences; much of a size, not tall. They were more English than the people in London streets. They came from parts of England where there was little mixture of foreign blood. Their worn, thin, washed-out khaki was wrinkled with heat. Dark patches of sweat showed between their shoulder blades and under their arms.' [11]

Olivia Manning observed that the shyer, more bewildered soldiers and non-commissioned officers yearned for the security of the respectable. They were easy prey for the more distinguished-looking Arab guides who hung around smart hotels in clean galabeiahs, leaning on walking sticks with schoolmasterly gravity. She also noted that they treated English civilians with the utmost deference.

Mrs Devonshire, to judge from the photograph of her talking to an earnest group of men and women in uniform, was used to respect. This remarkable Frenchwoman was a great expert in Islamic architecture, and a tour of the Cairo mosques in her company was a must for the cultivated visitor: she had become a historic monument in her own right, like Gertrude Stein in Paris or Bernard Berenson at I Tatti. On three afternoons a week, in both World Wars, Mrs Devonshire took members of the Services – free of charge – round the great Islamic buildings of the city.

Everybody wanted to see the Pyramids. Groups of five or six would hire a horse-drawn gharry in the late afternoon when the heat was more bearable. They would drive over the English Bridge, and watch the city give way to mud-brick villages, canals, and fields recently harvested of their crops of beans, barley and wheat. Schindler's *Guide to Cairo* of 1943 says that 'the Great Pyramid can be climbed in about fifteen minutes with the help of two strong Arabs, one to hold each hand'. One way or another, the sightseers scrambled up to admire the view, and carved their initials on the top as Napoleon's troops had done almost a hundred and fifty years before. Then they went to see the Sphinx, which was not looking its best. To protect it from possible bomb damage the British had thoughtfully built a blast wall between its paws, on top of which sandbags supported the four-thousand-year-old chin.

To escape the painful light and suffocating heat of the afternoon, there was always the cinema. In 1940 and 1941, films to be seen in Cairo included *Broadway Serenade*, *Elizabeth and Essex*, *Mutiny on the Bounty*, *Gone With the Wind* and *The Great Dictator*. The performance ended with the Egyptian National Anthem, composed by Verdi.* As soon as it had started, all the British troops in the audience sprang to their feet and started singing an extremely ribald song:

> 'King Farouk, King Farouk, you're a dirty old crook
> As you walk down the street in your fifty-shilling suit
> Queen Farida's very gay, 'cos she's in the family way . . .'

Muhammad Neguib, later President of Egypt's Revolutionary Council, was a lieutenant-colonel in the Egyptian Army. In his memoirs, he wrote that 'Farouk was never so popular as when he was being insulted by British troops, for we knew, as they knew, that by insulting our unfortunate King they were insulting the Egyptian people as a whole'.[12]

British insolence was not always tolerated. Neguib once threw a British soldier off a bus, and one pasha – when insulted beyond

---

* The story goes that Verdi jotted down the tune and gave it as a gift to the man who brought him payment for *Aida*: commissioned – but not delivered in time – for the inauguration of the Cairo Opera House.

endurance by a very drunken British officer – decided to take serious revenge. He invited the officer to dinner, by which time the latter had completely forgotten the man he had been so rude to; but there seemed no reason to turn down this unexpected offer of a free meal, so he accepted. He rang the bell of the pasha's house on the appointed night; but instead of being admitted by a polite sufragi, two huge Nubians hauled him into a room where his host announced, 'You insulted me the other night, and now you will pay for it.' His trousers were pulled down and, while the two Nubians kept him still, the British officer was sexually assaulted by six other Nubians before being thrown out of the house. Most men would have kept this humiliating episode to themselves; but, the following day, this particular officer was telling everyone, 'You'll never guess what happened to me last night – dashed unpleasant. I got buggered by six Nubians.'

Soldiers who could not afford the plush upholstery and blissful air-conditioning in the smarter theatres could watch films in open-air cinemas (the one in Ezbekieh Gardens was a great nuisance to people trying to sleep in the east-facing rooms of Shepheard's Hotel). Early on in the war, an entrepreneur called Thomas Shafto obtained the cinema concession for all military establishments. The films thus distributed were known as 'Shafto's Shufties'. Gabriella Barker, wife of Cyril Barker (the Barkers were one of the leading business families of Alexandria), organised a volunteer concert party called *Desert Angels*, which toured camps and hospitals. Gracie Fields was billed to inaugurate Cairo's Live Entertainment for the Troops, but she never came. The first two concert parties were *Spotlights* and *Hello Happiness*, which combined to give the first ENSA (Entertainments National Service Association) performance at the Cairo Opera House in October 1941.

The hostesses of Cairo, and especially Lady Russell Pasha, were active in setting up clubs where the men could relax in the shade after tramping about town in their woollen socks and hot boots. The soldiers who patronised them were considered rather cissy by their lustier comrades, but the clubs were used by thousands of men every week. The Tipperary Club had a long balcony overlooking Ezbekieh where tea, toast, eggs and cake were sold at minimal prices.

There were also showers, baths, a reading-room and a barber. The café was run by ladies who had spent their mornings working as VADs in the hospitals. On one occasion Lady Wavell, then in her mid-fifties, was serving tea in such a club when a soldier asked her what she was doing in a job like that in Cairo. She said that she had come with her husband, who was a soldier. 'Then it's a disgrace for an old man like that still to be fighting,' came the reply.

Lady Russell Pasha also started Music for All, which arranged concerts for the Forces in an old cinema. She and her helpers had only a gramophone, a few records and a piano to begin with; but excellent professional musicians started appearing once ENSA got going in Egypt. The Sunday concerts with the Cairo Symphony Orchestra under the baton of Squadron Leader Hugo Rignold were always packed out. On Monday afternoons, courtesy of Egyptian Hotels Ltd, the roof garden of the Continental was the venue for amateur concerts and shows: this was the only time that other ranks were allowed in the hotel.

The segregation between officers and men was visible everywhere. Along with the Continental, private soldiers were not allowed in Shepheard's, the Turf and Gezira Clubs, or the more expensive restaurants and night-clubs. The English soldier took this in his stride – he had been brought up with ideas of 'us and them' – but it caused considerable indignation among the Australians, New Zealanders and South Africans. Some of these men were rich landowners who had enlisted as private soldiers because they had been so keen to fight, and did not want to waste any time on an officers' training course. The fact that their patriotic ardour should keep them out of Shepheard's seemed grossly unfair. This segregation came in for even more criticism when American soldiers and airmen began to arrive in Cairo, so the rules were relaxed a little; though not at Shepheard's where, according to Cecil Beaton, gentlemen back from the desert were not always very civilised. He came down one morning to find the lobby in chaos: furniture and potted plants had been thrown about, while the floor was covered with earth, broken glass, and fire-extinguisher foam. The night-porter was almost in tears: 'Last night the same, all of them with red trousers from the same regiment, the chirry pickers. They all taker the chairs and puter them on the cars and I taker them back and they do this and they prakit and they say "put on bill", crash, "put that on bill", crash, and they go mad over that ebony woman. They are going back to the desert tomorrow, they say "put all on the bill".'[13]

Groppi's was one of the few smart places open to everyone – though it was not cheap, and the clientele therefore tended to be officers. There were two Groppi's: one on Midan Soliman Pasha, the other in Sharia Adly Pasha. The latter had a garden, with flowering creepers trained up the walls, and little tables and chairs set out on a sandy floor. No matter how full, this garden always preserved a feeling of intimacy. Pashas came to sip coffee and eat cream cakes with their Levantine mistresses, who draped their furs over the chairs; while officers on leave looked out for female companionship, and envied the man at the opposite table who suddenly rose to his feet with a smile, and pulled out a chair for the woman who had just joined him. As dusk fell, the garden was illuminated with strings of little coloured light-bulbs.

The need for English-speaking women was felt not only by those off duty. Demand for female clerical staff had increased dramatically since the previous year, when even women with employable skills like Lady Ranfurly had been evacuated. Many English-speaking refugees had been taken on as cypherenes, interpreters and censors; but still more women were needed to release desk-bound men for active service. Volunteer members of the South African Women's Auxiliary Army Service were summoned to fill the gap; and, on 2 August, their arrival in Cairo was celebrated on the front page of *Parade*, which announced 'The Waases are here!'

Discipline was strict for the Waases. They slept four to a room in beds that had to be fumigated for insects once a week, and had to endure drill sessions with a Scottish sergeant-major. But there were comforts: every month came a parcel from Oomah – Mrs Smuts. These were known as Glory Bags, and contained sweets, stockings, a pair of elasticated khaki bloomers and a box of Springbok cigarettes. On one occasion the Glory Bags were delivered to a detachment of South African soldiers at the front, who caused much hilarity by playing rugger in the bloomers. At first, the Waases were given only the most mindless office work;

but the situation improved in time and, when the first detachment of ATS (Auxiliary Territorial Service, the British women's army) arrived a few months later, they were not pleased to find that the Waases had all the best jobs. They were also allowed to wear silk stockings, whereas the ATS were obliged to wear hideous hosiery of khaki-coloured cotton.

A private was not allowed to live outside barracks and had to be back by midnight – an obligation not imposed on officers, nor of course on those whose jobs did not involve joining the Army. The most popular residential area was Gezira, and flats were usually shared by two or more friends, for rents were high. Yet because the Egyptian owners tended to remove the good furniture and rugs before renting them out, apartments maintained a gloomy sparsity. Bare tiled floors, too few chairs, and shutters closed against the sun emphasised that this was only temporary accommodation. Nevertheless, every flat had a minimum of two servants – a sufragi and a boy – and this basic team was often augmented by a cook. (Female servants were rare, since the majority of Egyptians thought it shameful for a woman to work outside her own house.)

Those women who lived in flats and were not in uniform could also spend a little of their money on clothes. Printed cottons and silks were readily available, and there were plenty of Greek or Levantine dressmakers who could perform miracles on their antiquated sewing machines. The atmosphere of cheerful improvisation also meant that clothes were freely borrowed and lent, though this sometimes happened through the sufragi network and without the owner's knowledge. Sometimes a woman would watch in astonishment as her dress literally walked out of the steam laundry (the boy who held it being invisible), and headed off in a completely unknown direction.

In British military establishments the working day started at nine, and broke off at one. Then the officers headed for the Gezira Club, to play tennis and swim, followed by lunch from the buffet piled with chicken, game pie, boiled and roast beef, ham and chops. Since other ranks were not allowed in the Club, and the Waases were forbidden to appear out of uniform even in the evening, the problem was solved by wearing their khaki coats and caps as far as the entrance where they were then removed to reveal day dresses. (Discovery would have meant being 'gated' for five nights.) The afternoon's work started at four or five.

It is worth remembering that most English-speaking people in Cairo at this time were under thirty, and involved in the immensely significant task of winning the war. It gave their world a glamorous, magazine feature quality; and within it, women were a privileged minority. By the time work ended at eight or nine, a small group of officers had collected outside the Waases' barracks in Sharia Champollion – some waiting for their dates, others just optimistic.

The evening began with dinner at Fleurent's, the St James's, or Le P'tit Coin de France, followed by dancing at the Scarabée, the Deck Club or the Kit Kat Club. The last two night-clubs were on boats moored by the river bank. The Kit Kat Club was always supposed to be full of spies, and officers were warned to be particularly discreet in front of the Hungarian dancing girls. At one point it was even made out of bounds.

Another favourite venue was the restaurant on the roof of the Continental Hotel, which had its own dance floor, and a rather disappointing cabaret which included belly-dancers, acrobats, and Mr Cardyman who did card tricks. They were introduced by a pretty blonde American in a long chiffon dress, who rounded off the show with a solo dance. This she began with the words 'and now, introducing myself, Betty to you, in a beguine' (or whatever dance she had chosen that evening). She was therefore known to all her fans as Betty-to-You.

A girl was not expected to pay for any of these entertainments, and could go for months without buying her own dinner. If sociable and even moderately attractive, she could find herself out on the town seven nights a week. Not all girls managed to keep their heads in the face of such adulation, and some became so contemptuous of the men at their feet that they made a habit of referring to them as 'meal tickets'.

In Olivia Manning's novel *The Danger Tree*, the first volume of the Levant Trilogy, Harriet Pringle asks the beautiful Edwina if she doesn't get bored going out so often. 'Well, yes, but what else is there for me? You're lucky. You have that nice husband. You've something to stay in for.'[14]

It was open season for husband hunting. Not many showed the determination of the MTC girl who drew a crumpled white satin wedding gown from the bottom of her kit bag, saying she'd get him in the end; yet the young women who found themselves in Cairo knew that they would never enjoy such a choice again, certainly not in post-war Britain.

'Abroad' in general, and the Orient in particular, has always had a subversive effect on British inhibitions, and buttons had a way of coming undone in Cairo. The war provided not only the first real romantic opportunity for these young women, but also the most powerful argument for giving in to male supplication. That the man in question might be killed next week lent not only a poignant intensity, but also a noble, generous element to the affair.

The rather sad and increasingly desperate Edwinas usually got their man, but he was seldom the one for whom they had aimed. The hundreds of weddings that took place in Cairo came about because men too had need of an anchor, in the violent, unpredictable world the war had created.

There were, however, women in Cairo whose first priority was their career. Eve Curie, daughter of the French scientists Marie and Pierre, arrived in Cairo in November 1941 determined to become the first woman correspondent to visit the front in the desert campaign. Women were not allowed in the fighting area, but with the help of Randolph Churchill – who enjoyed breaking rules – she achieved her ambition. Freya Stark only heard where Eve Curie was a few days later, over lunch with Brigadier Eric Shearer of Military Intelligence. She asked if he could arrange a similar visit for herself, but he managed to put her off – 'For one thing, he pointed out that all the sanitary arrangements are so public that everything simply *stops* when a woman is in the camp.'[15] Not only the men were inhibited. Alexander Clifford of the *Daily Mail* recalled that Randolph had to drive Eve Curie four miles into the desert and wait with his back turned. Nevertheless, being a woman in the all-male, monastic world of the desert held moments Freya would have relished. 'Several times in the desert I bumped into a dirty, sunburned

Englishman, hardly recognisable under a makeup of sand and sweat, and . . . heard a refined, slightly affected voice say to me "How very nice to see you here! We haven't met since that luncheon at the Ritz" or "since I saw you at Daisy's ball".[16]

Administrative Problems

The first wartime headquarters of the British Army in Egypt was the Semiramis, a luxuriously gloomy Edwardian hotel on the banks of the Nile. It remained the Headquarters of British Troops in Egypt,* while the actual administration of the war moved to a modern block of flats known as Grey Pillars at the southern end of Garden City, off Sharia Kasr el Aini. The speed with which GHQ was forced to expand encouraged the proliferation of offices rather than efficiency: planning, communications, supplies, intelligence, propaganda, and censorship were all split into sections, subdivided into departments, which in turn spawned sub-departmental satellites.

Sir Miles Lampson had been pleased with Wavell's co-operation in getting rid of Ali Maher, and hoped he could count on the weight of the Service Chiefs when he next needed to put pressure on the Egyptians. However, GHQ became very wary from then on of meddling in local politics:[1] in fact, it wanted to have as little to do with the Embassy as possible. A combination of obsessive secrecy and a reluctance to keep the Embassy up to date with events often left Sir Miles in an embarrassing position, when he found out that the Egyptian Prime Minister was better informed than he himself on the doings of GHQ. Cecil Campbell, who as an old legal adviser to the Embassy felt in a strong position to criticise it, told the Counsellor, Terence Shone, that the bad blood between GHQ and the Embassy was notorious. He warned that, when he went back to London, he would tell Lord Beaverbrook all about it.[2]

---

* The British garrison which, in peacetime, protected British interests and the Suez Canal was known as British Troops in Egypt, or BTE. Throughout the war it maintained a separate identity from the British Army in Egypt.

King Farouk and his bride Queen Farida, 20 January 1938

Prince Muhammad Ali

King George II of Greece

Princess Shevekiar

Field Marshal Smuts and Winston Churchill in Cairo, August 1942. Behind them are Sir Arthur Tedder and Sir Alan Brooke

Brigadier and Mrs (Momo) Marriott

Sir Thomas and Lady Russell Pasha

Christopher Sykes, Gertrude Wissa, Sir Miles Lampson and Mrs Salisbury Jones

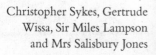

Sir Miles and Lady Lampson at the British Embassy in Cairo, September 1940

British armoured vehicles returning to camp after a day's training, July 1940

A British gun crew digging-in during artillery battle in the Western Desert, 1942

ENSA (Entertainments National Service Association) 'glamour girls' distributing cigarettes and beer to the troops in North Africa, July 1942

A garden party at the British Embassy

Innocent amusements for the Allied troops in the streets around 'the Berka', Cairo's red-light district, 1942

The terrace of Shepheard's Hotel, Cairo

Aziz el Masri

Three wartime Prime Ministers:
Ali Maher Pasha, Hussein Sirry
Pasha, Nahas Pasha

The trouble lay in the administrative structure: GHQ Cairo was responsible to the War Office, the British Embassy to the Foreign Office, and both War and Foreign Offices were in turn responsible to the War Cabinet. In other words, the only body with the authority to co-ordinate the work of GHQ Cairo and of British diplomats in the Arab world was on the other side of occupied Europe, and at such an Olympian level as to rule out day to day involvement in the rapidly changing situation in the Middle East.

In April 1941 Wavell wrote to the War Office that 'there is little doubt that events in Iraq and Syria, plans to revive the rebellion in Palestine, and fifth-columnist activities in Egypt are part of a co-ordinated German plan to cause us maximum trouble in Arabic-speaking countries . . . Germans have the great advantage of unified direction and execution of this policy . . . We on the other hand have no authority nearer than London who in major matters can decide on political policy in relation to strategy, authorise expenditure, or initiate important measures to counter enemy activities or propaganda when required on a Middle East basis. In almost every Middle Eastern problem local representatives of up to six departments of HMG have to be consulted and their views cabled home . . .'[3]

Averell Harriman, who visited Cairo in mid-June as President Roosevelt's special envoy, agreed with both Wavell and Lampson that a 'superman' of Cabinet rank was needed to regulate the often conflicting priorities of the diplomats and the military. The idea had been brought to the Prime Minister's attention, but he did not take action until he got a telegram from his son Randolph, who had been in Cairo for eight months and was bear-leading Harriman at the time.

The man Churchill chose to be the first Minister of State in the Middle East was Oliver Lyttelton, in whom he had great faith. Before the war, the far-sighted Lyttelton had harried the government about their dangerously low stocks of vital non-ferrous metals. Appointed Controller of Metals in an emergency nationalisation of the industry, he managed to buy up large reserves at remarkably low prices. Churchill had been so impressed that, in 1940, Lyttelton became President of the Board of Trade.

Now the Prime Minister told him that as Minister of State in the Middle East he would be a member of the War Cabinet, and thus the 'highest authority on the spot'. Lyttelton guessed that did not mean much. The ambassadors and commanders would still report first to their masters in Whitehall, and other departments he was expected to co-ordinate remained answerable to their overlords such as the Ministry of Transport, the Ministry for Economic Warfare, or the Colonial Office.

Lyttelton realised that all these groups would have to be persuaded, rather than ordered, to act in concert. His position, as highest authority on the spot with no authority to speak of, would have to retain its mystique without ever being put to the test.

The Minister of State moved into an office at No. 10 Sharia Tolumbat in Garden City, which inevitably became known as 'Number 10'. The first major task that faced Lyttelton was the drafting of the armistice with Syria. De Gaulle was understandably indignant when he read the terms of the agreement, signed on 14 July. Although his representative General Catroux was a member of the Armistice Commission, the document did not even mention the Free French, in spite of their important role in the campaign. He then discovered that General Wilson and the Vichy General Dentz had signed a secret protocol, preventing any contact between Free French officers and Vichy troops. This confirmed de Gaulle's worst suspicions: the British were taking advantage of France's present weakness to draw the Levant States into their own sphere of influence, and cut the Free French out altogether.

He stormed into Lyttelton's office with a paper declaring the withdrawal of all Free French troops from under the command of the C-in-C. Lyttelton boldly declared it *non-avenu* – a French diplomatic phrase which signified that he did not acknowledge its receipt – and tore it up.[4]

De Gaulle flew into a towering rage, damning Lyttelton, the British and all their works; but, on subsequent meetings, he and the Minister of State thrashed out what became known as the Lyttelton–de Gaulle Agreement, in which the British forswore any intention of seducing the Levant States away from France.

As well as re-tuning the relationship between the Embassy and

GHQ, Lyttelton overhauled the local dock and transport system, which had become appallingly congested. Ships sometimes had to wait for days to be unloaded, while army vehicles in wooden crates piled up on the quays. His office also had to deal with less urgent but equally inefficient anomalies, like the marmalade question. Palestinian orange farmers shipped their oranges to England to be made into marmalade for the troops. Marmalade was then shipped back to the Middle East, along with letters from England. These described the austerity of life and the shortage of, amongst other things, marmalade. When a soldier sent a tin of it home, as often happened, the contents would be taking up precious shipping space for the third time.

Lyttelton was very effective in a job that required a high order of administrative skill and great tact. But, since most of his work was secret, he came as something of a disappointment to the press. The writer Alan Moorehead, then in Cairo as correspondent for the London *Daily Express*, acknowledged that Lyttelton worked hard and was respected by his colleagues; but 'his press conferences were so appallingly dull, his words so banal and evasive that it was impossible to put him before the public as a leader'.[5]

The most important function of the Minister of State's office was to take a lot of domestic administration off the shoulders of the Service Chiefs, so that they could devote themselves to the running of the war. This was done, and very efficiently; but GHQ continued to expand. Soon it outgrew Grey Pillars. First it took over a large villa, then a street; and before long the compound of GHQ occupied an entire neighbourhood in Garden City, surrounded by check-points and coiled barbed wire.

In early July 1941, it had not yet reached such impressive dimensions; but in the hazy morning light, the staff of GHQ turned the street into a river of khaki uniforms as they walked briskly to work, and presented their passes to the guards. Inside the walls of Grey Pillars, the nerve-centre of the war in the Middle East, everything bore the marks of haste and improvisation. At the head of each flight of stairs was a battery of signposts, marked only with a bewildering array of initials. The interior architecture of the building had disintegrated into a warren: doors and sections of corridors were boarded up, while people came and went through adjoining bathrooms, knocked together to form passages between one flat and another. Sweaty shirt-sleeved brigadiers worked at their desks in converted kitchens and partitioned bedrooms. The war correspondent Alexander Clifford described the atmosphere of GHQ as that of a busy department store, valiantly trying to cope during alterations.[6]

In the summer of 1941, a remarkable soldier mounted a campaign against the formidable bureaucracy of GHQ, a campaign that nearly culminated in his own death. The imperfect instrument of a severe Puritan God, who had marked him for great things, Charles Orde Wingate had first come to Wavell's attention in Palestine in 1936. The latter thought him brilliant but dangerous, with his passionate Zionist opinions which echoed the thunder of the Old Testament; and, like all fanatics, Wingate was short on both tact and humour.

In 1940, to increase pressure on the Italians in Abyssinia, Wavell asked Orde Wingate to organise assistance to the supporters of Haile Selassie. From a base in Khartoum, Wingate managed to form his unit, with little help from an obstinate and sluggish military administration. He was a difficult man whose eccentricities were famous: he carried an alarm clock rather than a watch so as to time appointments, and instead of taking baths to keep clean he brushed himself all over with a hairbrush.

By January 1941, his mixed band of Sudanese, Ethiopian and British troops named 'Gideon Force' was ready; and, accompanied by Haile Selassie, they crossed the frontier into Abyssinia. As Gideon Force made its way over the mountains, Italian garrisons fell and patriots flocked to the Emperor. It was a brilliant military operation, which enabled Haile Selassie to return to Addis Ababa in triumph at the head of his troops.

Apart from the addition of a bar to the DSO he had won in Palestine, the congratulations of Wingate's superiors were brief. In Harar, he was told that Gideon Force was to be disbanded. He appeared to take the news calmly, and said he would return to Cairo to lobby for permission to raise a Jewish army in Palestine.

In June 1941, GHQ was still recovering from the three defeats of

Cyrenaica, Greece and Crete. No one had time for the guerilla hero of Abyssinia. He was ordered to revert to the rank of major; and, when he tried to get the allowances due to his volunteer soldiers in Gideon Force, he was informed that this was not possible because the claims had not been submitted at the correct time. The final straw was to be told that, because his men fought behind enemy lines, they did not qualify as 'a unit in the field'.

What happened next was gracefully passed over by Wavell, when he came to write up Wingate's life for the *Dictionary of National Biography*; but the incident is described at length in Christopher Sykes's book.[7] Sykes was well-placed to find out about it, for one of those involved in the story was his old boss Colonel Thornhill, for whom he had worked in SOE. Thornhill was an amiable, indiscreet man who was often to be found propping up the bar in Shepheard's or the Continental, and who had been so disastrously involved in the Aziz el Masri affair.

Wingate took a room in the Continental Hotel. There he wrote a blistering report on the treatment of Gideon Force, and how it had been hampered and obstructed by those he chose to call the 'military apes'. It did not make him any friends at GHQ, and Wavell – though he sided with Wingate on the subject of allowances – was heard to say that the report might almost justify placing him under arrest for insubordination.

Wingate was now seriously ill with malaria, but would not see an army doctor for fear of being relegated to a staff job. However, he did manage to visit a local doctor, who prescribed a drug called atabrine to reduce his temperature. He over-dosed himself liberally which inflamed his nerves, already ragged from brooding alone in his room. In the struggles he had had to set up Gideon Force, and the way the military administration had dealt with it, he saw a plot to absorb Ethiopia into the British Empire. It was too late to do anything. He had failed himself, his men, the Emperor Haile Selassie, and God.

On the afternoon of 4 July Wingate's temperature stood at 104° and he had run out of pills. He made his way out of the hotel in an effort to find the doctor and get some more atabrine, but so feverish was he that he could not remember the way, and thought he was going mad. He went back to the Continental, and decided to kill himself. On the way to his room, Wingate met the floor steward who brought him his food; and rather than arouse the man's suspicions, he closed but did not lock the door to his room. He had already stabbed his throat once with his hunting knife when he staggered back to the door, locked it, and then returned to the bathroom to try again. He plunged the knife into what he hoped was the jugular, and then collapsed on the floor.

As luck would have it, the next door room was occupied by the inquisitive Colonel Thornhill. Having heard a number of very strange noises coming through the wall, Thornhill knocked on Wingate's door. There was no answer. Thornhill alerted the manager. With the master key they got in, and Wingate was rushed to the 15th Scottish Hospital. He was operated on immediately and, thanks to Thornhill and the surgeon's skill, his life was saved.

The story provoked mixed reactions at GHQ; but as one brigadier put it, whether he was court-martialled or put in a lunatic asylum the career of the troublesome Major Wingate was over. Major Simonds, who had been part of Gideon Force, visited Wingate in hospital and asked the reason for his attempted suicide. The reply was: 'I did it to call attention to our wrongs.'

There was a verandah at the end of the ward and, as Wingate became stronger, he walked up and down it of an evening. Once, he heard a woman call him by name from the private wing. It was Pistol-Packing Mary Newall, whose No. 11 Convoy was soon to be amalgamated into the ATS. She was in hospital with duodenal ulcers.

In her straightforward, no-nonsense way, she told him that there had been a suicide in her own family; and that if he wanted to talk, he should talk to her. From then on Orde Wingate spent many hours sitting with Mrs Newall, talking and reading his Bible aloud. 'Isn't that marvellous?' said Wingate, as he finished reading the Book of Job. 'I don't know,' said Mrs Newall. 'I've been asleep for the last half hour.' Since she had many visitors, Wingate began to meet people again. His spirits lightened, and he began to feel that God had forgiven him. One visitor was rather taken aback, however, when

Wingate remarked that anyone who wanted to slit their own throat should have a hot bath first, otherwise – as he had found – the muscles would be too tense to cut.

Encouraged by Mrs Newall, Wingate sent a copy of his controversial report on Gideon Force to the recently-appointed Minister of State. Oliver Lyttelton was intrigued, both by the report and by the man who wrote it, and Wingate was invited to dinner. The Lytteltons lived in a villa on the Mena Road, some four miles outside Cairo, which had been lent to them by the geologist and collector Chester Beatty. The blue tiles adorning the walls gave rise to the name Beit el Azrak, the Blue House. It was full of Islamic art and had an oriental fountain in the courtyard, which was later to remind Noël Coward of the second act of *Kismet*. He also remarked that the grove of casuarina trees which encircled the house meant that one got no view at all, and a great many mosquitoes. The verandah looked onto the garden, and was protected from the evening breeze by a curtain at one end.

On the appointed night, Moira Lyttelton was sitting by herself on the verandah, reading. Suddenly the curtain behind her was pulled back, to reveal a pale face with blazing blue eyes above a tower of bandages. 'Major Wingate?' 'Yes,' croaked the apparition. He was not an easy guest. Neither his hostess, nor the Minister, nor any of his fellow-diners could engage him in conversation, and he remained monosyllabic till, towards the end of the evening, someone mentioned Ethiopia. Then Wingate launched into a brilliant and impassioned monologue that lasted over an hour.

Wingate's career did not end that summer. After a period of leave with his wife in England, he was sent out to Burma by Wavell, then C-in-C India. There, with his Chindits, he continued to develop the theory and practice of irregular warfare based on his experiences in Palestine and Abyssinia, which earned him another bar to his DSO and promotion to the rank of Major-General. He was killed in a plane crash over the Burmese jungle in 1944.

The Effects of War

For the Egyptians, the summer of 1941 was dominated by economic anxieties. Once again, the war effort had prevented Egypt from exporting her cotton crop: Britain was again obliged to buy it, but grudgingly. Sir Miles Lampson told London that 'The failure to limit cotton acreage more drastically was due to the fact that the Members of Parliament were mainly landowners and hoped to make more money on cotton, which was not wanted, than on wheat, which was essential for the feeding of the people.'[1]

Hussein Sirry handled the negotiations, but failed to warn Parliament that the British were not feeling generous. At the beginning of August he presented the figures as a fait accompli, and gave no explanations beyond saying that the British would not be moved. This resulted in such an uproar that the purchase price of the cotton was raised – but the Egyptian government had to pay the difference. As Sir Miles put it, '. . . the Egyptian tax payer was penalised in order to increase the receipts of the cotton owners.'[2] Nahas Pasha took this opportunity to launch a violent anti-British campaign. He accused the British, and Hussein Sirry who was their puppet, of infringing the Treaty and destroying the economy. Farouk evidently approved, and granted Nahas an audience – an event which provoked much discussion, considering their usually frosty relations.

Given the political undercurrents in Egypt, the progress of the war and the sight of refugee royal families fleeing the Balkans, it was not surprising that Farouk should want to strengthen his contacts not only with nationalist feeling in his own country, but with Britain's enemies. In his memoirs, Oliver Lyttelton observed that 'the King kept himself well-informed on politics and the movement of opinion, and was shrewder and more serious than is usually supposed'.

Lyttelton was in a good position to judge, since he saw the transcripts of the Palace radio messages that were regularly transmitted to Rome.[3]

The British might be angered by Farouk's flirtations with the Axis, but they had to recognise – if only in private – the difficulty of his position. Only two years after the war, the Foreign Office admitted that on Farouk's part, 'a certain degree of hedging was inevitable'.[4] The war that had come to Egypt was not his responsibility; yet his future might depend on the outcome.

It must also be remembered that the former Khedive Abbas Hilmi was still alive, and remained a threat – albeit distant – to Farouk's throne. Abbas Hilmi had decided to stay in Constantinople and side with the Germans on the outbreak of the First War; and, though he had been deposed and forbidden ever to return to Egypt, his descent from the dynasty's founder Muhammad Ali Pasha was more direct than Farouk's. A letter of 5 May, from the office of the German Under Secretary of State, Political Division, advises that 'the ex-Khedive appears . . . to consider himself a potential pretendant to the throne. In this he is neither to be encouraged, nor discouraged.'[5]

This letter was one of several captured German documents which came to light in 1947, and two in particular showed how many prominent Egyptians were keen to make themselves agreeable to the Axis. In April 1941 Assal Pasha, the Egyptian Ambassador in Switzerland, told the Hungarian Ambassador von Wettstein that every Egyptian nationalist fervently hoped the Axis would win the war – but Egypt did expect full independence when the British were defeated. Assal wanted the Hungarian Ambassador to sound out the German Ambassador on the subject, and emphasised that he made this request entirely on his own initiative.

The Hungarian Ambassador assured Assal that the Axis would come as liberators, to free Egypt from the British yoke. His assertions were, however, undercut by a leading article in the semi-official *Relazioni Internazionali*, which considerably rattled Assal when he read it the following day. It announced the imminent conquest of Egypt, and continued: 'the Egyptian bastion was bound to fall under Italian/German domination, and the fate of Egypt would be carved out in Rome and Berlin for all time.'

The most interesting document is a telegram written by Ettel, the German Minister in Iran, to Wilhelmstrasse. Dated 3 July 1941, it reports a conversation between himself and Youssef Zulficar Pasha, Farouk's father-in-law, who at that time was Egyptian Ambassador to Teheran.

Zulficar Pasha passed on the substance of a message from Farouk on 29 June, which gave precise details of a British plan to occupy the Iranian oilfields. The British considered this move vital if they were to protect themselves against a German invasion of Iran and Iraq through Russian territory, so the operation would be launched before long. Farouk charged Zulficar Pasha to bring this plan to the attention of the German Minister and the Shah, whose son Muhammad Reza Pahlavi had married Farouk's eldest sister Fawzia in 1939.

Ettel goes on to say that 'the Ambassador asked to transmit the views of the King to the RAM [the Reich's Ministry of Foreign Affairs], and to express in a telegram the King's desire for open and loyal relations with Germany. The Ambassador then described the King's situation, which had grown ever more difficult and dangerous . . . He was now regarded by the British as Enemy No.1.'

Large numbers of 'German tourists', crossing into Iran by train from Turkey, were the cause of growing concern in London. Anthony Eden had said Britain would not tolerate any threat to her eastern front, but between 3,000 and 5,000 Germans had entered Iran by July. The Shah insisted there were only 700. Farouk's warnings proved correct. On 25 August 1941, a large British force drawn from the Indian Army invaded Persia from the south and north. The Iranian government was co-operative, and agreed to the closure of all Axis and pro-Axis legations. All German and Italian subjects and sympathisers were interned, as were the supporters of the Iraqi rebellion – though the Shah's reluctance to expedite the arrests, particularly of the latter, led to British accusations of continuing ill-will. The Shah, forced to abdicate 'for reasons of health', was despatched to Mauritius; and in mid-September Farouk's brother-in-law was declared Emperor of Iran. Sir Miles Lampson wrote that the invasion of Persia and deposition of the Shah had had a salutary effect on the King of Egypt, in whom he detected a certain nervousness. The Ambassador added, 'Fear of his throne is the card to play if we are faced with further backslidings, which I fear we may.'[6]

On 17 September, the north-eastern district of Abbassia (where there were large British holding camps and an aerodrome) was bombed, leaving 39 dead. The Cairenes had thought that the enemy would respect Cairo as a 'sacred' city – an idea encouraged by the half-hearted black-out restrictions, under which car headlamps and street lights were dimmed with blue paint. But the raid did not cause so much anxiety as the dramatic rise in prices. Between August 1939 and September 1941, the cost of living index had risen by 45 percent.[7]

Ramadan, the Muslim month of fasting, began on 22 September; and, at the end of the month, railway and transport workers threatened to strike. Both the Wafd and Ali Maher hoped this would provide them with an opportunity to topple the Sirry government, and the King might have been expected to support Ali Maher in such a move; but he was more concerned by the activities of his cousin, Prince Abbas Halim.

Abbas Halim had fought in the First War on the German side, so forfeiting his royal title – though he was still accorded the respect due to a member of the royal family, in Cairo if not at court. He was a great admirer of Hitler and National Socialism, which was why he was now supporting the workers. This so disturbed the King, who saw Abbas Halim as a far greater threat to his throne in the event of a German victory than the ex-Khedive Abbas Hilmi, that he openly endorsed the government's moves to stop the strikes. At the end of September, the Prince attempted to change £2,000 sterling into Egyptian pounds through Sheffield's, the fashionable Cairo jewellers. The British had reason to suspect that this money came from German funds, but decided not to intern him for the present.[8]

Chaos in the transport services was thus averted, but Sirry's government seemed incapable of controlling the economy. The British Army was spending an average of four and a half million pounds a month in 1941, and the presence of over 100,000 British and Dominion troops in the Cairo area alone could hardly avoid pushing up prices; but most of the money generated was finding its way into the pockets of middle men. Even they found cause to complain: it was said that the financial side of GHQ was entirely run by Jews who discriminated against Muslim contractors. Only the young men who had found jobs in the workshops at Qantara and Tel el Kebir seemed to be doing well. Their average earnings had gone up from 3 to 30 piastres a day; and, with the help of those soldiers who were willing to deal in goods from Ordnance and Naafi stores, they did a fine trade in cigarettes, knives, bedcovers, shoes, and anything else that might turn up. The black market could provide anything from hospital supplies to weapons: an Italian automatic was valued at £E15, an English rifle at £E3.

WINTER 1941–1942

Auchinleck's Offensive

Having spent almost all his adult life in the Indian Army, General Sir Claude Auchinleck arrived in Cairo an unknown quantity. First impressions were favourable. He was tall and good-looking, with frank, friendly manners and a willingness to listen which made people like him at once. He was decisive; and, in sharp contrast to his predecessor, communicative. Yet in spite – or perhaps because – of his reserve, Wavell had inspired a devotion that made every soldier feel in touch with him. Auchinleck somehow remained distant. The new C-in-C had left his young American wife in India, and the comfortable house by the Gezira race-course, where Lady Wavell and her daughters had entertained, became spartan and workmanlike.

He had barely arrived when Churchill started bombarding him with telegrams urging an immediate offensive in the desert, to be led by Jumbo Wilson. Auchinleck disagreed. He kept General Wilson in Syria, and made Lieutenant-General Sir Alan Cunningham commander of the army in Cyrenaica, which from September became known as Eighth Army. His elder brother, Admiral Sir Andrew Cunningham, was C-in-C Mediterranean; and, to complete the confusion, the Air Force was under the direction of Air Vice-Marshal Arthur Coningham.

General Cunningham's brilliant victories in East Africa had made him far more famous than General O'Connor. He was keen and confident, his army was the best-equipped that the British had so far put into the field, and the prospects of his retaking Cyrenaica and relieving Tobruk looked excellent.

Rommel had been obsessed all summer by this obstinate outpost. Repeated attempts at storming the fortress with extraordinary ferocity had not budged the Australian garrison, and Royal Navy destroyers had managed to keep the troops supplied. Ships on 'the Spud Run' ran terrifying risks, because much of the cargo consisted of petrol and ammunition to build up a forward supply dump.

Living conditions inside the thirty-mile perimeter were grim, and made worse by almost constant shelling. Hours of boredom were relieved only by patrols, repair work, or undergoing a German assault. Water was rationed, and always brackish. In September the Australian garrison was relieved, and British troops plus a brigade of Poles took their place. The Poles were regarded with some awe by their companions. They were charming and polite; but their deadly hatred for the Germans, of whom they killed as many as possible as often as they could, was in sharp contrast to the complete indifference they showed for the Italians.

In Alexandria and Port Said, the docks worked around the clock, unloading prodigious quantities of equipment and a never ending stream of troops. Wavell's offensive against the Italians had been launched in complete secrecy. The only secret about this British offensive was when it would start. With Hitler poised over the northern Caucasus, the Egyptians wished it would start soon: they saw the Germans advancing on Egypt in a great pincer movement. The British, on the other hand, were remarkably confident.

Every war correspondent who wrote his account of the Desert War described this mood, which they found very alarming – at least in retrospect. Alan Moorehead said that there was 'something definitely and deeply wrong with the mental attitude of the British forces in the Middle East . . . The complacency was contagious. Everywhere you went the men were "in good heart" – or so their officers told you. Probably this was true enough, but it was largely the good heart of ignorance . . . Crete and Greece were sliding comfortably into the background. Everyone looked forward to the coming winter campaign in the desert with enthusiasm and dangerously brimming hope.'[1]

Despite the general optimism, plans for the winter offensive were not without problems. The infantry demanded tank support, but the commanders of the armoured formations refused to break up their units. Not surprisingly, the plan proved a not very satisfactory compromise.

The second Allied offensive, known as Crusader, began with a westward advance through all the rigours of a North African winter. As 100,000 men, 600 tanks and 5,000 cars and trucks drove across Egypt, their progress was slowed by continual breakdowns, icy winds and driving rain. Sand worked into the cold, wet clothes of the men and made them even more uncomfortable.

The offensive opened with two raids on the nights of 16 and 17 November. The 16th was marked by a violent storm with winds of thirty-five miles an hour. It was not a night for parachuting, and the first operation of the newly-formed SAS resulted in the death or capture of sixty-two men, with no damage to the enemy at all.

The other raids that took place on the 17th were led by Geoffrey Keyes, who at twenty-four was one of the youngest lieutenant-colonels in the Army. Their main purpose was to attack the German HQ at Beda Littoria, and capture Rommel in his villa to the west of the town. Though they burst into the HQ building and did a lot of damage, killing four Germans, this operation too was a disaster. Keyes was killed, and only two of the thirty-odd men who had taken part returned.

Rommel had not been anywhere near Beda Littoria that night – in fact he was in Rome, enjoying a few days' leave with his wife. His absence from North Africa was partly due to his most trusted spy, the 'Gauleiter of Mannheim', who led him to believe that the British had at present turned their attention from the desert and were looking north-east towards the Caucasus. Rommel did not know that the 'Gauleiter' had been captured as soon as he arrived in the Middle East, with his transmitter, codes, and transmission times. All information from this source was in fact being concocted by GHQ Cairo, to draw attention away from their next desert offensive.

These two catastrophic raids boded ill for the future, but after the first few days of heavy fighting around Tobruk, the British were very optimistic. They held the ridge of Sidi Rezegh, and soon hoped to join hands with the Tobruk garrison. By the night of the 22nd, everything had changed.

It was at this time that Eve Curie was up at the front. As she and the other war correspondents were driven to within fifteen miles of the fighting, the men they met told of a massive tank battle in which they had been totally outgunned by the Germans. They anticipated yet another 'strategical retreat', and this time their cynicism had a bitter edge. Eve Curie found herself comparing the unrestrained happiness of the Italian POWs with the arrogance of the German prisoners, and the tired, filthy, raw-eyed British.[2]

For both sides, the battle of Sunday, 23 November was one of the bloodiest and most costly of the Desert War. It fell, appropriately enough, on Totensonntag – the Day of the Dead.

The British tank losses so depressed Cunningham that he asked Auchinleck to fly up from Cairo to review the situation. Auchinleck arrived to find Cunningham prepared to withdraw to the Egyptian frontier, which the Commander-in-Chief declared out of the question. New plans were drawn up and the battle continued; but, on the flight back to Cairo, he decided that Cunningham was so tired and anxious that he no longer had the aggression and initiative to run the battle.

On the evening of Totensonntag, Eighth Army was exhausted and in disarray – but Rommel knew it would reorganise and attack again if supply lines from Egypt were not cut at once. The following morning he therefore set off at top speed in his command car for the Egyptian frontier, having ordered all units still battleworthy to follow him. The 'Dash to the Wire' was a brilliant, daring move which might have worked – but Rommel did not appreciate the extent to which his army had been drained by the battle. The distance between him and his forces grew longer and longer, and on the 27th he was forced to turn back.

On the morning of the 24th, however, the British and South Africans could hardly believe their eyes when the German tanks charged into their camps. They had only time to throw themselves, their boots and their half-eaten breakfasts into the nearest vehicle and start driving fast. Rommel swept all before him. No one knew what was happening and the panic was total – it was, as Alan Moorehead put it, 'the contagion of bewilderment and fear and ignorance'.[3] He and his companions were very relieved to get the other side of the Wire and into Egypt after a wild nine-hour drive. They rejoined the Correspondents' Base Camp at Fort Maddalena.

Randolph Churchill, then attached to the Intelligence Division, had brought some fresh eggs up from Cairo; and once they had been boiled, Alexander Clifford of the *Daily Mail* said he would make tea. The army drivers attached to the correspondents said that one should never re-use egg water, it made warts in the stomach. They were arguing about this when news came that stunned them all: General Cunningham had been relieved of his command, and replaced by Major-General Neil Ritchie.[4]

General Ritchie, Deputy Chief of General Staff at GHQ, was extremely reluctant to take on the job. He felt ready for promotion to corps commander, but no more.[5] To put him at the head of Eighth Army, over two corps commanders who were senior to him, was a risk determined by the facts that an unresolved battle was still being fought, and the less disruption there was at the front the better. Auchinleck also thought that Ritchie had the drive and boldness that Cunningham had lost. The latter, now suffering from severe nervous exhaustion, was flown back to hospital in Cairo on the same plane that had brought up his replacement.

Ritchie did possess drive, but he did not have the experience to handle such a complex battle. He was also unable to improve the relationships between some of his subordinate commanders, or raise morale in the ranks. The cynicism observed by Eve Curie in November had deepened even more by the New Year, and the men's loss of confidence in their commanders was mirrored by their unbounded admiration for Rommel. He was not only a brilliant tactician: he bullied, encouraged, inspired, and led his men into battle himself – unlike the British generals, whom their soldiers only knew by name.

But neither Rommel's leadership nor his superior armour could save him from the damage done to his supply lines in the first month of the campaign. Throughout November 1941, ULTRA was able to inform the Royal Navy and the RAF of the routes and destination of Italian supply ships bound for North Africa; and of the 22 ships sent that month, 14 were sunk. Rommel could not continue fighting any longer and, on the evening of 7 December, he began his withdrawal. With the British following warily, he pulled back to el Agheila, from where he had started so brilliantly in March. Since then, he had paid little attention to logistics: he had set the pace, and it was up to his quartermasters to keep up. Now he had been defeated – not by a superior force, nor superior generalship, but by lack of supplies.

The fact that the Germans had been forced to abandon Tobruk, which had so gallantly withstood nine months of siege, was given maximum publicity and made Rommel's retreat look more of a victory than it really was. The Japanese invasion of Malaya on 8 December did mean that a great many reinforcements destined for the Western Desert were diverted to India, but there was no question of repeating the Greek disaster by stripping Eighth Army. Auchinleck was determined to keep up the pressure, and Rommel too had no intention of giving up. Morale was high in the Afrika Korps, which had skilfully executed one of the most difficult manoeuvres in war – withdrawal in the face of the enemy.

December 1941 marked a pause in the battle, yet it was a black month for the Royal Navy. As well as losing the *Repulse* and the *Prince of Wales* in the Far East, the aircraft carrier *Ark Royal* and the *Barham* were hit by U boats in the Mediterranean, while the *Valiant* and the *Queen Elizabeth* were destroyed by 'human torpedoes' in Alexandria harbour. (On hearing of the sinking of the *Ark Royal*, King Farouk was supposed to have broken his rule and celebrated the event with a glass of champagne.) Now the tables were turned, in the Afrika Korps' favour. The Axis controlled the Mediterranean. Rommel's convoys of tanks and supplies, which had suffered heavy losses the previous month, were now safely reaching North Africa.

ULTRA kept Cairo informed on the German convoys, including No. 52, bound for North Africa with tank replacements. Among the ships in this convoy was the 4,700-ton *Ankara*, which successfully delivered her consignment of 22 heavy tanks in mid-December 1941. However, the Director of Military Intelligence, Brigadier Eric Shearer, had been advised in Cairo that there were no cranes or shearlegs strong enough to handle the heavier types of German armour. This was based on information gathered by the section involved with evaluating enemy transport and capabilities, which was headed by a formidable character called Lieutenant-Colonel C. M. Keble. Keble had detailed knowledge and experience in this field; but what he did not know was that the *Ankara* had been originally built for transporting locomotives to South America, and was fitted with specially reinforced derricks capable of handling the heaviest German tanks.

Shortly afterwards came a Long Range Desert Group report, describing German tanks of Marks III and IV travelling westward along the coastal road. General Messervy, in command of 4th Indian Division, also reported sightings of these heavy German tanks.[6] But Shearer still maintained his appreciation that heavy tanks could not have been unloaded.

Twenty-two tanks does not sound very much; but the heavier guns and armour of the German Mark IVs were enough to give Rommel a considerable advantage when he attacked on 21 January, an advantage all the more valuable since the British command was taken completely by surprise. Having seized the initiative and practically destroyed 2nd Armoured Brigade, Rommel plunged into Cyrenaica, driving the Allies before him.

Shearer's misjudgement, which led to his dismissal in early February, caused great concern in GHQ. Such a blunder must never happen again: and one man who set himself the task of ensuring it did not was Major Enoch Powell.

Powell, on becoming Professor of Greek at the University of Sydney in 1938 at the age of twenty-five, had made it clear that he would leave to enlist as soon as war was declared. From the rank of private he rose to major in two years, and wanted to see action; but his superiors decided that his intellect and capacity for work could be put to better use on the Staff. From the autumn of 1941, Major Powell worked in Lieutenant-Colonel Keble's section in GHQ Cairo.

Powell had been in the room when Keble advised Brigadier Shearer to ignore the LRDG report. He realised that Shearer had made his misappreciation as a result of faulty logic – namely, the use of negative information (that heavy armour could not be unloaded) to refute the positive evidence of the LRDG and other reports. He resolved that in future his own logic should be brought to bear upon the incoming material on North Africa, and Keble eventually decided to transfer the responsibility for this work to Powell.

A Joint Intelligence Committee which included members from all three services had been formed to analyse the latest reports and

ULTRA decrypts. Powell became the army representative; and the unremitting scrutiny of a mind as powerful and disciplined as his meant that from the spring of 1942 the Allied forces were remarkably well-informed on the enemy's supplies and logistics.

For the last months of the Desert War, Powell (who had been promoted to Lieutenant-Colonel) knew more about what was happening in the desert from his office in Cairo than most commanders on the spot. But, since those initiated into ULTRA had to swear on oath never to take part in operations where they might risk being captured, he had seen neither the battlefields, nor the landscape of Carthage and the Punic Wars – which were obviously of interest to a classical scholar. The opportunity came when Powell, whose outfit operated from Algiers during the final phases of the North African War, decided to return to base in Cairo in a three-ton truck accompanied by his assistant, Major Michael Strachan. Apart from anything else, it would be a good opportunity to learn to drive.

Strachan's account of their journey[7] is an affectionate view of an extraordinary individual. Among Powell's eccentricities was the wearing of full service dress with collar and tie, long trousers, tunic and Sam Browne, throughout a 3,000-mile journey across the desert. Strachan, who wore only a shirt and shorts, awoke each morning to the smell of tea and brass polish: for Powell put in as much work on his brass buttons and regimental badges as he would if about to go on parade. He seemed not to feel the baking heat, and declared that full uniform kept up his morale.

Although possessed of immense intelligence, energy and force of character, Powell had little physical co-ordination. His driving put a considerable strain on Strachan's nerves; yet this was amply made up for by the brilliant series of impromptu talks on Greek and Roman history, philosophy, art and literature which Powell delivered as they bowled along. Powell had insisted that Strachan instruct him in return. But there seemed to be no topic on which Strachan was better informed than his boss, except horses and hunting. To his surprise, Powell was fascinated by the subject. It had been his fate never to see action, but now he had discovered 'the image of war with none of the guilt and only five-and-twenty per cent of its danger',[8] and made up his mind to take up hunting as soon as the war was won. Over the two weeks of their journey, even Powell's driving improved; and, to his teacher's great surprise, he drove their three-ton truck through the obstacle course of Cairo traffic without hitting anything.

The Writers

After their flight from Greece in April 1941, Lawrence Durrell and his wife Nancy stayed a week in Alexandria. They then moved on to Cairo where they spent their first night in the Luna Park, a refugee hotel which was said to have been a brothel – the plush glitter of the cabaret downstairs gave way to rooms of dismal austerity on the upper floors.

Before long they found a flat in Gezira, thanks to Dr Theodore Stephanides, a friend from Corfu who had introduced Durrell to the work of the Alexandrian poet Cavafy, and was now a member of the Royal Army Medical Corps. For the first few weeks, Durrell wrote leaders and a weekly funny column for the *Egyptian Gazette*. Then, in August, he was interviewed by Walter Smart, the Oriental Counsellor at the British Embassy. Smart was impressed by Durrell's fluent Greek and his knowledge of Greece, and assigned him to the Information Department.

After only a few days in his new job, Durrell returned from an overlong lunch with an Egyptian poet to find a message to call Smart's office. Durrell rang back, expecting a rocket – only to find that his boss had been reading some of his poetry, and wanted to invite him home for a drink to discuss it.

Walter Smart, or Smartie as he was known, was an intellectual, and an orientalist of distinction. These qualities, which might have been awesome in a lesser man, were in his case illumined by a humour and modesty that made him one of the best-loved figures in Cairo. He was knighted in June 1942, and might have risen higher in the diplomatic service; but a divorce was sufficient, in those days, to bar a man from ambassadorial rank.

After his divorce in 1931, he married Amy Nimr, daughter of

Dr Fares Nimr Pasha, who had started the newspaper *el Mokkatam*. One of Amy's friends – the writer Patrick Kinross – described her as having 'a masculine mind in many ways but very oriental and feminine in others'.[1] She was a painter, though her own brightly-coloured exotic paintings were not much in evidence at 19 Sharia Ibn Zanki, the Smarts' house in Zamalek. This was full of beautiful Persian rugs and porcelain, the walls being largely taken up by bookcases. The books themselves were each enveloped in a dustwrapper of brown, silver or gold paper. Amy Smart took a keen interest in the work of young artists like Durrell, and was extremely generous to those she had taken under her wing.

One of these was the Greek poet Elie Papadimitriou, who had escaped from Greece with little more than her extended poem *Anatolia*, on which she had been working for many years. She was ascetic yet intensely alive and, although deeply religious, a Communist: the two faiths were not incompatible in Greece at that time. She had very little money, and there was always a bed for her at the Smarts'. Another woman who remembered Amy's kindness was Durrell's wife, who was also a painter. Nancy and Lawrence Durrell had married when they were both very young, and she was still at art school. Their relationship became stormy as Nancy struggled against his possessiveness; and in Egypt, where she was tied to their flat by the demands of a young child, she felt increasingly suffocated by her marriage.

The Durrells were frequent guests of Walter and Amy Smart, whose house – with its garden of palm trees and a sunken well – was one of the few bright spots in a country they found oppressive. 'Dust storms herald the spring; and summer comes in on such a wave of damp that the blood vessels in the body feel swollen and full of water. If one wrote poems here they could only be like marrows or pumpkins,'[2] he wrote to Tambimuttu, the editor of *Poetry London*.

He wrote in the same vein to Henry Miller, who replied, 'Listen, you gave me a stinking picture of Cairo. Don't tell me there's nothing more to it than that. What about the nightlife?'[3] Lurid and exotic though it could be, Cairo's nightlife included nothing to replace the taverna so missed by the Graecophiles. Bars in town were full of loud and unsteady soldiers, while the Egyptian cafés served no alcohol.

The closest thing to a taverna, where friends met to drink and above all to talk, was the Anglo-Egyptian Union at 179 Sharia Fuad el Awal. This became the haven of Cairo's English-speaking literary life. The Union's club house and library had once been the residence of the Sirdar (the commander-in-chief of the Egyptian Army), and its garden was graced by a magnificent cluster of old and exceptionally tall trees. During the previous summer, when the air-raids on Alexandria had forced people to remain in the sweltering heat of Cairo, the prospect of a cool garden had raised the membership of the Union to over four hundred. It had been a genteel place; but the influx of writers, refugees, and shade-seekers made it rather scruffy and battered about the edges. This contrasted sharply to the other side of the garden, which belonged to the Egyptian Officers' Club. Here immaculately-uniformed Egyptians, with rows of medals on their chests, played backgammon and baccarat.

It was in the Anglo-Egyptian Union that Robin Fedden, Bernard Spencer and Lawrence Durrell founded *Personal Landscape*, the most influential literary magazine to come out of the war years. Fedden and Spencer were now lecturers at Fuad el Awal University. They were not the first poets to grace the English Department. Its founder had been Robert Graves who came to Cairo with his wife Nancy in 1926 for a year, and wrote about it in his memoirs, *Goodbye to All That*. Although he mentions that Laura Gottschalk (better known as the poet Laura Riding) came to Egypt to stay with them, he does not record that the Egyptians – despite Islam's tolerance of polygamy – were rather shocked by their *ménage à trois*.

Robin Fedden had been an ardent pacifist since seeing his father suffer the tortures of shell-shock from the First War. In the spring of 1941, this attitude had been misinterpreted as 'defeatism', and the Embassy warned him to watch his step.[4] But, though he wanted no active part in the fighting, Fedden had spent the summer as an ambulance driver in Syria, for Mrs Spears' Hadfield Spears Hospital Unit. His friends were much relieved when he shaved from his pale, eighteenth-century face the long red beard that had made him one of the sights of the Middle East. His natural eloquence was hampered by a strong stammer.

Fedden had a very wide circle of friends, and only appeared

occasionally at the Union. Bernard Spencer was more of a regular. At home, he was already acknowledged as part of the new
wave of English poetry which included Stephen Spender and Louis
MacNeice. He was a quiet, elegant man; and, during his sojourn
in Egypt, he formed a deep attachment for Ruth Spiers, whose
translations of Rilke appeared in *Personal Landscape*.

In his memoir of the magazine's founding[5] Robin Fedden wrote,
'The title expressed our wish to emphasise the importance of personal
life and values when the current of all thought and feeling around
us was set strongly in the channels of war, and when it was growing
ever more difficult to exist outside the "war effort".' They wanted to
start a real literary magazine: not another wartime publication which
featured poetry about the war, and – as Terence Tiller put it – 'read
like the school mag or the parish mag'.[6] Terence Tiller had come
out to Cairo from Cambridge in 1939 to teach literature and history.
He had at first been very reticent about his poetry; but, with strong
encouragement from Durrell, he was persuaded to appear in *Personal
Landscape*. Tiller had small sharp features, and Durrell described him
as having the same sort of charm as the poet Philip Larkin – 'like a
mad policeman'.

The founders of *Personal Landscape* managed to borrow the print-
ing press of the French Institute of Archaeology, and their magazine
ran for eight numbers between January 1942 and 1945. Each issue
cost five piastres (a beer cost two). 'If you are interested,' the first edition announced on the back cover, 'you can obtain a copy by writing
to Bernard Spencer, 27 Sharia Malika Farida, Cairo; if you would
care to subscribe to two or three issues at a time it would help us.'

The taste of the war was inescapable in their lives, but the theme
that most preoccupied the poets of *Personal Landscape* was exile.
This exile was, to a certain extent, self-imposed: Fedden, Durrell,
and Spencer had been living out of England by choice before the
war started. It was not England they missed, but Greece. Quite
apart from their attachments to the country, the war had landed
them, in Durrell's words, 'on the wrong side of the Mediterranean.'

As they mourned Greece, and upheld its culture through the work
of Cavafy, George Seferis and Elie Papadimitriou, so the Salamander
Society looked towards France. *Salamander* started as 'an open house

... for literary expatriates and amateurs of the arts in early 1941'.[7] It was more traditional than *Personal Landscape*: as Roger Bowen put it in his excellent essay on Cairo literary life, 'in the five issues of *Salamander* the excesses of Eliot and Auden were clearly regretted, while Housman and Chesterton were translated into impeccable French.'[8]

The leading light of *Salamander* was Keith Bullen, a large, generous man who was headmaster of the Gezira Preparatory School. Meetings of the Salamander Society, with poetry and pink gin, took place on Sunday mornings at his house in Gezira, and he also held court at a table in a Greek grocery off Soliman Pasha. The difference between the poets of *Personal Landscape* and those of the Salamander Society was illustrated by Terence Tiller's irritation, when he heard that Keith Bullen – in all sincerity – had praised his work by saying he had written the best sonnets since Lord Alfred Douglas.[9]

While both *Salamander* and, to a lesser extent, *Personal Landscape* did include poems by serving soldiers, it was not until 1943 that an effort was made to collect and publish poetry written exclusively by the troops. The idea came to three private soldiers – Denis Saunders, David Burk and Victor Selwyn – in the Victory Club in Cairo. With the help of a friend in General Staff Intelligence, their appeal for poems was read on the Forces and Egyptian State Radio every day for a week. The appeal also appeared in the *Egyptian Mail* and Service magazines. Three thousand poems poured in and, in September 1943, over a hundred of the best appeared in a slim anthology called *Oasis: The Middle East Anthology of Poetry from the Forces*. It had a foreword signed by Jumbo Wilson, and proceeds from the sales raised £E250 for the Red Cross.

It might have ended there; but a generation later, the editors of *Oasis* got back in touch with each other, made contact with contributors to their own anthology and *Salamander*, and formed the Salamander-Oasis Trust, which has since put out two volumes of poetry and reminiscence by men who fought in the Middle East and Italy.

Olivia Manning's two novel-trilogies, collectively called *The Fortunes of War*, follow the lives of Guy and Harriet Pringle: the *Balkan*

Trilogy takes them through Rumania and Greece, the *Levant Trilogy* through Egypt and Palestine. The latter trilogy forms one of the most celebrated accounts of wartime Cairo, and is broadly based on the experiences of the author and her husband R. D. Smith.

They were married in England within a month of first meeting each other, and set off for Bucharest, where he was a British Council lecturer at the University. War broke out ten days after their wedding. It is ironic that Professor R. D. Smith, known to one and all as Reggie, is best remembered as Olivia Manning's husband and the inspiration for Guy Pringle. For, in the story of their early married life, it was Olivia who stayed in the background, and Reggie who was unquestionably the active principal.

He was a large, untidy man, whose boundless capacity for enjoying people's company was only matched by their desire to be near him. Always surrounded by a group of friends, students, and aspiring writers and actors, he could see the potential talent in everyone, and it blossomed in the warmth of his encouragement and enthusiasm. He was never too busy to put on a play or edit a magazine, and still found time to play the occasional game of chess, poker, or cricket (he dreamed of playing for Warwickshire). The poverty of his working-class upbringing made him an ardent if unconventional Communist. Money and comfort meant little, and what he had was easily shared or given away.

As long as he had books in his pockets and people to talk to, Reggie Smith could get on with his life wherever he happened to be. But for his wife, the middle-class daughter of a naval officer, the experience of being a refugee was profoundly unsettling – particularly since they were refugees twice over: first fleeing from Bucharest, and then from Athens. Her health, never strong, was further enfeebled by Cairo, and she felt constantly ill and run down.

One of the first people they contacted was Adam Watson, a diplomat with whom they had shared a house in Bucharest. He was now a Second Secretary in Cairo, and liaison officer between the Embassy and General Catroux. He offered them a room in his flat at 13 Sharia Ibrahim Pasha Naguib, overlooking the Embassy. 'Our room overhung the lawn of a rich businessman. We could look down between the dense, dark mango trees and see grass and we could hear the constant hiss of water drawn from the Nile.'[10] This room, and the flat, appear in the *Levant Trilogy*; and in the character of the relaxed and urbane Dobbie Dobson, there are recognisable traces of Adam Watson.

As the weeks went by, Olivia became more and more incensed at the negligence of the British Council. They seemed to make no effort to find Reggie – one of their most brilliant teachers – a job worthy of his talents; but there was little she could do, for Reggie preferred talking poetry and politics with students to cultivating influential colleagues. It did not take them long to discover the cool garden of the Anglo-Egyptian Union. Reggie was well-liked, though he tended to drink too much and Durrell remembers that he always had a gaggle of disreputable people in tow.

Olivia was less popular. Where Reggie was encouraging, she could be sharp, tactless, and (by her own admission) malicious. 'I would never do anything to injure anyone,' she explained in a conversation with Kay Dick; 'but I couldn't resist seeing through people, as one does; I couldn't resist letting them know.'[11] Her peculiar appearance was described by the poet G. S. Fraser, who had enlisted in the ranks and was then working on *Parade* magazine. She was 'slim and tubular, with a face at once oval and birdlike, whose pattern she completed with a turban, so that an artist of the school of Wyndham Lewis might have drawn her as a swathed, beaked egg balanced on a cylinder'.[12] Olivia felt that she and Reggie should have been taken up by Amy Smart, the unquestioned doyenne of Cairo's intellectual and literary scene. She bitterly resented the fact that Amy paid them so little attention: it amounted to a refusal to acknowledge their talents.

Reggie was finally offered a job in October, as lecturer in the new Farouk el Awal University (though the English Department was not officially opened till a year later, to the sound of the guns at Alamein). They moved up to Alexandria and shared a flat with Robert Liddell, also working at the University, who had known them in Athens. Soon after their arrival, Olivia heard of the death of her brother Oliver, who had joined the Fleet Air Arm. It was a shattering blow, for she adored her brother.

Alexandria was cool and Europeanised after Cairo, but the

presence of the war was disturbingly close. The raids were not as bad
as they had been in the summer, but the Germans were bombing
Alexandria regularly as part of the build-up to the winter offensive.
The air-raid warnings usually came in pairs: first to announce the
imminent arrival of the German planes, on their way to bomb Port
Said; and the second for their return, when any bombs they had not
dumped on Port Said were dropped on Alexandria. Tough though
she could be, Olivia was also nervous and hyper-sensitive. Liddell
found it very irritating that, whenever the sirens began wailing, she
would insist on them all trooping down to the basement. Before
long the raids became unendurable to Olivia, and she moved back
to Cairo.

In the winter of 1941 she found work as a press attaché in the
United States Legation, while in her spare time she was probably
making notes for *Guests at the Marriage*, an unpublished novel which
formed the prototype of the *Balkan Trilogy*. She was also writing
short stories, which she sent to her friend Stevie Smith in London, in
the hope of getting them published. Meanwhile Reggie had become
editor of a new magazine called *Citadel*. Over the six months of his
editorship he published poems by Keith Douglas, Robert Liddell,
Gwyn Williams, Terence Tiller and several Egyptian writers, as well
as an interesting piece by E. M. Forster entitled 'The New Disorder':
'To me, the best chance for future society lies through apathy, unin-
ventiveness, and inertia. If this war is followed – as it may be – by
universal Exhaustion, we may get the Change of Heart which is at
present so briskly recommended from a thousand pulpits.'[13]

One of Olivia's short stories, called 'The Visit', appeared in the
July 1942 issue (after Reggie had been succeeded as editor by David
Hicks). It is seen through the eyes of a child, whose mother takes
her to see the bed-ridden Lady Moxon. Lady Moxon gets out her
jewel box, saying, 'I may have something for the little girl'; but, after
picking over several pieces, she thinks better of it. The little girl,
tormented by envy and disappointment, is undoubtedly a portrait
of the young Olivia, who seldom wrote about anything beyond the
confines of her own life. 'I write out of experience,' she told Kay
Dick. 'I have no fantasy. I don't think anything I've experienced has
ever been wasted.'[14]

One important exception to this rule is Simon Boulderstone in the *Levant Trilogy*. Through his eyes, Olivia Manning not only describes the Desert War and Alamein, but does so with a remarkable immediacy, considering the novel was written thirty years after she had left the Middle East. In the interval, several books were published which described a soldier's life in the Western Desert, including Alan Moorehead's *African Trilogy* (1944), Keith Douglas's *Alamein to Zem Zem* (1946), Cyril Joly's *Take These Men* (1955). Perhaps these books made a contribution, but the book she kept on her desk for perpetual reference was Field Marshal Montgomery's *Memoirs*.

The focus of the *Levant Trilogy*, like the *Balkan Trilogy* that preceded it, is Guy Pringle. The way in which his wife Harriet (Olivia's more equivocal portrait of herself) becomes reconciled to life with a man who does love her, but whose gregariousness makes him neglect her emotional needs, is the real subject of the book.

Surrounding the two protagonists is a large cast of characters, some of whom can be associated with real people – but it must not be forgotten that Olivia Manning never drew precisely from life. She used her own experience and the characters of other people not as models, but as points of departure to be developed in her fiction.

The first novel, *The Danger Tree*, reflects Olivia Manning's early days in Egypt, though one of the main events of the story, the death of Sir Desmond and Lady Hooper's son, is based on a real tragedy which did not take place until Olivia and Reggie had left for Palestine. On 17 January 1943, Walter Smart – by then Sir Walter – had one of his rare days off; and, to honour the occasion, he and his family took a picnic into the desert. The party consisted of Sir Walter and his wife Amy; their eight-year-old son Micky; Amy's little niece, the future novelist Soraya Antonius; and the children's nanny.

After lunch Sir Walter took a nap, while Amy got out her easel and started to paint. Then came a muffled explosion: their only son had picked up a stick bomb, and it had gone off in his hands. He died soon after. The news of the tragedy spread; and it was said in Cairo that Sir Walter and Lady Smart, out of their minds with grief and shock, had taken the little boy home and tried to feed him through a hole in the side of his cheek. Amy Smart knew she was too old to have any more children. She filled her house full of photographs of Micky, and in the months to come was able to talk quite sensibly and objectively about what had happened – but it was years before she could bring herself to paint again.

Olivia must have heard the story when she and Reggie Smith stayed briefly in Cairo at the end of the war; and, in *The Danger Tree*, the feeding of the child is linked with the ancient Egyptian custom of bringing food to the dead. Walter and Amy Smart remained devoted to each other after the death of their son; but, in the novel, it prompts the bright and brittle Lady Hooper to leave her husband. She tries to forget her guilt in good times and whisky, and befriends Harriet Pringle.

Although both Walter and Amy Smart were no longer alive by the time the book came out, their friends were outraged that the story should have appeared in the novel, and that people might associate Amy's character with that of the feckless Lady Hooper. There is little doubt that Olivia used the incident as a form of subtle revenge for the fact that she and Reggie had not been 'taken up' by the Smarts, all those years ago in Cairo.

She also took her revenge on C. F. A. Dundas, who had been appointed the first Representative of the British Council in Egypt in 1938 and had been so slow in getting Reggie Smith a job. Flux Dundas was a hard-working man with a romantic but puritanical streak, and held a great admiration for T. E. Lawrence. Olivia made up a rhyme about him, called 'Dundas of the Desert':

> I'm so like the desert
> And the desert's so like me
> We're lean and bare, and full of hot air
> And we haven't got the OBE.

(Limericks and comic verses about well-known figures were a fea-ture of wartime Cairo, and both Olivia and Reggie enjoyed adding to the pool.)

Dundas had a very clear idea of the crisp, efficient lecturer the Council should be looking for, who would raise the prestige of his organisation within the British community; and he had a distinct prejudice against the staff who had come out of Greece and the Balkans. Writing to Lord Lloyd he said they had acquired a bad reputation, and had been described to him as 'pansies', 'long-haired' or 'soft'.[15] As Frances Donaldson points out in her book on the British Council, these are the sort of words that might well be used by the crustier members of the British community about anyone with the faintest intellectual pretensions; but similarly, people like Reggie Smith, who did not hide his political opinions, hardly conformed to Dundas's notion of the ideal Council lecturer.

In the *Levant Trilogy*, the head of the Organisation for whom Guy Pringle works is Colin Gracey, a cowardly, snobbish and effete nonentity who knows how to play office politics. (Guy Pringle makes up a verse about him called 'Gracey of Gezira'.) Gracey is too short-sighted to appreciate Guy's talents, and is far more concerned with making himself agreeable to Professor Lord Pinkrose.

The tiresome figure of Lord Pinkrose is loosely based on Lord Dunsany, who was evacuated with Reggie Smith and Olivia Manning in April 1941. The 18th Baron Dunsany was a magnificently bewhiskered Irish poet in his mid-sixties, who was sent out to Greece in October 1940 to occupy the Byron Chair of English at Athens University. Someone once asked him just what the Byron Chair of English was; to which Lord Dunsany is supposed to have replied he was not quite sure, but he was paid to sit in it and it was very uncomfortable. While he shared with Lord Pinkrose a certain cantankerousness, he did not suffer such a violent end: Pinkrose was assassinated by an Egyptian fanatic, while delivering a lecture on Byron.

Since Olivia heard of her brother's death while she was in Egypt, it is perhaps not surprising that the *Levant Trilogy* is much preoccupied with brotherly relationships. Simon Boulderstone loses his brother Hugo; and he is one of the wistful young officers who are drawn to Harriet Pringle, because she can give the sisterly comfort they need. They in turn provide her with the masculine friendship she cannot get from Guy, without being sexually threatening. Aidan Pratt, better known to his fans as the actor Aidan Sheridan, becomes very close to Harriet and accompanies her to Upper Egypt; but it is Guy, not Harriet, whom Aidan needs to comfort him for the fact that the war has ruined his acting career. When Pratt is posted to Palestine, he implores Guy to come and see him. Guy turns away. Aidan Pratt commits suicide on the train, by shooting himself in the corridor.

Once again, Olivia Manning recorded a curious death which actually happened. The figure of Aidan Pratt is based on a real life actor and poet called Stephen Haggard. Before the war, he had been hailed as one of the most handsome and promising classical actors of his generation. He came to the Middle East in 1942 and joined the Department of Political Warfare; and like Aidan Sheridan, Haggard felt the war had destroyed his career. He fell in love with a graceful Egyptian woman whose husband worked in Palestine, whom he went to visit in the winter of 1943. At the time he was on the edge of a nervous breakdown, being very overworked; and the last straw fell when the woman he loved said their relationship was over. Stephen Haggard shot himself in the corridor of a train travelling between Jerusalem and Cairo, in February 1943.

While her characters may depart from set points in real life and then take on their own existence, places such as the Anglo-Egyptian Union or Groppi's are described exactly as they were. The feeling of what it was like to be in wartime Cairo is not, for her, the pleasant recollection of glamorous parties where all the men were in uniform: it is the physical sensation of enervated liverishness, brought on by heat, which makes everything seem tawdry and insubstantial.

Although her work was praised by the critics, Olivia Manning felt she had never received the public recognition she deserved. She died in July 1980, two months before the publication of the last volume of the *Levant Trilogy*, and never knew of its belated success.

The Fall of Hussein Sirry

On 7 December, the Japanese bombed Pearl Harbor. Sir Miles Lampson and Alexander Kirk, the American Minister, were both gratified that America had at last joined the war, and 'purred together' at the prospect of being real allies.[1] Pearl Harbor was too far away to provoke much of a reaction in Egypt. But, although Lampson noted that German reverses in Russia and British successes in the desert in December had had a 'steadying effect' in the country, strong forces were at work against the British.

The banishment of Hasan el Banna, the leader of the Muslim Brotherhood, to Qena in April had only lasted a few weeks, and on his return it was seen that he had the protection of the Palace: reports from Egyptian sources on el Banna's doings dried up altogether. Meanwhile, British Military Intelligence was discovering that el Banna was not only engaged in propaganda, but was also preparing to sabotage British lines of communication to coincide with the next German offensive. Sir Miles asked Hussein Sirry to arrest the teacher, which was done in October; but thanks to the Special Branch of the Cairo police, in which Ali Maher had powerful friends, el Banna was released over the heads of the British less than a month later.[2] Lampson was furious, but the Prime Minister said he was unable to stop it. He had been equally unsuccessful over the matter of supplies.

After Hussein Sirry's unpopular legislation to reduce cotton acreage in the summer, merchants began hoarding cheap cotton; this was one of the first commodities to disappear from the local markets. The tendency to hoard and stockpile reached epidemic proportions, and was in part responsible for the absence of sugar, flour and kerosene. Then came a shortage of small change. This was linked to the fact that the price of basic foodstuffs – beans, oil and flour, the staples of the poor – had shown an average increase of 94 percent since August 1939.[3] Coins were hoarded by the money-lenders, who would only change notes for a commission. This racket was stopped by having 20 million small coins minted in India, and shipped to change-starved Egypt.

The only shortage that affected the richer classes more than the poor was the introduction of 'meatless days' in November for, since meat could no longer be imported from Turkey and the Balkans, Egypt's own livestock population had to be conserved. Otherwise, the enormous gap between affluence and poverty in Egypt meant that the well-off barely noticed any shortages at all: their parts of town remained reasonably well supplied, though prices seemed to rise almost by the hour.

With the government unable to control the economy, matters became worse as winter progressed. Despite the 200,000 *feddans** that had been reallocated for grain, bread was becoming scarce. King Farouk presided over a council of ministers convened to deal with the problem, and ordered all maize stocks in the royal granaries to be distributed – but by January 1942 people in the poorer parts of Cairo were storming the bakeries and accusing their bakers of mixing saw-dust with the flour. A Wafdist MP told a reporter of *El Misr*, 'On the eve of the French Revolution the people of Paris shouted, "We want bread." The people of Cairo have just done the same thing, attacking the wheat shipments. The situation in this country can be described as revolutionary.'[4] Hussein Sirry's administration was beginning to crumble: he had no support in the country, and Ali Maher had suc-cessfully eroded such influence as he had once had at the Palace.

The issue which brought down Hussein Sirry's government was its diplomatic relations with Vichy. Sir Miles had been urging their severance since October. The government managed to postpone the move for a few weeks because there were 300 students in France, not all of whom could be brought home immediately – some refused to leave at all. There were strong protests in Parliament, but Hussein Sirry bowed to British pressure in early January.

Both Lampson and the King were then in Upper Egypt. The

* one *feddan* equals 1.038 acres

former was spending the Christmas break as he had the year before, with his wife and Freya Stark in Luxor, while the King was at Aswan. The royal party took an entire floor of the Cataract Hotel. Prince Muhammad Ali, who disliked his nephew intensely and never lost an opportunity to spread a story about him, said he had been told that Farouk had been taking pot-shots at the little Nubian boys who paddled their boats under the windows of the Cataract Hotel, hoping for baksheesh.[5] The King's life was being made unbearable by the tensions between his mother Queen Nazli, and his wife Queen Farida.

Nazli would always arrive late for luncheon, which Farida took as a deliberate snub. So the younger Queen feigned illness, and took to her room – which was immediately above the dining room. As soon as Nazli had descended for lunch, Farida and her young ladies-in-waiting would start singing and dancing and making a terrific racket immediately above the Queen Mother's head. The bickering got so bad that Farouk left for a tour of the Red Sea coast.

When Lampson had first suggested closing the Vichy Legation in October, Farouk had seemed 'uninterested';[6] but, when the King heard that Sirry had broken relations with Vichy without consulting him, he was furious. According to Sir Miles, this mistake of Sirry Pasha's 'was quickly exploited by Ali Maher Pasha and his clique, who worked up the King by representing the Prime Minister's action as a violation of the Royal prerogative – His Majesty's most susceptible spot'.[7] The King demanded the resignation of the Minister of Foreign Affairs, Salib Sami Pasha. Hussein Sirry said that, if Salib Sami resigned, he would as well. Neither the King nor his Prime Minister was prepared to back down.

Meanwhile, public unrest continued. The demonstrations that took place in mid-January were not large, but given a dangerous edge by the mounting tension and sense of crisis. The Muslim Brothers helped whip up anti-British sentiment: members were specifically told to spread the word that the British were responsible for all shortages.[8] The students of el Azhar joined the disturbance with the usual complaint that graduates from their university were not getting posts in government schools, and their discontent spread to religious institutions in the provinces.

The fact that the King wanted to sack the Minister of Foreign Affairs for co-operating with the British naturally involved Lampson; but the incident pointed to a deeper political pattern which could not be allowed to continue. As he was at pains to stress in his reports, it had been clear for some time that 'no Government ... could hope to co-operate loyally with us and retain the King's support, without which, in the absence of popular backing, it could not handle the unrepresentative Parliament, on which the Government's continuance depended'.[9]

Sir Miles opened his campaign against Farouk and his mentor Ali Maher by demanding the eviction of the Palace Italians, and Abdel Wahab Talaat – who worked in the Royal Cabinet and was Ali Maher's chief agent. This move was aimed at the heart of Ali Maher's power base in Egypt. On 29 January, in conversation with Hassanein Pasha, the King's Chamberlain, Lampson let it be known that he might be prepared to give way on the matter of the Minister of Foreign Affairs Salib Sami, if these men were out of the Palace in reasonable time.[10]

As Ali Maher saw it, the King had become far angrier about the issue of the Vichy Legation than had been intended. He had staked his royal honour on the sacking of Salib Sami, and might be prepared to sacrifice the Italians to achieve it. If the Minister of Foreign Affairs was removed, Hussein Sirry would resign in protest. The British would then insist on the new government being dominated by the Wafd – the only party with sufficient strength in the country to stand up to the Palace. Ali Maher was in a corner, but not beaten. He realised that Sirry's government must be toppled as fast as possible, but in such a way as to discredit the Wafd in the process.[11]

With the King's tacit support, Ali Maher contacted Sheikh Maraghi of el Azhar University at the end of January to mobilise the nationalist extremists in the student body, and increase public disorder to a dangerous level. The purpose of this was twofold: to bring down the government, and raise discontent to such a temperature that extremist, anti-British elements in the Wafd boiled over. The leadership of the Wafd would then have lost control of its followers – and the confidence of the British, who would be forced to turn to the Palace for a government that could restore law and order.[12]

On top of all this, the German advance was causing a certain amount of panic. Axis radio reported that the capture of Benghazi on 28 January had put a great many British tanks in Rommel's hands, and it was now widely known that reinforcements on their way to Egypt had been diverted to the Far East. The feeling was that the British would not be able to hold Egypt any better than they had Greece. In Zagazig, rampaging students broke shop windows and beat up people known to have distributed Allied propaganda.[13]

On 1 February, encouraged by Ali Maher and Sheikh el Maraghi, the students of el Azhar erupted into the streets with renewed fervour. When Sirry found out who was behind the demonstrations he realised that the King had withdrawn his support, and his government had no hope of regaining control. He resigned on 2 February, while students in Cairo shouted, 'We are Rommel's soldiers', 'Down with the British', and 'Up Farouk'.

Ali Maher had succeeded in overthrowing Hussein Sirry, but had not managed to get the Wafd involved in civil disorder. Although Nahas was not shy of delivering anti-British speeches when it suited him, the conduct of the Wafd since the war had been designed to demonstrate two things. To its supporters, it was the only party that could wrest full independence from the British; while, to the British themselves, Nahas indicated that he was both keen to co-operate and ready for power.

These attitudes were, to some extent, contradictory. But the Wafd was a rallying call for nationalism and democracy more than a political party bound by a specific doctrine or manifesto. In the words of Jean and Simonne Lacouture, 'any attempt at defining [the Wafd] would involve a complete description of Egypt. It contained all the generosity, intellectual muddle, good nature, contradictions and mythomania of its millions of supporters. It united the unlimited poverty of some and the insultingly bloated fortunes of others, the demand for change and the demand for conservatism . . .'[14]

For these reasons the Wafd was more impressive in opposition than in power, for its strength lay in what it symbolised rather than what it was. But Egypt had been ruled by minority Palace-imposed governments for the last four years: what Britain needed was a strong and freely elected government, independent of the Palace and strongly supportive of the Allied cause.

Tanks at Abdin

As soon as Sirry had resigned, Sir Miles Lampson asked the King to summon the Wafd. Once again the King prevaricated, and suggested an interim government be set up before calling on Nahas to form a coalition – but Lampson was adamant. The Chamberlain, Hassanein, informed Sir Miles that the King would receive Nahas at three on the following afternoon, Tuesday 3 February.

On that day, Ali Maher made one last attempt to shake British confidence in the Wafd. He organised a 5,000-strong demonstration, which began at Cairo University, to prove that the democratic party's popularity was on the wane. But since the tone of the rally was as distinctly anti-Allied as that of el Azhar, with students shouting for Rommel and Farouk, it only reinforced British opinion that the Wafd must take power.

When Nahas Pasha was received in audience, Farouk did not ask him to form a government but to head a coalition. Nahas had already anticipated this move of the King's, and had been assured by Sir Miles that morning (via Amin Osman Pasha, the Wafd's liaison with the Embassy) that he would still have the British Embassy's full support if he refused.[1] He therefore told the King that he would head nothing less than a Wafd administration of his own choosing. When Lampson heard what had happened, he summoned Farouk's Chamberlain, Hassanein, and told him to tell the King that he must call Nahas again.

Lampson had no compunction about intervening so blatantly in Egyptian affairs. The commitment of the United States and developments in the Far East meant that the war was entering a new phase, while in the desert the British had been forced to withdraw to Gazala. The stability of Egypt had never been more vital and, to secure it, the power of King Farouk and Ali Maher had to be broken once and for all.

This was not the first time that the Foreign Office and Sir Miles Lampson had considered deposing Farouk. In July 1940, Sir Miles wrote that 'we may at any moment reach a stage where we shall have to take firm action with the King, which may (or may not) entail . . . the possibility of abdication'.[2] A few months later Sir Robert Vansittart, then Chief Diplomatic Adviser to the Secretary of State for Foreign Affairs, wrote, 'I have said for years that His Majesty's Government would have to get rid of Farouk, and I have consistently expressed my regret that it has not been done sooner.'[3]

The following morning, Wednesday 4 February, at a meeting of the Defence Committee – which consisted of Oliver Lyttelton, the Ambassador and the Service Chiefs – Lampson drafted an ultimatum to the King: 'Unless I hear by 6 pm today that Nahas Pasha has been asked to form a Government, His Majesty King Farouk must accept the consequences.'

Any pleas for soft-pedalling came from the military, whose attitude Sir Miles had often described as 'wobbly'. They did not like the idea of using British military power to force the King to abdicate. General Stone, the General Officer Commanding British Troops in Egypt, reluctantly consented to draft operational orders; but he warned Oliver Lyttelton and Sir Miles that there might be outraged demonstrations in Cairo, and a strike of all the civilian labour on which the British Army depended.

However, both the Ambassador and the Minister of State were determined to pursue their policy to the end. Throughout the afternoon, they made plans on the basis that King Farouk would refuse the ultimatum. If Nahas had not been called by 8 pm, a military cordon would be thrown round the Palace. Lampson would then march in, and demand Farouk's abdication. A warship at Alexandria was ordered to stand by, ready to take the ex-King to the Seychelles.

Meanwhile, an Instrument of Abdication was being drafted by Sir Walter Monckton, who had recently been appointed Director General of British Propaganda and Information Services at Oliver Lyttelton's request. This was the second time Monckton had formulated such a document: the first had been for King Edward VIII.

At 6.15 pm, a quarter of an hour after the ultimatum had expired, Hassanein arrived at the Embassy with a paper drawn up by seventeen prominent Egyptian leaders, including Nahas Pasha, who had been called to the Palace to advise the King: 'The British Ultimatum constitutes an attack upon the independence of Egypt, an interference in her domestic affairs, and a violation of the provisions of the Anglo-Egyptian Treaty. It is therefore beyond the King's powers to accept conditions which compromise the country's independence.'

On receiving the answer to the ultimatum, Lampson asked Amin Osman Pasha – Nahas's go-between – 'whether Nahas would take on the government in the event of the King being forced to abdicate or being deposed. Amin swore by all his gods that Nahas would do so.'[4] This seems to indicate that the leader of the Wafd was aware that the British intended to commit an even greater violation of Egyptian sovereignty – the removal of the King himself.

The original plan was that Lampson should arrive at the Abdin Palace at 8 pm. But, at the last moment, Oliver Lyttelton brought up the problem of whether or not they should insist on the King's abdication, if he gave in and agreed to call Nahas. After some earnest discussion, the Ambassador was reluctantly obliged to admit that 'we can't very well sack him at 9.00 for giving us what we would have welcomed at 6.00'.

Sir Miles Lampson was accompanied to the Palace by General Stone and two ADCs. The Ambassador's car was followed by all the officer cadets of the Officers' Training School – which was perhaps a significant choice: officer candidates were not only intelligent, but could be relied on to carry out their orders punctiliously. They arrived shortly before 9.00, by which time about a battalion of British troops (approximately 600 men) had been positioned to surround the Midan Abdin. A number of armoured cars were driven down from Heliopolis and crossed the city via Sharia Emad ed Din, to seal off all routes to the Palace itself.* By the time the Ambassador's

---

* Most accounts of the Abdin incident state that the British used tanks. Ian Weston-Smith, who was one of the officers involved in the operation, says that it may have included one or two of the British Army's new American 'Honey' tanks, which were small and manoeuvrable – but the bulk of the vehicles were armoured cars.

car appeared, the Palace guard had locked the gates – though they had been ordered to put up no further resistance. A British officer marched up and shot the locks off with a revolver. The first car to enter the Palace forecourt was that of the officer commanding the OTC platoon. His driver misjudged the turn, and damaged the gate. (Farouk later gave orders that it should not be repaired, but left as a reminder of the incident.)

The Ambassador's car rolled up to the front entrance, and Sir Miles noted in his diary that the ushers and chamberlains looked 'like startled hens' at his approach. He and General Stone were led upstairs, and after a few minutes were received in the King's study. Hassanein was standing behind the King's chair.

The Ambassador read out a statement, which accused the King of assisting the enemy, violating Egypt's commitments to Great Britain, and of unfaithful, wanton, and reckless behaviour. Sir Miles finished by saying he was 'no longer fit to occupy the Throne', and handed him the Instrument of Abdication. Farouk read it in silence, obviously shaken.

'We, King Farouk of Egypt, mindful as ever of the interests of our country, hereby renounce and abandon for ourselves and the Heirs of our Body the Throne of the Kingdom of Egypt and all Sovereign rights, privileges and powers in and over the said Kingdom and the subjects thereof, and we release our said subjects from their allegiance to our person.'

The King then remarked on the scruffiness of the document – with some justification, since it was written on a sheet of Embassy note paper from which the letter-head had been torn off. (This comment was later to remind Sir Walter Monckton of King Edward VIII signing his abdication, when he said there was no ink in the pot.[5])

Farouk was on the point of signing the document when Hassanein whispered to him urgently in Arabic. The King hesitated, and then asked Sir Miles for 'one more chance'. Lampson was not prepared for this response, and did not want to grant it – but the King said he was ready to call Nahas without delay; and, since Lampson and Lyttelton had decided not to force the abdication under these circumstances, the Ambassador was obliged to accede to Farouk's request.

According to Sir Miles's diary, the King now became quite affable, and actually thanked him for his help. This is in sharp contrast to the graphic account later given by Farouk to his friend Captain John Brinton, Assistant Military Attaché to the American Legation, as they stood in the same study. According to the King, he had treated Sir Miles with chilly dignity throughout. Farouk showed Brinton the pistol in his desk, claiming that he had been 'prepared to use it', and said that his guards – some of whom had been hiding behind a curtain – had orders to kill if anyone touched him.

Lampson admitted that he had thoroughly enjoyed his evening, but was disappointed that Farouk had been allowed to keep his throne. 'However regretfully, it seemed the right course.'[6] On reaching the Embassy, he received a frantic call from Hassanein at the Palace – Nahas had been summoned, but the cordon of British troops was refusing to allow him through. Nobody had remembered to tell them to stand down.

Among those at the Embassy on the night of 4 February were Duff and Diana Cooper. They had arrived in Cairo on 26 January on their way back from Singapore, where he had been Minister of State, and might have been gone by the 28th. But complications in their travel arrangements obliged them to stay on for a few more days, and become witnesses to one of the last great acts of British imperialism.

Diana was guest of honour that night at a dinner given by her 'new favourite', the American Minister Alexander Kirk. He was immensely tall and good-looking, and his white or lavender silk evening clothes made him something of a joke in Cairo; but beyond his rather too exquisite taste lay a sound judgement, and a talent for administrative efficiency. Events at Abdin called him away towards the end of the evening, and Diana was grateful to get back to the Embassy to hear what had happened.

'I found the Embassy hall a babel of huddled groups – Oliver and Moira Lyttelton, Walter Monckton, Mr Michael Wright, lots of ADCs and Military Secretaries . . . Wright and Walter see it as reminiscent of Munich in not getting an abdication signed, but Oliver and HE were "just certain" that they had been right in the present arrangement. HE came out of his den, dressed in a pearl-grey *frac*, arm-in-arm with Nahas Pasha, both grinning themselves in two.'[7] (Having received his appointment from the King, Nahas had come straight to the Embassy, on Farouk's orders. Lampson, Nahas and Oliver Lyttelton then had what Sir Miles called 'a satisfactory interview'.

Duff Cooper recalled a feeling of elated uncertainty: '... we found most of the principal actors in the hall of the Embassy discussing the evening as people discuss the first night of a play, when nobody is sure whether it has been a success or a failure.'[8]

There were also those who felt that the Abdin coup should never have been allowed to take place. General Stone wrote a paper addressed to General Jumbo Wilson, then General Officer Commanding British troops in Syria, saying how mistaken such a policy had been.[9] Stone had had an exceptional military career. He looked too young to have medals from the campaigns of the First War, but he also had one from the South African War, as a result of spending one school holiday with his father at the front. Before becoming GOC British Troops, he had commanded the British Military Mission to Egypt. He had made friends with Egyptian officers and sympathised with their nationalist aspirations, a feeling intensified by the Abdin Palace incident. The Ambassador later described General Stone as having 'inconveniently close contacts with local Egyptian circles',[10] and added that he did not take too many pains to disguise how much he disagreed with the Embassy's policy.

Sir Thomas Russell Pasha, Commandant of the Cairo Police, had not been informed of the final moves of the Abdin incident and was appalled by what had happened. According to his son-in-law Christopher Sykes, he 'set his face against these people [in the Embassy] whom he saw as destroying all the work of himself, his colleagues and his predecessors'.[11]

The BBC and British propaganda reported that the change of government had taken place with the unanimous approval of King and Parliament, and censorship forced the Egyptian press to do the same – but too many people had seen the armoured cars at Abdin. It was no secret that Sir Miles had compelled the King to appoint Nahas Prime Minister. 'How could he,' wrote Anwar Sadat, 'agree to be imposed upon by the colonising power?'[12] Lieutenant-Colonel

Muhammad Neguib, the first President of post-revolutionary Egypt, wrote a note to King Farouk saying, 'Since the Army was given no opportunity to defend your Majesty I am ashamed to wear my uniform. I hereby request permission to resign from the Egyptian Army.'[13] (The King sent a message to say that as he had forbidden the Royal Guards to resist the British, he could not accept Neguib's resignation.) Nasser was in the Sudan at the time, and was informed about what had happened in a letter. He too felt humiliated, and furious: bullies back down when challenged, he felt, and yet no Egyptian had been willing to sacrifice himself to make that challenge. 'Until now the officers only talked of how to enjoy themselves; now they are speaking of sacrificing their lives for their honour . . . This event – this blow, has put life into some. It has taught them there is something called dignity which has to be defended.'[14]

It was not only the nationalists who were outraged by what had happened. Lampson reported that 'our action has also caused much resentment among the princes and princesses and among the upper classes, more especially in Cairo and Alexandria. There has been a tendency towards a social boycott.'[15] One Muslim lady who worked for hospitals and war charities and was staunchly pro-Allied, said she felt unable to speak to her English friends. Some Egyptians returned their memberships of the Anglo-Egyptian Union and the Gezira Club; Sir Miles said that if they did, they would certainly not be allowed back. Though the social boycott thawed in time, Anglo-Egyptian relations were never the same again.

The Ambassador informed London that 'King Farouk . . . particularly asked, in my interview with him on the 4th February, that the abdication issue should remain a secret between the four people present at the interview'.[16] From Diana Cooper's account it was no secret at the Embassy, and the story soon spread; but an Italian account of the incident written eleven days after the event does not mention the question of abdication, and neither did the account addressed to the War Department, Washington, from Colonel Bonner Fellers – whose telegrams the Italians decyphered regularly.[17]

11 February was King Farouk's birthday, but Sir Miles did not attend the Palace to wish His Majesty many happy returns. They did not see each other until eight days later, when the Lampsons went to

the airport to greet the King's sister, the Empress of Iran. The marks of royal displeasure were evident. They were put into a small waiting room, and not told that the King, Queen Nazli, Queen Farida, the royal princesses and the Iranian Ambassador were all waiting in a hangar. Sir Miles sent a message to say that it would be gracious if Lady Lampson were invited to join the royal ladies. The invitation came, but Lady Lampson was given a very frosty reception; and, as they left, the King ignored Sir Miles altogether.[18] During the course of her visit, the Empress of Iran was shocked by the change in Farouk, and her account of him prompted the Shah to write a letter to his brother-in-law, urging him to mend his ways.[19]

When discussing the Abdin incident, even the most pro-British Egyptians who lived through that time condemn Sir Miles's action as an unforgivable outrage; but they also feel that, once Lampson had surrounded the Palace with armed men and pushed his way in, he should have gone through with his original intention and forced Farouk to abdicate. They believe that if he had done so, Nasser's revolution might never have happened. (Prince Muhammad Ali, the heir to the throne, also wished his nephew had been deposed: he had spent 4 February at home with his bags packed, waiting to move into Abdin Palace.) As it was, King Farouk was to remain on the throne of Egypt for another ten years. He had started with the very best of intentions; but, since no one had the authority to keep his self-indulgent nature in check, they had withered.

While Farouk was widely criticised for giving in too easily on 4 February, the British action was considered so brutal that it did rally patriotic feeling around the King, who now had the backing of 'all Muslim and disgruntled elements'.[20] Nevertheless, he had suffered an unforgettable humiliation, and his spirit never recovered.

It was a humiliation shared by those in court circles, but they confidently believed in the imminent overthrow of the British. 'You will have seen a report from secret sources describing the atmosphere at the Palace,' wrote Sir Miles, 'where it was being openly said that there was no need to trouble about this temporary success in bringing back the Wafd, since in a few weeks the German spring offensive would begin and England would be driven out of Egypt.'[21]

SPRING AND SUMMER 1942

Loose Talk in High Places

The Abdin Palace incident scarred Egyptian politics for years to come. Battle lines between King and Wafd were now drawn so deep that mutual co-operation was almost impossible. The Wafd lost much credibility among extreme nationalists for its continued accommodation of the British, and its prestige was to dwindle over the next few years to such an extent that it never regained its former power. Small cells of radical left-wing Egyptians began to expand from this time onwards; and 4 February became the most potent in a long line of trigger words and phrases that summed up hatred for the British, and formed the first link in the chain of events that led to the revolution of 1952.

The first measures of Nahas Pasha's new administration included the introduction of free primary education, and an office to supervise and audit the disposal of public funds. A law was also passed requiring the use of Arabic in all commercial company transactions. This was intended to repair the Wafd's image among nationalists and thoroughly inconvenience the British, which it did.

Despite this last bill (which did not come into force until August),[1] Sir Miles Lampson was very satisfied with the immediate effects of 4 February. Ali Maher was confined to his estate near Alexandria under heavy guard, and all the public disturbance and anti-British demonstrations of the previous few weeks ceased.[2] With a strong and popular government, the supply situation was soon expected to come under control, and the loan of large stocks of wheat from the British Army created a favourable impression. Nahas, while stressing that his primary motive was to spare Egypt the horrors of war, firmly declared his sympathy for the Allied cause and his determination to co-operate with Britain. At Easter, he gave a present of one packet

183

of cigarettes, two coloured eggs and some sweets to every fighting Allied soldier as a token of Egypt's appreciation.[3]

The 'German spring offensive' that the Palace was anticipating in the coming weeks did not materialise. Rommel's sudden advance in January had pushed the British back to a line between Gazala and Bir Hacheim, where they built a series of elaborate box-like fortifications and reinforced Tobruk. Meanwhile the Axis was concentrating on the destruction of Malta, which was the first step in the 'Great Plan'. This consisted of a huge pincer movement on the Midde East with one arm coming down from Russia through the Caucasus, and the other from the Western Desert, striking right across Egypt into northern Mesopotamia. Hitler would then be master of the Suez Canal, and of the oil-producing nations of the Middle East. The long lull in the desert campaign was mirrored by a relatively quiet spring in Cairo – though it was not without excitements.

The first of these was Ali Maher's dramatic escape from his country estate, in the back of his son's car: for, while Ali Maher had not been permitted visitors or telephone calls, Nahas had allowed his immediate family to see him. Once in Cairo he was taken to the house of his friend Shourbagi Pasha, who had been his Minister of Justice. Police surrounded the house, but by then Ali Maher had made his way to Parliament. On 8 April he burst in on a full session of the Senate, and gave an impassioned speech begging for justice and sanctuary. Nahas Pasha gave orders for his arrest as soon as he left the building: Ali Maher was still inside at 8 pm, but gave himself up two hours later.[4]

The new government set up a committee to deal with the internment of 'lesser undesirables', as Sir Miles called them. One member of this committee was Major Sansom of Field Security. He soon discovered that the emergency measures produced a situation entirely different to what he had imagined. Instead of an office full of weeping women pleading for the release of their husbands, he found that the majority of petitioners wanted their men out of the way – and were prepared to pay for it. One woman offered Sansom £E5,000 to intern her husband, while men came with similar sums to try and get their brothers or business partners locked up.[5]

Oliver Lyttelton missed these codas to the Abdin Palace story. He left Egypt for good on 26 February to take up the post of Minister of Production in England. Meanwhile, Sir Walter Monckton was left as acting Minister of State, with the use of the Beit el Azrak, which he had shared with the Lytteltons since his arrival in Cairo.

Shortly before the Abdin incident, Monckton had met Mrs Mary Newall, the elegant commandant of the ambulance drivers. He wrote in his diary that 'she added greatly to the gaiety of life',[6] and their relationship progressed rapidly. By early March, Mrs Newall had moved in to the Beit el Azrak, and Cairo was agog with the new scandal.

Although he was an exceptionally brilliant man, Walter Monckton in love was something of an innocent, for the next thing he did was to install her as his personal assistant in the office of the Minister of State. The sight of Mary Newall, wearing her beautiful uniform and her revolver as though guarding Walter Monckton's office, caused deep offence to the sensibilities of visiting Egyptian dignitaries.

On 24 March, Monckton came to see Sir Miles Lampson. He told him he had been unhappily married for twenty years and was now seeking a divorce. He was well aware of the scandal the affair had caused, and said that Mrs Newall would soon be moving out of the Beit el Azrak – although he planned to keep her on in her job, and would marry her as soon as he could. 'I did not feel called upon to say that I thought that a most unwise thing to do,' wrote Sir Miles; 'for, after all, it is evidently his own business and people do not relish such advice when they have obviously been swept off their feet as he has . . .'[7]

The new Minister of State, the Australian Richard Casey, arrived in Egypt on 4 May escorted by Arthur Rucker, the *chef de cabinet* who had set up the Cairo office with Oliver Lyttelton. Rucker was horrified by the scandal that had brewed up since his departure, and the complaints of the indignant office staff. He told Monckton that Mrs Newall must go, or he would resign. Monckton said shame-facedly that she was 'just a friend', and Mrs Newall left her job a few days later.[8]

Walter Monckton moved out of the Beit el Azrak to make way for the Caseys, and he and Mrs Newall stayed with Esther and Michael Wright (then First Secretary or Head of Chancery at the

Embassy). Monckton had been suffering from brain fever for some time – brought on by overwork, though Sir Miles said he was suffering 'from something amounting to an obsession'.[9] He and Mrs Newall left Cairo together on 26 May, but they never married.

The other subject of gossip for the British community that spring was King George VI's brother, the Duke of Gloucester, who arrived in Cairo in mid-April; but, considering all the trouble and expense, the visit was not a success. Brigadier John Marriott, who took him into the Western Desert, said his tour of the fighting area was embarrassing. He grumbled about the discomforts, had no knowledge of what was going on, and never stopped to say more than 'good morning' to anyone he was introduced to. Since he took so little interest in anything, his walk-abouts invariably finished early. The Duke only perked up at meal times, when he ate voraciously, saying the desert made him hungry.

His gaucheries became legendary. One evening, the Duke was taken out by a group of ADCs to Madame Badia's. This nightclub had been particularly popular with the British since Madame Badia had introduced comic anti-Nazi acts to her show, which also included the fabulous belly-dancer Tahia Carioca and a string of nubile chorus girls. When it was over, the performers changed into evening dress to talk or dance with members of the audience, which consisted largely of officers in uniform. One of the most beautiful of these girls, who spoke several languages including English, was selected by an ADC to dance with His Royal Highness. As they danced, she asked the usual polite questions: was this his first visit to Egypt? had he seen the Pyramids? did he like Cairo? She received such monosyllabic answers that they were soon drifting about in silence; until the Duke suddenly turned to her and said, 'D'you know Tidworth?'

The Duke of Gloucester did no better at a luncheon given in his honour by King Farouk on 25 April. Farouk announced that the Palace of Ras el Tin in Alexandria would be handed over to the British for use as a hospital. It was not the ideal site, being on the harbour's edge and very vulnerable to air-raids; but all the British present exclaimed that they were overwhelmed with gratitude by this gracious offer, except His Royal Highness who looked completely baffled. He had not understood the King's speech, which was in French; and when it was explained, all he said was, 'Oh yes yes yes, very good indeed.'

This story is recorded in the diary of Cecil Beaton,[10] who was then in the Western Desert as Official War Photographer. In the Minister of State's office, Owen Tweedy of Publicity reminded Beaton that 'we want "might" in our propaganda here, especially towards the Egyptians. Don't photograph one aeroplane, photograph sixty at a time – never four tanks, but a hundred!'[11] The theme was taken up again by Richard Casey himself, when he saw Beaton a few weeks later. Photographers were to show the British soldier as broadchested and muscular. All too often 'a freckled, spotty little chap, who may be as wiry and daring as bedamned, gets into the picture, and the impression he creates doesn't do any good'.[12]

After several interminable days waiting for his British Forces ID card, Beaton set off for the desert – which he described as 'so lacking in colour . . . that it might have been "fixed" by an interior decorator in 1928'. Over the next few weeks, he took hundreds of photographs in the early morning and late afternoon, when the light was at its most dramatic. He faithfully photographed large quantities of military machinery and strong soldiers, but his most interesting prints are those recording everyday life in the desert and the battered, broken ruins of Tobruk. Beaton returned to Cairo in mid-May, with the task of getting his photographs developed and captioned, and writing up his notes.

Cairo was impossible. He was not only irritated but alarmed by the bloated, indifferent bureaucracy of GHQ. 'Working hours did you say? Don't make me laugh; I was at the place most of the day and saw how much work people do there.'[13] This attitude was not helped by the heavily-censored English language newspapers, which Beaton thought were positively dangerous: they either encouraged the delusion that the war was going to be over in two months, or a deepening cynicism. 'This policy of pap feeding, of purveying "wishful thought" news (proven to be so disastrous in France) was aimed, it was said, at "heartening the Egyptians", yet did it not defeat itself by giving every incentive to complacency among the British?'[14]

Censorship of the English language press tended to reduce all news from the front as a resounding victory or a tactical retreat; and, in the interests of morale, all controversial or alarming topics were prohibited. Consequently there had been no mention of the arrival of refugees from Greece, or of the shortages and demonstrations that marked the last days of Hussein Sirry's administration, and certainly no mention of 4 February. Cairo as an Open City was not to be discussed; there was to be no notification of official or political transfers, and no allusions to the Muslim Brothers, Young Egypt,* or the Grand Mufti of Jerusalem.† There were to be no reports of untoward incidents involving imperial troops, air-raid communiqués were not to appear in conspicuous headlines, and the name of Rommel was not to enjoy unnecessary exposure: terms like 'the Axis Forces' or 'German Command' were preferable.[15]

The American journalist Clare Boothe Luce ignored these instructions, if she ever knew them, and made no attempt to moderate her caustic impressions of the British Army, which were – not surprisingly – stopped by the cable office. She had visited the front in March, and was shocked by the demoralisation of the men and General Ritchie's dislike of life in the field. He continued to insist on having his shirts laundered in Cairo, and sent up to the front. However, people had obviously talked to Mrs Boothe Luce, and on subjects more important than General Ritchie's laundry. Perhaps they felt it was the only opportunity of letting the Americans know what was going on at ground level.

Mrs Boothe Luce managed to get her notes out of Egypt in a bag with the British Censor's seal on it, which would have ensured their safe return to the United States – but she made the mistake of breaking the seal to start writing her report on the plane. She was stopped in Trinidad where she was put into custody for five days in early May. Her papers included top secret information on the defence of Egypt, and a letter to her husband saying that she had been very pro-British until she discovered their alarming inefficiency.[16] The papers

* A radical, nationalist group founded by a fanatical failed actor, Ahmed Hussein.
† The religious leader Haj Amin el Husseini, Grand Mufti of Jerusalem, had sided with Hitler rather than support the British, whom he saw as enemies of the Arabs.

were confiscated and sent to the British Ambassador in Washington, while Cairo buzzed with rumours of what she had heard and written. Cecil Beaton heard that she had referred to the RAF as 'the flying fairies'.[17]

A foreign correspondent passing through Cairo, like Clare Boothe Luce, could take more liberties than British correspondents on the spot. They naturally loathed censorship. Quite apart from trampling on principles held dear by journalists it took up so much time, since every article had to be passed by three separate censorship officers before being despatched. Alan Moorehead of the *Daily Express* once held a Censorship Derby: each correspondent had to set off in a gharry from Shepheard's with his latest article, get it stamped three times, and reach the telegraph office before completing the course: four hours was considered good going.[18]

Cecil Beaton's fretful and frustrated mood, brought on by GHQ's indifference and the blandness of the newspapers, was not made any better by the nagging stomach trouble known as 'Gippy Tummy'; and that in turn was made worse by too much rich food and drink – the penalties of being lionised.

The smartest woman in Cairo was still Momo Marriott, with her long red nails and simple, beautifully cut clothes. To be seen at her parties, in the company of generals, commandos and celebrities, was to be at the heart of Cairo's wartime society. As an active soldier, Brigadier John Marriott was usually absent, while Randolph Churchill was much in evidence. Momo lived with her mother, Mrs OK or Mother Bird as she was known, in an absurdly luxurious house rented from a rich Egyptian. A bank of clocks, radios, telephones and lights surrounded the bed, and the enormous bath was worthy of Cleopatra. Momo had been obliged to install a modest tub in its marble depths, since the boiler had not been built on the same scale.

'There is such . . . a social life here that I am harassed,' wrote Beaton; 'a lot of great characters and personalities, but I am preoccupied with my work . . . I feel as if I had too much cream, sugar and spice yet I go out every time a Cape gooseberry is in the offing,' he remarked gloomily in a letter to Juliet Duff.[19] He lunched with Walter and Amy Smart: 'the house rather slovenly, Amy too glib

– by her stream of quite witty talk she prevents any good talk.'[20] He lunched with Marie Riaz, another of Cairo's richest and most successful hostesses: '[she] lives in a house with a lot of lovely things jumbled up with a lot of continental junk. The atmosphere cosmopolitan, highbrow . . .'[21]

However, the nadir of interior decoration in Egypt seems to have been achieved by Mrs Nora Peel, the vivacious wife of the cotton magnate Edward Peel, whose house in Sharia Aboukir, Alexandria, was called 'The Bungalow'. Beaton described her as having 'a scraggy girl's figure . . . and Duchess of Windsor jewellery. Her house enormous, white and just wrong . . . badly proportioned furniture and curtains – a huge table with some hideous lots of silver on it. A huge dinner party – as artificial and nonsensical as only that sort of gathering can be – then to a night-club where the dance band is so good that one realised how seldom dance music is well-played, and how thrilling it can be – the gaiety here was absolutely terrific – young English officers on leave doing a frenzied hop that continued for hours without any alleviation.'[22]

He found a great deal more to admire in Alexander Kirk, the American Minister. 'He wore buttons covered in the same material as his suit, I was told, was very rich, had an Oedipus complex and very good taste. I expected something rather awful . . . I found a real surprise. I didn't know such a person still existed – he's the sort of apotheosis of an elegant man as seen on the stage at the beginning of this century.'[23] Beaton attended a party given by Kirk on a *dahabiya*. 'The houseboat on which we dined was done up in beige and white, with lighting from under the gold brass tables . . . the bowls of white ostrich feathers I thought was going a bit far – but for pleasure parties, as intended, it could not have been better done.'[24] Cecil Beaton did not know that Alexander Kirk had a phobia about flowers, and his decorations were always artificial. His Oedipus complex was flamboyant. A candle burned day and night in front of the photograph of his mother, and the water buffalo which provided his daily supply of fresh milk was called after her. Clare Boothe Luce evidently found the American Minister rather precious. As he showed her the breathtaking view from his house by the Pyramids, she could not resist putting on a puzzled expression and asking what they were for. The look on Alexander Kirk's face at that moment was, apparently, well worth the price of being thought a philistine.[25]

Cecil Beaton did his bit in Cairo. He attended various functions at the Embassy and visited hospitals with Maie Casey, the wife of the Minister of State, who was surprised at his kindness and genuine interest in the wounded men. 'The Caseys are very energetic,' wrote Beaton.[26] 'He gives me great pep, and I feel he will do a hell of a lot that is needed here.' His greatest praise, however, was reserved for Lady Lampson: 'She created a very good impression on me – fair and unbiased, and not minding the criticism of her enemies. Lady Russell hates her I know – but welfare work, like amateur theatricals, brings out the worst in everybody.'[27]

The welfare work factor chilled many relationships that might otherwise have remained cordial. Later in the summer Sir Miles was very displeased to find that his wife had not been invited to attend Mrs Casey's lecture on 'Interesting People I Have Met' at the YWCA, particularly since Lady Lampson was the founder of the Cairo branch – but Sir Miles had his doubts about Mrs Casey. She was extremely energetic, but rather odd and very unlike Moira Lyttelton – 'who was always so careful'.[28]

Cecil Beaton greatly enjoyed Lady Lampson's description of Mrs Casey's formal presentation to Queen Farida: '. . . it is a most formal and frightening ritual. Mrs Casey was primed – she must wear a long black dress – must wear gloves, one off one on – must never cross her legs – must curtsey three times on her way to the throne. Lady L went first – the Queen sitting in a lilac dress, her hair done in an elaborate coif (she has little else to do but have her hair done). They sat in a row on formal chairs – Lady L suddenly horrified to find Mrs Casey had put one leg across the other . . . She was appalled to see Mrs Casey lift her skirt and say to the Queen, "would you like to see my mosquito bites?" It appears all must walk out backwards – a favourite trick of the King's being to place a huge growling tiger rug on the slippery floor.'[29]

Tobruk

By May 1942, the British line from Gazala to Bir Hacheim looked impregnable. It consisted of a series of boxes, each stiffened with powerful artillery and armoured car units, underground shelters, reinforced ceilings to resist air attack, and generous supplies of food, water, medicine and ammunition. Between these boxes the desert had been planted with over a million mines. As Rommel pointed out, all mobility had been sacrificed to the construction of a rigid, static defence which petered out south of Bir Hacheim.[1]

Rommel took the bulk of his panzers deep into the desert below Bir Hacheim, hooked north, and smashed into the British armour on 26 May. Three days later, he had still not succeeded in destroying the British from the rear – but he was firmly dug into the middle of the British position in an area known as the Cauldron. The battles that took place there, in searing dusty winds that scorched the lungs and scoured skin and eyes till they were raw, were some of the bloodiest of the Desert War.

The British hoped to keep Rommel in the Cauldron, while they attacked in ever-decreasing circles; but one by one their boxes were attacked and destroyed. 150th Brigade's box surrendered on 1 June; Bir Hacheim, held by the Free French in their first major engagement of the war, fell on 10 June after a furious defence; and, three days after that, the Knightsbridge box was smashed. Rommel was once again within sight of Tobruk.

Both sides had sustained enormous losses as the fighting continued day after day. The outcome of the battle was still uncertain, but Eighth Army seemed to be collapsing from the inside. Administrative planning gradually lost coherence, leaving supplies and reinforcements to be juggled about and cobbled together as the moment dictated. Command Headquarters looked more and more like a harassed committee, and relations between some commanders had broken down completely. Rommel praised the Allied soldiers who still fought with astonishing courage and ferocity, in desperate situations which were largely the result of military incompetence. As for the men themselves, they had lost all confidence in their leaders.

General Ritchie now began pulling back. Auchinleck had at first been misled by Ritchie's optimistic reports but, even when he realised the gravity of the situation, he insisted that Tobruk be held at all costs. Defence of the harbour and fortress was given to the South African Division: and, by 15 June, no Allied troops remained west of Tobruk.

On the night of 20 June, when the battle for Tobruk began, the BBC announced that it might be lost and was not terribly important anyway – news which had a devastating effect on the men who were about to fight for it with their lives. Alan Moorehead wrote that '. . . almost the last message that was received from General Klopper [commanding 2nd South African Division inside Tobruk] said, "I cannot carry on if the BBC is allowed to make these statements."'[2]

The bombardment that fell on the harbour was the fiercest it had ever undergone, with wave after wave of Stukas. The assault came from the south-east and achieved almost complete surprise, for General Klopper and his 2nd South African Division had assumed that any attack would come in the south-western sector. On the following day, the Germans were masters of Tobruk, and could not get over the vast quantities of booty that was now theirs. Their exhilaration was in sharp contrast to the mood of their commander, who was nearly beside himself with rage: for the South Africans had burnt all the petrol and broached every water tank they could find.

That night Rommel heard he was now a Field Marshal, but there was no time for celebration. The advance must continue. He requested permission to take the Italian divisions up to and beyond the Nile. Mussolini was delighted, and informed Rommel that once he had got to the Delta he could step down, because the Duce himself would take over.[3]

Even *Parade* had forsaken its customary buoyancy after the fall of Tobruk. On 27 June, it reprinted an article by Alaric Jacob for the *Daily Express*. He reported that the troops were taking the news 'grimly, sardonically, realistically'. A sergeant of the Royal Army Service Corps was quoted as saying, 'If I hear any bluffer making excuses about this I'll sock him one.' The writer continues, 'The only thing that could upset our desert troops . . . would be for some politician or radio sunshine talker to take the line that Tobruk was no longer important, that our lines of communication are now happily shortened. Our troops are in no mood for such whimsicalities.'

The British in Egypt were stunned by the loss of Tobruk, but in England its fall was seen as nothing less than a catastrophe. Churchill's government suffered a sharp drop in public confidence, which Stafford Cripps was asked to look into. Cripps reported that a major factor responsible was over-optimistic news reports from Cairo.

In a broad sweep south so as to avoid the minefields, the Panzerarmee Afrika pressed on to the frontier, which they reached on 24 June. There was little resistance from the shattered Eighth Army, for Ritchie thought that the highest priority was to get as far from Rommel as possible. The following day Auchinleck relieved him of his command, and flew up to Maaten Bagush to take over. (In *Dilemmas of the Desert War*, Field Marshal Lord Carver argues that General Ritchie was not as incompetent a commander as history has made him out, and was not treated fairly by Auchinleck in his memoirs. However, Ritchie's loyalty to Auchinleck was such that he never attempted to defend himself in print. There is no doubt that he was blamed for a great many mistakes for which the higher levels of the British Army were responsible.)

To those who saw Mersa Matruh cut off on 28 June and the Germans pouring deep into Egypt, it must have seemed as though Auchinleck had arrived too late. Rommel's advance had been so fast that, beyond Mersa Matruh, units from both armies were going full tilt in the same direction, trying to avoid each other.

'I know how people at home are going to take this,' said one man in the desert – 'in their stride. I guess no one in the wide world can take bad news like we can, but then we've had so much practice, haven't we!'[4] As Eighth Army poured back into Egypt in full retreat, some men decided they had had enough practice. They had seen too many of their friends die as a result of clumsy leadership, and they saw no reason why they should suffer the same fate when Rommel had as good as won the battle. In ones and twos these deserters – who may have numbered as many as 25,000 – stole away from their units and lay low in the Delta. If caught, they would suffer severe punishment and disgrace; but it seemed more likely that they would end up in a German prison camp, along with the rest of Eighth Army, and the camp commandant would not care what they were. A South African captain set up a very lucrative racket, using organised gangs of deserters to rob Ordnance and Naafi stores in the Delta. He was so successful that SOE issued instructions that, if captured, he was to be handed over to them – his talents were just what they were looking for. Unfortunately for the South African, he evaded capture until the end of the war when nobody needed his services any longer. He was taken out into the desert and shot.[5]

On 29 June, Mussolini flew himself to Derna. Behind him came a large transport aircraft, containing – among other things – the white charger on which the Duce planned to enter Cairo in triumph. Four hundred miles in front, the men of the Panzerarmee were exhausted: for the last week they had been living on their adrenalin and driven like furies by Rommel. The following day they stopped, close to a railway halt called el Alamein: sixty miles beyond lay Alexandria.

The Flap

Alexandria was three hours from Cairo by car, and about one and a half by train. To go to one or the other for dinner was not unusual, and every summer saw a migration to the northern city to escape the suffocating heat of the capital. Yet, despite this constant shuttling, the two cities retained remarkably different characters. Cairo was an Islamic city, which looked to the east. Alexandria was Greek-Levantine, and faced the Mediterranean.

The Egyptian Muslims were concentrated in the lower echelons of society, as clerks, servants, or dock-workers, while the foreign communities dominated Alexandria – particularly the Greeks. They had been in the city for several generations, and important families like the Zervudachis, Benachis, and Salvagos had arrived as well-established merchants. Every non-Arab Alexandrian felt like an aristocrat in relation to the later waves of refugees and fortune hunters who settled in Cairo, and prided himself on being more cultivated, charming, good-looking, and better dressed than any Cairene.

The poorer quarters were to the west of the city. In a report at the beginning of the war, Captain Burt-Smith, Technical Supervisor of Air Raid Precautions to the Ministry of the Interior, wrote that 'the situation in Alexandria could hardly be worse or more inviting to an attacker: innumerable tanks of crude oil and benzine clustered together in a small area and surrounded by a highly-populated native quarter, interspersed with timber-yards and ware-houses.'[1] People who lived in these quarters were afraid of the dark, and Burt-Smith described the black-out restrictions as the cause of 'acute discomfiture – probably more than any other wartime restriction'. Nevertheless the Egyptians had great faith in its ability to render them invisible to the enemy, and would get very angry if any careless British troops on patrol showed a light after sunset.[2]

The influx of soldiers added a sense of excitement to the natural vibrancy of cosmopolitan Alexandria. The air was fresh and sparkling compared with dusty Cairo, and the sea was never far from sight. Elegant places like the Cecil Hotel, Pastroudis, the Union Bar and the Monseigneur restaurant abounded, and those who could afford it rented cabins on the beaches of Stanley Bay and Sidi Bishr. They also went racing, played golf, and – if they were very grand – enjoyed the exclusive luxury of the Royal Alexandria Yacht Club.

Alexandria also catered very well for those who were neither rich nor important. On the Corniche were innumerable little brasseries where entire families went to drink beer, eat *mezzes*, and watch Rumanian singers and gali-gali conjurors for a few piastres. At the San Stefano Casino on the beach, a single entrance fee provided access to a cinema, a café, a casino, and a walk along the promenade, though during the war most of it was used by the masters and pupils of Victoria College, whose own establishment had been turned into a hospital. Or one could take the train to Aboukir, where there were little wooden restaurants on the beach serving freshly-caught fish.

As in Cairo, entertainment and facilities had been organised for the Forces. The owners of large villas lent their spare rooms to convalescing soldiers and officers who needed a bed for the night. Georges de Menasce, head of one of the most important Alexandrian Jewish families, often gave piano recitals for the troops; but because of his phobia about hands, he always played from behind a screen. Both the Fleet Club, with its shady garden, and the Union Jack Club, were set up for the Royal Navy; but Army personnel were allowed in the latter, which was particularly well-appointed with everything from billiard tables and showers to a library.

The red light district was in the old part of town by the harbour, in a crumbling lane known as Sister Street. It was a dirtier, sadder version of the Berka in Cairo, and stood in marked contrast to the cleanliness and efficiency of Mary's House: the most famous brothel in Alexandria, where the girls were said to take on thirty-five men a night each. On one occasion a bomb sliced through the premises, leaving the bedrooms of sin unscathed while destroying the relatively innocent bar. In *The Danger Tree*, Olivia Manning quotes the joke about the nurse who, when she found out that almost every man on the ward had been wounded at Mary's House, remarked that Mary must have been throwing one hell of a party.

The Lampsons moved up to the coast on 17 June. Sir Miles was very irritated that Mutum, the Embassy butler, had lost both his bathing costumes and feared that he would be unable to buy a sufficiently large one in Alexandria. Even the resourceful Greeks who ran the black market would have been hard-pressed, though they did their best to keep the city well-stocked with goods of all sorts. In 1941, there had been a bad moment for blondes when Alexandria ran out of peroxide. Luckily a stash of the chemical was discovered on Malta, which at that time was enduring exceptionally heavy bombardment from German Stukas. Malta was also suffering from an acute shortage of alcohol. This made an ideal outlet for the Alexandrian hootch industry, which was soon providing Malta with home-made whisky and *zibib*, the local fire-water. The little Greek boats and their indomitable crews ran cargoes as far as Tunis and Algiers, from where they brought back Italian cheese and spaghetti, medical supplies, stockings and condoms.

The pleasant, slightly unreal life of the city continued in spite of the war. Air-raid sirens were so regular, it was said that you could set your watch by them. There were few direct attacks, for the bombers concentrated on the harbour to the west of the town, and the airfield at Dekhela. The harbour was partly defended by the activities of the Alexandria Volunteer Patrol, whose members took up their positions each night in boats designed for nothing more strenuous than an expedition down the coast, or a weekend's fishing. As bombs and shrapnel fell all around them, the volunteers noted the positions of mines dropped into the harbour, so they could be safely retrieved a few hours later.

Then came the day when Rommel's armour reached el Alamein. German radio broadcast a message to the women of Alexandria – 'Get out your party frocks, we're on our way!' Local dressmakers had no time now to do alterations for their English clients – they were too busy with fittings for the gowns that were to adorn 'the

Victory Ball'. Surreptitiously, shopkeepers made sure they had their photographs of Hitler and Rommel ready to slip into a frame, while their wives ran up red, white and black bunting. A few households, who rented rooms to officers then at the front, started burning the incriminating British uniforms their lodgers had left behind.

Lampson had broken off his stay in Alexandria as soon as he heard of the fall of Tobruk, and hurried back to Cairo on 21 June. There he found the American Minister, Alexander Kirk, in a frenzy about the incompetence of the British Army commanders. Sir Miles was impressed by the firmness of Nahas Pasha. On 24 June, the day Lord Haw Haw said that Cairo would be attacked by 200 Axis bombers, Nahas gave a bold speech in the Egyptian Parliament to say that scare-mongers would be ruthlessly punished. The Egyptian Prime Minister remained cheerful and confident, but there were allegations that he had hedged his bets. A letter to Rommel was said to have been drafted, assuring him that the sympathies of the Wafd were really with the Axis, but circumstances had forced them to co-operate with the British.[3]

At the end of June the threat to Alexandria reached its peak. Admiral Harwood, who had taken over the Mediterranean command from Admiral Cunningham, had to consider the possibility of heavier air-raids and the capture of the city itself. He therefore decided to split the ships at Alexandria between Port Said, Haifa and Beirut. The Alexandrians were given no warning, and fear mounted as the ships moved off, leaving the usually crowded harbour alarmingly empty.

This event signalled the start of what became known as 'the Flap'. There had been flaps before, but nothing like this. The European communities felt completely abandoned by the Navy's dispersal, and the BBC's bulletins only made things worse. They stated that the German success was due to greatly superior tactics and weapons, and referred to the fighting in progress around el Alamein as the 'Battle for Egypt' – which gave the impression that the British were already making a heroic last stand. In a report written a month later, E. G. D. Liveing (who became the first Director of the Cairo Office of the BBC) pointed out that 'while the British temperament may be able to stand up to unpalatable prophecies of serious crisis, such as the possible evacuation of the Delta, this does not apply to the local population'.[4]

Even a few British temperaments seem to have cracked under the strain. The retired naval officer in charge of the Ports and Lighthouses Administration of Egypt, Vice Admiral Sir Gerard Wells, left Alexandria 'without leave'. The Embassy managed to dissuade the Egyptian Minister of Communications from sacking him, for the British did not want his job to pass into Egyptian hands at such a crucial time. Admiral Wells returned to his post, and the matter was swiftly hushed up.[5]

While the military and consular offices of Alexandria started burning their files, British women and children packed up and joined the crowds at the station. The rest of the town appeared deserted; there were few people on the streets, and telephones rang interminably in empty houses. Lawrence Durrell went up to Alexandria to find the Press Service office had been shelled. There was nothing for him to do but walk around making a list of those shops decorated with signs of welcome for the Germans, and have them declared out of bounds to British troops as a punishment. Meanwhile the Italian women made their way to the western part of the city to form a welcoming committee – though the only person they might have welcomed was a single German motorcyclist, who made the heroic dash to Alexandria to bring the good news of his army's imminent arrival. He was promptly marched off under escort.

People loaded up their cars, strapped a mattress on the roof as a precaution against falling débris, and headed into the Delta. Here the rumour spread that, as the British withdrew, they would burn everything in their path – which caused mass evacuations from the villages. The British contingency plans were in fact limited to the destruction of power stations (with the exception of those harnessed to sewage and irrigation systems), all mechanised transport that could not be used in the withdrawal, and all stocks of tools, petrol and lubricants. Food supplies were to be spared. They also considered flooding the cultivated areas, which would have been easy enough since the Nile was almost at its height – but putting everything to the torch was never contemplated.[6]

Alexandria suffered heavy air-raids on 29 June; but in Cairo many believed the Germans planned to by-pass Alexandria altogether, and occupy the capital within the next twenty-four hours. That night, it was said, Cairo would witness an aerial invasion to rival Crete. Alexander Kirk heard this story from an American war correspondent and rushed to tell Sir Miles, who dismissed it as absurd and tried to present a brighter view of the situation. The thousands of lorries full of soldiers pouring into Cairo from the desert were hardly encouraging; yet the sight of these tired and beaten men prompted the kindness of the local people, who gave them soft drinks and cigarettes.

1 July became famous in Cairo as Ash Wednesday. This was the day the Embassy and GHQ started burning vast quantities of files. The air was thick with smoke, and charred flakes of paper floated over Kasr el Aini like black snow. The heat of the fires blew some papers high into the air before they had been properly burnt; and, days later, peanut vendors were still making little cones out of half-charred and strictly classified information. Lieutenant-General T. W. Corbett, Auchinleck's Chief of General Staff, was later criticised for his handling of the Flap. In what was thought to have been a case of severe over-reaction, he had ordered all officers to carry revolvers and made the centre of Cairo out of bounds from 8 pm to 7 am, without giving any explanation or reassurances to the civilian population. He had also been much too hasty in ordering the destruction of files.[7] Although the GHQ pen-pushers were to regret their loss bitterly, the more irreverent desert veterans said it could not make things worse, and might even improve them.

As in Alexandria, queues stretching for several blocks formed round the banks. Nahas Pasha made plans to transfer the Egyptian government and the gold reserves to Khartoum, but was in good spirits and made no move to do so. Sir Miles told King Farouk that the question of whether or not he left the capital was entirely up to him. Farouk declared that he was not 'un roi fantoche', and stayed.[8]

Cecil Beaton described Cairo as being in 'the most dreadful state of unrest, the streets jammed with traffic . . . Flap is the word of the moment. Everyone puts a stopper on their panic by calling it a Flap.'[9] The station was packed with women and children waiting to be taken to South Africa and Palestine.

Peter Stirling was one of the group of Embassy secretaries given the distressing job of allocating the three or four hundred places on the daily train to Palestine. Priority was given to women and children, and those who had 'helped us' and would therefore be in the Axis black book. Such was the panic that people were offering huge bribes to get themselves on the train. One official was rather shocked when, having refused the bribe, he was promptly offered the supplicant's wife.

Lady Lampson had brought her child down from Alexandria, and a special train was allocated to take Sir Miles, his family and staff to safety at the last minute. Adam Watson, the best German-speaker in the Embassy, was told he had better stay behind to liaise with the Germans. For the moment, however, neither Sir Miles nor Lady Lampson had any intention of leaving Cairo. In a conspicuous demonstration of sang-froid, the Ambassador ordered the Embassy railings to be repainted. He and Lady Lampson went shopping in the Mouski that afternoon, and dined later at the Muhammad Ali Club. Also present that evening was Prince Abbas Halim, who drank to Rommel's health and was heard to add, 'Now that he's got this far, let's hope he doesn't fall at the last fence!' The Prince was interned a few days later.

Cairene taxi-drivers made cheerful jokes like 'today, I drive you to Groppi's – tomorrow, you drive me!' The British joked too. Since their grandest hotel was known for its slow service, they said, 'Just wait till Rommel gets to Shepheard's – that'll slow him up.' It was also said that the Field Marshal had already telephoned to book the best rooms; but those who took a look at the hotel register found their curiosity unsatisfied.

For the Jews, on the other hand, the prospect of an Axis occupation was too horrible to be joked about. Although Auschwitz had not yet been heard of, Hitler's policy of a Final Solution to the Jewish 'problem' was common knowledge. The Bund Report on the fate of the Jews in Poland, of whom about a thousand a day had been gassed between the winter of 1941 and March 1942, was given wide publicity by the press of England and Palestine, as well as BBC coverage in all languages. Christopher Sykes was disgusted by the behaviour of the Palestine Administration, which did not allow visas to the group of a hundred or so German and Italian Jews working in high security jobs in Cairo, usually as translators. The British authorities in Cairo had specially requested priority for these people and their families, but the Palestine Administration refused to relax their immigration quotas. So, while SOE and certain sections of GHQ were moved to Jerusalem for safety, these Jewish employees – who could expect nothing but the worst from the Axis – were forced to stay behind.[10] Hundreds of Jewish businesses were sold up at the time of the Flap, at absurdly low prices. Many Jews saw no point in moving and stayed where they were, though the rise in anti-semitism since the war had been alarming. Muslim groups showed their solidarity with Palestinian Arabs by being hostile, and Jews were accused of being stockpilers and hoarders.

The Egyptians watched the Flap with varying degrees of alarm or anticipation. Anwar Sadat and a group of fellow-nationalists drafted a treaty to present to Rommel: in return for his guarantee of Egypt's complete independence, he could count on the support of a great army of resistance they were planning to raise. Sadat claims to have gone to the glass market in the Mouski and bought 10,000 bottles, suitable for making Molotov cocktails. Aerial photographs were taken of British military installations, and these plus the draft treaty were flown to Alamein. Once over German lines, the pilot gave a signal of friendship – but since he was flying a British Gladiator, he was shot down.[11] Several members of the Egyptian Royal Army Corps of Cairo were arrested for alarmist and subversive activities, and 250 British troops replaced Egyptian ones at vital defence posts.

Though British civilians might sense, like Terence Tiller, 'bright eyes, whiskers and teeth, gathering behind the wainscot and the dustbins',[12] the majority of roads, bridges and communications remained in the hands of the Egyptian Army, and no British soldiers were recalled from the front to deal with rebellion. Even the demonstrations were orderly, and these were more anti-Nahas than pro-German. 'One of the most remarkable features of the crisis,' wrote Lampson, 'was that once the enemy appeared at the doors of Egypt there was a general realisation of the unpleasantness of a German occupation and a reversion of feeling in favour of us. This sentiment and, it must be admitted, the patriotic attitude of the

Opposition dictated by Dr Ahmed Maher, greatly facilitated the task of Nahas Pasha.'[13] In sharp contrast to his brother Ali Maher, Dr Ahmed Maher had been urging greater co-operation with Britain, and the entry of Egypt into the war, since September 1939.

The run on the banks had brought the Note Issue up from £E57.9 million on 25 June, to £E76 million on 4 July. A meeting of the Board of the Bank of Egypt was hurriedly convened on the 2nd, when it looked as if the supplies of unissued notes might actually run out before new ones ordered from England had arrived. A choice would have to be made between issuing imperfect, cancelled notes that were pending incineration, or employing the skills of the Survey Office to make some new ones. The latter was deemed preferable, and in four days the Survey had produced £E6 million in £E100 notes.[14]

However, the line held at Alamein, and by 6 July the Flap was over. The Survey's beautiful new notes were never issued, and neither were the Italian campaign medals struck for the conquest of Egypt. These showed Mussolini and the Pyramids on the front, while the back was stamped with a figure of Victory, and the motto *SUMMA VIRTUS ET AUDACIA.*

Auchinleck had fired General Ritchie and taken personal command of the battle at the end of June. From then on, he had never lost sight of the fact that Rommel was being slowly strangled by his 1,000-mile supply line, which was being constantly harried by the RAF. Not only that, but the North African front had once again lost its priority with the German High Command, where all attention was focused on the summer offensive in Russia. Nevertheless Auchinleck displayed remarkable coolness and courage, as he turned a headlong retreat into a war of attrition which Rommel was bound to lose.

The railway halt of el Alamein lay inland from the coast and was fortified like a small Tobruk, with defensive boxes and minefields outside its perimeter fence. Two of these boxes were on the Ruweisat Ridge, a narrow bar running from east to west a few miles south of the railway. Twenty miles south of Ruweisat lay the Qattara Depression, formed as if by some gigantic hand scooping 7,000 square miles out of the desert plateau. Since its northern walls were too steep and its salty floor too soft for tanks or heavy transport, the Qattara Depression was a natural barrier, making a bottleneck of the desert between itself and the sea.

At 3 am on 1 July, Rommel launched his attack – but the defences in and around el Alamein held. Because of the shortage of supplies, the tiredness of his men, and the constant pressure of bombardment from the RAF, every attempt to burst through the lines cost the German and Italian force an enormous effort, and left them considerably weaker. By 5 July, Rommel knew for certain that he would not reach Alexandria. Then from 10 to 26 July he was on the defensive, while Auchinleck tried to tire the enemy out with repeated counter-attacks.

But Eighth Army was exhausted too. Before the last attempt to dislodge Rommel on the 26th, Auchinleck had issued an Order of the Day which ended with the words, 'We must not slacken. If we can stick it we will break him. STICK TO IT.' They stuck, but the energy was simply no longer there. On 27 July it was evident that no further progress was possible, and Auchinleck stopped the offensive. Sir Miles Lampson sent a telegram to London, saying that the Egyptians were dismayed by this pause in the battle which was having a very bad effect on local morale. Auchinleck, who had never got on with Lampson and was frequently at odds with Embassy policy, was furious.[15]

Churchill arrived in Egypt three days later, to put heart into Eighth Army and study the military situation for himself. On 4 August, at a meeting in Cairo which included Field Marshal Smuts and General Wavell, summoned from India, Churchill revealed plans for Anglo-American landings in North Africa, code-named Torch. He urged that Eighth Army return to the offensive immediately, and was very angry when Auchinleck insisted that would not be possible for at least eight weeks.

At dawn on 5 August Churchill went up to the front. Laudable as it was for Auchinleck to spare himself none of the discomforts endured by his men, it was unwise to inflict them on the Prime Minister in one of the hottest months of the year. Churchill did not enjoy his breakfast in what looked like a wire cage full of flies, and neither his temper nor his cigar improved the atmosphere in

Auchinleck's office – a stuffy caravan with no electric fan. He left Auchinleck around noon, and was driven to the RAF's base at Bourg el Arab, where his spirits lifted considerably. A magnificent lunch (driven up from Shepheard's) was served by the beach, at a table spread with a clean white cloth and laid with gleaming silver.

Churchill had been considering and discussing possible changes in the Middle East Command for some time, and it would be wrong to suggest that his day in the desert played a part in making up his mind. Yet it is more than probable that the senior RAF officers present, who did not miss the chance of expressing their views on the Army's incompetence, were listened to with some sympathy.

By the evening of 6 August, Churchill had made his decision. Lieutenant-General Sir Harold Alexander (then Deputy Commander, Torch) would replace Auchinleck in Cairo, and Lieutenant-General 'Strafer' Gott would take command in the field. Sir Alan Brooke, who had taken over as CIGS from Sir John Dill in December, disagreed. Gott had, after all, been fighting in the desert since the outbreak of war, and was probably too tired to be burdened with such a job. He had suggested Lieutenant-General Bernard Montgomery, but Churchill was adamant. Gott was highly experienced, he stood out as a desert leader, and he was one of the few commanders of the Desert War in whom the men retained complete confidence. Tragically, Gott's plane was shot down by enemy fighters on his way up to the front.

Churchill summoned Montgomery. He and Alexander had already worked together in May 1940, and Sir Alan Brooke later recalled the effectiveness of their partnership – despite the fact that they were such different characters. Montgomery thrived on danger, which kept his mind as sharp as a razor; while Alexander was so calm and composed that he seemed quite oblivious to it.[16]

Next day, Auchinleck received a letter from Churchill, informing him of the changes in the Middle East Command. He was offered a new command, that of Tenth Army in Iraq and Persia – but refused. His reason was that the men of Tenth Army should not be given a general who – in their eyes, at least – was tainted with failure. He returned to India.

The inhabitants of Alexandria and Cairo who had fled into the

Delta came back, and normal life resumed. The curfew that had kept British troops out of Cairo in the evenings was lifted, and once more the streets were full of soldiers.

There was a sense of anti-climax, a heavy calm made more oppressive by the heat – yet the upheaval of the Flap marked changes in many lives. Olivia Manning had left Egypt in the first wave of evacuations in early July; she settled down in Palestine and started reviewing for the *Palestine Post*, and Reggie Smith joined her that autumn to take up his new post as Controller of the English and Arabic programmes of the Palestine Broadcasting Services.

Lawrence and Nancy Durrell's marriage was now in its final stages. Durrell had left their flat and moved in briefly with Bernard Spencer, before moving to Alexandria on the day of the Flap. In the general evacuation of wives and children in July, Adam Watson arranged for Nancy Durrell and her daughter to travel to Jerusalem in a Free French vehicle.

Nancy was determined not to go back to her husband, but she had no employment and very little money. Olivia Manning lent her a room, and Nancy found work in the Censorship Department. Later Gershon Agronsky, editor of the *Palestine Post*, took her on as a sub-editor. Not long after, Olivia Manning introduced her to Aidan Philip, who was keen to hear more about Henry Miller who had stayed with the Durrells in Corfu and with whom they had later shared a house in Paris. Aidan Philip was director of the Near East Arab Broadcasting Station in Jaffa. He offered Nancy a job, and it was while working there that she met her second husband, the journalist E. C. Hodgkin, who succeeded Philip as Director in 1945. He and Nancy were married in 1947.

In late July 1942, after a long series of parties, Cairo society sadly waved goodbye to Momo Marriott. Her husband had been recalled to England. Sir Miles Lampson wrote that 'Cairo will hardly be the same place, without Momo and her salon'.[17] Julian Amery was posted back to England, and Randolph Churchill – who had spent the last two months in hospital with a broken vertebra – also returned home. He had joined the SAS in April, and a month later had persuaded David Stirling to include him in a mission to Benghazi, though his training was far from complete. The mission was not a success, but there were no casualties until they were within a few miles of Alexandria. David Stirling drove his car into a ditch while overtaking: one man was killed, and Randolph and Fitzroy Maclean (another recent recruit to the SAS) were badly injured. Six months later, Cecil Beaton wrote, 'Randolph took very little time to forget the existence of Momo. I'm afraid that really was a question of guest-room cupboard love, or cocktail lust.'[18]

Spies

They call me Venal Vera
I'm a lovely from Gezira
The Fuehrer pays me well for what I do
The order of the battle
I obtain from last night's rattle
On the golf-course with the Brigadier from Q
Ode to a Gezira Lovely (anonymous), *Oasis into Italy*

The Flap led to yet another series of internments and arrests master-minded by Major Sansom. Born and brought up in Cairo, Sansom had followed his father into the insurance business, and in 1940 had joined the Field Security branch of the Cairo Military Police. His employers were particularly interested in his talent for languages: Sansom spoke fluent Greek, French and Italian, as well as several dialects of Egyptian Arabic.

Two suspects high on his list at this time were the Endozzi sisters, who had once worked in the Italian Legation. In a dawn raid Sansom and his men burst into their flat and found themselves face to face with an ancient lady in bed in the first room, who screamed and fell back in a fit. The Endozzi sisters flew at Sansom and accused him of killing their invalid mother, and he had no choice but to back out with profuse apologies. However, he took the usual precaution of bribing the *bawaeb* (door-keeper) of the apartment block, who later reported that the Endozzi sisters and their mother had been heard screeching with laughter at the ease with which they had outwitted the policemen.

For the next raid on the Endozzis, Sansom was better prepared. Once again his men burst into the first room. Once again the old lady fell back in a fit while her daughters screamed murder, but this time their mother was swiftly brought to her senses with a bucket of cold water. The search uncovered some important information hidden in the lavatory cistern: it had been prepared for Rommel's occupying forces, and consisted of a list of those Italians who were loyal to the Axis and those who were not.

This, however, was relatively trivial information compared to what Colonel Bonner Fellers, the American Military Attaché, unwittingly supplied to the Germans. The British, who depended more and more on American arms, hoped to maintain the trust and goodwill of Fellers and his superiors by keeping him informed of the Army's every move. And, from autumn 1941, Fellers sent it all back to Washington in a cypher known as the Black Code, which had already been cracked by the Italians and Germans. The Axis intercept teams listened carefully, while Fellers gave information about the order of battle, the supply situation, spare parts, shortages, aircraft deployment and forthcoming operations. The code was not changed until Rommel reached Alamein. Fellers was then replaced by Colonel Dr Sivley, who made sure that his new Assistant, Captain John Brinton, changed the US Legation's codes on a regular basis. Brinton also had the difficult job of rebuilding GHQ's confidence in the American Legation.

A few weeks after that, the Germans also lost the only spy they had actually gone to the trouble of planting in Cairo. His name was John Eppler, and his capture crowned Major Sansom's wartime career. The decision to plant a spy in Cairo was taken in early 1942, and the Abwehr, Germany's military intelligence organisation, felt it had just the man for the job. John Eppler was born in Germany shortly before the First World War. He was still very young when his mother moved to Alexandria and later married an Egyptian, Salah Gafaar. Gafaar adopted her son, made the boy a Muslim, and gave him the name Hussein Gafaar. He was sent to school in Europe, but Alexandria was home.

With a generous allowance from his step-father, Eppler became one of the many idle and charming young men about town until 1937, when he was approached by the Abwehr. Eppler was then in his middle-twenties, and what really interested the Abwehr about him was that, although he was German, most people knew him as Egyptian. Eppler says that in 1937 he made contact with three nationalist groups in Egypt, who were prepared to work with him. These were the Muslim Brotherhood, Ahmed Hussein's Young Egypt, and members of Aziz el Masri's 'Ring of Iron' group in the Egyptian Army. He was then sent to Germany for training.[1]

Eppler's dramatic journey back to Egypt in the spring of 1942 began in Libya, where his German masters decided that the only way to get him and his wireless operator safely into Egypt was to travel overland: a journey of 1,700 miles, across the harshest wastes of the Sahara. The Hungarian Count Ladislaus Almasy, one of the greatest desert explorers of his day, was to lead the expedition.

Almasy was exceptionally tall and spare, with a huge beaky nose set in a predatory face. Before the war he had explored the desert with a few of those who formed the core of the Long Range Desert Group: H. G. Penderel and P. A. Clayton were both on the expedition to the Gilf el Kebir, the scene of Almasy's most exciting discovery. The Gilf el Kebir is a granite massif almost as large as Switzerland, in the south-western corner of Egypt. It has become as dry as the surrounding sand, but Almasy's study of the history and legends of Saharan Africa led him to believe that the area had once been blessed with water. He explored the area between 1932 and 1936, and high up in the rocks found the caves that proved his theory. They were decorated with paintings – of men and cattle, giraffes and buffalo, and even people swimming.[2]

Almasy was a familiar figure in pre-war Cairo, where he had many friends including King Fuad, his cousin Prince Kemal ed Din (also a desert explorer) and Russell Pasha. At the outbreak of war he had been living in Budapest. When the Germans came to the aid of their Italian allies in the desert, he was given leave of absence from the Hungarian Air Force Reserve to act as adviser to Rommel. He did so willingly – not from any personal commitment to National Socialism, but in order to return to the desert he loved. Rommel and his men knew nothing about the huge, waterless wastes they had to conquer, and there is evidence that Almasy worked on the Afrika Korps's *Guide to the Oases*.

Accompanied by his wireless operator Sandy, Count Almasy and two others, Eppler began his journey (code-name Operation Salaam) in mid-May. The first part was the most dangerous, but Almasy was a brilliant navigator and they arrived safely at Gilf el Kebir some two weeks later. There the party turned north-east, towards the Nile Valley. From then on the desert was easier – though the British had informers everywhere.

Eppler and Sandy parted company with Almasy a few miles outside Assyut, and they walked into town carrying their suitcases, one of which was full of money in British and Egyptian pounds, and the other with a 40-watt transmitter/receiver. Eppler re-adopted his Egyptian name, Hussein Gafaar, while Sandy posed as a young American called Peter Monkaster. Operation Salaam was over, and Operation Condor about to begin.

By the act of sending their suitcases ahead with a Nubian servant hired in the market place – a risk that terrified Sandy – their incriminating luggage was not searched by the Military Police. They arrived in Cairo one evening in early June, and Eppler got in touch with an old girlfriend, Hekmet Fahmy.

Hekmet was a belly-dancer, whose job brought her into close – if not intimate – contact with British officers, whom she occasionally entertained on her houseboat; but Eppler's idea that she would obtain information important enough to interest Rommel merely shows that he lived in a fantasy world of the movies. Eppler rented a houseboat near Hekmet's, on the Agouza side of the city by Zamalek Bridge, and while Sandy installed their wireless Eppler started to look up old friends who might be useful.

Eppler's houseboat seems to have been very luxurious, for it boasted a radiogram set into the mahogany bar. Underneath this, the transmitter/receiver was installed. Their next door neighbour was a major in Intelligence, at whom Hekmet managed to flutter her eyelids most effectively. She told him her friends were having trouble with the reception on their radiogram, and in almost no time he had presented her with an aerial which he boasted had a range of a thousand miles.

Eppler settled down to enjoy himself in Cairo, but felt he ought to do some spying to keep the Abwehr happy. He prowled around the Abbassia depot and made notes of what was being loaded and unloaded. In the uniform of a subaltern in the Rifle Brigade, he mixed with British officers, bought them drinks and listened to their stories. His English was by no means perfect; but the Allies included a number of different nationalities, so no one suspected him or his Army-issue drill. He thought himself a great success with women, and spent a lot of time and money on the Moniques and Suzettes, Nadias and Leilas who made a living out of entertaining officers. They were told he would pay handsomely for whatever indiscreet pillow-talk they could pick up.

The Cairo spies transmitted in a code based on Daphne du Maurier's novel *Rebecca*, but they did not have much opportunity to use it. According to Eppler, only the first transmission Sandy made was acknowledged by the German receiving station out in the desert. Further attempts to reach them on succeeding nights proved fruitless. The British had already begun to pick up this signal, though it was never on the air long enough to be traced. Nothing appeared to be wrong with the set, but Eppler decided to get a second opinion.

The man who came to look at the radio was Anwar Sadat, who at that time was a signals officer in the Cairene suburb of Maadi. He confirmed that the equipment was in working order, and was shocked at the life that Eppler and Sandy led on board the house-boat. Bottles of whisky and loose women were much in evidence, and Sadat described it as 'a place straight out of the *Thousand and One Nights*, where everything invited indolence, voluptuousness and pleasure of the senses. In this dissolute atmosphere the young Nazis had forgotten the delicate mission with which they had been entrusted.'[3]

Towards the latter part of June, the spies thought they had got hold of some really valuable information concerning the build-up of Allied arms and the arrival of a large convoy of American tanks. The incident is dealt with rather sketchily in Eppler's own book; but in another version of the story, by Leonard Mosley,[4] the victim is a certain 'Major Smith'. Smith is a young officer in GHQ, obsessed by Eppler's belly-dancing friend Hekmet Fahmy. And, before he leaves for the desert to deliver some highly classified information to General Ritchie, locked in his briefcase, she persuades him to come and have a drink on her houseboat. Rather predictably, Major Smith ends up having several drinks with Hekmet, who of course drugs him and calls in Eppler and Sandy. While the hapless Major sleeps it off, they go through his briefcase; but the valuable material they find is destined never to reach Rommel. Their frantic radio signals remain unanswered.

Eppler and Sandy must have viewed the rapid German advance towards Alamein with mixed feelings – if only for financial reasons. They had spent all their Egyptian currency, and all that remained was in sterling. The closer Rommel got, the further the value of the British pound fell – until it could not be given away, at least not on the black market. Perhaps the knowledge that the victorious German Army would shortly be entering Cairo made the spies careless; for they were spending their English pounds openly at the beginning of July.

On 10 July, Rommel's interception unit in the forward area was raided. Among the prisoners taken were two radio operators, and in their possession the British found copies of Daphne du Maurier's novel *Rebecca*. Neither man spoke English. They were taken to the Interrogation Centre at Maadi; and, although they were not very communicative, the British assumed that the novel was being used as a code book. This was confirmed by a message saying that five copies of *Rebecca* had been bought by the wife of the German Military Attaché in Lisbon, in March. Now all that remained was to find the spies and the transmitter.

Since families in England often sent money out to husbands and sons in the Forces, there was always a small quantity of sterling in circulation in Cairo. But, while it was accepted in bars and hotels, British Army and Empire troops in Egypt were paid in Egyptian pounds. The suspicions of the Turf Club barman, Peter, were therefore raised when he noticed a subaltern buying drinks with a seemingly limitless supply of British five-pound notes. Similar notes turned up in other places: bars and cabarets, as well as Shepheard's and Groppi's. On examination they proved to be expert forgeries, probably made in Germany. Field Security under Major Sansom began a discreet investigation to find the source of the dud fivers. The proximity of the Germans meant that hundreds of people were being hauled in for questioning every day, so the search did not attract attention – least of all from Sandy and Eppler, who continued their dissolute and rather desultory life in the flesh-pots.

According to Eppler, the Abwehr never told him the sterling was counterfeit. He was tipped off by his black-market money-changer, who warned him of the danger of using the notes. With this man's help, Eppler managed to offload the rest of his pounds sterling at a quarter of their face value. The money-changer also warned him of a girl he had been seeing. Eppler knew she was Jewish, but not that she was in the pay of Field Security.

Sansom's men surrounded the boat in the early hours of a morning in mid-July. Eppler woke and raised the alarm; and while Sandy was flooding the boat from below, he stood by to repel boarders. Once the door of the stateroom had been forced open by the police, Eppler won himself a few seconds by hurling a rolled-up pair of socks at them as if it were a grenade – but he could not escape the gun levelled at him by Major Sansom.[5]

Eppler and Sandy were captured and interrogated. Sadat was arrested for his part in the intrigue shortly after. The reason the spies were not shot was that the British would have had to shoot Sadat as well: and shooting an officer of the Egyptian Army was considered too dangerous and provocative a risk to take in July 1942. While Eppler and Sandy went to spend the rest of the war in a prison camp, Sadat was stripped of his rank and confined to the Aliens Jail. He was moved to a detention camp in Minia in December.

Eppler, Sadat and Major Sansom have all written their accounts of Operation Condor and, despite the differences, the shabby, amateurish quality of the affair cannot be disguised. Nevertheless, the story has inspired two novels, and two films: *Fox Hole in Cairo* (1960) based on Leonard Mosley's *The Cat and the Mice*, and *The Key to Rebecca* (1985), taken from the novel of that name by Ken Follett.

The spate of arrests and internments that took place over the summer of 1942 had not included two Germans, who continued to live in Cairo. The first was Dr Louis Keimer, a distinguished Egyptologist. Dr Keimer had been saved from confinement thanks to his friendship with Sir Walter Smart, and lived out the war in a small flat full of books and a magnificent collection of early Egyptian manuscripts, in Sharia Khawayati. The second was Mitzie Duhring, the quiet proprietress of the Salon Vogue at 37 Kasr el Nil. Mitzie was hairdresser to some of the most celebrated figures on Cairo's social scene, including Lady Lampson; but she owed her liberty to her most illustrious client – Queen Farida.

Both Walter Duhring, an engineer, and his wife Mitzie had refused to join the Nazi Party. This had led to their being ostracised by most of the German community, and the loss of several engineering contracts for Mitzie's husband. He had been interned in 1940, and was not allowed to communicate with her – while she had to be extremely careful. Her work at the Palace and the salon called for absolute discretion; the slightest slip of the tongue might result in her arrest and the sequestration of her business. Sir Miles Lampson did not like the idea of a German national listening to the well-informed gossip which evidently circulated in such a perfumed hothouse as the Salon Vogue. He suspected her of spying for the Palace, and had often tried to get her interned. The previous summer, he asked the then Prime Minister Hussein Sirry what was being done about Frau Duhring; Sirry answered that as they were relying on Queen Farida's beneficial influence on the King, it would be best to leave her hairdresser alone.[6]

Madame Zulficar, the Queen's mother and sister-in-law of Hussein Sirry, warned Mitzie Duhring that she was being followed. Mitzie was aware of it, and realised that the British would insist on her internment sooner or later. In an effort to save the Salon Vogue from sequestration, she arranged a fake sale of the premises to one of her hairdressers, who was a Greek.

Enemy aliens on Egyptian soil were issued with special passports: when opened, out spilled a concertina of stiff paper several feet long, covered in Egyptian and British seals, rubber stamp marks, fiscal stamps, dates, signatures, miniature forms and one sad photograph. When Mitzie Duhring went to the bank to withdraw money for the 'sale', she had to present her passport, and she felt bitterly ashamed when not only the manager, but all the bank tellers, crowded round to take a look at it.

Frau Duhring was not interned until October, and when she and her husband were released at the end of the war they had nothing. The Greek to whom she had given the money to 'buy' her business had run off with it, leaving the salon a wreck, while her husband's assets had all been confiscated to pay for war damage.

AUTUMN AND WINTER 1942

Alamein and After

Auchinleck had said he would hand over command of Eighth Army on 15 August, but Montgomery wanted to give the impression of a 'new broom'[1] confronted by a great pile of unnecessary dust. On 13 August he went up to the front, from where at 2 pm he signalled Cairo to say that he had assumed command of the Army, and ordered the immediate destruction of all plans for withdrawal. It was petty, insensitive, and grossly insulting to Auchinleck – yet Monty's abrasive character created a spirit which swept through Eighth Army like a breath of fresh air. A story circulated that the censors had opened a letter from an officer which read, 'The trouble is that to deal with a shit like Rommel we need someone of the same sort. Until now all our generals have been such frightfully good chaps – but now, thank God, we've got Monty.'

'There will be no more belly-aching,' said Montgomery, 'and no more retreats.' He was a natural teacher who never tired of putting forward his own ideas, in which he had the utmost confidence. Not only did the new commander want to meet and talk to as many of the men as possible, but he actually explained the coming battle. It would not be an offensive but a stonewalling operation, designed to make Rommel do more damage to himself than he would to his enemies.

The battle of Alam Halfa took shape as Montgomery had prophesied. Rommel had been unable to pierce the British defences. His army and his supplies were kept under remorseless attack from the RAF, and on 2 September he was forced to draw back for want of petrol.

The news that there was a commander in the desert who really knew his business soon got about. Now that it looked as if the Allies were going to win, the position of those who had stolen away in the long retreat from Gazala was much more serious. Rather than be caught and punished by their own side as deserters, they started returning to their units. The vast majority were private soldiers. They were greeted with sardonic amusement by their fellows, and were subjected to little more than black looks from the sergeants and spells of extremely hard work. Warrant officers and NCOs were stripped of their rank, but by dint of exceptional service they stood a chance of winning it back.

For the small proportion of officers who had deserted, things were not so easy: they could not be re-accepted in the tight community of an officers' mess. Paddy Mayne, David Stirling's second-in-command in the SAS, took several of these officers on as troopers, on the understanding that if they really excelled themselves he might be persuaded to fiddle their records. Others, under similar terms, joined the Long Range Desert Group.[2] It is interesting to see these two 'private armies' of the Desert War becoming latter-day alternatives to the French Foreign Legion, that military purgatory in which heroes used to redeem their honour.

Montgomery's arrival also created upheavals in GHQ. When Wavell became Commander-in-Chief Middle East, he had a very small army and was facing an enemy on several different fronts. He therefore recruited a great deal of manpower into GHQ, to study every conceivable angle of the war and prepare for any eventuality. By the time Auchinleck took over, the situation had changed so that much of that manpower was redundant. Auchinleck did his best to streamline the administration; but, having spent most of his professional life in the Indian Army, he had only the vaguest idea of the complex network of influence operating in the British Army. It was no secret that well-connected families still pulled strings to get their sons comfortable jobs on the staff; and despite Auchinleck's efforts, GHQ Cairo remained a haven for several officers whose only talent lay in who they knew. All this changed under Alexander. Suddenly everybody was expected to work. In the run-up to Alamein that meant at least a ten-hour day, seven days a week. Anyone who failed to keep up was packed off to his regiment at the front.

Never had the Eighth Army and the Panzer Army in Africa been so close for so long as they had been in September 1942. The desert had not shrunk; but the possibility of manoeuvre had been reduced by a thick band of static defences, running from the coast to the Qattara Depression. As a result, all preparations for the coming battle would have to be made under the enemy's eyes; and, for this reason, Montgomery employed the help of the celebrated illusionist, Jasper Maskelyne.

The attack was planned in the northern half of the enemy defences. Preparations in this sector of the front were so elaborate that they had a code-name of their own – Operation Bertram. Its purpose was to bring forward 2,000 guns and 1,000 tanks, plus all their logistical support for a twelve-day battle, without the enemy noticing. This was achieved by moving thousands of dummy tanks, lorries, and guns into the forward area, well in advance. This force, although enough for an attack, was so static that the enemy would not think it was for immediate use. As the time drew closer, real tanks and guns were moved up to replace the dummies. All this was done at night, while recce patrols plotted tracks through the minefields. This, the most important preparation, provided the spearhead's only chance of getting through.

On the evening of 23 October, Russell Pasha and his wife were dining in Cairo with Air Marshal Sir Arthur Tedder. During dinner, Tedder was handed a note. He turned to Lady Russell and asked her to keep an eye on the time for him. At precisely ten o'clock, the Air Marshal announced that a thousand British guns were opening fire at that moment. The third battle of Alamein had begun.

This great artillery barrage took the Germans completely by surprise. But, in spite of all the training and rehearsals, the first part of the plan – in which the infantry were to open up the way for the tanks of X Corps – proved over-ambitious. Heavy anti-tank screens blocked the lanes through the minefields, causing many casualties in front and unbelievable congestion behind. Rommel, who had been very ill for the past few months and gone home to recuperate after Alam Halfa, flew straight back to North Africa.

In the light of the lessons learnt from the first attack, Montgomery changed his plans on 26 October. He organised a more stream-lined assault, called 'Supercharge', launched on the night of 1–2

November. This succeeded in breaking a hole in the German defences, and by the night of 2 November Rommel had decided to withdraw.

Although he had many more tanks, guns and men than the enemy, Montgomery had never pretended that Alamein was going to be an easy battle to win. Out of a total strength of 220,000, Allied losses numbered approximately 1,000 a day. Despite his triumph, Montgomery was still a new commander, facing a formidable opponent who had been in command of the same well-seasoned German divisions for eighteen months. Montgomery could not risk engaging him again in the open, where Rommel was well-known for his ability to spring terrible surprises. He also could not risk any kind of set-back. It was imperative that the Allies should be in charge of the airfields of western Cyrenaica, still four hundred miles away, on 7 November – when the huge Anglo-American invasion force was due to land in North Africa.

One of those who took part in the third battle of Alamein was Keith Douglas, perhaps the greatest soldier poet of the Second World War – although, if he had followed orders, he would not have seen any action at all. 'The experience of battle is something I must have,' wrote Douglas, who had an unusually robust and athletic temperament for a poet. He was in his second year at Oxford when the war started. He joined the Sherwood Rangers in Palestine, and then moved to Egypt. Keen, intelligent, and courageous, Douglas was excellent officer material; but his insufferable impatience, which often came perilously close to insubordination, made senior officers reluctant to put him in action. In what was to be the decisive battle of the Desert War, his orders were to remain at Divisional Headquarters.

Six days after the battle started, Keith Douglas could bear it no longer. He drove his truck up through the lines and presented himself to the commanding officer of his regiment, saying he was acting on orders from Divisional Headquarters. As he had hoped, Colonel Kellett was much too busy to check. The regiment had also lost several junior officers in the early engagements. So, the following morning, Douglas found himself in the turret of a Crusader Mark III tank. 'I like you, sir,' said the fitter who had come up with him in the truck from Alexandria. 'You're shit or bust, you are.'

Keith Douglas was part of the force that swept Rommel out of Egypt, across Libya and into Tunisia, a journey he described in the narrative *Alamein to Zem Zem*. The first half was written in a page-a-day diary for 1943. G. S. Fraser remarked that when he came back to Cairo in September 1943, 'his talk was all of burning tanks and roasting bodies',[3] but in *Alamein to Zem Zem*, Douglas observes the living with equal and absorbing interest. On the opening page of his manuscript Douglas wrote,

> 'I look back as to a period spent on the moon
> almost to a short life in a new dimension.'

In the dimension of the war, every human action is spontaneous and, at the same time, extraordinary, almost freakish. A man in pain 'kicks his legs like a baby'; a man who thinks he's about to be shot cowers on the ground, 'like a puppy being scolded'. Douglas was one of the few soldiers to contribute to *Personal Landscape*. He twice met Lawrence Durrell and Terence Tiller, on whom he made a powerful impression, and left them with most of the poems he had written in the desert. Keith Douglas returned to England in December. Over the next few months he worked and reworked his poems and the text of *Alamein to Zem Zem*. He felt certain he would not survive the war, and was killed in Normandy shortly after D Day.

The 'Darling Belt'

How our Egyptian hostesses detested
The victories of our campaign;
'Assez de progrès,' they protested –
'Vous étiez bien à Alamein!'
Charles Hepburn Johnston, *In Praise of Gusto*

The news of Rommel's retreat from Alamein was greeted with as much relief as jubilation, but the celebrations were informal. After all, the fighting was not yet over, and GHQ could not relax until the safe completion of Operation Torch. This was not only the first joint operation the Allies had been able to mount: the commanders had no experience of landing huge forces on hostile beaches.

The first real sense of victory came on 12 November, when Eighth Army recaptured Tobruk. Montgomery's Order of the Day proclaimed: 'We have completely smashed the German and Italian Armies.' Three days later, on Sunday the 15th, the bells were rung all over England, as they were in the Anglican Cathedral in Cairo.

Sir Miles Lampson reported that the victory had had a salutary effect on the King. Not only did he make himself very agreeable, but the Italians and Abdel Wahab Talaat (Ali Maher's chief agent) were at last ordered to leave the Palace. Sir Miles did not entirely trust his motives, for Alamein had not altered Farouk's hatred of the Wafd. 'Apart from a healthy fear of antagonising the victor, King Farouk . . . may have been influenced by the idea that the eventual eviction of the Wafd will be facilitated if a friendly alternative is presented to us.'[1] The attitude of the King was reflected in that of the Turco–Egyptian élite, who had warmed considerably towards the British. Two months earlier their chic princesses would have scorned to dance with a British officer; now they accepted with pleasure.

Some of the finest descriptions of life in Cairo after Alamein come from a young diplomat, Charles Johnston. He had come from Tokyo, where he and the rest of the British diplomatic staff had been interned in their Embassy compound for the last eight months. Now he had been appointed to Sir Miles's Chancery staff, where his friend Peter Stirling had been working since 1940. They dined together on 18 September, the night of his arrival.

Peter Stirling was a few years older than his more famous brother David. He was extremely popular, very funny with his slow, magisterial voice, and was equally at ease in a louche night-club or an Embassy garden party. His main interests were horses and gambling. And, since most of his friends were now stationed in the desert or GHQ, their hours off duty were spent in much the same way as they had been in England – except that they now talked of Heliopolis and Gezira instead of Sandown and Newmarket. As for paying debts, the slowness of the Middle East post was harnessed to great advantage. Stirling and two others shared a bank account in Aleppo. A cheque drawn on this account always took at least two weeks to clear, giving the debtors a few days' grace to raise the money – which could be wired to Syria direct.

Stirling lived in a large, shabby flat overlooking the Embassy at 13 Sharia Ibrahim Pasha Naguib, immediately underneath that inhabited by Adam Watson and, until recently, Olivia Manning. The flat was looked after by the sufragi Muhammad Aboudi, better known as Mo. A powerful man of great character, Mo had stripped the English language to its bare essentials, so his speech made up in vigorous directness what it lacked in syntax. There were constant domestic dramas between Mo and the cook, Mahmoud. Mahmoud was an excellent cook, trained by that fastidious gourmet and ex-prime minister, Ali Maher Pasha, but he had an unfortunate predilection for hashish, of which Mo strongly disapproved.

The sitting room sofas were a nondescript grey, dotted with cigarette burns and stained with a grimy black line at head level. Haphazardly placed photographs of King George and Queen Elizabeth, cut from a magazine, had been hastily glued to the wall before the landlord came to lunch – to hide the marks of indoor revolver practice. On a table in the hall was a pile of letters, addressed to officers who might be dead, or in prison camps, or coming back at any moment.

In the corridor leading to the bedrooms and bathroom was a telephone, the wall above it grey with doodles and scribbled telephone numbers. The bathroom was piled high with uniform cases, captured German ammunition, and a pair of elephant tusks; while a fluctuating assortment of bedrolls, kit-bags and camp beds was strewn about the bedrooms.

Stirling liked Johnston, and offered him a room – though it was made plain that he was only 'on approval', for Stirling feared his friend might be too naive and bookish to fit in with life at the flat. As a test, he asked one of the most incorrigible gamblers in Cairo to come and stay as well.

Julian 'Lizzie' Lezard had been very handsome in his youth, and was better known as a tennis player than a barrister – a profession he had not practised for some time. He married a very rich woman called Hilda Wardell, and, when he had gambled away a good part of her fortune, she packed him off to Kenya. Here he had naturally gravitated towards the raffish set in the White Highlands, whose exotic depravities were brought to public attention with the murder of Lord Erroll in January 1941. Lizzie had been a witness at the trial of Sir Delves Broughton, and had come to Cairo after that.

He was fond of saying that his father kept a pack of cards in Leicestershire, and part of his great charm was that he had no illusions about himself. 'A drone is someone who employs spivs,' he once said. 'If only I could find a good drone, then I'd be fixed up for life.'[2]

However, Lizzie was not just a playboy. Xan Fielding wrote that 'He had been transferred from one unit to another probably more often than anyone else in the whole of the British armed forces; so that although still a captain at the age of forty, he had seen more varied service than most colonels. Obviously unsuitable as a regular officer . . . he had volunteered for a number of paramilitary missions in almost every "private army" then operating in the Middle East; and each one of his commanding officers, who had taken him on simply as court jester, soon discovered that his irreverent wit and unpractical jokes merely served to conceal a quality of which he seemed to be positively ashamed – courage.'[3]

He joined the SAS, and completed his parachute training in May 1943. The following year, when dropped with Fielding into the South of France, he cracked two vertebrae on landing. The news came back to Cairo that Lizzie had distinguished himself by becoming the Man who Broke his Back on Monte Carlo. Peter Stirling and Lizzie were always trying to borrow money off each other or Johnny Phrantzes, a young Greek diplomat. His Cairene friends declared that Johnny's Anglophilia made him *le prototype du English gentleman*.

One of Johnston's letters home describes Lizzie Lezard having an argument in the manager's office of the Auberge des Pyramides, about how much credit he should be given before a night of gambling at the Coptic Ball. 'All this time the band was playing the Gold and Silver Waltz and strings of Coptic beauties were passing back and forth outside the door of the little office where the drama was going on. I came by with Peter Bouverie and Samiha Wahba, and we guessed roughly what the form was by the grim, set faces we could see inside . . . credit is the one thing that is never joked about. As Lizzie came out with a stern expression and flashing eyes, I tried to whip the smile off my face and felt very frivolous and out of touch with reality.'[4]

A constant stream of officers from the front, plus the occasional appearance of David Stirling himself who was becoming widely known as the 'Phantom Major', gave the flat that excitement that comes from being at the centre of things. Its parties were famous, giving each guest the exhilarating sensation of being on top form, surrounded by the most attractive and interesting people in town. The food was delicious, the drink unlimited; and in spite of the dated dance records and battered furniture, the flat was considered one of the smartest places to be seen in Cairo.

It was not the sort of company that might immediately appeal to a young Wykehamist diplomat who had attained a first at Oxford, had ambitions as a poet, and was indifferent to gambling; but Charles Johnston had never seen anything like Lizzie Lezard or this café society in khaki, and he was completely bewitched.

Notebooks and letters home were devoted to describing the Cairene comedy of manners: how young officers described their education as 'Eton and Cyrenaica', or 'Harrow and Sidi Rezegh'; how Middle Eastern girls seemed to go for certain types: one for Yeomanry colonels, another for Brigadiers from GHQ, to say nothing of the regimental types – Greenjacket Annie, or Coldstream Milly. The novel Charles Johnston meant to write was never written; but he distilled his memories of Cairo and the transience of wartime life into a short volume called *Mo and Other Originals*.

Johnston's work in the Chancery kept him busy, but was not heavy enough to interfere with long lunches followed by a siesta back at the flat, or the parties that went on till the early hours. 'Cairo friendships are luxuriant but non-transplantable,' he observed. 'You are right in the middle of the "Darling belt". You arrive there from the material and emotional austerity of England, and before you know where you are your two hundred most intimate friends are dining with you by candlelight at small tables in a garden.'[5] But as the weeks passed, Johnston worried that he had not earned the right to enjoy himself as the soldiers had, coming back to Cairo from months of danger and hardship in the desert. It was shaming to be young, healthy and tied to a desk, and he made valiant attempts to get himself released for the duration. The Foreign Office had no intention of allowing it; but, around Christmas, it looked as though he might well succeed. He therefore went off to Marie Riaz's Christmas party with a light heart.

Marie Riaz, née Cavadia, had been married several times, and her present husband, Mamduh Riaz Bey, was director of one of Egypt's largest sugar refineries. At her sumptuous parties, the Cairo smart set was always well diluted with artists and writers, for she preferred their company to that of the bourgeoisie. She wrote poetry, was a great admirer of Communism, and would occasionally give clenched fist salutes to Stalin – a gesture which made the gold bracelets on her arm jangle heroically.

In a letter to his parents Charles Johnston described the party. It took place in the Riaz house in Sharia Mansour Muhammad, Zamalek, which was '. . . full of Italian pictures and Tang horses. From the windows of the ballroom one looked down into an enormous candle-lit hall entirely hung with red and black tapestries and with low tables and cushions grouped round a pool with fountains playing. You realised suddenly that this was the Pasha's garden, which had been enclosed in a tent for the evening and joined onto the house as a dining room. It was like something out of the Arabian Nights, or at any rate out of a novel by Disraeli. There was a full house of the curious Anglo-Egyptian society which has blossomed out during the war, Guards and cavalry officers, Turco-Egyptian princesses, war-profiteering pashas and a sprinkling of foreign diplomats, everyone very gay and knowing each other well and the English and Egyptians on very good terms. The locals have now seen that we are going to win the war and, after a tricky time earlier this year [a tactful way of describing the Abdin Palace incident], relations are pretty good and still improving. There was a first-class band clicking away and a couple of tummy dancers and unlimited whisky, which is about the only drinkable fluid left in Cairo . . .'

Johnston then proceeds to list his dance partners: Madame Lutfia Yusri, once married to Hassanein Pasha; Madame Melek Fawzi, once married to the Regent of Iraq; Betty Lampson, the Ambassador's niece; Philae Wissa, a pale, dark-haired Coptic beauty; Sybilla Szczeniowska, married to the Polish First Secretary; and Madu Faucigny-Lucinge, a Parisian mannequin once married to a French prince.

'I'm afraid this reads rather like a gossip column, but Cairo is like that and the great thing is to treat it as rather a joke and not let it impress you . . . For goodness sake please keep this description very quiet, because I think people at home would be horrified if they knew how unaustere Cairo is.'[6]

The last two months of 1942 were marked by the arrival of the Americans in Cairo. There had always been a few generals and advisers in Egypt since the start of Lend-Lease, and a handful of United States Air Force pilots had taken part in the air battle over el Alamein; but it was not until after the North African landings in November that their soldiers reached Cairo in any appreciable numbers. Even then they were few: at the beginning of 1943 there were only just over 1,000 American servicemen in Cairo, whereas British and Dominion troops numbered 126,000. Their impact, however, was out of all proportion to their numbers.

The reason for this was partly economic. Shortage of accommodation was a problem well-known to staff officers in Cairo, and rents were steep; but once Egyptian landlords discovered that American officers were willing to pay anything, and usually accepted the first price offered without bothering to haggle, prices trebled almost overnight. On top of that, the Americans thought that the British paid their staff disgracefully low wages. House servants working for Americans could hardly believe their luck, while local administrative staff received up to 50 percent more than they could have made in a British office.

Quite apart from the irritation of seeing their best workers lured away by American dollars, there were serious repercussions to be considered. The British reminded their rich allies that expenditure of the Allied Forces was one of the key factors contributing to inflation; and that, to an Egyptian, anyone who accepts the first price offered is a fool. It was not long before the Americans agreed that a combined front against rising prices must be formed and adhered to; but where there is little mutual understanding, co-operation is not easy.

One of the first priorities was to find a suitable site for an American camp. It took a long time, and the Americans felt that the British were being both inefficient and obstructive. For their part, the British thought it absurd that all American troops had to have huts rather than tents, and a ration of 40 gallons of water per man per day where no British soldier had ever had more than 20. On top of that, American insistence on water-borne drainage had made them turn down the otherwise perfectly acceptable Stadium site. There were more complaints when building material for the camp was shipped from the United States, causing congestion in the overworked docks.

On a more personal level, the natural reserve of the British character did not appreciate the informal breeziness of the American, and there was a feeling that they were unwilling to learn from British experience. One intelligence officer described working with his trans-Atlantic allies as like making love to an elephant: it was very difficult, you were liable to get trampled on, and you saw no results for a very long time.[7]

Among the men, a great deal of resentment was caused by the American Forces' very high rates of pay. In December 1942, a British private soldier earned 3/6 a day, a New Zealander 3/–, while an American earned the equivalent of 10/– which included a 20 percent increase for foreign service.[8] The United States serviceman arrived in Egypt not only with money, but with cigarettes of Virginia tobacco, chewing gum, nylons and the latest dance records – and, through the American PX (Post and Exchange), he also had access to such luxuries as kirby-grips and shampoo. In the competition for women, he therefore had advantages the British soldier could not hope to match – and the same went for his superior officers. General Barney M. Giles of the US Fourth Air Force was soon having an affair with Tahia Carioca, the most famous belly-dancer in Cairo (known to her fans as 'Gippy Tummy'). He also had sufficient whisky in his Gezira flat to soak lumps of bread in it, and then throw them up to the kites who swooped out of the sky to catch the bait. When sufficiently drunk, the kites entertained the General by reeling around and falling out of trees. Warm beer was good enough for the British, but Americans insisted on theirs being iced – a facility provided in their camps. The British were also contemptuous of the way the United States Forces seemed to give out medals like chocolates. It was said that all you had to do to get the Purple Heart was sit through a showing of *Desert Victory*, the film of the Battle of Alamein.

The Americans had some trenchant criticisms of their own. The British were snobbish, unfriendly, uninterested in learning about new technology, and obsessed with rank and privilege. The social gap between officers and men in the US Army was far narrower than in the British, and GIs thought it incredible that there should be hotels and restaurants that were out of bounds to Other Ranks. This caused as much resentment on the American side as pay did on the British. The Americans prided themselves on their vigorous determination to tear the guts out of Hitler, which they often displayed – only to be sneered at by the British, whose attitude to the war seemed to them alarmingly limp and cynical. The Americans also found it astonishing that the British should treat German POWs with such friendly respect, and could not understand their hero-worship of Rommel, inspired by the desert campaign. On the other hand, the British treated the Italians with an amiable contempt that made the Americans mad. This attitude sometimes provoked an Anglo-American fight among camp guards, much to the amusement of their prisoners.

All the American criticisms were bound up with a profound mistrust of British imperialism. This was supposed to be a war for freedom and democracy, but from Cairo it looked like a war to save the British Empire for the British – a suspicion confirmed by conversations with South Africans and New Zealanders, who also said that it was the Dominions who had borne the brunt of the fighting. In an attempt to ameliorate the situation, it was decided to use both British and American announcers and newscasters on the radio. Stories of Anglo-American co-operation would be given maximum coverage, and Anglo-American films would emphasise the buddy-buddy image. But it was the anti-imperialist arguments which caused particular concern in the Minister of State's office, for this was exactly what enemy propaganda had been saying for the last three years.

The intensity of America's disapproval really became apparent thirteen years later. Eisenhower, who had seen British and French colonialism in North Africa at the time of Torch, was to react devastatingly in 1956 when the British and French tried to crush Nasser and take back the Suez Canal. His determined use of the dollar against the pound on the international exchanges brought this last major attempt to assert imperial power to an abrupt and ignominious end.

SPRING AND SUMMER 1943

Scandals and Quarrels

1943 was the year in which both King Farouk and Nahas Pasha started to look towards Egypt's post-war future. They each hoped to dominate its development and, not surprisingly, relations between them did not improve. In April the King decided he would not attend any public function at which his ministers were present, and Nahas's party to celebrate Accession Day was remarkable for its lack of representatives from the Palace; yet 1943 was marked more by scandals and quarrels than by real political crises.

The year began well for Sir Miles Lampson, who in the New Year Honours list became the first Baron Killearn. It was a rare honour for an Ambassador to be raised to the peerage while he was still *en poste*, and Nahas Pasha gave a great banquet to celebrate the event at the Zafaran Palace. This mark of high esteem from the British King and his government was not lost on King Farouk, but other Anglo-Egyptian relations were on his mind: Queen Farida had been visiting the studio of a British portrait painter called Simon Elwes.

A handsome man in his early forties, Elwes had come to Egypt in November 1941 with the 1st Armoured Division. Attached in theory to GHQ's public relations section, Elwes's main occupation was painting the luminaries of Cairene society. In the summer of 1942, his sitters included the British Ambassador, and the beautiful Consuelo Rolo. Cecil Beaton was not impressed. He dismissed the portraits as weak and fashionable, while admitting that the one of Consuelo was very pretty, and another 'good enough to hang in a small sitting room'. The painter himself he described as 'intolerable – affected, long-winded and utterly egotistical'.[1] Elwes fancied himself as a lady-killer, and told one Egyptian friend that he could never paint a good portrait of a woman unless he had slept with her. He was also ambitious, and he did not want to leave Egypt without having painted the King and Queen.

The suggestion was put to Their Majesties by Nahed Sirry, wife of the ex-Prime Minister and Queen Farida's aunt. The King agreed to commission a pair of portraits for which Simon Elwes was to be paid £1,000 each, with half in advance; and it was decided that he should paint Farida first. Both the Ambassador and Elwes's friends in the Embassy told him how important it was, given Muslim sensibilities, to behave with the utmost decorum in the presence of the Queen.

The first sittings took place at the Abdin Palace, where the chatter of the ladies-in-waiting and the constant interruptions of a Middle Eastern court drove the artist to distraction. He said it was impossible to work in such surroundings; and, if he was to do any justice to the portrait at all, the Queen must come to his studio. If this sounded quite innocent to Western ears, the ladies-in-waiting were shocked at such a suggestion being made to the Queen of Egypt; but Simon Elwes insisted that he could not work at Abdin, and after some persuasion Farida consented to come to his studio.

Queen Farida was only twenty. She had given birth to two daughters, Ferial and Fawzia, but had not yet produced an heir for the House of Muhammad Ali. While she could dismiss her husband's affairs with women she considered little better than tarts, she was deeply hurt by his liaison with Princess Fatma Toussoun, a lady of the royal family. From then on, Farida was barely on speaking terms with Farouk, and perhaps this was why she did not ask his permission for her portrait to be finished at Elwes's studio. Yet, by omitting to do so, the Queen put herself in a dangerous position, for the strictness of Muslim morality meant that she had to keep the sittings at Elwes's house a secret; and, if she were found out, only the worst interpretation would be put on her visits.

Accompanied by a lady-in-waiting named Akila, Queen Farida went several times to Simon Elwes's house; but she did not go unnoticed. The Palace had an impressive intelligence service, built up by King Fuad and passed on to Farouk – who kept himself as well-informed as his father. It was said that almost every Nubian and Sudanese sufragi in Cairo was linked in a network controlled by Muhammad Hassan, the King's Nubian butler. Another source of domestic information was supposed to be the *khassandara*, or 'holder of the keys'. This woman was in charge of the Royal Wardrobes, and received information from a grapevine of ladies' maids throughout the city. Farouk soon knew about his wife's visits to the studio; and, one afternoon, he decided to go there himself.

Simon Elwes shared his flat with two RAF officers: Sonny Whitney, and (confusingly) Air Commodore Whitney Straight (Air Officer commanding a new transport group under Sholto Douglas). Straight, a wealthy Anglo-American, had been shot down over France, and his escape was an extraordinary story. (Noël Coward described him as having great charm; but the fact that such an immensely rich man had decided to contribute to the war effort by living only on his pay was considered more stingy than patriotic in Cairo.) The two officers both knew that the Queen was coming in secret to have her portrait painted, and were both in the house when, to their horror, the King arrived. He stayed for some time, taking satisfaction in the evident discomfort of his hosts, while the Queen and her lady-in-waiting made a hasty exit by the back door.

In years to come, Farida and Elwes were alleged to have met in the intimate darkness of cinemas, even to have been caught *in flagrante* at Abdin; but very few people knew the story at the time. The King let it be known that Elwes had better leave Egypt as soon as possible, and Lord Killearn was only too keen to avoid a major scandal. On 16 January, Simon Elwes was sent to South Africa. In his diary, Killearn noted that, in view of the rumours that Farouk was going to divorce his wife, it was just as well that Elwes had been got out of the way. (He later admitted that he had been 'a little alarmed for Simon's safety' at the time.[2]) The Ambassador also remarked that the King had been behaving very strangely since he had grown a beard.

Many people believed that his beard, a symbol of piety in Egypt, was an indication that Farouk had aspirations to the Caliphate. The first Caliph was the Prophet Muhammad's successor Abu Bakr, and the last man to hold the title in Egypt died in 1171 (the Fatimid Caliph 'Adid). Yet the idea of a leader who would unite the Islamic world had a new relevance, at a time when pan-Arabism seemed to be the most logical development for the countries of the Middle East.

In a series of articles Farouk wrote for the *Empire News* after his abdication in 1952, the ex-King denied any ambitions to the title of Caliph. He grew the beard, he told his readers, because it is the most sacred thing that a Muslim can swear on – and on it he swore to divorce Farida.[3]

Elwes seems to have been quite oblivious to the explosive situation. He genuinely thought he was going to South Africa just to paint a portrait of Mrs Smuts. When he found out that the Embassy was preventing his return to Egypt, Elwes wrote Queen Farida a letter containing an impassioned diatribe against the British Ambassador. It never reached her, but was intercepted by the censor and passed to Killearn.[4] From South Africa he was sent to India, because – as Killearn later explained to Wavell – he was less likely to cause trouble there than if he were in London, where he could have carried on an indiscreet correspondence forwarded by the Egyptian Ambassador. The last episode in the story came a month later, when the King sent Hassanein to the Embassy to demand that Elwes return to Egypt for two weeks to finish the portraits, for which His Majesty had paid half;[5] but this was more of a prank to annoy and embarrass the Ambassador than a serious suggestion.

The Eighth Army marched into Tripoli on 23 January, an event which caused much celebration in Egypt. The threat of invasion was well and truly over, and news of a great conference at Casablanca was offered as a sign that the Allies would shortly enter Europe. Mussolini was prophetically described in one Egyptian newspaper as 'an empty drum hanging on a tree'.[6]

Churchill passed through Cairo on his way back from Casablanca. He was travelling incognito under the name of Commodore Frankland, but that did not lessen the upheaval at the Embassy. His party consisted of the CIGS Sir Alan Brooke, the Prime Minister's son Randolph, his doctor, two detectives, two private secretaries, two stenographers and a valet. One of the decisions reached during this visit to Cairo was the refusal to continue supporting the French

Admiral Godfroy and his men, who were still sitting in Alexandria Harbour. Godfroy complained bitterly, and negotiations dragged on throughout the spring. Eventually, the French ships raised steam on 15 May and sailed to join General Giraud in Algiers.

On 27 January Churchill was presented to King Farouk. He mentioned that King George invited him to lunch once a week in London. Did the King of Egypt not think this a habit worth adopting with his own prime minister? Farouk pulled a face and said that would be very agreeable if his prime minister was Winston Churchill, but unfortunately it was Nahas. Killearn was rather shocked that the King called his distinguished visitor 'Churchill' throughout, without any prefix;[7] but the King evidently enjoyed the meeting, and later presented the Prime Minister with a six-inch long cigarette instead of a cigar.[8]

At about this time, the news finally reached Cairo that David Stirling of the SAS had been taken prisoner, while harassing enemy supply lines beyond Tripoli. Charles Johnston wrote that it was in fact a relief, 'for he was bound to get himself killed before long if this had not happened. In a way David's capture marks the end of a phase of the war out here. It will be a terrible loss not to have him turning up mysteriously and living in the flat between operations, with maps being unrolled in the dining room late at night, and comings and goings of staff officers and parachutists and soldier servants and a line of jeeps drawn up outside the flat, and David himself very modest and embarrassed by his fame and dodging parties in order to sit and drink beer and read a book by the fire . . .'[9]

Two months later, Peter Stirling heard that his brother was safely in an Italian prisoner of war camp, and Johnston passed the good news on in his letter home. 'He [David] is a terrific gambler and celebrated the night of his arrival by winning £150 at roulette with his fellow captives. The story is that several officers planning to escape can now no longer afford to.'[10]

The winter of 1942/43 was harsh, by Cairo standards. Typhoid was on the rise, and there were severe rainstorms in and around the capital. The poor endured the cold and wet as best they could, by wrapping their heads in woolly scarves and shivering in their thin cotton clothes. However, there was room for hope: the British troops would surely go away now the fighting in Egypt was over, and that would bring prices down. The Cairenes also looked forward to the spring.

With the warmth came the short flower season, and in front of villas in Zamalek and Garden City gardeners tended borders of larkspur and snapdragon, sweet peas, pinks and marigolds. On the Monday after the Coptic Easter, Egyptians of all religions celebrate the spring festival: *Sham el Nessim*, the Smelling of the Breeze. The air that day is supposed to be particularly beneficial, and hundreds of families go out for a picnic to take advantage of it. Every park and patch of grass is crowded with people eating the traditional foods of the season: salt fish, eggs, spring onions, and a drink made from dried apricots.

However welcome to some, the spring of 1943 brought little good to Nahas Pasha. In March he was said to be suffering from congestion of the prostate,[11] while his government was in the throes of an acrimonious political scandal, engineered by Makram Ebeid Pasha. When Nahas became Prime Minister the previous year, he had appointed his right hand man, Makram Ebeid Pasha, as Minister of Finance. Makram Ebeid was an able politician, and a Copt: the Wafd had always insisted on collaboration with the Coptic minority, and every Wafd administration had one or two Coptic ministers. However, Makram's elevation did not please Nahas's wife, Zeinab el Wakil. Madame Nahas was a formidable and ambitious woman. Killearn had noted that her *Semaine de Bonté* of the previous spring caused much local resentment, for in raising money for charity she relied more on her own talents for extortion than other people's goodwill.[12] In the rise of Makram Ebeid, she saw a threat to her husband's power and prestige within the Wafd. She taunted Nahas by suggesting it was common knowledge that Makram ran the party, while he was a mere figurehead.[13]

Nahas, who had relied closely on Makram in the past, now started closing doors against him. Makram retaliated. He accused the Prime Minister of unjustly sacking certain officials, who were then replaced with Wafdists on well-fattened salaries. He challenged Nahas head on over certain inter-governmental appointments: but Nahas was

Ahmed Bey Sadik, the Sequestrator of German property in Egypt

Mrs Devonshire and party in a Cairo mosque

Olivia Manning, Cairo

R. D. (Reggie) Smith

Lawrence Durrell

Charles Johnston

Lord Dunsany with members of No. 11 Convoy, sailing to Egypt

'Pistol-Packing' Mary Newall

Sudi Southby, Elizabeth Holberton and Anita Rodzianko (née Leslie), Hilmiya Camp

King Farouk with Nahas Pasha

The Duke of Gloucester greeting troops in the desert

The Prince of the Atlantic Ocean:
Christopher Sykes's fictional version
of Colonel John Metherall

Grabbing sword and dagger he DASHED down the
dining-room table —   and—

Two sketches of
Julian 'Lizzie' Lezard
by Mollie Bishop

The Two Types by Jon:
the triumph of comfort
over conformity in
Desert War uniforms
was a standing joke

Princess Shevekiar (left), King Peter II of Yugoslavia (opposite)
and General Stone (right)

The wedding of William Moss and Sophie Tarnowska

too strong for him, and in May 1942 Makram was forced to resign from the Ministry of Finance.

The vehemence of Makram's repeated attacks on Nahas in Parliament alienated many of his supporters, and he was expelled from the Wafd. The party had been severely weakened by the conflict; but Nahas's firm handling of the country during the German advance of the previous summer, and the energy with which he tackled fifth-columnists, had given him great authority.

This however was not sufficient to still the increasing agitation from the Opposition and Makram Ebeid about corruption within the Wafd. Makram Ebeid was known to be compiling a 'black book', which would set out in detail all the offences of the government. In March, just as the book was expected to appear, Nahas organised raids on a number of printers in an attempt to confiscate the whole edition. He failed to find the right one, and by the end of the month thousands of copies of Makram Ebeid's 'black book' were in circulation.

The Foreign Office was naturally keen to read it, but the Embassy's translation seemed to take a very long time. On 17 April, Killearn had to explain that 'it is a matter of infinite industry and patience to disinter from masses of Arabic verbiage the main charges against the government'.[14]

The book took the form of a petition to the King, and was divided into two sections: 'General Survey' and 'The Facts'. Makram Ebeid accused the government of favouritism, particularly towards Madame Nahas's family, the Wakils. She and her brother were lining their pockets with government money, and selling privileges and concessions. Using the clout of his position, Nahas had made several private deals advantageous to himself, and was filling the Civil Service and the administration with his cronies. Furthermore, the internment of Ali Maher and Prince Abbas Halim was the act of a dictator, and Egypt's sovereign rights had been pushed aside in favour of Britain's interest. From the evidence put forward in the 'black book', it was clear that Makram Ebeid had done much of his research before leaving office. He had also had considerable collaboration from the Palace in preparing the book.[15]

For most of the month of March, Nahas was very ill. He returned to Parliament in April and, after much argument about restrictions and procedure, Makram Ebeid was given three whole days to set his case before the Chamber. This should have given him ample time, but when Makram Ebeid was not allowed to continue his speech on the fourth day he and the whole of the Opposition withdrew. Two days were devoted to the Government's replies – and since the Opposition had walked out, the vote of confidence in the Government was unanimous.[16]

Nahas refuted everything, but his arguments against the more solid accusations had been rather unconvincing. Nevertheless the Wafdist press screeched abuse at Makram Ebeid, calling him 'the professional liar', the 'master cretin', and even 'the bat'. Local Wafd committees spread the rumour that the 'black book' was a British idea to frighten Nahas, and make him look to Britain for help. The work of Parliament came to a standstill, while its members devoted themselves to heated discussions about the conduct of the Prime Minister and his relations.

Reactions in Egypt were mixed. The foreign communities, who had always hated the Wafd because they felt threatened by its nationalist policies, were far more indignant than the average educated Egyptian. He was not particularly impressed by the 'black book', and expected a measure of corruption in any government. Beyond a certain point it was, of course, reprehensible – but it was not regarded as unnatural to profit from one's political position. The illiterate classes, who tended to hero-worship their leaders, still thought of Nahas as the heir to Zaghloul, rather than the villain of the 'black book'. But their faith in the Wafd had been severely shaken, and the scandal was followed by a wave of cynicism and political apathy.

Makram Ebeid had personally given a copy of his book to King Farouk, who now had the perfect excuse to dissociate himself completely from his government. The King began to boycott the Wafd in society, and the charities associated with it. The Wafd reciprocated: with the result that no supporter of the King could give any money towards the Alamein Club, while no Wafdist would have anything to do with Hospitals Day. Farouk learnt that Nahas had arranged for Wafdist workers from the arsenal and government workshops to join the processions of students, who came to Abdin to cheer the King on the anniversary of his accession. The workers would be instructed to call for Farouk *and* Nahas. The Palace told the Public Security Department that there were to be no workers in Abdin Square that day. Nahas said that if that were the case, there would be no students either.[17]

Beneath this high-level game of tit for tat lay a deeper rivalry. The Axis had been beaten at Alamein, and suffered a massive defeat at Stalingrad in January. The Allies looked set to win the Second World War, and Egypt was out of danger. Both Farouk and Nahas were aiming to lead not only a fully independent Egypt, but the post-war Arab world.

The Wafdist press kept up their glowing reports of Nahas; but, although they could describe him as the 'Leader of the Orient and Pan-Arabism' when he visited Palestine in June,[18] the Prime Minister knew that there were other Egyptian politicians in the Opposition who had a better grasp of the problems and issues of Pan-Arabism than he did himself. In Egypt, it was harder to idealise Nahas. Even more important than the shadow cast by the 'black book' was the fact that his administration had failed to control the economy.

The Allies were still spending around 3 million pounds sterling in Egypt every month. Between 1940 and 1943 bank deposits had risen from 45 million to 120 million, and anyone who had shares in Egyptian Hotels Ltd (which owned Shepheard's, the Continental, and the Semiramis, among others) had seen their value doubled. Since imports had been cut to a minimum, local industry was booming.[19]

But none of this alleviated the hardship of the poor. Their wages had not kept up with inflation, and the restrictions on cotton acreage hit them from two directions. If the landowners grew cereals, which made less money than cotton, this was reflected in wages. At the same time, the price of cotton had been kept deliberately high to appease the powerful landowners' lobby in Parliament.[20] This encouraged them to ignore the restrictions on cotton acreage, leading to fresh shortages of cereals, which would consequently go up in price – and, again, it was the poor who suffered. The cost of living index had risen even more sharply since Nahas came to power, and the shortages of sugar and paraffin were almost permanent.

In contrast to his government, King Farouk had got off to a good start in 1943. In January he made a donation of £E400 to the Monastery of St Catherine's in the Sinai. The Abbot had expressed his appreciation of this generous present from a Muslim King, and Farouk replied that he was King of all Egyptians.[21] The press applauded enthusiastically, and several inspiring articles were written on the subject of Egyptian unity. At the Muslim New Year Farouk was described by *el Mokkatam* and *el Ithnein* as the pattern of good Islamic conduct, and, on the occasion of his birthday, the latter publication referred to the King as 'The Man of the Hour'. Another article compared Farouk, who sought contact with his subjects and helped the poor, to Caliph Haroun al Rashid – that exemplary ruler whose virtues are extolled in the *Thousand and One Nights*. *El Ithnein* wrote that the Hedjazis considered Farouk to be the only monarch who could unite the Middle East, and *el Mussawar* hailed him as King of the Muslims.[22] Whatever his later denials, it was not surprising that Farouk's recent beard was taken as a sign that he was grooming himself for the Caliphate.

Indignant at the way her son and daughter-in-law had been ignoring her, Queen Nazli had retreated to Palestine in February. After a few months her absence from court became a matter for comment; but Nazli would only return on condition that her arrival at Cairo station be accorded a full-dress official reception, with the King and Prime Minister present. They reluctantly agreed, and she came home in July – though, at the last minute, the King decided not to attend.

The next royal flight from Egypt was more permanent. On 23 March, the voice of the King's cousin Prince Mansour Daoud was heard broadcasting in Arabic from Rome. He said he had come to 'join the Axis cause', though now that the Allies were winning it looked as if he had made his move rather too late. The Prince's subsequent talks about British oppression and the need for an Axis victory were not taken very seriously in Egypt, where the Prince enjoyed very little esteem. Everybody knew Mansour Daoud was short of money, and the Italians had obviously paid handsomely for his support.[23] The following month, the King deprived him of his royal rank and privileges.

Mansour Daoud's defection did no harm to the King's prestige. Farouk still had the respect of his subjects who saw him as the symbol of his country's nationalist aspirations. Their respect for him as a man was not so high, for he had been humiliated by the British; but Lord Killearn's action was bitterly resented, and every word in the King's favour was therefore an act of patriotic defiance against the oppressors. The Egyptian newspapers vied with each other in singing Farouk's praises. People knew there was a less wholesome side to his character but the Egyptians are very tolerant, and the King was very young. The British Embassy, on the other hand, had little respect of any kind for Farouk, and took his misdemeanours far more seriously.

Lord Killearn had kept London well-informed of the King's activities. One night in December 1939, Farouk had raided a sequestrated German bookshop. The policeman on guard had been told that a party was coming to break the seals and enter the premises, and he was not to stop them.[24] In early 1940 he appropriated the collection of swords belonging to the brothers George and Habib Lotfallah,[25] and a year later he appropriated the magnificent collection of weapons belonging to Mahmoud Khairy Pasha. Farouk had apparently sent Khairy a list of what he wanted from the collection. Khairy said that the value of the collection would be ruined if it were split; but the King made it known that if he were thwarted, he would stop the royal pension of £E120 a month paid to Khairy's wife Princess Kadria. This was not a great sum of money; but the loss of the King's patronage could severely affect the family's prestige, and the career of their young son. Khairy Pasha agreed to part with the collection for £E20,000, though he doubted he would ever see the money, and Farouk's 'experts' would no doubt value the collection at half the sum.[26]

It must be said that Lord Killearn, too, had whims that were sometimes indulged. A party of people playing competition golf were astonished to see the Ambassador come striding over the Gezira golf course one day, with a pair of guns, a loader, and two boys. His targets were the scavenging kites that floated over the city, for which he had a passionate hatred because they stole his golf balls – in the mistaken belief that they were eggs.

Since they performed a useful service in Egypt by eating the parasites that feed on cotton plants, the kites were a protected species. And in British eyes it is considered very bad form to go shooting on golf courses. Neither of these considerations prevented Killearn from killing between twenty and thirty kites that afternoon, and the two boys were kept busy picking up the dead birds as they thumped on to the grass among the golfers. The latter included Gertie Wissa and Brigadier Charles Fraser, who was deeply shocked by his Ambassador's behaviour.

Both Killearn and Russell Pasha, Cairo's Chief of Police, were considerably more concerned when King Farouk's acquisitive instincts were drawn to the Wadi Rishrash. Russell Pasha was a passionate conservationist as well as a keen shot. He had persuaded Farouk's father, King Fuad, to make the Wadi Rishrash a state reserve. Farouk visited the reserve in the summer of 1941, shot an ibex, and announced that from henceforth it would be his private shoot.[27] Russell Pasha was understandably furious, and it would appear that he finally managed to save it from Farouk's depredations; for in his memoirs, published in 1949, he wrote: 'Today, by order of His Majesty King Farouk, the Rishrash is closely guarded and remains the one safe refuge for ibex in this country.'[28]

The King was a manic collector of almost anything: hunting trophies, cars, weapons, patent medicines, gold objects, practical jokes, naughty postcards, pornography, jewels, coins and matchboxes. All this junk and treasure was piled into room after room in the palaces of Koubbeh and Abdin. It seemed as if Egypt's royal magpie was trying to fill some insatiable emptiness inside him. He had a voracious appetite, preferring simple food to the rich concoctions served at royal banquets, washed down with milk or sweet lemonade.

Farouk enjoyed showing off the rows of latchkeys, which let him into the apartments of his different girlfriends. He liked to pose as a Casanova and, in one sense, women were objects for collection like everything else; but he also enjoyed the company of women for their own sake. Irene Najjar, a beautiful blonde Cairene with whom the King was for some time obsessed, spent one weekend alone with the King during which they frolicked for hours in the swimming pool – but two days passed with no more than a kiss on the cheek from Farouk.

He also enjoyed watching women squabbling amongst themselves for his favours. When the King organised informal shooting parties in the Fayoum for his friends, the role of hostess was taken by his current *maîtresse en titre* – in this case, Irene Najjar. At dinner, she put the King next to a pretty, mischievous-looking young Englishwoman. None of the guests knew much about her, but there was no doubt that the King was enchanted by the newcomer. A furious Irene watched the King and her latest rival retire upstairs, and plotted revenge.

Among the tables laid for breakfast she ordered a small one laid with three places, and invited Farouk and the Englishwoman to join her when they finally appeared the following morning. Accompanied by roars of laughter from Farouk, Irene Najjar was scrupulously polite to her rival, whom she plied with coffee and toast. Meanwhile the servants, on Irene's instructions, were packing the unwelcome guest's bags. As soon as the bags were loaded into the car, Irene turned to her rival and said, 'My dear, it is too sad you have to leave us so soon' – and before the Englishwoman knew what was happening, she was being helped into a chauffeur-driven car and whisked back to Cairo. Farouk watched the scene with the greatest delight, and clapped heartily at the end.

Male companionship he found among the rich Egyptians who played for high stakes at the Royal Automobile Club: they included Shukri Wissa, Emile Adès, and Georges Sednaoui. Farouk also spent time with non-Egyptians, many of whom found, to their surprise, that they liked him for himself. One of these was Air Marshal Sir William Sholto Douglas, the head of Fighter Command between 1940 and 1942.

Douglas arrived in Cairo in January to take over as Air Officer Commander-in-Chief from Air Marshal Sir Arthur Tedder. His friendship with the King really began on 1 April 1943, when King Farouk attended a gala performance of the film *Desert Victory*. The main reason for inviting the King was so as to attract the rich Cairenes, who would be willing to pay handsomely for the charity tickets. But Douglas had also observed the Embassy's patronising treatment of Farouk, which he thought very misguided. Farouk was, after all, the most powerful man in Egypt, and the British were guests in his country.

On the night of the gala, Douglas organised a magnificent reception for the King with full guard of honour. 'He had certainly never been accorded such a smart turn-out as the respect paid to him at that film première,' wrote Douglas in his memoirs. 'The poor man even admitted to me that he felt that at last the British were taking some notice of him. His pleasure was both evident and sincere, and I came to feel that it might do some good if we went on making a bit of a fuss of him.'[29]

He then invited Farouk to dine at Air House, and the King began to drop by whenever he felt like it. He often took the Air Marshal round the night-clubs of Cairo, at every one of which a table was permanently reserved for the King. These outings became exhausting, for Douglas could not leave before Farouk who regularly stayed up till four or five in the morning, and seemed oblivious of other people's working lives. The King liked to keep the conversation well-leavened with jokes; but he could be serious, revealing himself better read and informed than one might have imagined. One thing he took seriously was money. Farouk told Douglas that his personal fortune was estimated at six million pounds, and increasing it was one of the main interests of his life. In politics his opinions were well to the right, and anything else – Douglas's moderate socialist principles, for example – was Communism.

At this time, the King had a number of English and American friends. One group he enjoyed visiting spent their summers in a cool, spacious house at Bulaq Dacrour just to the west of Cairo. The house belonged to Roger Low, who moved his family up to Alexandria every summer. It was said that Rommel had picked out the house for his headquarters; and, during the Flap the previous year, British Army personnel had laid mines in the ditches and threatened to uproot the trees. They had turned their attention to the roof when a swarm of wild bees drove them off, much to the delight of the servants.

The group which took the house during the summer months consisted of Robin Fedden, co-founder of *Personal Landscape*, and Renée Catseflis, an Alexandrian Greek whom he married that autumn; Bernard (later Sir Bernard) Burrows, then Second Secretary at the Embassy, and Inez Walter, who were married in 1944; John Brinton, the American Military Attaché, and his wife Josie; and David (later Professor) and Mary Abercrombie. David, like Robin Fedden, was a lecturer at Cairo University.

On party nights, Bernard Burrows and John Brinton would bring out the *goula*, a huge earthenware jar, which would then be filled up with grapefruit juice, and as much whisky or gin as the rest of the household had managed to lay their hands on. This would not have been real whisky or gin, which by this stage in the war had become rare enough to be treated with respect; but imitations from Cyprus or Palestine which even their makers admitted were inferior, by advertising them as 'suitable for cocktails'.

Bulaq Dacrour was much cooler than Cairo; and for the guests who had spent the day sweltering in town, 'it really is delightful to drive out along an avenue which leads away from the English Bridge and turns abruptly into a country lane; going through fields and crowded villages and then more fields, and then a clump of trees with a cool English country house in it, and a garden with yews clipped into cones, and a pool . . .'[30]

Bathing at midnight was a regular feature of parties at Bulaq Dacrour. Before that, there was dancing – much enjoyed by the young King Peter of Yugoslavia, who took charge of choosing the records and winding up the gramophone. King Farouk liked to drop in unexpectedly, an event which would send the servants running off to fetch His Majesty a glass of fresh buffalo milk. As well as the informality, Farouk enjoyed the light-hearted teasing which was possible to accept from foreigners more easily than from his own subjects. On one occasion, John Brinton mischievously asked the King if he were going to join General Jumbo Wilson on United Nations Day (14 June 1943), at which Wilson was going to take the salute before a procession of Allied troops and tanks. 'Why should I?' replied Farouk, 'they usually bring the tanks to me.'

Farouk found another friend in a young British officer called Patrick Telfer-Smollett, who tried to bring him out of his luxurious, over-sheltered world. Telfer-Smollett was attached to the British Military Mission, which acted as a cover for his work in Intelligence under Brigadier Clayton. He was amazed at how little Farouk appeared in public, far less than the British royal family.

Royal tours in the provinces were very rare; and Telfer-Smollett discovered, to his astonishment, that the King had never been to the Egyptian Officers' Club. A visit was arranged, and the officers – who included some of the King's staunchest supporters – were delighted to have Farouk in their midst, talking easily and dressed in the magnificent uniform of a Field Marshal. Encouraged by his reception, Farouk returned to the Officers' Club on several occasions.

That the King had British and American friends who were sympathetic to his cause was naturally a source of anxiety to Lord Killearn – though he could not stop the King enjoying their companionship. Douglas was one of the senior officers in the Armed Forces, while other friends like Telfer-Smollett or Max Aitken had influential connections.

Relations between the Palace and the Embassy were further complicated when Wendell Wilkie's volume of memoirs *One World* came out that year. In it, Wilkie had described Killearn as 'the British Ambassador to Egypt and for all practical purposes its actual ruler'. The book was banned in Egypt.

A Glittering Summer

The official victory over the Axis forces in Africa came on 15 May, an event which was greeted with satisfaction in Egypt. The poorer inhabitants of Alexandria were particularly pleased, since they thought it would signal the end of the hated black-out restrictions – but, to their great disappointment, Colonel Burt-Smith refused to let them lapse while Greece and Crete remained in enemy hands. By August the rich, too, seemed to feel that the blackout was no longer necessary. At a party given in aid of the Alamein Club the Antoniades Palace was ablaze with lights, and Burt-Smith sharply reprimanded the organisers for their irresponsibility.[1]

The Opposition parties in Egypt had hoped that, once the war was effectively out of North Africa, the British would allow Nahas's obviously corrupt and inept government to be overthrown; but, when they saw that Lord Killearn was still prepared to support the Wafd, they turned against the British. At an Opposition rally in Menoufia in June, the anti-British speeches were distinctly violent and a number of well-known nationalist agitators were present. Killearn expected this trend to continue, and confided in his diary that what they needed was a good aerial bombardment to bring them to their senses.[2]

Meanwhile, the British and American commanders were preparing for one of the most ambitious and complex operations of the war – Operation Husky. Unlike the North African landings in November, the landings in Sicily planned for 10 July would be heavily opposed; and Husky involved landing half a million men over the course of the campaign. The headquarters for the Cairo end was housed not in GHQ but in a separate office off the Sharia Emad ed Din, known as 'George'.

While the planners assessed the likely British casualties, one officer was more concerned with the damage they might inflict. The archaeologist Mortimer Wheeler had raised an anti-aircraft battery at the beginning of the war, and – although he was seven years over the age-limit for active service – went on to fight at Alamein. In the break-out and pursuit that followed, he had ample opportunity to observe that, though the Afrika Korps had done very little damage to the classical ruins in Cyrenaica, the victorious Eighth Army was more inclined to destruction. As he so tolerantly put it in his auto-biography *Still Digging*, 'The colonnades of Leptis and its underclad statuary was fair game.'[3] Measures were taken to protect the monu-ments in North Africa; and, having seen the damage there, Brigadier Wheeler (he was promoted in May 1943) felt it vital that the Army pledge its protection to the monuments of Sicily before the Allied invasion.

He flew to Cairo at the beginning of June, and from GHQ was directed to 'George' – where he was pleased to find Lieutenant-Colonel Lord Gerald Wellesley, heir to the Duke of Wellington. An architect in civilian life, Wellesley was naturally sympathetic. He was not sure what could be done, but the question was put to Allied Forces HQ in Algiers. Meanwhile, Wellesley said he would do all in his power to protect the monuments in his sphere of influence in Sicily, though the task would be difficult without a guide book. And, while there were probably several copies of Baedeker's guide to Sicily dotted around the bookshops of Cairo, it was too risky for a British officer to be seen buying one.

Later that afternoon, Mortimer Wheeler went to have tea with one of the most scholarly Englishmen in Cairo: Archibald Creswell, Professor of Muslim Art and Architecture at Fuad I University, who lived at the top of a crumbling tenement in the Rue Hassan el Akbar near the Citadel. While Creswell was busy in the kitchen, Wheeler quickly scanned the bookcases that lined the tiny sitting room – and there he saw Baedeker's *Guide to South Italy and Sicily*. The book was in his pocket by the time Creswell returned with the tea.

Back at 'George', Wellesley reported that a message had come from Algiers to say that two Americans were going to be keeping an eye on the ruins and churches of the island during the invasion. It did not sound very reassuring; but Wheeler was glad to be able to give Lord Gerald the purloined book, and know that at least one guide to the monuments of Sicily would be joining Operation Husky.

Gerry Wellesley, known in Cairo as 'the Iron Duchess', was one of the handful of Englishmen who, like Professor Creswell, preferred to live in the older part of Cairo. He had found a house which formed a sort of annexe to the ninth-century mosque of Ibn Tulun, and from the roof one could look into its vast colonnaded courtyard. He shared the house with David Balfour, a man whose religious career had been more confusing than contemplative.

Having begun as a Benedictine monk, Balfour joined the Orthodox Church and became a priest, first in Russia and then in Greece. During this time he was known as Father Dimitri Balfour. When Greece fell he came to Egypt, where the war began to undermine his vocation. Captain Bryan Guinness, the son of Lord Moyne, worked in GHQ and described the transformation of Father Dimitri Balfour to his wife Elisabeth: '. . . Father Balfour is trimming himself away piece by piece, and . . . I think it is a pity. First he cut off his bun of hair, then he shed his long black robes and inverted top hat, then he clipped his beard. He says that next week he expects to be clean-shaven and in uniform . . .'[4] The change was then complete: he became Captain David Balfour, and got a job in GHQ – though he still retained a certain asceticism.

For Wellesley, the inconvenience of living so far from the centre of town began to outweigh the charm of the Ibn Tulun house. He moved out in the autumn of 1942, ceding his place to Patrick Kinross. Kinross had recently been appointed press officer to the RAF. 'I think I shall have [the house] to myself,' he wrote to his mother, 'as he [David Balfour], hermit-like, is going to live on sour milk in a hutch on the roof.'[5]

Patrick Kinross, who was in the process of divorcing his wife, had to set most of his income aside to pay his lawyers. The Ibn Tulun house cost only £10 a month, and in January 1943 he was joined by Eddie Gathorne-Hardy from Cyprus, which reduced overheads even further. Gathorne-Hardy was one of the lecturers whose dubious reputation caused so much concern to Flux Dundas, the head of the British Council. His outrageously camp gestures and sparkling conversation made no concession to the stuffier members of the British community; but behind his frivolity was a well-stocked, incisive mind which believed in the classical tradition, and had no time for the innovations of writers like Henry Miller. Lawrence Durrell had once tried to bring them together in Greece, but both took an instant dislike to each other. Robin Fedden was also of the party, and recalled how at one point an enraged Miller struck his belly and said, 'But I write my books here' – to which Gathorne-Hardy immediately replied, 'Do tell me *just* where, my dear.'[6]

Thanks to the inexpensiveness of life in the old quarter, Kinross and Gathorne-Hardy were able to invest in a sofa, 'so we can relax in the evening instead of sitting bolt upright on the Iron Duchess's pompous chairs'.[7] David Balfour left his hutch on the roof and moved in below them, and tried to get over his first disastrous romance with the aid of a piano. 'He plays Bach all evening while his cat, who doesn't like Bach, screams outside our door.'[8]

In the winter months, Kinross enjoyed walking to work; but as the heat increased, all exercise became increasingly unpleasant. 'Summer is upon us and we rather dread it,' he wrote to his mother in April. 'Already it is getting muggy and one feels liverish and stale.'[9] By July the weather had become unbearably steamy, but evenings were the reward for living through the day. As the twilight deepened the streets would come to life. People went to sit up on their roofs or put chairs out on their balconies to eat their plate of bread, beans and pickled vegetables.

Kinross's birthday happened to coincide with the *mulid*, an annual festival in honour of the local saint, 'so we had a party on the roof and watched the junketings in the street below. Someone gave me a couple of turkeys and we had Nile fish and prawns and strawberries and cream and Palestine wine cup. There are six nice, attractive girls in Cairo and they were all there. The festivities were wonderful: absolutely spontaneous with dervishes and sword-swallowers dancing among gay crowds, and native orchestras everywhere, and barrows selling melon and honey-cakes and rice and beans, and coloured lights and flags. It was all focused around our house, as we are the lords of the manor.'[10]

Farouk's attempts to have Lord Killearn replaced as Ambassador did not succeed, but his campaign continued by every means available. In the late summer of 1943, he asked Patrick Telfer-Smollett to arrange a meeting with the Commander-in-Chief, Jumbo Wilson. His friend explained it would be extremely difficult, and naturally Wilson would be reluctant to be seen going behind the Ambassador's back. However, a meeting was arranged through Telfer-Smollett and Mark Chapman-Walker, General Wilson's ADC. It took place at Farouk's villa on the Nile just outside Cairo, in September 1943 — while the Ambassador was on leave in South Africa.

Patrick Telfer-Smollett was the first to arrive, followed shortly after by Farouk — who had an entire gold tea-service in the boot of his car, thrown in anyhow. A sufragi was summoned to whisk the tea-service into the villa, while Farouk waited to greet General Wilson. The Commander-in-Chief, having only met the King officially, was slightly taken aback when the King shook his hand and said, 'Jumbo, I couldn't be more pleased to see you.'

The meeting was private; but it seems likely that, as well as discussing Farouk's troubles with the Ambassador, they touched on an idea that Farouk was ready to put into practice. At the time of the Khedive Ismail, some difficulty with the British had been satisfactorily solved by the Khedive sending an emissary direct to Queen Victoria. Farouk now proposed to try something of the sort again. A large box of chocolates would be sent from Farouk's daughters to the Princesses Elizabeth and Margaret, to be distributed to children in hospitals. Patrick Telfer-Smollett would accompany the chocolates, which would provide him with an entree to the royal family — and the chance to deliver a private letter from King Farouk into the hands of King George himself.

The journey to England was arranged with the help of Mark Chapman-Walker, and on the appointed day Telfer-Smollett went to Abdin to collect the King's gift. Until then, he had not quite realised the scale of the operation. Farouk had ordered about 230 pounds of chocolates from Groppi's, which were now laid out in rows on a huge table. He watched in amazement as the King worked his way round the table, tasting each flavour, while a magnificent lacquered box emblazoned with the royal arms of Egypt and Great Britain was gradually being filled.

Telfer-Smollett and the chocolates travelled from Cairo to Khartoum, and from there to Nairobi, Entebbe, Stanleyville, and Dakar. Whenever possible the chocolates were put on ice for a few hours, but ice was not always available and they must have been in a sorry state by the time the cooler part of their journey began. From Dakar they continued on to Lisbon, Ireland, and finally London. Telfer-Smollett delivered the chocolates to Buckingham Palace, but he did not see the royal family who were then at Sandringham. Unsure of what to do next, he went to the Foreign Office where he saw the Permanent Under Secretary, Sir Alexander Cadogan, and explained his predicament. The interview was brief, for Cadogan did not want to hear: if Killearn were deposed, he himself might be appointed the next Ambassador to Cairo.

Farouk's letter was still undelivered when Telfer-Smollett was ordered back to Egypt. He was sent straight to the Canal Zone, and his every attempt to get to Cairo was blocked. Friends were evasive, and said they were trying to help; but the Foreign Office had evidently given orders that he was not to return to the capital. From the Canal Zone he was posted directly to Italy. It was not until two years after the war that he had the opportunity to tell King George the story, at a dance at Buckingham Palace. Telfer-Smollett expressed his regrets at having been unable to deliver King Farouk's letter. King George smiled, and said he had known about it all along.

The abundance of delicacies like fresh fruit and coffee, butter and chocolate always staggered those arriving from ration-obsessed London. On 1 September, Vivien Leigh wrote to her mother that 'the war is non-existent in Egypt and to see huge tables spread with every sort of deliciousness, and bowls of cream was extraordinary'.[11] The war had been vivid enough in July 1942, but all that had passed. The capital, which remained a vital pivot in the Allied war machine, was now out of all danger, and this summer it had the added glamour of the stars.

With Vivien Leigh were Beatrice Lillie, Dorothy Dickson, Nicholas Phipps and Leslie Henson, in a revue called *Spring Party* produced by John Gielgud. They had played to thousands of enthusiastic soldiers across Algeria and Tunisia before arriving in Cairo in late June, where they performed at the Opera House – a cheerful building with ornate plasterwork painted in white, crimson and gold. It was made almost entirely of wood and plaster, had ominously creaking floors and was probably one of the greatest safety hazards in the city.

'The show was much too sophisticated for the troops,' wrote Patrick Kinross. 'B. Lillie singing the stuff she sang at the Café de Paris from years ago, D. Dickson too old, Henson also trying to be too subtle, and Vivien Leigh pathetic, reciting *You are Old, Father William* with goo-goo eyes, a song about Scarlett O'Hara and Clark Gable, and a sentimental recitation about Plymouth in the Blitz. However she looked nice, and the troops get so little anyway that they seemed quite pleased.'[12]

There was no shortage of people keen to entertain the principals of *Spring Party*. The Ambassador had arranged a supper after the show on 29 June, but it was postponed due to the arrival of the Killearns' second child, Jacquetta. The stars did not come to the Embassy until three nights later, when other guests included Consuelo Rolo and the Aly Khans.

Lord Killearn wrote that they sat late after supper and then moved onto the terrace, by which time Beatrice Lillie was so drunk that her theatrical colleagues were rather alarmed. But the Ambassador recalled that 'Beatrice Lillie is more amusing than words can say, and the tighter she got the more amusing she became'. The stars stayed until a quarter to four, having drunk nothing but whisky – 'So our exiguous stocks must have been considerably punished.'

Patrick Kinross was invited to a luncheon party given for them by Maie Casey, 'at which the stars and the generals and admirals and air marshals all sat at one end of the room, and all the amusing people at the other being witty about them'.[13] He had only a few words with Miss Leigh before Sholto Douglas claimed her attention, and 'monopolised' her for the rest of her visit.

The summer of 1943 also saw the opening of the Auberge des Pyramides, a luxurious new night-club on the Mena Road. It had a large open-air courtyard with a dance-floor in the middle, and was judged the most pleasant night spot in Cairo. The Auberge became a venue for charity galas, and – along with the Club Royal de Chasse et de Pêche – a favourite haunt of the King's. Lord Killearn first went there on 5 August with his niece Betty. They were summoned to Farouk's table where he was sitting alone with two ADCs. The King was evidently amused by Betty's forthright humour and, when the King left at ten, to Killearn's astonishment he was told that His Majesty had settled the bill.

This unusual event was repeated on 18 August, when Killearn brought Noël Coward to the Auberge des Pyramides after a dinner with the American Minister. Their entrance, wrote Coward, was impressive – 'Any entrance with Miles is impressive.' They were put at a table next to the King, who was in the company of Sholto Douglas and Connie Carpenter, an actress now with ENSA who had been the first to sing 'Poor Little Rich Girl' in the United States. Douglas was often seen with Miss Carpenter, and the King seemed equally attracted to her. People said that Douglas was in her room in Shepheard's one evening when the King came to call, and the Air Marshal had to make a flying exit via the service lift. The Ambassador presented Noël Coward to the King, who left early having paid their bill. Coward rather regretted having only ordered a beer and two packets of Gold Flake.[14]

Coward saw Josephine Baker outside Shepheard's on 8 September, the day Italy surrendered. She was dressed in the uniform of a Free French colonel, 'looking the last word in chic and bright as a button ... She is doing a wonderful job for the troops and refuses to appear anywhere where admission is charged or where civilians are present.' Unlike Josephine Baker who only sang for the fighting men, Coward performed whenever he was asked. On 11 September he was invited to a party by Sholto Douglas to meet the King again. The entertainment began with two short propaganda films 'which', Coward wrote in his diary, 'would have been enough to persuade the King to hand over the whole of the Nile Delta to the Germans in sheer irritation'. (Lord Killearn, however, did not trust Coward's ideas about propaganda. *In Which We Serve* was all very well for home consumption, he thought, but a film about the drowning crew of a sinking British warship did not create the right impression in Egypt.[15]) They were then treated to the Hollywood version of *Arsenic and Old Lace*. At 1.30, Coward was told that the King would like him to sing, and Sholto Douglas's memoirs recall that he was not on top form.

'I do not doubt that Coward was weary. He had been working hard and travelling great distances in his generous effort to entertain the troops. But what had caused him to perform so badly at our party – and it was an embarrassingly poor show – was a comment that King Farouk made when I asked Coward if he would be so good as to play for us. In his high-pitched voice, which rang out so that nobody could escape hearing it, Farouk exclaimed: "Yes . . . come and sing for your supper." If looks could have killed, the one shot at Farouk by Coward . . . would have resulted in his losing his throne far quicker than he did.'[16]

No day went by without a tour of at least one hospital, and Coward was deeply impressed by the men he saw: 'One can privately, very privately allow oneself a little personal compassion for their broken bodies, but their spirit is clear and high above pity.'[17] He usually did two shows a day for the troops, and on 14 September three. A show starring Larry Adler, Winnie Shaw, Anna Lee and Jack Benny had been organised in an open-air cinema in Cairo, which was packed with thousands of RAF men on the night – but, at the last minute, Anna Lee and Jack Benny were unable to appear. Larry Adler sent an SOS to Coward, which reached him after he had completed two concerts at the Heliopolis hospitals; but he rushed back to Cairo, and put in a much-appreciated half hour performance before dining with Alexander Kirk.

Coward did not leave Egypt without visiting Alexandria, where he had the distinction of being asked to leave the premises of the Royal Yacht Club for wearing shorts and a shirt – a costume which Coward thought was 'eminently suited both to the climate and the setting'. Coward's host Oswald Finney, one of the most influential printer-publishers in Egypt, was similarly dressed; but despite his threats and remonstrations, they were forced to go. 'We had a delicious lunch in town,' wrote Coward, 'and comforted ourselves with the reflection that as long as the Alexandria Yacht Club maintained its high moral standards, the war for freedom and civilisation really was worth winning.'[18]

The morals of the rest of Alexandria were, of course, more

dubious. Readers of Lawrence Durrell's *Alexandria Quartet* still like to think of a city bathed in glamorous corruption. When talking of it to a foreigner, almost every Egyptian begins by saying rather defensively that Durrell got Alexandria all wrong in the *Quartet*. This is merely a way of saying that it is not full of sexual perverts and child brothels. Yet perhaps what really irritates the Egyptians is that the *Quartet* – written by an Englishman and inspired by two other foreigners, Constantine Cavafy and E. M. Forster – makes more of an impact than the modern-day city itself. Alexandria is still viewed, by most tourists and particularly foreign journalists, through Durrell-tinted lenses.

The *Alexandria Quartet* had a very long gestation, and was not published until after the Egyptian revolution. But its beginnings can be traced back to the early forties, and the war that had brought Durrell to Egypt in the first place.

In the latter half of 1942 Durrell left Cairo to become Press Attaché in Alexandria; and, in September, he was joined by the poet Gwyn Williams. Williams had been sent up from Cairo to become the first head of the English Department of Farouk I University. He was also the initiator of the War of the Poets, in which Durrell, Robert Liddell, Harold Edwards and Williams himself represented Alexandria, while Robin Fedden, Bernard Spencer, Terence Tiller and Bryn Davies represented Cairo. '. . . not since Troy was there such a bash-up,' wrote Durrell to Tambimuttu at *Poetry London*.[19] This light-hearted slanging match in verse, bristling with insults, private jokes and literary allusions, continued for three years, until Williams called a truce in 1945.[20]

The way people allowed the real war to absorb their every waking minute irritated Durrell, and he looked on his own job with no small degree of irony – but this did not stop him being highly effective. Lesley Pares (later O'Malley), who worked at the Ministry of Information in Cairo, once had to go up to Alexandria for a week to organise press coverage for an exhibition on the RAF. She introduced herself to Durrell, and explained what had to be done: but, instead of getting to work, he swept her off on a round of picnics, parties, and lazy days on the beach. This impetuosity may be explained by the fact that Durrell later described Lesley Pares as 'so beautiful that the effect was like Hiroshima. She made men forget about the war. Montgomery had the greatest difficulty in attracting any attention to himself while she was around.'[21] As the days wore on, Lesley Pares felt increasingly anxious about how little work was being done. It was not until the last day that Durrell said, 'Right! Down to business.' They visited the RAF exhibition together, and found it much as one might expect. But, when Durrell summoned the reporters, he gave them such a stirring brief on the importance of the exhibition that it received maximum coverage; and Lesley Pares returned to Cairo to accept, somewhat sheepishly, the glowing praises of her superiors in the Ministry.

For the tourist, Alexandria's prime attractions are pleasant restaurants and good bathing. The modern apartment blocks look as dated as the crumbling baroque villas, there is almost nothing left of the city of classical antiquity, and such sightseeing as there is can be done in an afternoon. But to explore Alexandria as Durrell did, with E. M. Forster's guidebook and the poems of Cavafy, is to discover another, intangible city that shimmers just behind the real one. Durrell was impatient with the day-to-day Alexandria, 'this smashed up broken down shabby Neapolitan town, with its Levantine mounds of houses peeling in the sun', as he described it to Henry Miller. '. . . no music, no art, no real gaiety. A saturated middle European boredom laced with drink and Packards and beach cabins. NO SUBJECT OF CONVERSATION EXCEPT MONEY.'[22] At the same time, he was fascinated by the contiguity between this small-minded Alexandria with its sinister corruptions, and the ancient capital of beauty and arcane learning which Forster and Cavafy had awakened.

In the autumn of 1943, Durrell left the place he had been sharing with Gwyn Williams and went to live in a large flat with Paul and Diana Gotch. The flat also had access to a little tower on the roof from which one could see Pompey's Pillar, and the salty expanse of Lake Mareotis in the distance. It was around this time that he met Eve Cohen, the woman who was to become his second wife, and much of whom can be recognised in the character of Justine in the *Alexandria Quartet*.

Eve Cohen was the eldest child of a Spanish-Jewish mother and an Egyptian-Jewish father who was not very good at his trade of money-lending. They were poor, moved house often, and as a child she was often hungry and barefoot. Yet her mother had her pride, and spoke Arabic only to servants. At home, the family spoke that curious hybrid, Alexandrian French. When Eve had finished school she got herself a job, typing for a film company – a move which enraged her father. The fact that she worked at all was an insult to his honour; and, when she could no longer bear the rows and beatings at home, she moved in with her boss and his wife.

The youth of Alexandria moved in large noisy groups, from the beach to the café, and the café to the cinema. Sometimes they would row out to the middle of the harbour, and continue the party on an old raft tied to a buoy. It was a pleasant life, but Eve Cohen was restless. She was bored by her friends, with their comfortable aspirations and their talk that was at once flowery and banal. They in turn could not understand her impatient intensity, her desire to rub ideas together, and called her 'Miss Psychoanalyse'. Since Eve could not share her thoughts, nor her disgust at the way Alexandrians could ignore the squalor and misery that surrounded them, she became silent; and what she could not communicate became a suffocating weight inside her.

Lawrence Durrell met her at a party. Eve Cohen, a beautiful young woman with dark, dramatic looks, was not particularly impressed by this short, solidly-built man who said he was a poet. However, he found her attractive – and, being Alexandrian, she did not fail to notice. This encouraged her to ring him up one evening, when she was very lonely and depressed. They went out to Pastroudis, where Durrell was not only sympathetic: for the first time in her life, Eve Cohen found herself talking to someone who was on the same wavelength.

Talking to Durrell was not, however, a cosy experience. Over the weeks that followed he bombarded her with questions and forced her to question everything, a painful process that felt as if she were being turned inside out. In Eve Cohen, whom he called Gypsy Rose, Durrell found a passionate integrity which rendered her, as he wrote to Henry Miller, 'completely at sea here in this morass of venality and money. The only person I have been able to talk to really; we share a kind of refugee life' . . . At the same time, Durrell's imagination was changing her into a creature of his own Alexandria. The letter continues: 'She sits for hours on the bed and tells me about the sex life of Arabs, perversions, circumcision, hashish, sweetmeats, removal of the clitoris, cruelty and murder.'[23]

In the company of Durrell's friends, Eve found herself in a world where people had the conversations she had only dreamed about. She had no wish to join in, only to listen – which perhaps explains why Charles Johnston described her as 'beautiful as a tigress, and about as articulate in English'.[24] Charles Johnston's diplomatic high life had not stopped him writing poetry, but so far none had been published in Egypt. He met Eve Cohen and Durrell in Alexandria at the Union Bar, and the following day went round to the Press Office in the Rue Toussoun. 'What's happened?' said Durrell. 'You arrived a year ago, we were told you wrote poetry, and since then you have relapsed into total obscurity.' Johnston refrained from pointing out that his life in Cairo was hardly spent in obscurity; yet he was flattered that Durrell should want to see his poems, and sat down in a little office to type them out. 'Larry came in after a bit and gazed at me in stupefaction. "But," he said, "how can you possibly [transcribe them] like that – from memory? I can never remember a word of mine."'[25]

'The poetry I exude these days is dark and streaky, like bad bacon,' wrote Durrell to Henry Miller in the spring of 1944. His letters still raged against the money-grabbing pettiness of Alexandria, and he longed to get out of Egypt. Yet Diana Gould (who was to marry Yehudi Menuhin), in Egypt with Cyril Richards's production of *The Merry Widow*, formed a rather different impression. Robin Fedden had told Diana in Cairo that she must meet Durrell, and they were delighted with each other's company. As they walked through the streets or sat talking in cafés she felt he was totally at ease in the city, and 'wore Alexandria like a cape'.[26] Eve bitterly resented Durrell's attentions to other women. Durrell told Miller that although she understood perfectly the Taoist texts of Lao-Tse, 'it doesn't prevent her from scratching my face open for infidelities which in this landscape and ambience are as meaningless as she, I, or Pompey's Pillar are.'[27]

After the war Durrell and Eve Cohen went to Rhodes where

Durrell had been appointed Director of Public Relations, and in 1947 they returned to Egypt to get married. This involved an enormous amount of paperwork; for although Eve Cohen's birth certificate was in order, her family – who had been in Alexandria for generations – had originally arrived as refugees, and had never taken Egyptian or any other citizenship. Officially, Eve Cohen was a 'stateless alien'.

At the same time, her parents were so opposed to the idea of her marrying Durrell that they were prepared to have their daughter declared insane and committed, and had even hauled the Chief Rabbi of Alexandria into their camp. Things became so bad that Eve had to escape to Tanta, where she found sanctuary with Durrell's old friend Paul Gotch – who had received a telegram from Durrell saying, 'Lock this girl in the loft and don't let her out of your sight.' Eventually the Chief Rabbi managed to calm Eve's parents, the paperwork was completed, and they married in Cairo. Their marriage certificate did not, however, look very impressive; and, in order to increase its status in the eyes of Eve's parents, Durrell persuaded a friend in the Embassy to emblazon the document with the largest and most magnificent red seal the British Embassy could provide.

Behind Closed Doors (SOE Cairo)

'The trouble with war is that it puts people like you in charge of
people like me. Your heart is as false as your teeth!'
>Captain Christopher Sykes, reputedly addressing
>Brigadier C. M. Keble

We've got hundreds of mugs
Who've been trained like thugs
And now they're at the mercy of
The Greeks and Jugs
And the man at the helm's
A peer of the realm
And nobody's using us now, oh no
Nobody's using us now

We've got a partisan itch
And there's Mihailovitch
And the Foreign Office never seems
To know which is which
We're the talk of the town
We'd better close down
'Cos nobody's using us now, oh no
Nobody's using us now'
>Song about SOE Cairo by George Morton

As a centre of international politics and administration, the great
days of wartime Cairo came after Alamein. The Minister of State's
office was the focus for all British diplomatic missions in the Near
and Middle East, and the Middle East Supply Centre co-ordinated
supplies from Aleppo to Khartoum, Damascus to Tripoli. Every
nationality in occupied Europe had its national branch of the Red

Cross and its military office in the city. It was also the home of the Greek Government in exile, and of their sovereign King George, from March 1943. In August, King Peter of Yugoslavia came to Egypt to be closer to events in Yugoslavia. Including the King of Egypt, that made three Kings in Cairo (John Brinton was once in a lift with all three at the same time). The war's progress westwards naturally called for other headquarters, most notably Allied Forces Headquarters in Algiers; but GHQ Cairo retained its significance as a supply base, and the pivot for co-ordinating operations in the Middle East, the Mediterranean and North Africa.

After working for Colonel Thornhill between 1940 and 1941, Christopher Sykes spent a year in Persia before returning to SOE Cairo. He wrote two novels about GHQ and SOE Cairo and, according to at least one witness, they are disturbingly accurate. 'Nobody who didn't experience it can possibly imagine the atmosphere of jealousy, suspicion, and intrigue which embittered the relations between the various secret and semi-secret departments during that summer of 1941, or for that matter the next two years,' wrote Bickham Sweet-Escott. 'Those who have read Christopher Sykes's two brilliant novels may find it hard to believe that he does not exaggerate. But I can assure them that . . . his account of the way people behaved is severely objective.'[1]

High Minded Murder was set in 1941, and it seems quite extraordinary that the book was published only three years later, when the war was still in progress. Quite apart from his criticisms of GHQ, he mentions three people who were there at the time without bothering to conceal their names. One was Momo Marriott; and, though it was hardly a breach of security to mention her as a great Cairo hostess, her name gave weight to what followed: 'That the contents of "Most Secret" files were so often discussed with Mrs Marriott did not worry us unduly, for few women are more discreet; but that her guests would not speak of these things in such loud boastful voices was our constant and unanswered prayer.'[2] Other real names that crop up include those of Brigadier Shearer, and Adrian Bishop who worked for SOE in Persia. The villain of the novel, a character called Major Anstey, is based on Major John Metherell: a tall man with a moustache and monocle, who had been

Thornhill's staff officer. Sykes had developed a hatred for this man which amounted to an obsession, and described him as the most evil creature he had ever met. He wrote a song about Metherell's rampant ambition called 'Promotion: A Ballad of World War II'; and, in a story Sykes wrote and illustrated for his four-year-old son Mark, Metherell again appears as the wicked Prince of the Atlantic Ocean.[3]

Both *High Minded Murder* and *A Song of a Shirt*, published in 1953, describe a world of frigidly polite committees, split into power-hungry factions representing the interests of rival departments. Withholding vital information from a committee was a common ploy in the quest for power, as was what Basil Davidson dubbed 'the Rule of Three'.[4] Although there was nothing in King's Regulations to support the idea, the custom had developed that an officer with three captains working for him should be a major; an officer with three majors, a colonel; three colonels should be commanded by a brigadier, and so on – though the rule became harder to apply at the top end of the scale. But even more disturbing than the mechanics of power was the effect of petty-minded bureaucracy.

'Here was the civilised world rent by the most terrible of all its conflicts,' wrote Sykes. 'Here we were close to the great events, in daily communication with men whose names will be remembered in history . . . and yet we never seemed to discuss anything but precedence, procedure, and trifling matters of organisation.'[5]

The atmosphere became even worse in 1943, when GHQ was no longer as important nor exciting as it had been the year before. For a regular officer, one of the benefits of a long war is that it brings quick promotion, and GHQ was now full of officers with war-inflated ranks and salaries, and not enough to do. Not unnaturally, they tried to hold on to their jobs and not fall back in the hierarchy; a struggle which became increasingly competitive and acrimonious, as the fighting moved further and further from GHQ.

Not far from GHQ was the headquarters of SOE Cairo, in a block of flats called Rustum Buildings. Politically it took its directives from London, while GHQ exercised operational control through the Special Operations Committee. 'The atmosphere was rarely agreeable,' wrote Bickham Sweet-Escott, 'and the Force

133* representatives often felt and were treated more like prisoners in the dock than members of a committee.' Despite the fact that the activities of SOE were so secret, there never seemed to be fewer than twenty people present, 'all smart with the smartness only wartime Cairo knew'.[6] Sweet-Escott wrote that he never forgot the look of horror on their faces, when he asked Colonel Tom Barnes to come in with the latest news from Greece. Barnes had just returned from the mountains of Epirus: his battledress was filthy, and he sported a huge black beard. The incident was, in its way, indicative of the way things were going: GHQ was cooling down, turning in on itself, while SOE was generating activity.

Despite the thirty-year rule, very few documents concerning SOE have been released. As for the files of SOE Cairo, it is doubtful if any of real interest remain at all. The Flap of July 1942 saw the burning of a great number of records, and a further burning of SOE Cairo's files was authorised and carried out in 1945. This lack of documentary evidence keeps both scholars and those involved at the time arguing amongst themselves. Within the scope of this book, there is only space to raise a few questions, and describe some of the more controversial moments in what every Cairene taxi-driver knew as 'Secret Building'.

In the summer of 1942, Lord Glenconner took over both branches (operations and propaganda) of SOE Cairo. Glenconner was also in charge of the Arab Bureau, and the wide range of his duties meant that he was not a familiar figure to his subordinates in Rustum Buildings, who referred to him simply as 'God'. He seemed to operate in high circles; and those to whom he had delegated authority were expected to get on with their work without constantly referring to him, a policy that suited Brigadier C. M. Keble very well.

Keble came from GHQ, where he had been head of the intelligence section monitoring supplies to Rommel. He was made Director of SOE's Military Operations after Alamein, and has been

---

* One of the ways SOE protected its secrecy was to hide behind a barrage of names: MOI (SP), MO4, 'the firm', and towards the end of the war, Force 133. The organisation is referred to as SOE Cairo or SOE London throughout, to avoid confusion.

described as 'the last man to hold this position who knew all that was going on all the time'.[7] Whatever the criticisms against him – and there were many – no one could deny that 'Bolo' Keble was an energetic and effective officer, with a remarkable head for detail. His stout red figure, sweating profusely and dressed in no more than shorts and a vest, stamped about Rustum Buildings from morning till night. The aggressive, bullying tone he adopted with his subordinates did not make him popular, but Keble did not care. He was an empire-builder, and at last he had a job which gave full scope to his talents and ambitions.[8]

A few months before Keble's appointment, the Chiefs of Staff in London had decided that SOE missions should be sent into Yugoslavia to find out more about the Partisan resistance. The official royalist resistance, backed by the Yugoslav Government in exile and by Britain, was led by Colonel Draja Mihailovic and concentrated in Serbia. However, reports were coming through that groups of guerillas independent of Mihailovic were operating in Slovenia and Croatia.

In order to contact them SOE turned to Canada, where many Croats had emigrated in the 1930s. The Croats whose help they enlisted were all Communists, which made negotiations extremely delicate as they had to be undertaken without the official knowledge of the King or the Yugoslav Government in exile, who were anti-Communist and pro-Serbian. In August, the Canadian Croats began their long sea journey from Montreal to Suez, via the Cape.

Victory at Alamein in October was followed by one of the most successful of SOE's operations, the destruction of the Gorgopotamos viaduct on 25 November which put the Athens–Salonika railway out of action for thirty-nine days. This severely disrupted Rommel's supplies to North Africa, and encouraged expectations of a dramatic rise in guerilla activities in the Balkans.

By virtue of his previous job, Keble's name was still on the circulation list for certain highly classified information. Soon after his appointment, he became intrigued by a series of German intercepts which referred to fighting with the Partisans. Two of Keble's team were now put to work on the intercepts. The first was Basil Davidson, an adventurous extrovert with a flamboyant style, who

had been working as a journalist on the *Star* when recruited by
SOE. After a mission to Hungary from which he escaped ahead of
the advancing Germans, he became head of the Yugoslav Section of
SOE. The second was Captain F. W. D. (later Sir William) Deakin,
an academic who before the war had taught history at Wadham
College, Oxford. He had also been Churchill's research assistant on
his biography of the first Duke of Marlborough.

The purpose of Davidson's and Deakin's study on the intercepts,
which began shortly after the latter's arrival in late 1942, was to plot
safe places in Yugoslavia to drop new missions, by using Axis information to establish how their forces in Yugoslavia were deployed.
What it revealed was that nine divisions were in the areas controlled
by Mihailovic, while thirty divisions – just over half a million men
– were dotted over the rest of the country. Clearly the bulk of Axis
forces were being held down by other resistance organisations.

When Churchill came through Cairo on his way back from
Casablanca, he lunched with Deakin on 28 January. The Prime
Minister asked what he was up to, and the answer intrigued him.
He questioned Deakin in detail, and the result was that Brigadier
Keble was summoned for an interview that evening. Keble arrived
with a paper, addressed to the Service Chiefs with a copy to Richard
Casey, the Minister of State.[9] The main intention of this report was
to get SOE more aircraft, for unless the organisation could keep pace
with developments its work in the Balkans would be useless. The
paper summarised what had been deduced from the intercepts, and
suggested that aid should be sent to both Mihailovic's Cetnicks *and*
the Partisans. It was the first document to do so; and it argued that,
if Great Britain did not support the Partisans, sooner or later the
Americans or the Russians would. Churchill asked for a copy, and
took it back with him to London.

From then on, Deakin's and Davidson's work on the intercepts
changed. Instead of marking places free of Germans, they began to
chart the positions and activities of the Slovene and Croat guerillas.

SOE London strongly resisted the idea of a change in policy. Lord
Selborne, who had taken over from Hugh Dalton as Minister for
Economic Warfare and was now the minister responsible for SOE,
was convinced that Mihailovic should be backed to the exclusion

of every other group. He disapproved of any alliance with the Communists, even though not all the Croat and Slovene guerillas were. The Chiefs of Staff were also against the idea, since there were not enough planes to supply both Cetniks and Partisans – but Churchill was determined that SOE should have them, and in due course ten Halifaxes joined the organisation's overworked Liberators.

The Canadian Croats reached Cairo in February under the strictest secrecy, and were taken to a villa near the Mena House Hotel. The group of around a dozen men were naturally impatient to begin dropping into Yugoslavia, but were obliged to remain in the villa for nearly a month. They were briefed by Davidson, Deakin, and James Klugmann.

At Cambridge, where he got a Double First in Modern Languages, Klugmann was part of that group of ardent young Communists which later achieved notoriety through Guy Burgess and Donald Maclean. From 1935 to 1939, he was Secretary of the World Student Association against War and Fascism. In this capacity Klugmann travelled to the Middle East, the Balkans, and China, where he met Mao Tse-tung.

After his conscription into the Royal Army Service Corps (Klugmann refused to violate Stalin's non-aggression pact with Hitler by volunteering) he was transferred to the Intelligence Corps. In Cairo, he joined SOE as a corporal clerk, and one day happened to bring a cup of tea to Lieutenant-Colonel Terence (later Sir Terence) Airey. Airey had come to SOE in 1941, as part of the first influx of officers from GHQ. He and the Corporal had been at school together, and Airey remembered him as an exceptionally brilliant student. He thought it absurd that Klugmann's talents should be held back by his lowly rank, and sent to London for security clearance before promoting him. The security files had been sent to Wormwood Scrubs Prison for safe-keeping at the start of the war, but many were destroyed when the place was bombed in the Blitz. A message came back saying that there was nothing on Klugmann, and he was duly promoted to captain.

Had the security checks been more thorough, it is very unlikely that Klugmann would have been employed in a secret and politically sensitive organisation. The World Student Association was well-known for its Communist ideals, even if it wisely avoided admitting this in public. However, Klugmann worked hard and conscientiously. His knowledge of the Balkan anti-fascist groups he had met in the thirties, and how Communist cells were set up, gave his work – and especially his briefings to Balkan agents – a dimension that others lacked. By the summer of 1943 he had been appointed Intelligence Officer.

There are those, including the American historian David Martin, author of a book defending Mihailovic,[10] who believe that the presence of Klugmann in SOE Cairo automatically points to Communist infiltration. He was a committed Communist, ergo the instrument of the NKVD. From August 1943 there was a Russian Legation in Cairo, so it would have been possible for him to make contact; but until the files of the NKVD are opened for public inspection, this cannot be proved one way or the other. Unlike those who are known to have worked for the NKVD, Klugmann never hid behind a smoke-screen of right-wing credentials; but the supporters of the SOE Cairo infiltration theory believe that any intelligence about Mihailovic's anti-German activities was being deliberately suppressed by Klugmann in Cairo, and that this was what led to the British government's decision to abandon the Cetniks in favour of the Communists.

The first group of Canadian Croats was parachuted into Yugoslavia on the night of 20–21 April. Their operation was purely technical: to identify resistance groups in key areas of Croatia, to which British missions would be sent as soon as possible. As luck would have it, they landed almost on top of Tito's headquarters.

Tito had led the Communist resistance since the German invasion of Russia in June 1941, when the Comintern told all loyal party members to fight the Germans day and night, whatever the cost, to take the pressure off Russia. At first, Mihailovic's Cetniks and Tito's Partisans had formed an uneasy alliance, in the face of the first ferocious attempt by the Germans to crush the resistance; but this partnership had disintegrated and, from 1942 onwards, a state of civil war existed between them. Both sides knew that, sooner or later, the Germans would go. The real battle, for a post-war Yugoslavia, was between the Cetniks and the Partisans.

As far as the Second World War was concerned, the difference between them was that Tito was concentrating his efforts on the Germans, and his Communist followers had little to lose. For Mihailovic, it was more difficult: any action against the Germans unleashed savage reprisals on the Serbian peasants, whose property and way of life he was pledged to protect.

Brigadier Keble (he was promoted soon after his appointment as Director of Military Operations) covered two areas within SOE Cairo. The first was the Arab world and Persia, in which British stay-behind missions were organised by Patrick Domvile – one of the few Arabists who could also sing in Arabic. The second was the Balkans. Military missions to Greece, Albania and Yugoslavia were administered by the appropriate country section, as were projected missions to Bulgaria, Hungary and Rumania.

The country sections were headed by Colonel Guy Tamplin, who in pre-war life had been a banker in Poland, Esthonia and Latvia. He knew these countries well and had a Latvian wife – so the joke was that he had been sent out by some ignorant official in London, who did not know the difference between the Baltic and the Balkans. Tamplin failed to survive the pressures of his job. In October 1943 he was found slumped over his desk one morning, having suffered a massive heart-attack, although some believed the cause of death was more sinister. All that day, Keble was pestered by anonymous internal telephone calls of sardonic congratulation: for it was well-known that he had been speculating on the efficacy of a certain poison, designed for use in enemy-occupied territory.[11]

Keble and Tamplin had assembled a remarkable staff. As well as Davidson and Deakin there was the historian Hugh Seton-Watson, who specialised in Balkan languages, and Mrs Hasluck, who had devoted her life to studying the language and customs of Albania. Captain Wigginton organised the air sorties, which – as SOE's commitments spread – required not only administrative skill but immense tact. He had started his career on the Nottinghamshire tramways, and later co-ordinated SOE's air sorties over the whole of Europe. But, despite Tamplin's non-stop work and the tireless dedication of his staff, SOE was growing too fast. People came and went at a moment's notice, either to take up another appointment or to parachute into the Balkans. Whoever succeeded was hardly briefed, and often had little more than a pat on the back and an assurance that he'd soon get the hang of it. Important signals came pouring in every day and not all of them were seen by the right people, while a huge backlog of uncoded telegrams built up due to a chronic shortage of cypherenes.

Officially, SOE was still secret; but the size and scale of its operations (Keble was to have around eighty separate missions in the Balkans by October) meant that its character was changing from that of a covert organisation to an increasingly overt one. In spring 1943, Keble's demands for more facilities, more men and officers, and more administrative staff became so clamorous that GHQ started to complain. At the same time, Keble had got on the wrong side of Lord Selborne, over the case of Julian Amery.

Julian Amery had worked as press attaché in the British Embassy Belgrade before the war, and was recruited into 'D' section – a secret department of the War Office that became absorbed into SOE in 1940. His support for those Yugoslav politicians in favour of a coup d'état, at a time when the British were officially backing the Regent Prince Paul, was seen as insubordination by the Foreign Office – though he had been proved right by events. Since June 1941 Amery had worked on Balkan affairs in SOE, concentrating on Yugoslavia. He had no wish to spend the war chained to a desk, and wanted to put his experience and knowledge to practical use in the field.

His keenness to be sent on a mission to Yugoslavia had the full approval of Lord Selborne; and when in March 1943 Colonel S. W. 'Bill' Bailey asked for Julian Amery to join him at Mihailovic's headquarters, Selborne exerted some pressure on SOE Cairo on Amery's behalf. Brigadier Keble, who had a heavy chip on his shoulder, reacted strongly. He sent a brutal telegram to London saying there was every objection, on security grounds, to parachuting the brother of a notorious traitor into enemy-occupied territory.*[12]

---

* Julian Amery's hopeless brother John had made several broadcasts from Berlin in 1942, and continued his propaganda work for the Germans till the end of the war. He pleaded guilty to all charges of treason at his trial, and was hanged in November 1945.

Selborne was outraged by this response. From then on, he watched for the opportunity to dismiss Keble but was prevented, for the time being, by the impressive results of the Brigadier's department.

No one in SOE had expected contact with the Yugoslav Partisans to be made so swiftly. There was a flurry of excitement in Cairo when the Canadian Croats signalled that Tito would be willing to accept a British mission. William Deakin was chosen to command one of two joint missions to the Partisans, which were kept secret by SOE Cairo until despatch.

As well as discussing targets and supplies with the Partisans and finding out as much as he could, Deakin was to ask Tito whether he would be willing to accept a larger and more important British mission, to be headed by a senior British officer. It was Keble's plan to have an officer of brigadier's rank or above commanding all his main missions in occupied Europe.[13] The prevailing myth was that all resistance groups would be happy to be led by a British officer, and the more senior he was, the better he could lead them. But Basil Davidson believes that Keble was encouraging promotions within his department of SOE, according to the 'rule of three' already described, to increase the power and importance of his empire.

On 31 May, Deakin signalled from Yugoslavia that Tito was willing to accept a larger and more important British mission. The news reached London four days later, and Churchill now decided to intervene personally in the affairs of SOE. Despite cries of protest from Eden and Lord Selborne, he chose Captain Fitzroy Maclean to be his own representative to the Partisans.

Maclean spoke Russian and had close experience of Communism, having been Second Secretary in the Moscow Embassy. When war broke out, Maclean was determined to fight – but knew that the Foreign Office never released their men for active service. The only acceptable reason for a diplomat's resignation was if he wanted to stand for Parliament: so that is what Maclean did. He became Member of Parliament for Lancaster; and with the blessings of his constituents he enlisted, came to the Middle East, and joined the SAS. He had excellent references, of the sort Churchill valued: from Randolph Churchill, Rex Leeper and Sir Orme Sargent, and – as luck would have it – he was immediately available.

In early June an operation involving a detachment of the 1st SAS had been cancelled, leaving its commander, Captain Maclean, at a loose end. He had suggested to Rex Leeper, Ambassador to the Greek Government in exile since March, that he was keen to parachute into Greece if he could be of use there. This resulted in a prompt summons to England, where he was told he would be parachuting into Yugoslavia, to head a mission to the Partisans.

Maclean was briefed by the Prime Minister at Chequers, and told to return to Egypt with the rank of Brigadier; his own account of what happened next was not revealed until thirty years later.[14] Maclean was told by SOE that there were no planes to Cairo due to bad weather. After several days he found this to be untrue. Then, after an extraordinary interview with Lord Selborne, who tried to make him swear an oath of loyalty to SOE and intimated that such loyalty might earn him a DSO, Maclean was again summoned by the Prime Minister. In Downing Street, Churchill showed him a message he had received from the C-in-C Middle East. In it General Wilson, a personal friend of Maclean's, expressed his opinion that Maclean was totally unsuitable for the job. The Prime Minister showed him his reply: 'Do as you're told.'

In Cairo, General Wilson was completely baffled by Churchill's rebuke – which, as far as he knew, he had done nothing to provoke. It was not until Maclean arrived, and told Wilson about the first message, that the C-in-C realised that someone had sent it in his name and without his knowledge. Maclean was then told to have himself gazetted Brigadier; and, having put up three pips and a crown on his tunic, he went to visit Brigadier Keble.

The newly appointed Brigadier had all the confidence which goes with good looks, a swashbuckling spirit, and a commission from the Prime Minister himself. He had heard some very strange things about SOE from his conversations with Rex Leeper, but they hardly prepared him for his experiences at Rustum Buildings.

Maclean was shown into an office, where Keble was sitting back in shorts, vest and socks, with his feet on the desk. Keble started the conversation by saying, 'How dare you come in here dressed like that?' Maclean replied that he was acting on the orders of the Commander-in-Chief. Why had he gone to see the

Commander-in-Chief? Because, answered Maclean, he had been asked to. Keble said that, if the Commander-in-Chief sent for him again, he was not to go. Maclean replied that, as a serving soldier, he certainly would go. It was not a promising start, and for Brigadier Keble Maclean's appointment was a disaster. He had no authority over this young officer, who as Churchill's representative would take over the direction of his most important mission. It was the first step to SOE becoming nothing more than a military department store supplying air sorties and wireless operators, with Keble its glorified quartermaster.

He refused Maclean any access to SOE files, and told him that no matter what Churchill or General Wilson might say, Keble would ensure he never got there. The indignant Maclean returned to the office of General Wilson, to ask him to signal the Prime Minister that he would not take the job if it involved SOE. By that time, the Commander-in-Chief had been joined by Paul Vellacott, Director of Political Warfare in the Middle East – part of whose job was to spread rumours around Cairo in the Allied cause. Someone in SOE Cairo had asked Vellacott to put it about that Maclean was an active homosexual and drunkard, who had shown consistent cowardice and unreliability throughout his time with the SAS. Unable to believe his ears, Vellacott had sought confirmation from Wilson. The ridiculous rumour got no further, but Wilson was not about to let the matter drop. At an urgent meeting summoned by the C-in-C and attended by the Minister of State, Maclean, and Lord Glenconner of SOE, General Wilson told the latter that his organisation was 'rotten to the core', and he subsequently wrote a very unfavourable report to London on SOE.

Maclean was made directly responsible to the Commander-in-Chief, but he would still have to depend on SOE to get him to Yugoslavia. Having failed to block his mission, SOE reluctantly agreed to show Maclean a selection of their files on Yugoslavia – though there was nothing very up to date, since there was a six-week time-lag on most coded signals. Of more interest was a series of memoranda and telegrams concerning Maclean's appointment. These stressed the importance of frustrating the sinister activities of an organisation called 'PX', with whom Maclean was surprised to learn he had connections. He asked his temporary assistant what 'PX' stood for: the answer was the Foreign Office.

At the same time as Fitzroy Maclean was on a collision course with Brigadier Keble, another crisis was developing – which, if the Foreign Office had had its way, would have broken SOE. The subject of the quarrel was Greece.

The Foreign Office supported the Greek King and his Government in exile. It was very disturbed to discover that not only the Nationalist and Republican EDES forces had been involved in SOE's operations in Greece, but also the Communist ELAS. (EAM was the political branch, and ELAS the military, of an organisation founded and controlled by the KKE, the Greek Communist Party.) This was an illogical attitude, considering the British government's increasing warmth towards the Communists in Yugoslavia – but there were differences.

Though the senior diplomats of the Foreign Office were uneasy about Tito's politics, he was built in a herioc mould they could admire. It was understandable that men should follow such a leader even if he was a Communist, and his independent mind contrasted sharply with the conformist mentality of Stalin's apparatchiks. In Greece, however, the power of the Communist EAM/ELAS was wielded by a series of faceless committees and tribunals, for which the British tended to have a profound mistrust.

SOE had deliberately kept the Foreign Office and the Greek government in the dark about their collaboration with EAM/ELAS in the field, both in Cairo and London. George Taylor described the meetings of the Anglo-Greek Committee as a farce, since 'in order not to provoke tremendous trouble from the Greek government, the Committee only discussed plans in Greece that were acceptable to the Greek government . . . the real operations of SOE were not mentioned at all.'[15]

SOE's justification for pursuing a policy so different from that of the Foreign Office, or the Greek Government in exile, rested on Churchill's directive of 18 March. The Prime Minister stressed the operational importance of subversive activities in Greece, and said that though SOE should always lean towards groups that favour the

Greek King and his ministers, 'there can be no question of SOE refusing to have dealings with a given group merely on the grounds that the political sentiments of the group are opposed to King and government . . .'[16]

In July 1943, the chief British Liaison Officer (BLO) in Greece, Brigadier Edmund Myers, requested permission to come to Cairo with his political assistant, Major David Wallace, and a member of each of the three main resistance parties – EAM, EDES, and EKKA. The groups had been persuaded to work together, when they thought the liberation of Greece was imminent; but the British strategy of striking up through Italy instead of the Balkans demanded that their resistance energies be cooled down, and put on ice – for a period that might last several months if not more. Myers warned that this would almost certainly lead to civil war, since the Communists were determined to consolidate their control over the country, and had already set up an embryo free state in the mountains. The only way to avert bloodshed was to establish stronger common ground between the resistance groups, and the Greek Government in exile.

Permission was granted by SOE Cairo, and the delegation was to travel to Egypt by plane. At the last moment, when the party was about to take off, EAM insisted on sending another three delegates. Myers had no choice but to accept, and signalled the news to Cairo – though he could not wait for a reply. The delegation of six, plus Myers and Wallace, reached Cairo on 10 August.

Although those concerned had been warned of the arrival of the andarte (resistance fighter) delegation in Cairo, they were quite unprepared for its size and importance. Leeper 'had been led to expect a small group of two or three individuals coming for a friendly chat and a pat on the back. Instead there arrived six men representing three organisations which were coming to regard themselves as the future rulers of Greece.'[17]

The andarte delegation was united on one point – that King George II should not return to Greece without a plebiscite. The King, who had already declared that he would hold elections within six months of returning to Greece, refused to alter his position. He was supported by Roosevelt and Churchill; but the Greek Government in exile, which had been painstakingly put together on a series of compromises, was nearly split on the issue. The andarte delegation went back to Greece empty-handed in mid-September, and within a month of their return civil war had broken out in Greece.

In so far as SOE had been so secretive about its dealings with the Greek Communists, and had flown the andartes out of Greece to drop their political bomb-shell in Cairo, it was bound to be blamed. But Bickham Sweet-Escott points out that it was also a scapegoat for the blinkered attitude of higher authorities:

'The Embassy were shocked to find that guerilla fighters should have any political views to which any importance was attached. The military were shocked to find that the guerilla activity which had been asked for by the Chiefs of Staff and Allied Forces Headquarters could lead to political demands. Neither seemed to have any alternative but to put the blame on SOE for creating such a situation.'[18]

In the purge that followed, Lord Glenconner was ordered back to London, and SOE Cairo was put under General W. A. M. Stawell – who had held several high appointments in the War Office and GHQ, but had no experience of secret organisations. A few weeks later Brigadier Keble, his empire now well out of his hands, was returned to 'routine duties'.

Fitzroy Maclean was parachuted to the Partisans on 17 September, the same day the andarte delegation went back to Greece. In conversations with Tito and Bill Deakin, as well as Partisan operators in the field, he learnt a great deal about the organisation and activities of the Partisans. He was also presented with evidence concerning Cetnik collaboration not only with the Italians, but the Germans as well.

He left Yugoslavia with 'a detailed report on the military and political situation as seen from Jajce, and a list of requirements for military aid'. Back in Cairo on 25 November, he discussed his report over dinner at the Muhammad Ali Club with Sir Alexander Cadogan. He then ran through it again with Anthony Eden the following day. The report stressed that Tito's National Liberation Army must be officially recognised as an Allied Force, and that its leader would be the power in post-war Yugoslavia. It suggested sending a great deal more aid to the Partisans, and that 'support for Mihailovic should be discontinued'.

In the course of the Teheran Conference, which opened on 28 November, the Big Three authorised a military directive to say that Tito should be supported to the greatest possible extent. Mihailovic was not mentioned, and he received no more British supplies from then on; while in the last three months of 1943, the Partisans received over 2,000 tons of supplies.[19]

While the conference was in progress, Fitzroy Maclean had gone back to Yugoslavia. A few days later he returned with Bill Deakin, and a delegation of three Partisan leaders. The Prime Minister flew back from Teheran via Cairo, where on the morning of 8 December he saw Maclean, Deakin (now promoted to Major), and Ralph (later Sir Ralph) Stevenson – who had recently been appointed Ambassador to the Yugoslavian Government in exile. Churchill received them in bed, in the house of the Minister of State. Maclean summarised his conclusions that Mihailovic's contribution to anti-Axis operations in Yugoslavia was negligible, and that any operations undertaken were largely the work of British officers attached to the Cetniks. He also emphasised his conviction that Tito would be the decisive political factor in post-war Yugoslavia, and that his régime would be Communist.

'The Prime Minister's reply resolved my doubts,' wrote Maclean in *Eastern Approaches*.

'"Do you intend," he asked, "to make Jugoslavia your home after the war?"

'"No, sir," I replied.

'"Neither do I," he said. "And, that being so, the less you and I worry about the form of Government they set up, the better."'[20]

The most important decision taken at Teheran was to set the next Allied offensive in northern France, rather than the eastern Mediterranean as Churchill would have preferred. From then on, Mihailovic was lost. There was no hope of his survival in an Eastern Europe that was to be 'liberated' – and therefore dominated – by Soviet Russia. Yet, in order to clarify things in his own mind, the Prime Minister questioned Bill Deakin for many hours over the next two days. He also gave Deakin the heavy task of telling young King Peter that the Allies would henceforward be backing Tito.

Fitzroy Maclean was told that his mission to the Partisans would be expanded, and he returned to Peter Stirling's flat to look for more recruits. The *Daily Express* had dubbed Maclean 'The Kilted Pimpernel', about which he was teased mercilessly – but Mo the sufragi was kinder. 'Bugadier fine fellow,' he said, 'one day he catchit scissors' – referring to the crossed sabre and baton of a major-general. There was no shortage of volunteers for the Yugoslav mission, and one of the four officers chosen was Randolph Churchill. Maclean thought Randolph's rumbustious approach to life would endear him to the Yugoslavs, and he certainly had the courage and endurance for life on operations. However, he was not a natural diplomat.

Before being sent into Yugoslavia, Randolph had to be vetted by Major Vlatko Velebit – Tito's liaison officer to the British mission, who had flown to Cairo with Deakin and Maclean as a member of the Partisan delegation. A lunch was arranged for Randolph and Velebit to meet, which included Captain David Smiley and Major Billy McLean, who had set up SOE's first mission to Albania.

McLean and Smiley were then on leave, and had spent the morning buying presents at Ahmed Soliman's Palace of Perfumes in the bazaar. They had sampled so many different scents on their arms that they appeared for lunch smelling 'like a couple of tarts', and Major Velebit was visibly taken aback. David Smiley hoped that Randolph's arrival would correct the unfavourable impression he and McLean had made; but Randolph's first words were, 'Well, Major Velebit, it seems your Cetniks are doing some splendid work.'

Considering that Randolph Churchill's job was to be Public Relations Officer between Tito and the Allied Forces, it was hardly a promising start – but he took part in two missions to Yugoslavia. The first was in Bosnia, where Randolph stayed until the Germans overran Tito's headquarters in May. The Partisans had to fight their way out, and were impressed by his courage in the retreat. Tito and his staff escaped to Bari, and were back in Yugoslavia shortly after.

During his time in Bosnia, Randolph Churchill had perceived the need for a Catholic BLO who would make discreet contacts with the large Catholic community. Britain's long-term interests in Yugoslavia would, he felt, be best served by nurturing those elements most likely to resist absorption into Communism.

Randolph decided that Evelyn Waugh was the man for the job: for he was not only a Catholic, but a stimulating companion. Their mission in Croatia was, however, a dismal disappointment. From September to December 1944 they lived in a farmhouse outside the village of Topusko, and the enforced tedium of their existence made both men more irritable and intolerant than usual. Both Waugh and Randolph abhorred Communism and made no effort to hide their feelings from the Partisans, while Waugh's attempts to forge links with the local Catholics were half-hearted to say the least. The most significant work that Waugh did in Topusko took up one week in late November, when he corrected the proofs of *Brideshead Revisited*. Otherwise there was little to do but quarrel with Randolph, who wallowed in slivovitz and self-pity.

WINTER 1943

Statesmen and Buccaneers

When Stalin agreed to a conference in Teheran of the Big Three, Churchill suggested to Roosevelt a preliminary meeting in Cairo; but the American President did not want to go to Teheran arm in arm with the British Prime Minister; and so, while agreeing to the idea, Roosevelt also invited the Chinese nationalist leader Chiang Kai-shek. The first plenary session of 23 November was dedicated to the Far East, with Chiang Kai-shek stressing the importance of an amphibious operation across the Bay of Bengal. On the following day, Churchill and Roosevelt discussed the conflicting claims of the Mediterranean and cross-Channel theatres, and heard from the Commanders-in-Chief over the next two days that the Mediterranean should be secured before attempting an invasion of France. On 27 November, Churchill flew to Teheran.

Although the preparations for the conference had provoked a great deal of excitement and curiosity, hardly anyone in Cairo knew what was being discussed. On 14 November, the *Egyptian Gazette* announced that Mena House was to be taken over for some important talks, and the rumours began. An American in Aleppo was heard to say that no plane was allowed within ten miles of Mena House on pain of being shot down, and someone else heard that the King David Hotel in Jerusalem had been requisitioned as well.

As soon as word got out that all villas in the area were to be requisitioned for the accommodation of some very important people and their retinues, the owners raised the rents for the occasion. One tenant refused to move out of his villa, which was wanted by the Americans, and referred them to his landlord. It turned out that the man owed six months' back rent – which the Americans were forced to pay, just to evict him. An American general selected the ideal camp site for the men detailed to guard the conference area. He and two colonels drew up a plan of how it was to be laid out, and organised a team of workers to prepare the ground and to pitch sleeping and mess tents. But the site belonged to a farmer, who chose that night to irrigate his land so that when the workforce arrived next morning, the place was flooded.

The conference was lavishly equipped. In Mena House, a switchboard with 27 extensions, three of them 'secrophoned', was installed with three operators, and backed up by a three-man, twenty-four-hour despatch service. Special clerks were detailed to take waste paper to special incinerators, and the garden was guarded by four sappers. The native staff in the surrounding villas were replaced by military personnel, and one side of every relevant flight of steps was equipped with a ramp for the President's wheel-chair. Since malaria was now widespread in Upper Egypt and the numbers of mosquitoes in Cairo had increased, three men of No. 3 Malaria Field Laboratory were kept busy spraying every corner with Flit, seeing every door and window was covered with netting and keeping a firm eye on the kitchens. Twenty-one field tented houses and four Indian-type mess tents were erected for the staff, who also had their own cook-house and a Naafi store. There was in addition a specially-constructed clothes room, fitted with brushes and an electric iron as well as washing and starching facilities.[1]

'Everything about this whole business was very secret except that nearly everybody knew about it,' said Chester Morrison of the *Chicago Sun*. He was intensely frustrated by all the secrecy and censorship, which provoked so much rumour and speculation it seemed counter-productive. Soon it was well-known that Churchill, Roosevelt and Chiang Kai-shek were in Egypt; and the hundred-odd correspondents in the city all flocked around a small, bald-headed bureaucrat, who seemed to have been told to feed the journalists copy without telling them anything of any importance. He would relate '. . . how General Chiang went to visit Mr Roosevelt, and how Mr Churchill gave a tea and who all came to it. He used to talk about how Mr Churchill wore a white linen suit on Tuesday and black socks with white shoes on Wednesday; how Mme Chiang wore something very picturesque only he couldn't describe it because he didn't know much about Chinese costumes.'[2]

These quotations come from a broadcast by Chester Morrison. Although passed by the censor and transmitted after the conference was over, it caused a great deal of embarrassment to the Embassy. First of all, the broadcast contained an unintentional leak of classified information which caused a flurry of indignation from the security services. But Morrison's talk was also a sardonic comment on the absurdity of trying to cover such an event, when all that could be reported was trivia. He criticised not only the publicity machine but also the journalists: on the afternoon of the 23rd Churchill had taken Roosevelt to see the Pyramids, accompanied by an Egyptian drago-man. The following day, the dragoman was able to sell his exclusive story of the trip to three or four different papers, and probably made more money in that afternoon than he did in a year. As far as the Embassy was concerned, the only good thing to come out of the broadcast was the fury it provoked in A. P. Ryan of the Ministry of Information: this official had made himself very unpopular by sweeping in a few days before the conference started, and taking control of all publicity arrangements.

So much secrecy, publicity and rumour did, however, manage to mislead the Germans, who made a great show of what they had found out. On the last two nights of November they broadcast that Roosevelt, Churchill and Stalin had all met 'in a tent in the shadow of the Pyramids', and that they were all flying on to Teheran together.[3]

On 15 November, while preparations for the Cairo conference were getting under way, King Farouk was racing towards Ismailia with his foot, as usual, hard down on the accelerator. As he was overtaking a British Army truck he saw another car approaching him at speed. Farouk winged the truck as he pulled in sharply ahead of it; the impact made him lose control, and he smashed into the trees at the edge of the road. He was rushed to the British military hospital at Qassassin, where he was found to have two fractured ribs and a crack in the pubic bone of the pelvis.

After a few days, the King's physicians suggested that His Majesty might be more comfortable in his palace than in an iron bed in the field hospital, but Farouk refused to be moved and insisted on being treated just like any other patient – though there were noticeable differences. A telephone was installed, and a truck brought his food from the royal kitchens every day. It was a measure of the King's popularity that poor peasants flocked to the hospital to wish him well, and offer him small gifts of eggs or cakes as well as their prayers for his recovery. Even after three weeks, the King was enjoying himself too much to want to move back to Cairo. He was far from the cares of state, unhampered by protocol, surrounded by nurses who blushed and scolded when he teased them, and had a constant stream of visitors. But the massage and physiotherapy had done their work and, after much persuasion, the King went home.

In the hot-house atmosphere of the Egyptian court, there was much whispering and consultation about what other damage the King might have suffered when his pubic bone was cracked. Two days after the accident, Prince Muhammad Ali had gleefully told Lord Killearn that the King was in a much worse condition than anyone was prepared to let on.[4] It was rumoured that certain glands were irreparably crushed. Some said that the British had urged the King to undergo surgery, but that the Egyptian physicians had forbidden it saying the risks were too great. Others declared that he had had an operation, but the British surgeon had bungled it, leaving him worse off than before. The only sign that the King's accident had triggered some sort of hormonal imbalance was that his normally heavy body rapidly became obese.

As the weather turned cooler, the days became more pleasant – particularly for Lord Killearn, who had his own shoot at Ekiad in the Delta. During the war, import restrictions had severely curtailed the import of cartridges, with the result that only a handful of the most influential people in Egypt had access to supplies. Killearn bought his from Boudi the gunsmith, and ordered some three thousand at a time for £E2.10 a hundred. Those who were invited to shoot with the Ambassador would then buy their cartridges from him, a ceremony that could be very disconcerting for those who were not good shots. Each gun would be issued with cartridges, and the account was not made up until the end of the afternoon when a long table was set up, behind which sat one of the Embassy staff. Each guest would approach the table accompanied by a bearer carrying the duck and snipe he had shot, return his spare cartridges, and then suffer the humiliation of having his bird–cartridge ratio calculated before being told how much he had to pay.

In Cairo itself, things went on as before, but that sense of excitement and solidarity that the war had brought the Allies was gone. People still called each other by their Christian names with little preamble, and soldiers went to informal parties in no more than shorts and a bush shirt; but there was a jaded feeling in the air, as in a play which is nearing the end of its run and in which the actors are losing interest. In one house to the north of Zamalek, however, the fun had only just begun.

The house belonged to a group of young officers, most of whom had been involved in SOE's military missions to Greece and Albania. One of the exceptions was Captain William Stanley Moss of the Coldstream Guards. He had fought at Alamein and followed the campaign to its conclusion in Tunisia, after which he had been recruited into SOE – though, so far, he had not been sent into the field.

In the autumn of 1943, he met Captain Patrick Leigh Fermor, an SOE officer who had spent the last fifteen months in the mountains of Crete. Leigh Fermor could quote poetry in several different languages, and sing 'It's a Long Way to Tipperary' in French and Arabic. The loyalty and affection he had inspired in the Cretans attested his soldierly virtues; but these were masked by the romantic ebullience, half Byron and half pantomime pirate, which enchanted his friends. He and Billy Moss decided to leave Hangover Hall, one of the dreary hostels provided by SOE Cairo, for a spacious villa Moss had found at the northern end of Gezira. A flight of steps led up to the *piano nobile*; and, as well as several bedrooms, the house boasted a great ballroom with parquet floors. Its new inhabitants called it Tara – the legendary home of the High Kings of Ireland, and (on another continent) of Scarlett O'Hara.

Since they could only use the house when on leave, they asked three women to share it with them; but two dropped out, leaving only Countess Sophie Tarnowska. She was separated from her husband, an officer in the Polish Carpathian Brigade, and had founded the Cairo branch of the Polish Red Cross. She did not want to be the only woman in an all-male household; yet no other female tenant could be found, and Paddy Leigh Fermor and Billy Moss pleaded with her not to let them down. So Sophie moved in, with her few possessions – a bathing costume, an evening gown, a uniform and two pet mongooses. Her reputation was protected by a fictional tenant called Madame Khayatt, who suffered from distressingly poor health.

The household grew. The next to arrive was Arnold Breene, who worked in SOE Headquarters, and he was followed by four more SOE agents: Billy McLean and David Smiley, who had just returned from Albania; Rowland Winn (later Lord St Oswald), who took part in another of SOE's Albanian missions; and Xan Fielding, who had worked with Leigh Fermor in Crete. For one brief period, over the winter of 1943–44, they were all in the house together. 'One must accept the fact that we were all pretty pleased with ourselves in those days,' wrote Billy Moss five years later.[5] They were all under thirty, back from enemy-occupied territory and rejoicing in the fact of being alive. A fortune in back pay sat in their bank accounts, ready to be spent on slaking appetites sharpened by months of hardship, and the glamour of secret operations meant they were greeted as heroes.

Theirs was an enviable position, compared to that of GHQ staff officers. There were those who deserved the name of 'Gabardine Swine', but even those who did not were seen as effete military drones. No matter how hard they worked and worried, no matter what lengths some of them went to to get to the front, there was that inescapable social obligation to sound bashful and describe themselves as members of Groppi's Horse, or the Short Range Shepheard's Group. (On the other hand, those going off on hazardous missions could never quite believe the words 'Wish I was going with you, old boy' from the mouth of the staff officer who accompanied them to the plane.)

The young buccaneers of Tara, who wanted to live like princes for their few weeks' leave, found that back pay never lasts as long as it should. Real whisky and gin had been taken off the list of essential imports from the United Kingdom in January, and the

Naafi ration currently stood at a quarter-bottle a month, which did not go far. Although beer, Cyprus brandy, and the fake Palestinian gins and whiskies ('suitable for cocktails') were relatively cheap, the lavish hospitality of parties at Tara made steep inroads into the communal budget. Their sufragi thought he might relieve the situation by standing at the top of the steps with his tarboosh in his hands, requesting a donation from the departing guests. This embarrassing habit was stopped as soon as Sophie found out about it, but some economies would have to be made. She remembered how, on her father's estates in Poland, plums, apricots or peaches were added to vodka to make the most delicious liqueurs; and the household decided to experiment on the same lines with raw alcohol, available from the local garage, and prunes. The results were very disappointing; perhaps because Tara's occupants – who might, after all, be ordered back to Greece or Albania at any minute – decided they could not wait three weeks for the mixture to mature, and started drinking it after three days.

The intoxicating atmosphere of life at Tara even affected one of Sophie's mongooses, which escaped into the neighbouring garden and savaged Lady Keown-Boyd's parrot. Sir Alexander Keown-Boyd was a person of consequence, being immensely rich and involved with the Middle East Supply Centre – and the incident had repercussions. Brigadier Keble summoned Captain Smiley and Major McLean to his office, where he gave them a furious dressing down and told them to keep the animal under control. Unfortunately, it escaped again and, this time, the parrot did not survive. Lady Keown-Boyd insisted the errant mongoose be shot. McLean told the story at a dinner one night, expressing great indignation at such heartlessness – but the story was not appreciated by his listener, who turned out to be Lady Keown-Boyd herself.

Like Peter Stirling's flat before it, Tara became the most exciting place in the city. Apart from the usual crowd of diplomats, officers, writers, lecturers, war correspondents, and sparkling Coptic and Levantine party-goers, Tara's parties were unpredictable. They could get very wild, as happened when some Polish friends of Sophie's shot out all the light bulbs; or they might be graced by generals, princes, the British Ambassador, or King Farouk who once brought a case of champagne. Over the course of that winter, a piano was borrowed from the Egyptian Officers' Club; a variety of objects from golf balls to sofas were thrown out of the windows; and Tara was alive with the high spirits one might expect to find in an Oxford college at the end of Trinity term.

Yet the house was more than just a good place to give parties. During his time in Crete, Billy Moss wrote that he often thought of those who had come to wish him and Paddy Leigh Fermor good-bye on their last night in Tara: David Smiley, Gertie Wissa, Denise Menasce, Alexis Ladas, Inez Burrows, and Sophie Tarnowska, whom he married in 1945. David Smiley came in with a towel round his waist and a present for them – the *Oxford Book of English Verse* and a one-volume Shakespeare. He said they had been with him in Albania and would surely bring them luck. At four in the morning there were still grouped around a red table, their faces lit by candle-light as they drank and sang and sat with him till it was time to go to the aerodrome. The warmth of such evenings and the dreams of coming back became enormously important; not only to him, but to all those who thought of Tara as home as they sat through anxious, hungry nights hidden in a cave and too cold to sleep.

By the following winter, Sophie and her fellow-tenants had left their now rather battered villa and moved into a flat. It was not quite as glamorous; but the new Tara was distinguished by the same brass plaque that had adorned the old. Above the word TARA written in large italics were inscribed the names of its inhabitants: Princess Dneiper-Petrovsk, Sir Eustace Rapier, the Marquis of Whipstock, the Hon. Rupert Sabretache, Lord Hughe Devildrive, Lord Pintpot, Lord Rakehell, and Mr Jack Jargon.*

A round of charity parties took place in the run-up to Christmas. The King donated £1,000 for the entertainment of the troops, and Lady Killearn's Christmas Stocking Fund was given a good boost

---

* The real names were later given as Countess Sophie Tarnowska; Lieutenant-Colonel Neil McLean, DSO; Colonel David Smiley, LVO, OBE, MC; Major the Hon. Rowland Winn, MC; Major Xan Fielding, DSO; Arnold Breene; Major Patrick Leigh Fermor, DSO; and Captain W. Stanley Moss, MC.)

by Princess Shevekiar's magnificent Christmas Stocking Ball at the Auberge des Pyramides. The Ambassador noted in his diary that the Princess was dressed in black velvet, the better to display one of the most stunning diamond necklaces he had ever seen – made up of very large stones of the highest quality.

The Princess, now in her early seventies, had been the first wife of the late King Fuad, whom she married in 1895 – long before he had any pretensions to the throne. Spoilt and capricious, Shevekiar was as well-born as her husband and considerably richer. Their marriage nearly cost Fuad his life.

Prince Fuad was short, earnest and punctilious, and sported a moustache with waxed ends that stood rigidly to attention either side of his nose. His Italian upbringing had given him a taste for gambling and Italian mistresses, but he had very old-fashioned ideas about the seclusion of Muslim women, and Shevekiar deeply resented being kept in the harem from morning till night. Their only son died at the age of nine months; and, after the birth of her next child, Shevekiar decided she could no longer bear her husband's violent temper and finicky habits, and returned to her family.

Her husband got her back, as he was entitled to do under Muslim law; but Shevekiar had an elder brother, Seifeddin, who swore to deliver her from this tyrant. On 7 May 1898, Seifeddin rushed up the stairs of the Khedival Club, found Fuad in the Silence Room, and shot him several times before anyone could stop him. Fuad was so badly wounded that his doctors decided to operate there and then, on the floor. They took a bullet from his ribs and another from his thigh, but the one lodged in his throat was too near an artery to be removed. From that day until his death, Fuad's speech was occasionally interrupted by what Laurence Grafftey-Smith described as a 'high spasmodic bark',[6] that astonished those who had not been warned about it.

Seifeddin was sentenced to five years' hard labour, after which he was declared insane and sent to an asylum; but his dramatic action did succeed in turning Fuad against his wife, whom he divorced shortly after. Shevekiar had three more husbands in the first decades of the twentieth century before marrying her fifth, Ilhami Hussein Pasha, in 1927. Some said it was she who had corrupted Farouk by indulging his tastes and encouraging him to gamble, because she had a grudge against Fuad and his family. For the same reason she was said to have encouraged the alleged love affair between her son, Wahid Yusri, and Queen Farida. However the King seemed well-disposed towards Princess Shevekiar, and was always seen at her New Year's Eve party – one of the most spectacular events of the social calendar.

To give some idea of the scale of Princess Shevekiar's entertaining, no one at her dinner table was expected to take a slice from a fish or a bird which had already been served to someone else. The footman behind each chair presented each guest with a whole fish or bird, from which to take the choicest cuts. This naturally resulted in a fair amount of food left uneaten; and this was sent to Coptic monasteries and charitable institutions the following day.

On New Year's Eve, Princess Shevekiar's five hundred-odd guests were met on the steps of her pink and grey baroque palace by a double line of beautiful Circassian girls, in traditional embroidered costumes and gauze headdresses, who bowed and murmured words of welcome as guests moved forward. (It was said that the Princess's Circassian girls were to balance the regiment of good-looking footmen, in eighteenth-century livery, kept by her husband.) Inside, the whole garden had been tented over, enclosing the heavy scent of tuberoses. As the great reception rooms filled with Turkish and Egyptian aristocracy, the display of rubies, emeralds and diamonds became ever more dazzling – leaving the European women with their modest strings of pearls looking rather under-dressed. Buffets were piled high with lobsters and quail, and the guests had a choice of three bands in the palace to listen to: tzigane, jazz and classical. As for Shevekiar's party favours, these were more inclined to be Cartier evening bags and gold cigar clippers rather than chocolates or miniature bottles of scent. Lord Killearn noted that the King was smoking a pipe at Shevekiar's New Year's Eve party to welcome 1944, and was behaving very boorishly. When Prince Abdel Moneim (who was briefly to become Regent after Farouk had been deposed in 1952) congratulated the King on such a rapid recovery from his accident, Farouk said that his return to health had disappointed many people on whom he would be revenged. Perhaps his mood was due to the disappointment at the birth of his third daughter, Fadia, on 15 December (evil tongues said it was the child of Wahid Yusri). The King had declared that even though the child was not the long-awaited son, she would be loved just the same.

SPRING 1944

The Greek Mutinies

The health of the fellahin in Upper Egypt had been relatively good until the early years of the century, when British engineering had built the first Aswan Dam. By 1912, the cotton and sugar crops were doubled; but all the mistakes that had been made in Lower Egypt, where perennial irrigation had been introduced almost a century before by Muhammad Ali, were repeated. Canal systems were dug without proper drainage and, since the canal had to be higher than the surrounding land, seepage led to the creation of warm, stagnant pools where disease hatched and spread. Bilharzia and ankylostoma became endemic, as they were in the Delta. Malaria was still virtually unknown; but news of its emergence in the provinces of Qena and Aswan had reached Cairo in January 1943, and by the end of the year it had caused the deaths of 150 people in Luxor.

The British were keen to do something, but it was a politically sensitive area. Any aid would have to be sufficiently low-key so as not to show up the Egyptian government; and yet, as the diplomat Edwin Chapman Andrews pointed out from London, if the British did not do anything about the situation the Americans would. He added gloomily that, even if the malaria relief programme were a joint Anglo-American project, the Egyptians would give all the credit to the Americans anyway.[1]

King Farouk went to visit the stricken provinces himself in mid-February. The fact that the government had done almost nothing to alleviate the situation played into Farouk's hands, and much propaganda was made of his concern; though, according to Lord Killearn, some of the worst conditions in Upper Egypt existed on Farouk's own properties.[2] Egypt at that time was still a feudal society: most landlords never visited their lands, and thought that all was well as

303

long as their income was regular. Whether the peasants on their estates lived in tolerable conditions or abject misery depended on the estate managers and bailiffs, who were often careless and corrupt. Patrick Kinross wrote that 'when you do find a landlord who is conscientious the difference is incredible: decent villages, healthy peasants, and a real spirit of feudal loyalty.'[3]

Conditions in Upper Egypt were, for the most part, a long way from this ideal. Inadequate distribution of supplies had resulted in widespread malnutrition over the past two years; and the lack of cotton meant that not only were the people in rags, but those suffering from malaria could scarcely be kept warm and there were not enough shrouds to bury the dead.

The government had voted £E750,000 towards the epidemic; yet despite the importance of stamping out the disease in the dormant stage of the mosquito's life-cycle, the administration still dragged its heels. Nahas was deeply irritated by the mounting criticism. Lord Killearn heard that he had been very rude to two influential Egyptian ladies, who had come to his house to ask Madame Nahas for her assistance in the relief work.

The King's tour had given wide coverage to the gravity of the situation in Aswan and Qena, and the public were now responding. Branches of the Red Cross, and private organisations like the Muhammad Ali Institution run by Princess Shevekiar began to organise aid to Upper Egypt. The Princess was overheard on the telephone to Cairo, saying that the Palace was now in a position to break the Wafd and sack Nahas.[4]

Anti-British sentiment was rising again. On 2 February the Opposition leaders again staged a rally at which the most violent methods against the British were advocated. The Wafd were more moderate, but reaffirmed their desire to get the occupiers out of Egypt. The press reflected the prevailing mood by bringing up a subject which always exasperated the British: the use of Arabic in daily life. *El Mussawar* attacked the neglect of Arabic at race meetings and restaurants, and questioned the legality of the government's decision to permit the use of French and English in diplomatic correspondence. The Egyptian press became more sensitive to criticism of Egypt in the English-speaking papers. Now that the war had left

Egypt, it was time the British remembered they were guests in the country, and start to behave as such.[5]

On top of this, the Wafd started spreading the usual rumours that the lack of food in Upper Egypt was due to the voracious consumption of the Allied forces. This was refuted by a well-reasoned communiqué from the British Embassy, laying the blame squarely on Nahas's administration; and, when the news leaked out that the Wafd had turned down Britain's offer of expert aid, people were inclined to believe it.[6]

Curiously enough, the King chose to stand aside from this wave of anti-British feeling. Lord Killearn had written that Farouk 'was unlikely ever to forgive February 4th . . . He would indeed hardly be human if he did.'[7] And yet, only two days after the second anniversary of the Abdin coup, the Ambassador was the King's guest at the royal shoot at Darshour. This friendly attitude had begun after Alamein, but it was not only due to the fact that the Allies were winning the war. Farouk realised that Lord Killearn would not allow him to dismiss the Wafd unless he put a co-operative government in their place; the King therefore needed to convince the Ambassador that he was positively pro-British, and would ensure that any new government was too.

Farouk knew that Egypt was no longer as overwhelmingly Wafdist as it had been when Nahas was in opposition. There was a general sense of disillusion with Nahas and his party, which had failed to curb rising prices as well as the malaria epidemic. Corruption in the party was as bad as ever, and it was known that Mme Nahas's brother, Ahmed el Wakil, was demanding 80 percent of the profits of any deal he put through.[8]

In an attempt to revive his popularity, Nahas made two tours of Upper Egypt in early April: first to Assyut and Minia, and then to the provinces of Qena and Aswan. He laid a number of foundation stones for new social institutions that were to bear his name, rather than the sovereign's as was the usual custom. Meanwhile the Wafd was busy putting pressure on local landowners and companies to finance them. To King Farouk, the Nahas Pasha Relief Institutions were an assault on the royal prerogative. He was even more incensed when the Prime Minister made a press statement saying that the people of

Upper Egypt were healthy, well-fed, and well-content with their government – implying that His Majesty had obviously overreacted to the situation. The last straw came when he heard that Nahas was planning a tour of the Delta as well.

King Farouk summoned Lord Killearn to the Abdin Palace on Thursday 12 April, and presented him with a memorandum declaring that His Majesty had decided on a change of government. Nahas's ministry was not only corrupt and inefficient, but 'openly and fla-grantly disrespectful towards the Throne'. He proposed to replace it with what the Ambassador described as 'a colourless collection of officials, ex-officials and comparative nonentities', to be headed by Hassanein Pasha as Prime Minister.[9] Since the fall of Ali Maher, Hassanein's influence in the Palace had been gaining strength. He had always got on well with Lord Killearn, and often acted as a skilful negotiator between him and Farouk.

The Ambassador tried to keep the meeting informal and light-hearted, and asked the King not to do anything rash while the fate of the world was still in the balance; but the fact that the King had received Lord Killearn in audience provoked speculation in the press that another crisis was looming. The Cairo police reported that the Royal Bodyguard and the King's ADCs were on standby with all leave cancelled, in case of emergency; while the Opposition was greatly looking forward to seeing the Wafd thrown out of power. Nahas kept discreetly in the background, but many Wafdists felt it was humiliating that any argument about the future of an Egyptian government should be entirely between the King and the British Embassy.

In May 1940, by which time he had already spent over half a decade in Egypt, the Ambassador had written: '. . . in my own mind I have for many years often thought that the best form of permanent relationship with Egypt lay in her incorporation, in some shape or form, within the British Empire.'[10] This conviction lay at the root of his policy in Egypt, and if he had a single regret about the Abdin Palace incident it was that the King had been left on the throne. After his meeting with Farouk on 12 April, Killearn sent Anthony Eden a very secret telegram, suggesting that perhaps the time had come to take 'some more direct control of Egypt' rather than be faced with these continual petty crises provoked by the Palace.

Despite having promised Killearn that he would not act too fast, by 18 April the King was ready to sack Nahas. A meeting of the Defence Committee was called. Lord Killearn was in favour of using force. The Service Chiefs included a new Air Officer Commander-in-Chief, Sir Keith Park, and a new Commander-in-Chief, Sir Bernard Paget, but they were as against the idea as their predecessors had been on 4 February two years before, and stated that, even on orders from London, they could not produce enough troops to carry out such a policy. Apart from anything else, they might be called upon to quell the mutiny in the Greek armed forces based in Egypt, which had blown up that month.

Killearn thought that London would probably agree with the Service Chiefs and instruct him not to use force. However, Churchill was right behind the Ambassador, and the following day he wrote that the War Cabinet 'will be very likely to support a democratic administration against a Palace clique headed by an oriental despot who on every occasion has proved himself a poor friend of England . . . make sure the C-in-Cs have at their disposal sufficient forces to deal with any troublesome Egyptians as well as cope with Greeks.'[11]

General Paget duly drew up contingency plans. But, on being presented with the military alternatives, Killearn felt that the political situation was too fluid and uncertain to commit himself to any one of them. The most important thing was to push the Egyptian government into the foreground, so that if British force were used it would be on Nahas Pasha's authority. They were all agreed, Killearn included, that there could be no repetition of 4 February.

Over the next few days, veiled threats and solemn warnings from the Embassy did their work, and there was no need for force. On 24 April, Farouk declared he would leave the government in office for the time being; but the Ambassador thought one more threat was necessary to drive the message home. That evening, at a party given by Dora Plant (a Copt of the Khyatt family, who had recently married a British officer), Lord Killearn had a long conversation with Nahed Sirry, Queen Farida's aunt. Knowing that what he said would get back to the King, the Ambassador told her that the British had armies coming from all directions to 'put people in their place'.[12]

The British owed Nahas their loyalty, since he had kept Egypt stable over the dark days of July 1942. But now that his government had lost so much public confidence, and the Opposition accused the British of keeping a quisling in power, it may well be asked why Lord Killearn was so determined to support it. The main reason was that the Wafd in opposition was a potentially dangerous and vindictive animal, which was liable to turn vehemently anti-British. As Lord Killearn put it in one report, 'whatever the Wafd's shortcomings as an administrative machine, its nuisance value as an irresponsible force in opposition should not be underrated.'[13]

On 1 May, King Farouk grudgingly agreed to see Nahas Pasha; but instead of keeping the interview on a mild and agreeable note, as his advisers had suggested, the King attacked him on several subjects, and accused him of ignoring Egypt's sovereign rights. Later the same day, His Majesty received Killearn, who said that, with a little trouble, Farouk could have Nahas in his pocket. Farouk retorted angrily that he wouldn't want anything so dirty in his pocket.[14]

That Farouk backed away from a confrontation with Killearn on 24 April was hardly a coincidence. News had just arrived of the suppression of the Greek Army mutiny by British troops.

The Royal Hellenic Forces in Egypt consisted of volunteers and conscripts from the Greek community, troops who had been evacuated after the fall of Crete, and refugees who had made their way to Egypt in the months that followed. In April 1942, they were formed into the First and Second Greek Brigades. The Greeks also formed air force and naval units, the latter backed up by a strong merchant fleet.

Most men serving in the Greek armed forces favoured a liberal government; but their ranks also included a proportion of ardent socialists and Communists, many of them Egyptian Greeks or refugees from the Greek islands, who wanted to see a radical change in the way their country was governed. There had already been two mutinies in the Greek Army. The first took place in Syria in the winter of 1942, when right-wing officers were arrested by the men and units came under the control of 'soldier committees' composed of left-wing extremists. After it had been put down, Montgomery declared that the possession of subversive pamphlets by members of the Greek forces would be a crime punishable by court martial. The Greek Army was purged of subversive elements, as it was after the second mutiny in July 1943 when 200 'hardline leftists' were interned in the Sudan; but dissaffection continued to grow.[15]

In March 1944, the Greek Communist Party set up a provisional government for the administration of areas liberated from the Germans. It was known as the Political Committee of National Liberation, or PEEA. This organisation invited support from Greeks around the world, and called on the Prime Minister of the Greek Government in exile to form a government of national unity representing all parties and resistance groups.

In Egypt, a group of officers from the Greek Army, Navy and Air Force came to Tsouderos to demand a government of national unity, which would represent all parties and resistance groups and support PEEA. Tsouderos refused, and the trouble began. On 2 April a small group of rebels came into Cairo from their camp at Mena, burst into the office of the Greek Provost Marshal which had once been a Greek school, and barricaded themselves inside. They were persuaded to give themselves up two days later, when a British mobile unit surrounded the building.

The next to join the mutiny was the First Greek Brigade, then at Bourg el Arab. They were due to sail to Italy on 8 April but, two days before that, soldiers' committees arrested all right-wing officers and formed pickets. The British tried to persuade them to surrender, and a troop of tanks was brought forward. Some Greeks did leave the camp at that point; but, when the mutineers manned the Bofors batteries, the tanks pulled back. The British surrounded the rebel camp, and cut all supplies – though this did not cause much hardship. The Greeks were over 2,000 strong; but they had plenty of stores, drew their water directly from the Matruh pipeline, and had money to buy eggs and bread from the local Arabs. By 8 April they were well entrenched in the camp, and the revolt had spread to Alexandria. Three ships of the Royal Hellenic Navy mutinied, while the Communist leader of the Greek Seamen's Union organised two hundred Greek seamen armed with knives and rifles to occupy the Union's office in Muhammad Ali Square.

On 11 April a delegation from the First Greek Brigade at Bourg el Arab tried to open negotiations with the Commander-in-Chief, but General Paget insisted on an unconditional surrender. This was refused and the next twelve days passed in stalemate, while clouds of leaflets with messages from King George II, the new Prime Minister Sophocles Venizelos, and General Paget rained down on the mutineers.

The gathering political crisis in Egypt, triggered by Farouk's decision to sack the Wafd, meant that the mutiny could not be allowed to continue indefinitely. In the early hours of 23 April, a small British force opened fire on the rebel camp at Bourg el Arab, and the First Brigade agreed to surrender the following day. By the evening of 24 April the rebel ships had surrendered, and the First Greek Brigade was split among three prison cages near Alexandria. The most militant group, shouting for their comrades, shook their fences so violently that the British thought they were going to break them.

Only two days after the end of the Greek mutiny, one of the most celebrated small-scale operations of the war took place in Crete. A small party of Cretans (which included soldiers of the Greek Army, as well as local andartes), led by Major Leigh Fermor and Captain Moss, kidnapped General Heinrich Kreipe, who commanded the 22nd Sevastopol Division then occupying central Crete. With the General immobilised by three Cretans in the back of his car, Leigh Fermor sat in the front seat wearing the General's hat. With Moss at the wheel, they drove through the capital Heraklion and twenty-two German check-points before abandoning the car and vanishing into the mountains. Among the Germans, reactions to the kidnapping were evidently mixed. Bickham Sweet-Escott records a story told after the war by a German friend of his, who had been on Kreipe's staff at the time. When Kreipe's abduction was announced in the officers' mess in Heraklion, there was an uneasy silence – followed by someone saying, 'Well, gentlemen, I think this calls for champagne all round.'

Although the raiders had tried to give the impression that the Navy had picked them up off the north coast, the Germans were not convinced; and suspicions were confirmed a week later by the BBC, which announced that 'Kreipe *is being* taken off the island'. To avoid search parties, Moss and Leigh Fermor were obliged to subject the General to a gruelling march over the crest of Mount Ida, the highest point on Crete, to the south coast. After an anxious week trying to organise a rendezvous while hundreds of Germans patrolled the nearby beaches, the party was safely evacuated from the Rodakino area and returned to Egypt.

During the last few days on Crete, Leigh Fermor had been suffering from weakness and cramps. His condition deteriorated on returning to Cairo, where he was taken to hospital with a strange form of rheumatoid paralysis. He was still there when General Paget pinned the DSO onto his khaki jacket, worn over striped pyjamas, while Moss was awarded the MC. Their friends in Cairo were astonished at the success of the mission: the kidnappers had cheerfully told everyone they were going to Crete to bag a German general, but no one had seriously expected them to succeed.

The kidnapping idea had arisen following the successful evacuation of an Italian general, which Leigh Fermor had organised after the Italian surrender. (One planning session took place in the bathroom at Tara: while David Smiley and Billy McLean advised the would-be kidnappers on ambush techniques, Leigh Fermor drew maps of the target area on the steamy bathroom walls.) At that time, the Divisional Commander of Crete was General Müller, hated by the Cretans for the savage brutality of his reprisals. Leigh Fermor had been successfully parachuted into Crete in February; but bad luck had kept Moss and the rest of the team from joining him until 4 April. By that time, Müller had been replaced by General Kreipe.

SOE Cairo now had to decide whether or not the operation should proceed. Bickham Sweet-Escott, then in Cairo as political adviser to SOE's chief General Stawell, was very much against it. But others in SOE felt that the boost it would give Cretan morale, plus the sheer fun of making the Germans look so foolish, provided sufficient reason to go ahead.

Moss and Leigh Fermor were much concerned about reprisals. They had assured the Germans by letter that the operation had been entirely carried out by British and Greek soldiers without the help of Cretan andartes; and that the General was an honourable prisoner of war, who would be treated with the consideration due to his rank. Yet, in concluding his criticism of the kidnap operation, Bickham Sweet-Escott writes that 'I was afterwards told that nearly 200 Cretans were shot', implying that those lives would have been saved had General Kreipe not been taken.

Both the figure and the implication seem exaggerated. While German reprisals could certainly be severe, the Cretans are a fierce mountain people much given to blood-thirsty feuds. Resistance operations and reprisals were going on all over the island: three villages were destroyed while the kidnappers and their prisoner were in the mountains, in retaliation for a gun-running operation the month before. The final judgement must surely rest with the Cretans themselves; and, if the tremendous welcome they gave to Patrick Leigh Fermor in the post-war years is anything to go by, they clearly do not share Sweet-Escott's view.

One problem Moss and Leigh Fermor had brought out of Crete came in the form of a Russian called Piotr Ivanov, who had escaped from a prisoner of war camp in Retimo with three comrades. During his hard days on the run, Piotr Ivanov had become so weak and ill that the SOE officers felt obliged to bring him back to Cairo. The British authorities had strong doubts about this surly and unpleasant man, and they held him for some time without allowing him contact with the Russian Legation. This provoked a terrific scene from Nicolai Lovinov, the Russian Minister, who started shouting and threatening in such a violent way that Lord Killearn was quite shocked. Ivanov was only released when the British military authorities had been given a pledge that he was a bona fide member of the Red Army.

SUMMER AND WINTER 1944

Lord Moyne

Cairo had changed little in the weeks Leigh Fermor and Moss had been away. In the hot, bleached light of summer the shoe-shine boys and fly-whisk vendors were still as raucous and persistent as ever, and the same man stood outside GHQ shouting, 'Chocolates! Cigarettes! OBEs!' The kites still circled slowly in the warm draughts, while above the hooting traffic one could occasionally hear the clatter of a tram, and the self-important blast from the tram conductor's cornet. Groups of men in pale galabeiahs still sat on the rough patch of grass in the middle of Midan Khedive Ismail. They took no notice of the din and fumes of the traffic, but talked and smoked peacefully as though on the lawns of Paradise. The British and Egyptians seemed only to make contact at the very edges of each other's existence. Little boys dashed in between the wicker tables on the terrace of Shepheard's Hotel with the latest edition of the *Bourse Egyptienne* crying, 'Bourse! Bourse!', or tried to thrust them under the nose of an important general whose black Daimler was caught in between honking cars, and mules whose distended panniers were so much broader than their emaciated haunches. On several afternoons a week, as had been his habit for many years, Russell Pasha would ride about the town on his white horse. In his sombre black uniform and red tarboosh, he was the very embodiment of law and order.

Lady Russell Pasha had been awarded the OBE, while the troublesome Makram Ebeid, author of the 'black book', had been interned. This provided yet another example of the repressive way in which Nahas tended to deal with his opponents; but for all that, the news was greeted with some relief. Everybody had got rather tired of Makram and his rantings. In June, the American Minister Alexander Kirk was replaced by Pinkney Tuck (the last in the series of 'monosyllabic Ministers' as Bert Fish, Kirk and Tuck became known). Lord Killearn was sad to lose Kirk, who had been a close friend and very pro-British – but Tuck was a popular appointment in Egypt. The son of a Mixed Court judge, he had been consul in Alexandria and spoke passable Arabic.

The Ambassador was also sorry to note how Cairo was winding down, after the excitements of the war. Administrative offices were becoming smaller or closing altogether, and flats were breaking up as officers left for Italy and England. 'I am impressed more and more each day,' wrote Lord Killearn on 18 May, 'how we seem to be reverting to pre-war Cairo. This I devotedly trust is only a passing phase . . .' The war might yet take a turn for the worse, and catch Cairo napping; but beneath this anxiety was the sad reflection that 'things in general have become definitely drab and dull of late'.[1] Even the arrival of the Embassy's new seven-seater Packard, and the lavish Coptic Ball at the Auberge des Pyramides failed to lighten the Ambassador's mood, and on 27 July he again remarked on how 'flat and bored' Cairo had become since the war left.

However, the war occasionally drifted back. A few days later, on 3 August, a dangerous type of Italian acoustic mine was washed up on the beach of the royal palace of Montazah, at the eastern end of Alexandria. King Farouk was very excited, and gave orders for the mine to be dismantled by the Egyptian Navy; but, since they had no experience of such mines, the Egyptian Navy wisely called in the British. Demolition experts set to work, but Farouk was furious that the British had been involved, and commanded them to stop immediately. The experts warned him that, though they had removed the detonator, the mine was still live; but this did not stop Farouk from having it put on the back of a truck, where it bumped and jolted all the way down to Cairo. Lord Killearn was informed that the mine was on its way to the Abdin Palace, and managed to contact Hassanein. The Chamberlain, appalled by visions of Abdin being blown to pieces, gave urgent orders that no one in the palace was to touch it; but in the event it was taken to the Egyptian Ministry of Defence and safely neutralised. The mine then vanished into the King's vast collection of weapons.

On a more peaceful note, the King attended the gala première of

Irving Berlin's show, 'This is the Army, Mr Jones!', on 17 August. Lord Killearn made it clear to Madame Sirry, who was organising the event, that he was not going to pay £E25 a ticket only to be cut dead by His Majesty in the interval, as had happened on the last two occasions they had appeared in public together.[2] The show did indeed turn out to be an embarrassment, but for different reasons – the chorus line was made up of beefy GIs dressed up as glamour girls, which the Cairene audience found rather distasteful. In spite of Killearn's forebodings, however, Farouk behaved most graciously, and not only summoned the British Ambassador to his box in the interval but kept him there for the second half. The King was very disappointed by the chorus line, and kept asking why on earth they had not got real girls instead.

While Farouk was prepared to be agreeable to the British Embassy, the same could not be said for the Egyptian government. After the crisis in April, the Wafd tried to increase its waning popularity with an anti-British stridency. Workers' syndicates, government officials and the Muslim Brethren all found themselves being wooed assiduously by the Wafd. Revision of the Anglo-Egyptian Treaty and Egypt's rights over the Sudan were well aired in Parliament, and Nahas also emphasised his nationalist credentials by releasing Ahmed Hussein, the fanatical leader of the Islamic National Party (once Young Egypt) – much to Killearn's irritation.

Towards the end of August an attempt was made to improve relations between Nahas and the Palace, and on 3 September Farouk grudgingly agreed to receive Nahas. Once again, instead of being conciliatory, Farouk rudely upbraided the Prime Minister for doing nothing about the Sudan question, and boycotting the Palace ceremonies during Ramadan. On 15 September, the next crisis of the year blew up over the trivial subject of banners. On his way to prayers at the Mosque of Amr, the King was much offended by the sight of some patriotic banners saying 'Long Live Farouk – Long Live Nahas'. Farouk ordered Ghazali Bey, the Director General of Public Security, to take the banners down at once. Ghazali Bey did so, and was promptly sacked by the government the following day. The Palace insisted on his reinstatement, and once again the King and the Wafd were in deadlock. Lord Killearn was on leave in South

Africa. Lord Moyne, who was looking after the Embassy, tried to make both sides see how idiotic and unseemly the squabble was, but then received instructions from the Foreign Office to 'sit back' and watch developments.

At the same time preparations were under way for the first conference of Arab leaders, due to begin on 26 September. This was a great achievement for Nahas Pasha, whose policy of Arab unity had been viewed with scepticism by those who thought it merely a public relations exercise. But Nahas had persevered; and, after sounding out the leaders of the Arab world, he had come to the conclusion that there was enough common ground to warrant the organisation of a preliminary meeting in Egypt. Lord Moyne was much in favour of the conference, and facilitated the attendance of an Arab representative from Palestine. The conference was a great success, and culminated in the signing of the Alexandria Protocol – a document containing resolutions for the formation of a League of Arab Nations.

With this triumph behind him, Nahas thought the time had come to take the initiative. In protest at Britain's unforgivable meddling in Egyptian politics (in other words, Lord Moyne's mild remonstrations over the banner dispute) he proposed to present his resignation to the King that evening and force an election. But the King forestalled him. On the morning of 8 October Nahas Pasha received a Royal Rescript, informing him in the bluntest terms that he had been dismissed.

In February 1942, Mustafa el Nahas Pasha had taken office with the full weight of the British and the country behind him. Two and a half years later, his government had lost so much popularity that the King was able to brush him aside like a flunkey. In Cairo, there were one or two demonstrations and the odd incident, but otherwise little protest. British consuls reported that in the villages, where the Wafd had always been strong, some people were even pleased to see Nahas go – for this particular Wafdist administration had not only been corrupt, but incapable of handling the supplies question. Lord Killearn was still on leave in South Africa, and the British did not lift a finger to help the man they had brought to power. Nahas's humiliation was complete.

The King summoned Dr Ahmed Maher to form a new coalition government, a choice of which the British approved. Ahmed Maher had begun his political life in the Wafd. He and another member of the party, Nokrashi Pasha, had been acquitted of complicity in the murder of Sir Lee Stack in 1924. In 1937, the year of Farouk's accession, Ahmed Maher and Nokrashi were among a group of Wafdists who thought the party should end its absolute hostility to the throne, and encourage an evolution towards a constitutional monarchy. Nahas expelled them from the Wafd, and the following year they founded the Saadist Party: so called because its members claimed to be closer to the spirit of Saad Zaghloul – the founding father of the Wafd – than the Wafd under Nahas.

Despite his alleged involvement with the murder of Sir Lee Stack, Ahmed Maher had won the friendship of the British on the outbreak of war by urging Egypt to forsake her neutrality and join the Allies. The British were also impressed by his behaviour in the summer of 1942, when Rommel stood at Alamein. As Leader of the Opposition, Ahmed Maher was Nahas's most important political enemy. Yet he fully endorsed the Prime Minister's co-operation with Britain, and Nahas would have had a much harder job keeping Egypt calm in those anxious days had he not done so.

The new government had hardly been assembled when Egypt was rocked by the murder of Lord Moyne. Walter Edward Guinness, 1st Baron Moyne, was the sort of public servant the British most admired. With a famous Irish name and immense wealth, he was a gentle, quietly-spoken man who had distinguished himself in both the Army and the administration. His intellectual curiosity had led him to explore a broad range of subjects from archaeology to biology, and he was a close personal friend of Churchill's. Lord Moyne had first been in Egypt during the Great War; and, in August 1942, he was sent out to Cairo as Deputy Minister of State under Richard Casey, whom he replaced as Minister Resident in January 1944.

The men responsible for his death were a group of Jewish terrorists who referred to themselves as the Fighters for the Freedom of Israel, often confused with the Stern Gang, though they were separate organisations. Their reasons for his assassination go back to the autumn of 1940, when both Churchill and Eden had agreed to the formation of a Jewish Army of some 10,000 men, to be drawn up along the lines of the Polish and Czech armies then being funded by Britain. The Jewish leaders had hoped that their army would be raised and led by Orde Wingate, whose passionate devotion to the Zionist cause was well-known; but the latter was ordered to Ethiopia. He was a loss, but Dr Chaim Weizmann and his colleagues were satisfied that at least they had the British government's commitment to the project.

Unfortunately, Churchill had made the mistake of giving his word without first consulting the Palestine Administration and the Commander-in-Chief, Middle East. For both political and economic reasons, the High Commissioner, Sir Harold MacMichael, and General Wavell were solidly opposed to the formation of a Jewish Army. Churchill found it impossible to change their minds. The Jewish community in Palestine were told that the idea could not be put into practice at the moment, though the possibility might be considered again in six months' time.

The man who had to tell them was not Churchill but Lord Moyne, who, following the sudden death of Lord Lloyd, had become Colonial Secretary in February. Both Moyne and his predecessor were pro-Arab, although not unsympathetic to Zionism; but Moyne's manner was more detached and practical, which perhaps conveyed a cold impression. He twice had to inform Chaim Weizmann and Ben-Gurion that the formation of a Jewish Army had to be postponed: first in February 1941, and then in October when the subject came up for review and was again turned down.

From that time on, extreme Zionists saw him as an enemy – a view which did not change when he was posted to Cairo. It was well-known that the Minister of State's office contained a group of dedicated pro-Arabs, of whom the chief was Brigadier Iltyd Clayton. It is to Lord Moyne's credit that he did not invite Clayton to dinner on the night he entertained Field Marshal Lord Gort, who was about to take up his appointment as High Commissioner in Palestine. Clayton, he felt, was too biased in his pro-Arab views and might give the new High Commissioner the wrong impression.

But the Stern Gang were not particularly concerned with Lord

Moyne's sense of fair play. His encouragement of the conference on Arab union, and the help he had given the Palestinian delegates, provided reason enough for eliminating him; and, as they saw it, the killing would bring other advantages. The resulting outcry would put the Palestine problem onto an international level: the British would see that this was no longer an issue they could settle at their convenience in London. The Stern Gang also believed that the British presence in the Middle East was what threatened their cause, not the Arabs whom they saw as fellow-sufferers from the same British oppression. The assassination would show the Egyptians that the British were not as strong as was supposed.

The Stern Gang did have a cell in Cairo, consisting of eight men and four women; but they had done nothing more subversive than print a few pamphlets and look for weapons. They could provide no more than assistance, so the assassins would have to be sent in from Palestine.

There was no shortage of volunteers for the mission, and two were chosen. The first, Eliahu Hakim, had joined the Fighters for the Freedom of Israel in 1940 while still at school. His family were horrified, forced him to leave the organisation, and persuaded him to join the British Army. Posted to Cairo, he became involved in small-time gun-running with the Stern Gang cell, and deserted in February 1944. He then returned to Palestine and went underground. By the time he was selected for the mission, he had already killed at least six people and had taken part in several abortive attempts on Sir Harold MacMichael. He was twenty years old. The second man, Eliahu Bet-Zouri, was three years older. He had a job in the Survey Department; and what he lacked in operational experience he made up for in fanatical zeal.[3]

Hakim came to Cairo in the autumn of 1944, and got in touch with his old accomplices. He took a small room in the Mouski quarter, found himself a girlfriend called Yaffa, and together they ate in little restaurants and went dancing. Yaffa also provided him with an innocent-looking cover. They would stroll like any other courting couple through the curved streets of Garden City, around Moyne's office, and the broad residential avenues of Zamalek near his house (which had once been Momo Marriott's) while Hakim carried out the grim work of studying his victim's daily habits and movements. Bet-Zouri joined him from Palestine, and the murder was fixed for 6 November. They decided to make their get-away by bicycle; for it would take only a few minutes to turn from Moyne's house in Sharia Gamalaya onto the Zamalek Bridge, and vanish into the shabby backstreets of Bulaq.

At lunchtime on Monday 6 November, the Minister's black Packard turned into the gravel drive of No. 4 Sharia Gamalaya. Lord Moyne was accompanied by his personal secretary Dorothy Osmond, his ADC Captain Andrew Hughes-Onslow, and his chauffeur, Lance-Corporal Fuller. Hughes-Onslow got out and walked towards the house when he heard a voice telling him not to move. Fuller, who had walked round the back of the car to open the door for Lord Moyne, was shot several times in the chest by Bet-Zouri; then Hakim ran forward, and started firing at Lord Moyne as he tried to get out of the car. By the time Dorothy Osmond and Hughes-Onslow had recovered from their initial shock, Fuller was dead, Lord Moyne was in shock with multiple wounds, and the two murderers had bolted out of the compound.

Hughes-Onslow rushed after them and raised the alarm at a nearby sentry box. A policeman commandeered a passing car, and though the murderers had slipped down a side street the police were on their heels by the time they got within sight of the bridge. Someone shouted from a window, alerting a member of the Egyptian Ministerial Protection Squad on a motorbike who cut off their escape. The terrorists fired shots into the air, but Amin Muhammad Abdullah did not turn aside and the terrorists were swiftly overpowered. Hakim and Bet-Zouri might still have been able to make a get-away had they been prepared to shoot Amin; but he was Egyptian, and they did not want to alienate Arab opinion.

Meanwhile, Lord Moyne had been taken to hospital. In the course of the afternoon, he was given four blood transfusions and underwent surgery; but he had little chance of surviving the shock and loss of blood, on top of severe internal injuries. He died at 8.40 that evening.

The Egyptians were appalled. They had not forgotten the murder of Sir Lee Stack. On that day, in the space of a few minutes, a handful of nationalist extremists had set Egypt's struggle towards full independence back twenty years. The British felt justified in taking the harshest and most repressive punitive measures; they also increased their control over the Sudan, which Egypt was never to reclaim. Both the King and the new Prime Minister were horrified by the idea of such a set-back in 1944. So, when they found out that the assassins were Jewish rather than Egyptian, their relief was considerable.

The bodies of Lord Moyne and Corporal Fuller were given a state funeral in Cairo. A long procession of British and Egyptian troops followed the coffins, Corporal Fuller's being in front. Behind Lord Moyne marched his son Bryan, who had hurried back from Palestine but had not reached the hospital in time to see his father alive. He marched stiffly, head high, his face streaming with tears.

'If our dreams for Zionism are to end in the smoke of an assassin's pistol,' thundered Churchill in the House of Commons, 'and the labours for its future produce a new set of gangsters worthy of Nazi Germany, then many like myself will have to reconsider the position we have maintained so consistently and so long in the past.'[4] The Prime Minister's grief and rage were such that it was many weeks before anyone dared broach the subject of Palestine in his presence.

Under interrogation, the murderers gave their names as Cohen and Saltzmann, but said nothing else for twenty-four hours to give their friends a chance to get away. Then they admitted to being members of the Fighters for the Freedom of Israel. Hakim and Bet-Zouri were brought to trial in January, and hanged on 22 March 1945. They died secure in the knowledge that they were martyrs to their cause. As Hakim stood on the scaffold, he looked down at the coarse red burlap in which condemned men were tradition-ally dressed, and declared it to be the finest suit of clothes he had ever worn. The bodies were buried in a special cemetery outside Heliopolis, and a guard was mounted over them to prevent them being exhumed and returned to Palestine. One individual was seen approaching the graves. He was arrested, and the names of 60 people associated with the Stern Gang were found on him.[5]

The majority of Jews, and their leaders, saw the Stern Gang terrorists as murderers rather than martyrs. Even the more radical

Jewish Agency condemned their action, and it was a measure of that condemnation that the Agency committed the Haganah (the secret Jewish Army) to help the police root out the Stern Gang. It also appealed to the Jewish community in Palestine not to give shelter to terrorists, but to turn them over to justice.

Thirty years later, however, the mood in Israel had changed significantly. In 1975, the Egyptian government released the remains of Eliahu Hakim and Eliahu Bet-Zouri, in return for twenty Arabs jailed in Israel as enemy spies. The bodies were taken back to Jerusalem, and mourned as heroes. Thousands, including the Prime Minister Yitzhak Rabin, filed past their coffins. The two assassins were then buried with full military honours among the founders of Israel.[6]

SPRING 1945

Burying the Hatchet

Elections were called in January. Although they were boycotted by the Wafd, the new Prime Minister, Dr Ahmed Maher, managed to put together a respectable coalition government; and one of his first actions was to release those interned under the previous administration. These included his brother Ali Maher, who had been Prime Minister when war broke out and had been removed by the British for his pro-Axis sympathies; and Makram Ebeid, who was given a standing ovation as he re-entered the House.

The Speech from the Throne took place on 18 January 1945. According to the King's express command, the new Prime Minister pledged himself to provide adequate food and clothing for the poor. This was the main point in a speech some thirty pages long, and most of the audience did not give it their full attention. They were much more intrigued by Queen Farida's refusal to attend. This was in protest at the fact that King Farouk had invited his mistress Princess Fatma Toussoun, and her sister-in-law Princess Mahavesh.[1]

On 15 February, Winston Churchill came for his fourth wartime visit to Cairo, on his way back from Yalta. He arrived with his daughter Sarah at Alexandria, in such secrecy that the guard only realised whom they were protecting when they heard the senior officer ask if the brandy and cigars had arrived. Churchill's first appointment was on board the American ship SS *Quincy*, and here he had what turned out to be his last meeting with Franklin D. Roosevelt (who died on 12 April). Then Churchill went down to Cairo where once again he was lodged at the Beit el Azrak, as the guest of Lord Moyne's successor Sir Edward Grigg (later Lord Altrincham).

'Am now near the Pyramids receiving Potentates,'[2] he telegraphed to his wife. After a meeting with Haile Selassie, who expressed no gratitude for the help the British had given in regaining his throne, Churchill went to the Fayoum. The Fayoum Oasis, a beautiful green bowl in the desert some seventy miles south-west of Cairo, had been chosen as the site for Churchill's meeting with King Abdul Aziz ibn Abdurrahman el Feisal al Saud, better known as Ibn Saud. The King and his vast retinue were lodged at the newly-built Hotel du Lac, since neither Ibn Saud nor King Farouk thought it sensible for him to be seen in Cairo. Ibn Saud was a magnificent figure of a man and, as Lord Killearn was presented, the King remarked with a smile that he seldom met anyone bigger than himself. 'I don't think anyone could help being immensely impressed by him,' wrote the Ambassador.[3] Churchill too was impressed, and noted that he had around seventy women in his harem and forty living sons. The meeting went well, and was followed by an immense banquet.

Churchill had been told that Ibn Saud would not permit smoking or the drinking of alcohol in his presence; but he told the King that if this was a religious proscription, then his own religion insisted that drinking and smoking were hallowed rites, to be indulged in whenever the believer saw fit. However, so as not to offend the King, the whiskies and sodas for Churchill, Eden and Killearn were served in coloured glasses and described as 'medicine'. The King only drank water from the sacred spring at Mecca. Churchill was persuaded to try some, and wrote that it was the sweetest water he had ever tasted.

After the banquet, Churchill presented Ibn Saud with a casket of precious perfumes which his ADC had bought in the Mouski for £E100. It had seemed like a handsome gift, until Ibn Saud started presenting his. As jewelled swords and daggers, diamond rings, costly scents, jars of spices, a case of attar of roses and a trunkful of gold-embroidered robes were spread out at Churchill's feet, the gift of the British dwindled into embarrassing insignificance. The Prime Minister therefore told Ibn Saud that the casket of scent was only a token, because his real present – a very special Rolls-Royce – was not yet ready. Churchill warmed to his theme as he described the car's innumerable comforts, its magnificent upholstery, and its ability to withstand armed assault; while Anthony Eden listened with a sinking heart, and wondered how much this palace on wheels was going to cost.

That afternoon Churchill, Eden and Lord Killearn drove back to the Beit el Azrak near the Pyramids, where they had a meeting with King Farouk, followed by another with the Syrian President Shukri Kuatli. After the departure of these distinguished guests, the British party stayed on for dinner; after which they retired to the drawing room, to admire the gifts of the Saudi King. Eden and the Ambassador looked on in amusement as the Prime Minister tried on his ceremonial robes, and Sarah Churchill opened the huge portmanteau which the King had given her father 'for your womenfolk'. This contained more robes embroidered with gold, as well as necklaces of pearls and diamonds. Lord Killearn valued the treasure at £3,500; and – much to his daughter's disappointment – Churchill decided everything must be sold, to pay for the Rolls-Royce he had promised Ibn Saud.[4]

At his meeting with King Farouk that afternoon, Churchill had stressed the urgency of improving the lot of the fellahin, and even ventured to say that no country on earth showed such a contrast between vast wealth and grinding poverty. The King heartily agreed, but said that this was largely the concern of his government. He also agreed that there was no reason to delay the execution of Lord Moyne's murderers any longer – a subject that had begun to cause Churchill some anxiety. On an international level, Churchill told the King that one of the results of the Yalta Conference would be a convention of the Allied nations in San Francisco in April. Only those states which had declared war on Germany and Japan before 1 March 1945 might participate. He urged Egypt to declare war, so that she could claim her place at the conference, and become a founder member of the United Nations.

King Farouk's immediate reaction was that Egypt would look foolish if she declared war at this late stage; but Churchill stressed that Egypt had a right to be there, and should not lose it. When he heard that the Turks were also being invited to join the conference, Farouk shifted his position and said that Egypt would probably act in concert with Turkey. In any case, he added, it was a matter for his government to decide, and he asked Anthony Eden to bring the matter up with Dr Ahmed Maher at their meeting the following day.[5]

Though he had failed to get Egypt into the war in 1940, Ahmed Maher was determined to succeed this time. The Wafd, as Lord Killearn predicted, had become vehemently anti-British as soon as they were in opposition, and were very much against the idea; with the support of extreme nationalists like the Muslim Brethren, they spread rumours that Egypt would have to send a workforce to the Far East if she became a combatant ally. However, on Saturday 24 February, Ahmed Maher managed to secure Parliament's approval for the declaration of war. The next step was to put his case before the upper house.

Leaving the Chamber of Deputies, Ahmed Maher was walking down the corridor on his way to the Senate, when a fanatical young lawyer called Mahmoud Isawi shot him three times at point-blank range. The Prime Minister died almost immediately, and his assassin surrendered without a struggle. When Russell Pasha arrived fifteen minutes later, the doors of the Parliament buildings were still wide open. Inside, he found a large crowd had gathered round a scene of hysterical confusion. In a letter to his father-in-law, Russell Pasha wrote that it was '. . . a very bad case of disgraceful police work by the Parliament Police who, I will have you and sundry know, do not come under my command but are a fancy body of men under the direct and only control of the President of the Chamber; they are dressed in a splendid uniform of their own, carry Webley revolvers which they have never fired and which were none of them loaded at the time of the crime!'[6]

Russell Pasha brought in a hundred of his own men and took control; but, when they had shut the doors and searched everybody in the building, fifty-two people were found who had no admission tickets or passes. Lord Killearn and Sir Walter Smart came hurrying to the scene, and they were soon joined by a British army doctor; but by that time, Ahmed Maher's body had been removed and was on its way to the family home in Avenue el Malik, Koubbeh Gardens. The Ambassador and Sir Walter followed shortly after, to pay their respects to the bereaved family.

As they walked into the house, they could hear the women of the family wailing with grief behind closed doors. Servants were sobbing and moaning; while in the main room, surrounded by a group of silent male relatives, sat Lord Killearn's old enemy of 1940 – Ali Maher Pasha. Sir Walter Smart thought the situation was extremely embarrassing, but Lord Killearn decided to rise above any personal feelings. He shook Ali Maher by the hand, and extended his most sincere condolences.[7]

Ahmed Maher had been murdered for bringing Egypt into a war that she had never wanted any part of; and, as the autocratic figure of the British Ambassador shook hands with the man he had thrown out of power for his pro-Axis sympathies, that war – at least in Egypt – had come to an end.

EPILOGUE

EPILOGUE

Fire and Revolution 1951–1952

In 1946 Lord Killearn was appointed Special Commissioner in South-East Asia, after thirteen years' service in Egypt. He had his farewell lunch with King Farouk on 6 March. 'He was outwardly very friendly,' wrote Killearn, 'as indeed he always has been latterly; however pleased at heart he must be . . . to see my back, he is a good actor and does not show it.'[1]

The end of the Second World War saw Egypt a great deal richer than she had been at the beginning. Quite apart from the huge sums of money the Allies had spent in Egypt, the restriction on imports had given a much-needed boost to local industry; and Britain still owed Egypt three hundred million pounds for supplies, damages and compensations. Yet all this money was going into the hands of the rich rather than the poor. Prices had gone up by at least two thirds since 1939 and showed no signs of descending, while wages lagged behind. The local industries that had sprung up could not all compete with the resumption of normal trade in the post-war world, and many of them foundered. This, plus the jobs lost through the dismantling of the Allied war machine, put over 300,000 out of work.

The immediate post-war years saw a period of painful change in Egypt. Up to the mid-1940s, the poor had pinned their hopes on the Wafd or the King, but those hopes had shrivelled. The Wafd had proved itself corrupt and inefficient, incapable of helping them; and, where the Egyptians had once been tolerant of their young King, they now deplored his self-indulgence.

Farouk had also lost their love and respect. He had offended Muslim opinion by acquiring a *fattweh* (religious edict) to say that he was a Descendant of the Prophet, a statement most people found hard to believe; and there was much sympathy for Queen Farida when the King divorced her in 1948. In fact, it was the Queen who had wanted the divorce. She had not lived with the King since the birth of her third daughter, after which she had quietly left Abdin and taken up residence in the Koubbeh Palace. On 6 May 1951, Farouk married Narriman Sadek, daughter of the Secretary General to the Ministry of Communications, and futher alienated public opinion by being on honeymoon when Ramadan began on 25 May. Queen Narriman gave birth, on 16 January 1952, to Farouk's only son, Prince Ahmed Fuad.

Apart from growing older and stouter, the King had not changed very much; but the mood of the country had hardened. Socialist ideas were discussed rather as democracy had been in the twenties and thirties, and the emergence of the Soviet Union as a great power helped give a new impetus to the struggle of the working classes. The Egyptian Socialist Party (originally called Young Egypt) of Ahmed Hussein was gaining strength, as were the Marxist Partisans of Peace and the Communist National Democratic Liberation Movement – assiduously nurtured by the Russian Legation.

Every extremist, nationalist group, whether right- or left-wing, flourished in the general dissatisfaction. The message of the Muslim Brethren became increasingly potent, and the organisation in its own daily paper denounced the failure of government and King to relieve the plight of the poor. For its poorer members, the Brethren offered loans, insurance programmes, and free medicine; it also raised a secret army, the *Jawwala* (Rovers), which at one point numbered 2,000. Within this corps was another even more secret group, trained in the arts of terrorism and assassination.[2]

On 1 September 1947, the United Nations Commission decided to partition Palestine. The British Mandate ended on 15 May 1948, and on that day the Arab States – represented by the armies of Egypt, Iraq, Transjordan and Syria – invaded Palestine in an attempt to strangle the new state of Israel at birth. In Cairo, various Jewish and foreign owned businesses were attacked and a bomb was set off in the Jewish quarter. Since martial law had been established with the declaration of war on Palestine, the government was able to dissolve the Muslim Brotherhood, which was dangerously powerful. In less than a month, the Prime Minister Nokrashi Pasha had been assassinated by one of the organisation's terrorists; and, in early 1949, the leader of the Muslim Brotherhood himself, Hasan el Banna, was murdered in his turn – probably on the orders of the government.

In the first phase of the Palestine War the Egyptians advanced rapidly and linked up with the Arab Legion in Transjordan. But the Egyptian Army was badly equipped, and its territorial gains were unconsolidated. In the second phase of the war they were driven back. Colonel Gamal Abdel Nasser was one of those who refused to surrender the last besieged position of Faluja, and in December he launched a counter-attack that enabled the Egyptians to hold out until the following month. Then even he had to give up, and the armistice was signed in February. He returned to Egypt feeling bitterly ashamed at the defeat of the Egyptian Army. Above all he was enraged by the way it had been the victim of a political deal in defective arms which the King had helped to cover up. He was not alone. The small, clandestine group of officers within the Army swelled in secret. From 1949, a Constituent Committee of five was formed under the sole leadership of Nasser.

The most significant aspect of politics in Egypt in the late forties was that the dissident groups, whether religious or secular, inclined to the right or the left, all believed that the fight against imperialism – as represented by the continuing presence of British troops – was inextricably linked with the fight against their country's corrupt *ancien régime*. There was a feeling in the air that the days of the pashas were drawing to an end, and that nothing could stop the wave of revolt building up beneath the surface.

Compared to London or Paris, Cairo had undergone little change since the war, and the Anglo-Egyptian upper crust carried on as they always had. The British still sipped their gin-slings on the terrace of Shepheard's Hotel; some were in uniform, for the British continued to maintain a force of 80,000 men in Egypt, largely in the Canal Zone, but the majority of men were in linen suits with the women in straw hats and flowered cotton frocks. There was still polo and racing at the Gezira Club, dancing at the Auberge des Pyramides or Madame Badia's. It was not until Saturday, 26 January 1952, that Cairo went through one of the most extraordinary upheavals in its long history; and the city the British had known and loved, and which was largely created for their benefit and enjoyment, virtually vanished overnight.

The build-up to what became known as 'Black Saturday' began in October 1951, when Nahas Pasha and the Wafd were back in power. They had repealed martial law and released interned members of the Muslim Brotherhood, a favour they hoped would reap benefits by keeping the extremists on their side. But their negotiations for the revision of the 1936 Anglo-Egyptian Treaty, Egyptian rights to the Sudan and evacuation of British troops had come to nothing. Bands of extremists had begun sabotage operations in the Canal Zone, and the British had not been afraid to use force in return. To break the deadlock, Nahas Pasha unilaterally abrogated the Anglo-Egyptian Treaty, and the Sudan Agreement of 1899.

The British protested that this was illegal, intolerable, and Egypt would have to accept the consequences. To the Egyptians, however, the abrogation meant that the British presence in Egypt was now illegal, and whatever the results Britain would have no one but herself to blame. Small bands of students, peasants and Muslim Brethren, known as 'phalanxes of liberation', launched into a spirited campaign of guerilla warfare. At the same time the government started to cut off transport and supplies, and Egyptian contractors and labourers refused to work for the British any longer. On 30 December, the government passed a law declaring it an offence, punishable by imprisonment – and in some cases, death – to offer any service to the British.

The Wafd tried to achieve control over the extremists by giving them aid and support. It undertook the military training of young men, in the hope of gaining some authority over the militias being formed by the Muslim Brotherhood and the phalanxes of liberation. Fuad Serag-ed-Din Pasha, the Minister of the Interior, was giving arms, money and police protection to the Young Egypt Socialist Party – all of which he hoped would be used in the anti-British campaign in the Canal Zone.

The British Ambassador, Sir Ralph Stevenson, sent repeated notes of protest to the government, while the British garrison took control of the Canal Zone, concentrating on the areas around Ismailia and Tel el Kebir. All communications had been cut, and General Sir

George Erskine, the General Officer Commanding British troops in Egypt, anticipated that the Egyptian government might even cut off food supplies to the area in an attempt to force the British out by starving the local population. Rations were calculated for 400,000 people, suggesting allowances of flour, sugar, onions, rice etc., and '6oz. tinned herrings – if required for religious reasons'. (A puzzled note in the margin reads, 'Who needs a tinned herring for religious reasons?'[3]) Life for the troops was getting more and more unbearable – and expensive. With every lorry having to be accompanied by an armed escort, the British government soon realised that their presence in the Canal Zone could not be maintained without Egypt's co-operation. At the same time, they were determined not to leave under pressure.

On 31 December, an article in *Gamanhour el Misri* gave an accurate idea of how violent a hatred had been unleashed against the British. The paper offered a reward of £E1,000 for the murder of General Erskine, and £E100 for the murder of any of his officers. It then boasted that '*El Gamanhour el Misri* has led the national campaign against the red-faced bandits in the Canal Zone, and its news and articles always inspired the hero-commandos who kill, every day, in the name of the Egyptian people, a number of British officers and soldiers'.[4]

The crisis in the Canal Zone had developed with such alarming rapidity that the Wafd did not know what to do next. Yet the radical groups in Egypt realised that, whatever happened, their government could not send Egyptian troops into the Canal Zone and declare war, even when General Erskine began a series of cleaning-up operations which brought British troops ever closer to Cairo. From mid-January onwards, radical demonstrators made it plain that they had lost patience with both government and King.

The violence grew worse in the new year, and anti-British sentiment was kept at white heat by the Minister of the Interior, Fuad Serag-ed-Din. On 21 January the British cordoned off a cemetery and searched it for weapons. The following day, they forcibly evacuated three blocks in a poor residential district of Ismailia. No doubt the British involved were rougher and angrier than they might have been; but the Minister of the Interior gave a broadcast on 23 January which one can only hope was exaggerated: 'British action in Ismailia exceeded anything the human mind could conceive. Women were turned into the streets half-clothed and taken to camps where their fate is still unknown. Mosques were desecrated, cemeteries profaned and great numbers of Egyptians killed or wounded and crucified on trees.'[5]

Two days later, General Erskine sent an ultimatum to the police and auxiliary police (*buluq nizam*) in Ismailia, demanding the immediate surrender of all their weapons. The *buluq nizam* were recruited from those conscripts rejected by the Army, and were normally armed with no more than staves; but, since the abrogation of the Treaty in October, large numbers of them had been issued with rifles and sent to the Canal Zone. The British saw them as a particularly volatile and undisciplined force which was working closely with the guerillas; but the guerillas were difficult to find, whereas the *buluq nizam* were concentrated in specific places. The police compound and barracks were surrounded by 1,500 British troops supported by tanks, and the Governor of the Province and Chief of Police were given a warning that, unless the police and the *buluq nizam* were immediately disarmed, the British would be obliged to do the job themselves. This warning was delivered at 6.30 am, on Friday 25 January. The Chief of Police replied that his men would fight to the death, as they had been ordered by the Minister of the Interior.

Loudspeaker vans told the besieged that they were completely surrounded, and gave them forty-five minutes to surrender their weapons. The men inside started firing at once and, after the allotted three-quarters of an hour, the British answered with blank rounds from the tanks and small arms fire.[6] The British then stormed the compound, which led to a pitched battle. The Egyptians put up a fierce resistance, though they had no chance of winning. They surrendered at midday, by which time fifty men of the Egyptian police and *buluq nizam* were dead.

The first signs of the ensuing storm came that evening at Cairo airport, when four BOAC planes were forcibly detained. Passengers and crew were molested and threatened by an angry crowd that included airport officials. The British Consul advised great caution, and Egyptian servants told their employers it would not be wise to go out on Saturday.

At seven in the morning, three hundred *buluq nizam* left their barracks at Abbassia and marched to Giza, where the students of Cairo University were organising a massive demonstration of their own. People watching were astonished to see students *and* police shoulder to shoulder; and the crowd, now two thousand-strong, crossed the bridge and gathered in front of the Cabinet Offices (the former palace of Princess Shevekiar, who had died in 1947). Here they were addressed by the Minister of Social Affairs, Abdul Fattah Hassan, who told them that the day of vengeance had arrived. There was, however, a certain nervousness in his voice. The crowd listened, its mood hardening. Police were seen with their arms around the students, and some even threw off their uniforms in protest. Their anger was intense, and not only against the British. The *buluq nizam* had borne the brunt of the fighting in the Canal Zone, and were expected to die rather than surrender at all times. They felt they were doing the work of soldiers: but they were given none of the status accorded to the Army, and far less pay. At this point, the government should have scented danger, and broken up the demonstration while it was still possible; but nothing was done.

The police were behaving very strangely. In a subsequent report, Russell Pasha (who had retired as Commandant of the Cairo Police in 1946, but still had his contacts in the force) wrote that the police had taken no measures to deal with the trouble even though they knew it was coming. Normally, they would have rounded up all dangerous hot-heads the night before, and flooded the city with their men. This had been done in Alexandria on the night of 25 January, and there was very little trouble next day. But, according to Russell Pasha's unnamed informant, the Ministry of the Interior had ordered that the rioters should not be interfered with.[7]

The demonstration in front of the Cabinet Offices turned into a debate, and Abdel Fattah Hassan was horrified by the demands of the crowd. When he said that, in the battle for the Canal Zone, surely Egypt should not ask Russia for arms – they roared, 'Yes, Yes!'[8] Large numbers of people were moving into the town centre from al Azhar and the Mouski, and at 11.30 the first fire broke out. The target was Madame Badia's Opera Casino, where a police officer was having a drink on the terrace. An angry group of demonstrators cursed him for drinking when his colleagues were being slaughtered in the Canal Zone; and when he replied equally rudely, they stormed the premises. Well-dressed young effendis burst into the restaurant, and started ripping down curtains and throwing furniture into the street. Barrows with cans of petrol were brought forward, passed inside the building, and someone else poured petrol onto the pile of furnishings outside. Soon the restaurant was blazing hard. There were no casualties; but nearby police did nothing to stop the arsonists and, a few yards away, another policeman calmly continued to direct traffic. Eyewitnesses were shocked to see that the crowd – not demonstrators, but ordinary people – looked on quite impassively, as though they were watching a film.

The assault on Madame Badia's Opera Casino may have been partly spontaneous, but all the destruction that followed had clearly been planned. Just after 1.30 the Turf Club was attacked. For the past few weeks, the Club had been protected by a police guard of some forty men, but this had mysteriously dwindled to four by the time the gang arrived. Under orders from a young man in a blue uniform (possibly of Air Misr, the state airline) they broke down the front door, and immediately started smashing furniture and making piles of it on the ground floor, which were set alight with bundles of hessian, and rods capped with inflammable wicks and paraffin.

Of the forty-odd members who were in the Club at the time, most were on the ground floor and managed to get out by the back door. But several were prevented from escaping by the crowds outside, and were pushed back into the flames. Two Englishmen who were trapped on an upper storey jumped out of the windows. The first broke his back on the roof of a small shed beneath, and must have died soon after; but the second let himself down into a small courtyard on knotted sheets. He was kicked and beaten to death with iron bars. The bodies of the two men were brought together, and a great pile of material was put on top of them to make a bonfire. The *bawaeb* (doorman) of the Turf Club protested, saying that such an act was barbarous and deplored by Islam; but the crowd told him to get out of the way or they would burn him too. While the Turf

Club was under attack, a lorry full of police drove by. They did not stop, and the crowd cheered. Inside the building, a number of other Britons were savagely mutilated before being tossed onto bonfires.

The gangs of arsonists had appeared from nowhere. All appeared to be well-dressed young men who knew exactly what they were doing. Each group of between ten and thirty men had its own list of targets, and moved from one to the next with such ruthless efficiency that four or five buildings were in flames at any one time. They enlisted the help of demonstrators and bystanders who willingly joined in, while a crowd collected to watch and cheer. The gangs were well-equipped, and brought petrol and tools with them. For one building, protected by metal shutters, they even produced an oxyacetylene torch. For the most part, they did not repeat the sort of atrocities that took place in the Turf Club; but the manager of the Rivoli Cinema was hounded through his premises by murderous fanatics. They also tried to track down the Canadian Trade Commissioner, who had got out of the Turf Club and was hidden by some courageous Egyptians in a partially completed building. After two hours he was eventually found, dragged out and stabbed to death.

Barclays Bank, the BOAC building, Thomas Cook's, W. H. Smith's, the British Council offices and the British Institute were all burning by early afternoon. The gang attacking the Morris Motors car showrooms forced their way in by using a twelve-foot 'No Parking' sign as a battering ram. A gunsmith's was set on fire, his stock going off in a series of violent explosions that caused considerable damage to the onlookers. British firms were the most obvious targets, but they also burnt anything that smelled of foreign money and decadence. Every cinema, bar, cabaret and wine-merchant in the city centre was destroyed. The fire brigade could do little, since the crowds that gathered to watch the fires were on the side of the arsonists, and regularly cut the fire hoses. On three occasions policemen were seen cutting hoses, and they also encouraged and applauded the gangs busily slashing, tearing, breaking and burning their way through the town. As the Rivoli Cinema was being burnt, one Egyptian – whom the investigating committee described as not particularly pro-British – saw the Assistant Commandant of Police,

Imam Bey, watching the blaze. One hand was in his pocket, the other playing with his worry beads. The Egyptian approached, and asked if the police were going to do anything. Imam Bey turned to him with a smile and said, 'Let the boys have their fun.'

Most senior officers of the police and Army were in the Abdin Palace that day, at a luncheon for 600 given by King Farouk to celebrate the birth of his son. Those attending the lunch were very much aware of what was going on. Couriers came and went with messages for His Majesty, who was on several occasions seen in earnest consultation with Haidar Pasha, the Commander-in-Chief of the Egyptian Army. They must have known that the police were siding with the mob, but no move was made to send in the Army to restore order.

It was not until 2.30 that Shepheard's Hotel was destroyed. As usual the gang burst in and started tearing curtains and smashing furniture to make a bonfire, while people rushed to escape. The Moorish Hall drew the heat upwards, and its dome of coloured glass had crashed into the flames within twenty minutes. Two members of an Italian Opera Company were seen rushing out in their underwear, clutching their jewels – while one unfortunate girl jumped to her death from the fourth floor to escape the flames.[9]

By four in the afternoon, almost every street that lay within the area bounded by Opera Square, Sharia Kasr el Nil, Sharia Soliman Pasha and Sharia Alfi Bey had one or more buildings on fire. Everywhere, burnt cars lay overturned in the road. Then the looting started in earnest. The crowd stumbled into the smoking ruins of department stores like Cicurel's, Davies Bryan's and Robert Hughes, and squabbled over the spoils. One Greek grocer kept looters at bay by giving them money. Having gutted the centre of town, the incendiarists set off in lorries down the road to the Pyramids, where they destroyed the Auberge des Pyramides and the Club Royal de Chasse et de Pêche. Mena House was only saved at the behest of the camel drivers and pedlars who begged the gang not to ruin their livelihood. As it was, fifteen thousand people were made jobless in the destruction of that afternoon. A great pall of smoke hung over the centre, though Gezira and Garden City had been left unmolested. In the latter quarter, the police maintained a strong presence, and at

3.30 had even barred the way to a mob trying to get to the British Embassy. The British thought their Embassy might have been less well protected, had the houses of Serag-ed-Din and Nahas Pasha not been in the vicinity.

The British were alarmed by the lack of response from the Egyptian authorities, and considered moving on Cairo – but wisely decided against it. In a telegram to the CIGS, General Sir Brian Robertson – the Commander-in-Chief Middle East Land Forces – wrote that 'any idea that we can waltz into Cairo and find some moderate elements whom we could set up to restore order is out of the question. Our former expectation that the Egyptian Army might offer only token resistance will not be realised.'[10] It was not until six o'clock that afternoon that the Egyptian Army was called in to restore order. They advanced through the streets in line abreast, and did not hesitate to fire on anyone who attempted to stop them. King Farouk afterwards announced how proud he was of the Army, and of the efficiency they had shown in bringing the disturbances to an end. He thought it demonstrated their loyalty to the Crown; but the behaviour of his troops was more influenced by the officers' movement, which did not approve of mob violence. Even within the Army there were signs of ambivalence. Some units restricted themselves to firing over the heads of the crowd, which was then allowed to disperse.

To this day, nobody knows for certain who was responsible for the well-organised gangs of arsonists. Some of the gangs were raised by the Muslim Brotherhood, and these attacked bars and night-clubs. Several other gangs seemed to be made up of members of Ahmed Hussein's Socialist Party. The British thought it unlikely that Ahmed Hussein could have organised them so well – but there were cleverer people than him in the organisation, which was known to be infiltrated by the Communists. The Socialist Party had also had the advantage of being well-equipped and funded by the Minister of the Interior, Fuad Serag-ed-Din. 'Right up to the end,' reads a Chancery report on information offered by Farkhani Bey, a source who had proved reliable in the past, 'Serag-ed-Din had been stupid enough to think that these facilities [money and weapons] would be used in the Canal Zone. He had, of course, expected and wanted a riot on the 26th, but only a "normal riot".'[11]

Fuad Serag-ed-Din wrote an article in his own defence which would have appeared in the Wafdist *El Misr* on 10 February, but the whole issue was confiscated. Serag-ed-Din said he had been trying all afternoon to get Haidar Pasha to call out the Army, but that he and the King had deliberately held it back until it was too late.[12]

The events of Black Saturday were sparked off by the British attack on the *buluq nizam* in Ismailia; but hatred of the British was not the only motive for the destruction that took place that day, and neither were Islamic fundamentalism and xenophobia. At the root of it all was a strong revolutionary tension, which had been building up for a long time. Its spontaneous eruption left the city emotionally drained, and the revolution which followed a few months later was far less dramatic as a result.

On 23 July 1952, the people of Egypt woke up to find that the Free Officers of the Egyptian Army had seized power in the night. Ali Maher was appointed Prime Minister, and on 26 July he was sent with an ultimatum to the King. It was the Will of the People that he should abdicate in favour of his infant son, Prince Ahmed Fuad; and he and his family were ordered to leave Egypt by 6 pm that evening.

Accompanied by his wife Narriman and their son on board the royal yacht *Mahroussa*, the ex-King of Egypt left his country just as his grandfather Ismail had done seventy-three years before. He exchanged polite farewells with General Muhammad Neguib, and was given a twenty-one gun salute as the yacht sailed out of sight. As for the people in whose name the revolution had been launched, they knew little of their new rulers or of how things would change. But Egypt had been promised a just society, and they looked forward to it with hope.

Notes

PROLOGUE

1. Gordon Waterfield, *Morning Will Come*, John Murray 1944, pp10–13

THE BRITISH IN EGYPT

P. J. Vatikiotis, *The History of Egypt* (second edition), Weidenfeld & Nicolson 1980
Tom Little, *Egypt*, Benn 1958

THE KING AND THE CITY

1. Barrie St Clair McBride, *Farouk of Egypt*, Robert Hale 1967, p73
2. Harold Macmillan, *War Diaries*, Macmillan 1984, p393
3. During the intervening months, the premiership was held by Muhammad Mahmoud, who resigned due to ill health in August
4. Magdi Wahba, *Cairo Memories*, Encounter magazine, May 1984, pp74–79
5. Amy Smart to Burnet Pavitt
6. In Charles Johnston's *Mo and Other Originals*, the character of Lord Hassocks is based on Sir Robert Greg.
7. Pennethorne Hughes, *While Shepheard's Watched*, Chatto and Windus 1949, p15
8. Sir Charles Johnston, letter to his parents, 18 September 1942

PREPARING FOR WAR

1. At that time, all the countries of the Middle East together were estimated to have 33,000 trucks between them, most of them having been in service for an average of nine years. Undated report on the activities of the Middle East Supply Centre, Furness Papers, St Antony's College, Oxford

2. General Sir Henry Maitland Wilson, *Eight Years Overseas*, Hutchinson 1950

3. Lord Killearn's Diaries, 3 January 1940

4. FO 371/24623, pp99–102

5. FO 371/24609, report by General Macready of 31 January 1940

6. Anwar Sadat, *Revolt on the Nile*, Allan Wingate, 1957, p32

7. Lord Killearn's Diaries, 21 March 1940

8. Wavell to V.C.I.G.S.; see John Connell, *Wavell, Soldier and Scholar*, Collins 1964, p229

9. Jean Lugol, *Egypt in World War II*, Cairo 1945, p77

10. Alexander Clifford, *Three Against Rommel*, Harrap 1943, pp34–35

11. Jean Lugol, op. cit., p16

12. FO 371/27446, report of 5 December 1940

13. Jeanne de Schoutheete, *Jeanette of Cairo*, Editions France Empire 1975, p146

14. FO 371/24626, report entitled *The Case against Ali Maher*

15. Lord Killearn's Diaries, 30 August 1940

16. Ibid., 11 September 1940

THE BENGHAZI HANDICAP

1. FO 371/27428, file on Anglo-Egyptian relations. Churchill's words were, 'Where was the need [for Italy] to invade Egypt, which is under British protection?'

2. John Connell, *Wavell*, p301

3. FO 371/24634, report of 26 December 1940

4. Lord Killearn's Diaries, 17 June 1940

5. Jean Lugol, op. cit., p135

6. Freya Stark, *East is West*, John Murray 1945, p68

7. *The Diaries of Sir Henry Channon*, ed. Robert Rhodes James, Weidenfeld & Nicolson 1967, 1 January 1941

8. Ibid., 4 January 1941

9. Ibid., 4 January 1941

10. Lord Killearn's Diaries, 24 January 1941

DISASTER IN ALL DIRECTIONS

1. FO 371/27430

2. David A. Thomas, Appendix C of *Crete 1941: The Battle at Sea*, André Deutsch 1972

3. FO 371/27431, report of 7 June 1941

4. Brian Roberts, *Randolph: a Study of Churchill's Son*, Hamish Hamilton 1984, p209

5. FO 371/27431, report of 11 August 1941

6. Christopher Sykes, *Orde Wingate*, Collins 1959, p329

7. Freya Stark, *East is West*, p130

NEW ARRIVALS

1. Lord Killearn's Diaries, 1 April 1941

2. Peter Coats, *Of Generals and Gardens*, Weidenfeld & Nicolson 1976, pp92–93

3. Lord Killearn's Diaries, 11 April 1941

4. Ibid., 11 April 1941

5. Neil Balfour and Sally Mackay, *Paul of Yugoslavia: Britain's Maligned Friend*, Hamish Hamilton 1980

6. Lord Killearn's Diaries, 1 April 1941

7. Ibid., 18 April 1941

8. Peter Coats, op. cit., p104

9. E. E. P. Tidsall, *The Royal Hellenic Cousins*, Stanley Paul 1955

10. Lord Killearn's Diaries, 5 June 1941

11. Ibid., 21 and 23 April 1941

12. Olivia Manning, *Cairo: Back from the Blue*, Sunday Times Colour Supplement, 17 September 1967

13. *Spirit of Place*, ed. Alan G. Thomas, Faber & Faber 1969. Letter from Lawrence Durrell to Anne Ridler, Cairo 1942, p75

14. Olivia Manning, *Middle East Letter*, Modern Reading No.9, 1944

15. Anita Leslie, *A Story Half Told*, Hutchinson 1983

16. Lord Killearn's Diaries, 31 July 1941

17. Ibid., 16 April 1941

A TIME OF IDEAS

1. Cecil Beaton, *Near East*, Batsford 1943, p74

2. W. B. Kennedy Shaw, *The Long Range Desert Group*, Collins 1945, p147

3. *The Letters of Evelyn Waugh*, ed. Mark Amory, Weidenfeld & Nicolson 1980. Letter from Evelyn Waugh to his wife Laura, Christmas Day 1940, p149

4. *The Diaries of Evelyn Waugh*, ed. Michael Davie, first published Weidenfeld & Nicolson 1976. Penguin Books 1979, p492

5. Julian Amery, *Approach March*, Hutchinson 1973, p285

6. Evelyn Waugh, *Officers and Gentlemen* (second volume of the *Sword of Honour* trilogy), first published by Chapman & Hall 1955; Penguin Books 1984, p123

7. *The Diaries of Evelyn Waugh*, p154

8. Christopher Sykes, *Evelyn Waugh*, Collins 1975, p215

9. Virginia Cowles, *The Phantom Major*, Collins 1958, pp15–16

10. Philip Warner, Appendix 3 of *The Special Air Service*, William Kimber 1971

11. Lord Killearn's Diaries, 8 December 1940

12. Ibid., 24 March 1941

13. Bickham Sweet-Escott, *Baker Street Irregular*, Methuen 1976, pp74–75

14. Freya Stark, letter to her mother, 30 June 1941. *Letters* vol. IV, ed. Lucy Moorehead, Michael Russell 1977

15. Ibid., letter to Jock Murray, 8 October 1940

16. Freya Stark, *Dust in the Lion's Paw*, John Murray 1961, p69

17. Peter Partner, *Arab Voices: The BBC Arabic Service, 1938–1988*, BBC Publications 1988, p52

18. John Connell, *The House at Herod's Gate*, Sampson, Low, Marston & Co. 1947, p32

19. Alan Moorehead, *African Trilogy*, Hamish Hamilton 1944, p191

PATRIOTS OR FIFTH-COLUMNISTS?

1. Charles Tripp, *Ali Mahir and the Palace in Egyptian Politics, 1936–1942*. London University Ph.D. Thesis, 1984, pp245–287

2. P. J. Vatikiotis, *The Egyptian Army in Politics*, Indiana University Press 1961; see Chapter 3, The Free Officers Group

3. General Sir Henry Maitland Wilson, op. cit., p19

4. Lord Killearn's Diaries, 20 October 1941

5. Anwar Sadat, *Revolt on the Nile*, p35

6. The variations in Sadat's autobiographies are analysed in David Hirst's and Irene Beeson's *Sadat*, Faber & Faber 1981.

7. Charles Tripp, op. cit., pp219, 221

8. FO 371/31570: the Ambassador's report of 9 April 1942, reviewing the political situation in Egypt between October 1941 and March 1942, p1

9. Lord Killearn's Diaries, 3 April 1941

10. Ibid., 12 April 1941

TROOPS

1. Erik de Mauny, *Silver Fern Leaf Up the Blue*: vignette in *Return to Oasis*: War Poems and Recollections from the Middle East, 1940–1946, ed. Victor Selwyn, published by Poetry London for the Salamander-Oasis Trust 1980, p221

2. Alan Moorehead, op. cit., p193

3. WO 222/1337, Quarterly Medical reports for the Cairo area, July 1940 – December 1946. Reports include figures of average ration strengths

4. A. E. W. Sansom, *I Spied Spies*, Harrap 1965, p46

5. WO 222/1337, op. cit.

6. WO 222/12, Note to Regimental Medical Officers called upon to lecture on the Prevention of VD among troops

7. WO 222/1337, op. cit.

8. J. H. Bailey, *From My Middle East Diary*: passage appears in *From Oasis into Italy*: War Poems and Diaries from Africa and Italy 1940–1946, ed. Victor Selwyn, published by Shepheard-Walwyn for the Salamander-Oasis Trust 1983, p4

9. WO 222/1337, op. cit.

10. A. E. W. Sansom, op. cit., pp42–43

11. Olivia Manning, *Middle East Letter*

12. Muhammad Neguib, *Egypt's Destiny*, Doubleday 1955, p78

13. Cecil Beaton, *Near East*, p37

14. Olivia Manning, *The Danger Tree* (first volume of *The Levant Trilogy*), first published by Weidenfeld & Nicolson 1977; Penguin Books 1979, p169

15. Freya Stark, *Letters*, op. cit.: to Flora Stark, 30 November 1941

16. Eve Curie, *Journey Among Warriors*, Heinemann 1947, p39

ADMINISTRATIVE PROBLEMS

1. Lord Killearn's Diaries, 21 July 1940
2. Ibid., 20 May 1941
3. See Peter Partner, op. cit., p38
4. Viscount Chandos (Oliver Lyttelton), *Memoirs*, Bodley Head 1962, p247
5. Alan Moorehead, op. cit., p185
6. Alexander Clifford, op. cit., pp118–119
7. Christopher Sykes, *Orde Wingate*, pp329–337

THE EFFECTS OF WAR

1. FO 371/31570 (review of political situation between October 1941 and March 1942), p2
2. FO 371/31569: the Ambassador's report of 12 February 1942, reviewing political developments in Egypt during the year 1941, p3
3. Chandos, op. cit., p238
4. FO 371/63073: file of German documents captured at the end of the war, concerning Egypt. Minute from R. G. Howe to Sir Orme Sargeant, 7 February 1947
5. Ibid. The file does not contain the original documents, only their translations.
6. Lord Killearn's Diaries, 4 October 1941
7. Figures compiled by the Middle East Supply Centre. From M.E.S.C. papers in St Antony's College, Oxford. (See also FO 371/35529, report on the cost of living in Egypt, 28 January 1943)
8. Lord Killearn's Diaries, 1 October 1941

AUCHINLECK'S OFFENSIVE

1. Alan Moorehead, op. cit., p185
2. Eve Curie, op. cit., pp45–47
3. Alan Moorehead, op. cit., p227
4. Alexander Clifford, op. cit., p156
5. Field Marshal Lord Carver, *Dilemmas of the Desert War*, Batsford 1986
6. John Strawson, *The Battle for North Africa*, Batsford 1969, p100

7. *Teaching the Professor*, by M. F. S., Blackwoods Magazine, May 1949
8. R. S. Surtees, *Handley Cross*, 1843

THE WRITERS

1. Patrick, 3rd Baron Kinross: letter to his mother, 23 July 1944
2. Lawrence Durrell, *Airgraph on Refugee Poets in Africa* (undated), Poetry London vol X, 1944
3. Letter from Henry Miller to Lawrence Durrell, *A Private Correspondence*, ed. George Wickes, Faber & Faber 1963, 21 November 1942, p178
4. Lord Killearn's Diaries, 3 March 1941
5. Robin Fedden, *Personal Landscape* (a memoir), Turret Books 1966
6. Terence Tiller, letter to the author, 12 June 1987
7. John Cromer, Introduction to the Salamander *Miscellany*, 1947
8. Roger Bowen, *Monologue for a Cairo Evening*, London Magazine, December 1982/January 1983
9. Terence Tiller, letter to the author, 23 June 1987
10. Olivia Manning, *Cairo: Back from the Blue*
11. Kay Dick, *Friends and Friendship*, Sidgwick & Jackson 1974, p35
12. G. S. Fraser, *A Stranger and Afraid*, Carcanet New Press 1983, p125
13. E. M. Forster, *Citadel*, issue of March 1942
14. Kay Dick, op. cit., p31
15. Frances Donaldson, *The British Council: the first Fifty Years*, Jonathan Cape 1984, p95–96

THE FALL OF HUSSEIN SIRRY

1. Lord Killearn's Diaries, 7 December 1941
2. Charles Tripp, op. cit., p234
3. FO 371/27434, report compiled by Statistical Department of Shell Co. of Egypt Ltd
4. Jean and Simonne Lacouture, *Egypt in Transition*, Methuen 1958, pp99–100
5. Lord Killearn's Diaries, 14 January 1942
6. Ibid., 4 October 1941
7. FO 371/31570 (review of October 1941 to March 1942), p4
8. Charles Tripp, op. cit., p238

9. FO 371/31570 (review of October 1941 to March 1942), p2
10. Lord Killearn's Diaries, 29 January 1942
11. Charles Tripp, op. cit., p239
12. Ibid., pp241–242
13. FO 371/31567, report of 4 February 1942
14. Jean and Simonne Lacouture, op. cit., p91

TANKS AT ABDIN

1. Lord Killearn's Diaries, 3 February 1942
2. FO 371/24626, 23 July 1940
3. FO 371/24626, 30 October 1940
4. FO 371/31567, report of 4 February 1942
5. Lord Birkenhead, *Walter Monckton*, Weidenfeld & Nicolson 1969, p199
6. Lord Killearn's Diaries, 4 February 1942
7. Diana Cooper, *Trumpets from the Steep*, Rupert Hart-Davis 1960, pp 146–147
8. Duff Cooper, *Old Men Forget*, Rupert Hart-Davis 1953, p308
9. Lord Killearn's Diaries, 24 April 1944
10. Ibid., 13 January 1944
11. Christopher Sykes, Introduction to Ronald Seth's biography *Russell Pasha*, William Kimber 1966, p13
12. Anwar Sadat, *In Search of Identity*, Harper & Row 1977, p32
13. Muhammad Neguib, op. cit., pp80–81
14. See Peter Mansfield, *Nasser*, Methuen 1969, p35
15. FO 371/31570 (review of October 1941 to March 1942), p4
16. Ibid., p5
17. FO 371/63073, translations of enemy accounts of 4 February 1942
18. Lord Killearn's Diaries, 19 February 1942
19. Ibid., 9 May 1942
20. FO 371/31567, report of 4 February
21. FO 371/31570 (review of October 1941 to March 1942). p5)

LOOSE TALK IN HIGH PLACES

1. FO 371/31574, report of 18 August 1942
2. FO 371/31570 (review of October 1941 to March 1942), p5

3. *Parade* magazine, April 1942
4. FO 371/31570, report of 8 April 1942
5. A. E. W. Sansom, op. cit., p96
6. See Lord Birkenhead, op. cit., p198
7. Lord Killearn's Diaries, 24 March 1942
8. Lord Birkenhead, op. cit., pp201, 202
9. Lord Killearn's Diaries, 22 May 1942
10. Cecil Beaton's Diaries, 30 April 1942
11. Cecil Beaton, op. cit., p27
12. Ibid., p87
13. Cecil Beaton's Diaries, 18 May 1942
14. Cecil Beaton, op. cit., p32
15. Furness Papers, St Antony's College: censorship instructions issued between July 1940 and June 1942
16. Lord Killearn's Diaries, 7 May 1942
17. Cecil Beaton's Diaries, 31 May 1942
18. Nina Nelson, *Shepheard's Hotel*, Barrie & Rockliff 1960, pp158–159
19. Cecil Beaton to Juliet Duff, 3 June 1942
20. Cecil Beaton's Diaries, 2 June 1942
21. Ibid., 20 May 1942
22. Ibid., 14 May 1942
23. Ibid., 6 June 1942
24. Ibid.
25. Stephen Shadegg, *Clare Boothe Luce*, Leslie Frewin 1973, pp149–152
26. Cecil Beaton to Juliet Duff, 3 June 1942
27. Cecil Beaton's Diaries, 30 May 1942
28. Lord Killearn's Diaries, 7 July 1942
29. Cecil Beaton's Diaries, 7 June 1942

TOBRUK

1. See Barrie Pitt, *The Crucible of War*, vol. II: Auchinleck's Command, Papermac edition 1986, p184
2. Alan Moorehead, op. cit., p347
3. Barrie Pitt, op. cit., p267
4. *Parade* magazine, issue of 27 June 1942
5. Barrie Pitt, letter to the author, 16 January 1988

THE FLAP

1. FO 371/24612, Burt-Smith's report of April 1940
2. FO 371/31564, report of 25 November 1942
3. P. J. Vatikiotis, *The History of Egypt*, p351
4. Peter Partner, op. cit., p51
5. Lord Killearn's Diaries, 25 June 1943 and 9 December 1943
6. FO 291/25, 26: minutes of a series of meetings on contingency plans held in the Minister of State's office
7. Philip Warner, *Auchinleck: The Lonely Soldier*, Buchan & Enright 1981, p162
8. FO 371/31573, report of 3 July 1942
9. Cecil Beaton, op. cit., p132
10. Christopher Sykes, *Cross Roads to Israel*, Collins 1965, p256
11. David Hirst and Irene Beeson, op. cit., p63
12. Terence Tiller, letter to the author, 23 June 1987
13. FO 371/34374, report of 23 October 1942, p3
14. The National Bank of Egypt: A Short History, produced on the 50th Anniversary of its Foundation (Middle East Centre, St Antony's College, Oxford)
15. Lord Killearn's Diaries, 11 August 1942
16. Arthur Bryant, *The Turn of the Tide*, Collins 1957, pp107–108
17. Lord Killearn's Diaries, 28 July 1942
18. Cecil Beaton, letter to Patrick Kinross, 12 December 1942

SPIES

1. John Eppler, *Operation Condor: Rommel's Spy*, Macdonald & Jane's, 1977
2. Plate XIII, *Récentes Explorations dans le Désert Libyque (1932–1936)*, L. E. de Alamsy. Printed in Cairo for the Société Royale de Géographie d'Egypte, 1936
3. Anwar Sadat, *Revolt on the Nile*, p47
4. Leonard Mosley, *The Cat and the Mice*, Arthur Barker 1958
5. A. E. W. Sansom, op. cit., p130
6. Lord Killearn's Diaries, 2 June 1941

ALAMEIN AND AFTER

1. Field Marshal Lord Montgomery of Alamein, *Memoirs*, Collins 1958, p102
2. Barrie Pitt, letter to the author, 16 January 1988
3. Desmond Graham, *Keith Douglas*, Oxford University Press 1974, p225

THE 'DARLING BELT'

1. FO 371/35529, the Ambassador's report of 19 February 1943 reviewing the political situation in Egypt between October 1942 and January 1943, p1
2. Charles Johnston, letter to his parents, undated
3. Xan Fielding, *Hide and Seek*, Secker & Warburg 1954, p224
4. Charles Johnston, letter to his parents, 28 May 1944
5. Charles Johnston, notebook
6. Charles Johnston, letter to his parents, 25 December 1942
7. Bickham Sweet-Escott, op. cit., p145
8. FO 921/39, report on Anglo-American relations, December 1942. Salaries for US Forces based on exchange rate of $4.035 to £1

SCANDALS AND QUARRELS

1. Cecil Beaton's Diaries, 23 May 1942
2. Lord Killearn's Diaries, 4 January 1944
3. *Empire News*, 16 January 1952
4. Lord Killearn's Diaries, written between 19 February and 30 March 1943
5. Ibid., 17 February 1943
6. FO 371/35529, report of 28 January 1943
7. Lord Killearn's Diaries, 27 January 1943
8. Ibid., 2 February 1943
9. Charles Johnston, letter to his parents, 28 January 1943
10. Ibid., 14 April 1943
11. FO 371/35530, report of 1 March 1943
12. Lord Killearn's Diaries, 4 June 1942
13. FO 371/34374, the Ambassador's report of 28 September 1942 reviewing the political situation in Egypt between April and September 1942, p2

14. FO 371/35532, report of 17 April 1943

15. FO 371/35536, the Ambassador's report of 16 June 1943 reviewing the political situation in Egypt between March and June 1943, p2

16. Ibid., p3

17. FO 371/35534, report of 9 May 1943, and weekly review of 29 April to 5 May 1943

18. FO 371/35535, weekly report covering the period 10–16 June 1943

19. Jean and Simonne Lacouture, op. cit., p99

20. FO 371/35529 (report on the political situation in Egypt between October 1942 and January 1943), p3

21. FO 371/35529, report of 7 January 1943 on the King's visit to Sinai

22. FO 371/35529, 35530, 35531

23. FO 371/35531, report of 30 March 1943

24. FO 371/24622, report of 9 January 1940

25. FO 371/24623, report of 9 April 1940

26. FO 371/27446, report of 18 January 1941

27. FO 371/27428, August 1941

28. Sir Thomas Russell Pasha, *Egyptian Service 1902–1946*, John Murray 1949, p121

29. Lord Douglas of Kirtleside with Robert Wright, *Years of Command*, Collins 1966, pp198–199

30. Charles Johnston, letter to his parents, 18 June 1944

A GLITTERING SUMMER

1. Lord Killearn's Diaries, 12 August 1943

2. Ibid., 2 June 1943

3. Mortimer Wheeler, *Still Digging*, Michael Joseph 1955, p153

4. Bryan Guinness, *Personal Patchwork*, Cygnet Press 1986, p67

5. Patrick Kinross, letter to his mother, 28 October 1942

6. Robin Fedden, op. cit.

7. Patrick Kinross, letter to his mother, 18 January 1944

8. Ibid., 29 December 1943

9. Ibid., 10 April 1943

10. Ibid., 9 July 1943

11. Vivien Leigh, letter to Mrs Hartley, 1 September 1943

12. Patrick Kinross, letter to his mother, 9 July 1943

13. Ibid.

14. Noël Coward, *Middle East Diary*, Heinemann 1944, 18 August 1943

15. Lord Killearn's Diaries, 16 June 1943
16. Sholto Douglas, *Years of Command*, p200
17. Noël Coward, op. cit., 9 September 1943
18. Ibid., 17 September 1943
19. See Preface to *Return to Oasis*, pxx
20. Gwyn Williams, *War-time Flyting in Cairo and Alexandria*, Planet No. 62, April/May 1987
21. Lawrence Durrell, conversation with the author, 2 September 1987
22. Lawrence Durrell to Henry Miller, spring 1944, *A Private Correspondence*, p187
23. Ibid., p189
24. Charles Johnston, 'My first steps in Bloomsbury', undated entry in notebook
25. Ibid.
26. Lady Menuhin, conversation with the author, 17 September 1986
27. Lawrence Durrell to Henry Miller, 23 May 1944, *A Private Correspondence*, p192

BEHIND CLOSED DOORS (SOE CAIRO)

1. Bickham Sweet-Escott, op. cit., p73
2. Christopher Sykes, *High Minded Murder*, Home & Van Thal 1944, p17
3. Christopher Sykes, *Albert and Emerald*, Hollis & Carter 1961
4. Basil Davidson, *Special Operations Europe*, Gollancz 1980, p112
5. Christopher Sykes, *A Song of a Shirt*, Derek Verschoyle 1953, p71
6. Bickham Sweet-Escott, op. cit., p198
7. Ibid., p170
8. Keble was brilliantly portrayed by the actor Geoffrey Hutchings as 'Colonel Hippo', in the Royal Shakespeare Company's 1985 production of *Desert Air* by Nicholas Wright. The play is based on Basil Davidson's description of these events in his book *Special Operations Europe*
9. FO 371/37579
10. David Martin, *Patriot or Traitor: the Case of General Mihailovic*, Hoover Institution Press 1978
11. Xan Fielding, op. cit., p99
12. Bickham Sweet-Escott, unpublished material held by the Library of Balliol College, Oxford

13. Bickham Sweet-Escott, op. cit., p172
14. Statement by Brigadier Sir Fitzroy Maclean to the conference organised by the History Department of the School of Slavonic and East European Studies in July 1973. See P. Auty and R. Clogg (eds.), *British Policy towards Wartime Resistance in Yugoslavia and Greece*, Macmillan 1975, pp221–228
15. Ibid., p263
16. See David Stafford, *Britain and European Resistance 1940–1945*, Macmillan and St Antony's College Oxford 1980, p124: Churchill's instruction to SOE Cairo, 18 March 1943
17. C. M. Woodhouse, *The Apple of Discord*, Hutchinson 1948, p150
18. Bickham Sweet-Escott, op. cit., pp174–175
19. David Stafford, op. cit., p121
20. Fitzroy Maclean, *Eastern Approaches*, Jonathan Cape 1949, pp402–403

STATESMEN AND BUCCANEERS

1. FO 921/137
2. FO 921/134
3. Ibid.
4. Lord Killearn's Diaries, 17 November 1943
5. William Stanley Moss, *Ill-Met by Moonlight*, Harrap 1950, p7
6. Laurence Grafftey-Smith, *Bright Levant*, John Murray 1970, pp47–48

THE GREEK MUTINIES

1. FO 371/35598,16 June 1943
2. FO 371/41316, report for the week 10–16 February 1944
3. Patrick Kinross, letter to his mother, 17 April 1944
4. Lord Killearn's Diaries, 22 February 1944
5. FO 371/41316, report of 27 January to 2 February 1944
6. Lord Killearn's Diaries, 18 February 1944
7. Ibid., 18 April 1943
8. Ibid., 20 November 1943; reported to Lord Killearn by Amin Osman Pasha
9. FO 371/45921, the Ambassador's report of 4 May 1945, reviewing political developments in Egypt during the year 1944, p2
10. Lord Killearn's Diaries, 30 May 1940

11. Ibid., 19 April 1944
12. Ibid., 24 April 1944
13. FO 371/35536, report on the political situation in Egypt between March and June 1943, p5
14. Lord Killearn's Diaries, 1 May 1944
15. WO 201/2522: report of June 1944 on the Greek Mutinies

LORD MOYNE

1. Lord Killearn's Diaries, 18 May 1944
2. Ibid., 13 May 1944
3. John Bowyer Bell, *Terror out of Zion*, Academy Press Dublin 1979, pp95–100
4. Speech to the House of Commons, 17 November 1944. See Martin Gilbert, *Churchill* vol VII, *The Road to Victory*
5. Lord Killearn's Diaries, 23 March 1945
6. John Bowyer Bell, op. cit., p349

BURYING THE HATCHET

1. Lord Killearn's Diaries, 18 January 1945
2. Martin Gilbert, op. cit., p1223
3. Lord Killearn's Diaries, 17 February 1945
4. Ibid.
5. Ibid.
6. See Ronald Seth, op. cit., p208
7. Lord Killearn's Diaries, 24 February 1945

FIRE AND REVOLUTION

1. Lord Killearn's Diaries, 6 March 1946
2. P. J. Vatikiotis, *Nasser and his Generation*, Croom Helm 1978, p91
3. FO 371/96860, 29 December 1951
4. Ibid., 31 December 1951
5. FO 371/96872, report of the Investigation Committee on the events of 26 January 1952
6. Ibid.

7. Russell Pasha's report is attached to that of the Investigating Committee, FO 371/96872
8. Jean and Simonne Lacouture, op. cit., p109
9. Nina Nelson, op. cit., p203
10. FO 371/96870, telegram of 26 January 1952
11. FO 371/96872
12. See Jean and Simonne Lacouture, op. cit., pp112–114

PRIMARY SOURCES

GOVERNMENT FILES

Foreign Office	Public Record Office, Kew
War Office & GHQ Middle East	Public Record Office, Kew
Office of Minister of State, Cairo	Public Record Office, Kew

PRIVATE PAPERS

The complete diaries of Lord Killearn,	St Antony's College, Oxford
The Furness Papers,	St Antony's College, Oxford
Papers of Lord Kinross,	National Library of Scotland
Papers of Sir Charles Johnston,	Private collection
Papers of Sir Cecil Beaton,	Private collection

INTERVIEWS AND CORRESPONDENCE

Much of my material comes from interviews or correspondence with those who have personal experience or knowledge of Egypt during this period.

Sir Philip Adams; Julian Amery MP; Luis Awad; Brigadier Bagnold; Mary Benson; Lady Bowker; June and Neville Braybrooke; John and Josie Brinton; the Viscountess Camrose; Field Marshal Lord Carver; Mr and Mrs Walter Clarke; Hilda Clouet des Péruches; Anthony Contomichaelos; Pamela Cooper; Company Sergeant Major T. Cosgrove, In Pensioner; Elizabeth David; Dan Davin; Walter and Mitzie Duhring; Lord Dunsany; Eve Durrell; Lawrence Durrell; Ibrahim Farag; Fayed Farid; Renée Fedden; Xan Fielding; Sir Edward Ford; Mrs V. Greer; Irene Guinle; Michael

Haag; Mr H. Habergam, In Pensioner; Mary Hadkinson; Samira Hansa; Max Harari; Prince Hasan Aziz Hasan; Edward Hodgkin; Albert Hourani; Jean Howard; Yusuf Idriss; Mollie Izzard; Lord Jellicoe; the late Sir Charles Johnston; Marie Louise Khomsy; Lord Killearn; Jacqueline, Lady Killearn; Commander Bill King; Wagih Kotb; Joan and Patrick Leigh Fermor; the late Anita Leslie; Robert Liddell; Admiral Lucas; Sir Fitzroy Maclean, Bart.; Adel Mahmoud Sabit; Mahmoud Muhammad Mahmoud; Lady Menuhin; Sophie Moss; Samih Moussa; Brigadier and Mrs Edmund Myers; Lesley O'Malley; Princess Osmanoglu; Jean Papasian; Burnet Pavitt; Stewart Perowne; Barrie Pitt; J. Enoch Powell, MP; Sir James Richards; André Rouxel; Abdel Salaam Osman; the late Christopher Scaife; Rodney Searight; Fares Serafim; Victor Simaika; Colonel David Smiley; Diana Smith; Major Patrick Telfer-Smollett; Colonel David Stirling; Peter Stirling; Dr Hammed Sultan; the late Terence Tiller; Ivor Treavett; Sergeant S. Tweedale, MM, In Pensioner; Richard Usborne; Magdi Wahba; Samiha Wahba; the late Gordon Waterfield; Professor J. H. A. Watson; Sir Peter Wilkinson; Gertrude Wissa; Nolly Zervudachi; Kyril Zinovieff; and Mme I. Zulficar.

Bibliography

Abu Lughod, Janet, *Cairo: A Thousand Years of the City Victorious*, Princeton University Press 1971

Aldridge, James, *Cairo*, Boston 1969

Amery, Julian, *Approach March*, Hutchinson 1973

Auty, P., and Clogg, R., *British Policy towards Wartime Resistance in Yugoslavia and Greece*, Macmillan 1975

Balfour, N., and Mackay, S., *Paul of Yugoslavia: Britain's Maligned Friend*, Hamish Hamilton 1980

Barnett, Corelli, *The Desert Generals*, Allen & Unwin 1983

Beaton, Cecil, *Near East*, Batsford 1943

Bell, John Bowyer, *Terror out of Zion*, Dublin University Press 1979

Berque, Jacques, *Egypt: Imperialism and Revolution*, Faber & Faber 1972

Birkenhead, Lord, *Walter Monckton*, Weidenfeld & Nicolson 1969

Borden, Mary, *Journey down a Blind Alley*, Hutchinson 1946

Carver, Michael, *Dilemmas of the Desert War*, Batsford 1986

Chandos, Viscount (Oliver Lyttelton), *Memoirs*, Bodley Head 1962

Channon, Sir Henry, *Diaries*, ed. Robert Rhodes James, Weidenfeld & Nicolson 1967

Clifford, Alexander, *Three Against Rommel*, Harrap 1943

Coats, Peter, *Of Generals and Gardens*, Weidenfeld & Nicolson 1976

Connell, John, *Wavell, Soldier and Scholar*, Collins 1964

Coward, Noël, *Middle East Diary*, Heinemann 1944

Cowles, Virginia, *The Phantom Major*, Collins 1958

Crimp, R. L., *The Diary of a Desert Rat*, Leo Cooper 1971

Curie, Eve, *Journey Among Warriors*, Heinemann 1947

Dardaud, Gabriel, *Trente ans au bord du Nil*, Lieu Commun 1987

Davidson, Basil, *Special Operations Europe*, Gollancz 1980

Davin, Dan, *For the Rest of our Lives*, Michael Joseph 1965

Deakin, E. W. D., *The Embattled Mountain*, Oxford University Press 1971

Dean, Basil, *The Theatre at War*, Harrap 1956

Dimbleby, Richard, *The Frontiers are Green*, Hodder & Stoughton 1943

Douglas of Kirtleside, Lord, *Years of Command*, Collins 1966

Durrell, Lawrence, *Spirit of Place*, Letters and Essays on Travel, ed. Alan G. Thomas, Faber & Faber 1969

Eppler, John, *Operation Condor: Rommel's Spy*, Macdonald & Jane's 1977

Fedden, Robin, *Personal Landscape*, Turret Books 1966

Fielding, Xan, *Hide and Seek*, Secker & Warburg 1954

Fraser, G. S., *A Stranger and Afraid*, Carcanet New Press 1983

Gilbert, Martin, *Churchill* vol. VII, *The Road to Victory: 1941–1945*, Heinemann 1986

Grafftey-Smith, Laurence, *Bright Levant*, John Murray 1970

Graham, Desmond, *Keith Douglas*, Oxford University Press 1974

Guinness, Bryan, *Personal Patchwork*, Cygnet Press 1986

Hart-Davis, Duff, *Peter Fleming*, Jonathan Cape 1974

Hirst, D., and Beeson, I., *Sadat*, Faber & Faber 1981

Hughes, Pennethorne, *While Shepheard's Watched*, Chatto & Windus 1949

Johnston, Charles, *Mo and Other Originals*, Hamish Hamilton 1971

Joly, Cyril, *Take these Men*, Harmondsworth 1956

Kennedy Shaw, W. B., *The Long Range Desert Group*, Collins 1945

Lacouture, Jean and Simonne, *Egypt in Transition*, Methuen 1958

Leslie, Anita, *A Story Half Told*, Hutchinson 1983

Little, Tom, *Egypt*, Benn 1958

Lugol, Jean, *Egypt in World War II*, Cairo 1945

Maclean, Fitzroy, *Eastern Approaches*, Jonathan Cape 1949

Macmillan, Harold, *War Diaries*, Macmillan 1984

Mansfield, Peter, *Nasser*, Methuen 1969

Martin, David, *Patriot or Traitor: The Case of General Mihailovic*, Hoover Institution Press 1978

Montgomery of Alamein, Field Marshal Lord, *Memoirs*, Collins 1958

Moorehead, Alan, *African Trilogy*, Hamish Hamilton 1944

Moss, William Stanley, *Ill-Met by Moonlight*, Harrap 1950

Mure, David, *Master of Deception*, William Kimber 1980

Neguib, Muhammad, *Egypt's Destiny*, Doubleday 1955

Nelson, Nina, *Shepheard's Hotel*, Barrie & Rockliff 1960

Partner, Peter, *Arab Voices: The BBC Arabic Service 1938–1988*, BBC Publications 1988

Pitt, Barrie, *The Crucible of War* (three volumes, second edition), Papermac 1986

Roberts, Brian, *Randolph: A Study of Churchill's Son*, Hamish Hamilton 1984

Rowlatt, Mary, *A Family in Egypt*, Robert Hale 1956

Rugh, Andrea B., *Family in Contemporary Egypt*, the American University in Cairo Press 1985

Russell Pasha, Sir Thomas, *Egyptian Service: 1902-1946*, John Murray 1949

Sadat, Anwar, *Revolt on the Nile*, Allan Wingate 1957

Sadat, Anwar, *In Search of Identity*, Harper & Row 1977

St Clair McBride, Barrie, *Farouk of Egypt*, Robert Hale 1967

Sansom, A. E. W., *I Spied Spies*, Harrap 1965

Schoutheete, Jeanne de, *Jeanette of Cairo*, Editions France Empire 1978

Sedat, Jehan, *A Woman of Egypt*, Bloomsbury 1987

Seth, Ronald, *Russell Pasha*, William Kimber 1966

Shadegg, Stephen, *Clare Boothe Luce*, Leslie Frewin 1973

Spears, Sir Edward Louis, *Fulfilment of a Mission*, Cooper 1977

Stark, Freya, *East is West*, John Murray 1945

Stark, Freya, *Dust in the Lion's Paw*, John Murray 1961

Stark, Freya, *Letters* vol. IV, ed. Lucy Moorehead, Michael Russell 1977

Storrs, Ronald, *Orientations*, Nicolson & Watson 1937

Strawson, John, *The Battle for North Africa*, Batsford 1969

Sweet-Escott, Bickham, *Baker Street Irregular*, Methuen 1976

Sykes, Christopher, *Orde Wingate*, Collins 1959

Sykes, Christopher, *Cross Roads to Israel*, Collins 1965

Sykes, Christopher, *Evelyn Waugh*, Collins 1975

Tidsall, E. E. P., *The Royal Hellenic Cousins*, Stanley Paul 1955

Tripp, Charles, *Ali Mahir and the Palace in Egyptian Politics 1936–1942*, London University Ph.D. Thesis, 1984

Vatikiotis, P. J., *The History of Egypt* (second edition), Weidenfeld & Nicolson 1980

Vatikiotis, P. J., *The Egyptian Army in Politics*, Indiana University Press 1961

Vatikiotis, P. J., *Nasser and his Generation*, Croom Helm 1978

Vickers, Hugo, *Cecil Beaton*, Weidenfeld & Nicolson 1985

Warner, Philip, *The Special Air Service*, William Kimber 1971

Warner, Philip, *Auchinleck: the Lonely Soldier*, Buchan & Enright 1981

Waterfield, Gordon, *Morning will Come*, John Murray 1944

Waugh, Evelyn, *Letters*, ed. Mark Amory, Weidenfeld & Nicolson 1980

Waugh, Evelyn, *Diaries*, ed. Michael Davie, Weidenfeld & Nicolson 1976

Wikan, Unni, *Life among the Poor in Cairo*, Tavistock Publications 1976

Wilson, General Sir Henry Maitland, *Eight Years Overseas*, Hutchinson 1950

Woodhouse, C. M., *The Apple of Discord*, Hutchinson 1948

Young, Desmond, *Rommel*, Collins 1950

ARTICLES

Bowen, Roger, *Monologue for a Cairo Evening*, London Magazine, December 1982/January 1983

Durrell, Lawrence, *Airgraph on Refugee Poets in Africa* (undated), Poetry London vol. X, 1944

Manning, Olivia, *Middle East Letter*, Modern Reading No.9, 1944

Manning, Olivia, *Cairo: Back from the Blue*, Sunday Times Colour Supplement, 17 September 1967

Wahba, Magdi, *Cairo Memories*, Encounter magazine, May 1984

Williams, Gwyn, *War-time Flyting in Cairo and Alexandria*, Planet No.62, April/May 1987

FICTION

Barber, Noel, *A Woman of Cairo*, Hodder & Stoughton 1984

Chedid, Andrée, *Le Sixième Jour*, Flammarion 1960

Connell, John, *The House at Herod's Gate*, Sampson, Low, Marston & Co 1947

Durrell, Lawrence, *The Alexandria Quartet*, single volume edition, Faber & Faber 1962

Enright, D. J., *An Academic Year*, Seeker & Warburg 1955

Liddell, Robert, *Unreal City*, Jonathan Cape 1952

Liddell, Robert, *The Rivers of Babylon*, Jonathan Cape 1959

Lively, Penelope, *Moon Tiger*, André Deutsch 1987

Mahfouz, Naguib, *Midaq Alley*, Heinemann 1975

Mahfouz, Naguib, *The Beginning and the End*, American University in Cairo Press 1985

Manning, Olivia, *The Levant Trilogy*, single volume edition, Penguin 1982

Mosley, Leonard, *The Cat and the Mice*, Arthur Barker 1958

Newby, P. H., *Kith*, Faber & Faber 1977

Newby, P. H., *The Picnic at Sakkara*, Jonathan Cape 1955

Sykes, Christopher, *High-Minded Murder*, Home & Van Thal 1944

Sykes, Christopher, *A Song of a Shirt*, Derek Verschoyle 1953

Tsirkas, Stratis, *Drifting Cities*, translated by Kay Cicellis, Alfred A. Knopf 1974

Waugh, Evelyn, *The Sword of Honour* (trilogy), Chapman & Hall 1955

POETRY

Douglas, Keith, *Collected Poems*, eds. John Waller and G. S. Fraser, Editions Poetry London 1951

Durrell, Lawrence, *Collected Poems 1931–1974*, ed. James Brigham, Faber & Faber 1980

Hore-Ruthven, Patrick, *Desert Warrior*, John Murray 1944

Personal Landscape: An Anthology of Exile, with introduction by Robin Fedden, Editions Poetry Ltd 1945

Selwyn, Victor (ed.), *Return to Oasis*: War Poems and Recollections from the Middle East 1940–1946, published by Poetry London for the Salamander-Oasis Trust 1980

Selwyn, Victor (ed.), *From Oasis into Italy*, War Poems and Diaries from Africa and Italy 1940–1946, Shepheard-Walwyn Publications for the Salamander-Oasis Trust 1983

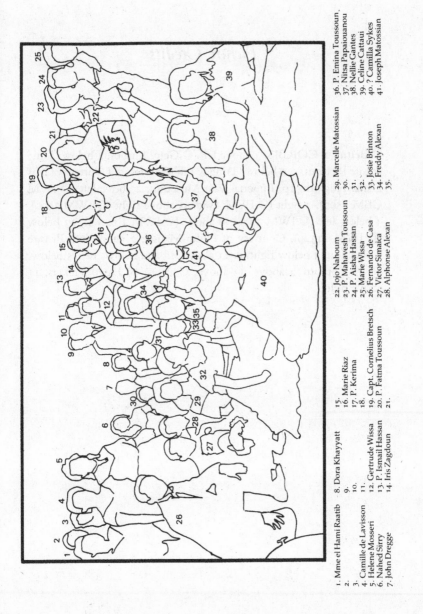

1. Mme el Hami Raatib
2.
3. Camille de Lavisson
4. Helene Mosseri
5. Nahed Sirry
6. John Dregge
7.

8. Dora Khayyatt
9.
10.
11.
12. Gertrude Wissa
13. P. Ismail Hassan
14. Iris Zagdoun

15. Marie Riaz
16. P. Kerima
17.
18.
19. Capt. Cornelius Bretsch
20. P. Fatma Toussoun
21.

22. Jojo Nahoum
23. P. Mahavesh Toussoun
24. P. Aisha Hassan
25. Marie Wissa
26. Fernando de Casa
27. Victor Simaica
28. Alphonse Alexan

29. Marcelle Matossian
30.
31.
32.
33. Josie Brinton
34. Freddy Alexan
35.

36. P. Emina Toussoun.
37. Nitsa Papaiouanou
38. Nellie Gantes
39. Celine Cattaui
40. ? Camilla Sykes
41. Joseph Matossian

Picture Credits

© Bettman/CORBIS: 3 above left. © Getty Images: 4 below/Time & Life Pictures, 5, 6 below/Time & Life Pictures, 7. Courtesy of Mrs Diana Hogarth: 10. Imperial War Museums: 2 above left (© IWM CBM 1597), 2 right (© IWM 1587), 3 above right (© IWM 1600), 3 below left (© IWM 1578), 6 above (© IWM E11064), 13 below (© IWM 11329). Courtesy of Philip Mansel: 2 below left. Private Collection: 3 below right, 9, 11 above left and below, 12, 15 below, 16. © Topfoto: 4 above, 13 above. Courtesy of Hugo Vickers: 11 above right.

Index

Ranks and titles are generally the highest mentioned in the text

Brotherhood of Freedom, 101–3
Broughton, Sir Delves, 228
Bulaq Dacrour (house), 250–1
Bullen, Keith, 158
buluq nizam (auxiliary police), 340–1, 346
Burgess, Guy, 273
Burk, David, 158
Burrows, (Sir) Bernard, 250–1
Burrows, Inez, 296
Burt-Smith, Colonel, 196, 253

Cadogan, Sir Alexander, 258, 282
Cairo: conditions, 4–5; Waterfield visits,
    4; dereliction under Ottomans,
    9; centre rebuilt under Ismail, 10;
    communities, 26–7; languages,
    27; social life, 28, 30–4, 189–90,
    229–31; architecture and layout,
    34–6; declared an Open City (1940),
    47, 188; enemy agents in, 58; SOE
    branch, 97–100; 9th General Hospital,
    116; brothels, 116, 118–20; facilities
    and entertainments for troops, 116,
    118–24, 127–8; climatic conditions,
    117; troops' behaviour, 119–21;
    bombed by Germans, 141; prices
    and earnings increase, 141–2, 167;
    nightlife, 155; literary life, 156–61,
    256; goods hoarded and stockpiled,
    166; unrest and anti-British
    demonstrations, 168, 170; under
    threat of German assault, 200–1;
    evacuees return at end of German
    threat, 206–7; internments, 209–10;
    Americans in, 231–4; typhoid, 241;
    blackout retained after defeat of Axis
    in Africa, 253; entertainments, 258–61,
    265; importance after Alamein,
    267–8; Churchill–Roosevelt–Chiang
    meeting in, 289–91; Christmas
    celebrations (1943), 297; winds down
    (1944), 316; post-war complacency,
    337; post-war violence and riots
    ('Black Saturday'), 337–46
Cairo Symphony Orchestra, 124
Campbell, Cecil, 130
Campbell, Major Colin, 33
Campbell, Robin, 94
Canada: declares war on Italy, 47
Canal Zone: anti-British violence in,
    338–41

Capitulations (Ottoman system), 10
Capsalis, Madame Dmitri, 60, 62
Capuzzo, Fort, Libya, 57
Carioca, Tahia, 186, 233
Carpenter, Connie, 260
Carter, Howard, 33
Carver, Field-Marshal Michael, Baron:
    Dilemmas of the Desert War, 194
Casablanca Conference (1943), 240
Casey, Maie, 191, 259
Casey, Richard, 185, 187, 319
Castellani, Sir Aldo, 61
Catroux, General Georges, 51, 132
Catroux, Margot, 51
Catseflis, Renée (*later* Mrs Robin
    Fedden), 250
Cattaui Pasha, Madame Joseph, 30
Cauldron (area), 192
Cavafy, Constantine, 154, 157, 262–3
censorship, 187–9
Cetniks (Yugoslavia), 274, 282
Chad, 88
Channon, Sir Henry ('Chips'), 61–3
Chapman-Walker, Mark, 257
Chesterton, G. K., 157
Chiang Kai-shek, 289
Chiang, Madame (Mayling Soong),
    290
Churchill, Randolph: in Layforce,
    90, 93–4; life in Cairo, 91–2, 189;
    Freya Stark criticises behaviour, 101;
    broadsheets, 115; helps Eve Curie
    to visit front, 128; and Lyttelton's
    appointment, 131; attached to
    Intelligence Division, 148; returns
    to England, 207; accompanies father
    on June 1943 visit, 240; recommends
    Maclean, 277; on mission to
    Yugoslavia, 284–5
Churchill, Sarah, 327, 329
Churchill (Sir) Winston: and Wavell's
    taciturnity, 43; as Prime Minister,
    47; and attack on French fleet, 50;
    harasses Wavell, 58, 71; demands
    Syrian campaign of Wavell, 74; sends
    tanks to Egypt, 74–5; moves Wavell
    to India, 76; encourages imaginative
    ideas, 86; supports SOE, 96; appoints
    Oliver Lyttelton Minister of State in
    Middle East, 131–2; urges Auchinleck
    to offensive action, 145; government